Birth of the Other

Birth of the Other

Rosine Lefort,
in collaboration with
Robert Lefort

Translated by
Marc Du Ry, Lindsay Watson,
and Leonardo Rodríguez

Foreword by
Russell Grigg

University of Illinois Press
Urbana and Chicago

Naissance de L'Autre © 1980 by Éditions du Seuil
English-language translation, foreword, and translators' note
© 1994 by the Board of Trustees of the University of Illinois
Published by arrangement with Éditions du Seuil, Paris
Manufactured in the United States of America
P 6 5 4 3 2

This book is printed on acid-free paper.

Library of Congress Cataloging-in-Publication Data
Lefort, Rosine
    [Naissance de l'autre. English]
    Birth of the other / Rosine Lefort, in collaboration with Robert
Lefort : translated by Marc Du Ry, Lindsay Watson, and Leonardo
Rodríguez ; foreword by Russell Grigg.
        p.   cm.
    Includes bibliographical references.
    ISBN 0-252-01900-8 (alk. paper). — ISBN 0-252-06393-7 (pbk.)
    ISBN 978-0-252-01900-5 (alk. paper). — ISBN 978-0-252-06393-0
    (pbk.)
    1. Child analysis—Case studies. 2. Autism in children—Case
studies. 3. Psychoanalysis—Case studies. I. Lefort, Robert.
II. Title.
RJ504.2.L4413 1994
618.92'89'17—dc20   93-40386
                                             CIP

Contents

Foreword

The pages that follow, in which Rosine Lefort and Robert Lefort relate and discuss the psychoanalyses of two young children, constitute a major contribution to the literature of psychoanalytic case studies. Rosine Lefort's case notes, recorded every evening after the sessions with her two young patients, are set out here in their entirety. They are meticulous in their recounting of day-to-day details of two children taken into treatment by her in the early 1950s at the Fondation Parent de Rosan, a clinic in the unit headed by Jenny Aubry, a pediatrician. These notes are accompanied by, but clearly distinguished from, a theoretical commentary written in the late 1970s that, in centering on an argument about the emergence and structure of subjectivity in relation to the Other, presents an analysis of the treatment that is explicitly Lacanian in orientation.

We should be grateful for the circumstances that produced this unusual separation in time between the original case notes and the subsequent commentary, as it renders the case notes all the more valuable, having been recorded without any commitment to a particular theoretical framework. These circumstances are quite fortuitous: Lacan had only just begun to give his now famous Seminar and the theoretical advances that made the commentary possible here were only to unfold in Lacan's teaching over subsequent years. Nevertheless, Rosine Lefort's treatment with these young children was of sufficient interest to Lacan for him to invite her to speak of one of her cases, Robert the Wolf Child, at his Seminar in 1954.

Rosine Lefort began working at Parent de Rosan in 1950 as an observer of a small group of young children, a number of whom she took into individual treatment. She had already been in analysis with Lacan since early that year and, she says, the treatment of the two children reported here was an integral part of her own analysis. Apart from a period of eight months at the William Alanson White Clinic in 1952–53, Rosine Lefort continued to work at Parent de Rosan until 1955. During this same period Robert Lefort was also employed at the hospital as a pediatrician. Rosine Lefort and Robert Lefort were both members of the Freudian School of Paris until its dissolution and are currently prominent members of the Ecole de la Cause Freudienne, where the interest in their clinical and theoretical approach to psychoanalysis with children has led to the creation of an international network, CEREDA, Centre d'Etudes et de Recherche sur l'Enfant dans le Discours Analytique.

At the time of the Leforts' employment Parent de Rosan was an institution in the French public health system for the temporary care of young children between the ages of one and four who had either been abandoned by their parents and were awaiting placement or had been left in respite care during extended periods of illness of their mothers. This was still the time of large institutions with residents living in a highly structured environment, and Parent de Rosan was no exception. Forty-five to fifty children resided in two villas in the northwest of Paris and were lodged in dormitories of eight to ten beds. Although most suffered no illnesses, and indeed the ailments they did contract were often due to the circumstances of their hospitalization, they all were still treated as hospital patients. The medical staff did daily rounds and the children had their temperatures taken morning and evening. The children would often pass the entire day in bed, with perhaps the exception of a couple of hours spent in the hospital nursery, and during their residence they at no time left the confines of the hospital. They were fed individually by a nurse who would pass from bed to bed, while the other children waiting would be crying for their turn. Today Parent de Rosan still operates as a hospital for young children, now largely as a service for mentally ill children; it should be noted, though, that the strict and rigid medical regime is a thing of the past.

The first subject of the cases reported here, Nadia, who was thirteen and a half months old at the beginning of her treatment, was seen by Rosine Lefort for a period of ten months between October 1951 and July 1952. The following pages describe her condition at the beginning of the analysis, recount the course of her progress, and end with a description of the treatment's conclusion. Though brief, Nadia's treatment contains the three logical moments of a complete analysis: establishment of the transference, the process of working-through that locates her as a subject in the Real, the Symbolic, and the Imaginary, and the dissolution of the transference and "fall" of the object. The case is of special interest not just because of its rich and detailed account of an analysis with a child but more particularly because it is a child who is at an age where she is beginning to speak. The momentous consequences of this step for the human child are captured in the discussion of the analysis, where the focus is on the creation of the subject's lack and the emergence of what Lacan calls object *a*, the primordial lost object, as the cause of desire. We find confirmation here that this lack is initially located, not in the subject, but in the Other, which is the place or locus occupied here in the transference by Rosine Lefort. This function of a lack, located both at the level of the subject and the Other, can arguably be regarded as the key to the dialectical unfolding of the emergence of the subject, Nadia. It is important in this respect to observe Rosine Lefort's refusal to occupy the maternal position of satisfying Nadia's needs and demands, thereby confronting her with her own lack, initially in the Real and the Imaginary, and subsequently, through symbolic castration, in the three registers together. It is noteworthy that in the anonymity of the care provided in the hospital setting at Parent de Rosan, at a time when the concept of "maternal deprivation" was dominant, Rosine Lefort nevertheless assumed the properly psychoanalytic role of interrogating Nadia's demands and interpreting her desire, rather than satisfying her at the level of her needs—a position that enabled the introduction of the lack essential to the advent of subjectivity.

While Nadia's treatment had a logical conclusion, Marie-Françoise's treatment was prematurely interrupted, which inevitably leaves some questions unresolved, not least that of diagnosis. On admission to Parent de Rosan Marie-Françoise was diagnosed as schizophrenic or autistic, and in Rosine Lefort's view the treatment tends to confirm this diagnosis of psychosis, since for Marie-Françoise the absence of the Other meant that the object remained in the Real, unable to be raised to the dignity of the signifier. While certain signifiers were present for Marie-Françoise there was no Other to give them a place and a structure, thus the issue for Rosine Lefort was not that of securing Marie-Françoise's desire by refusing the position of satisfying the child's needs, but of providing the conditions for the emergence of the Other for a psychotic subject. This gives a certain poignancy to events at the end of the treatment, just prior to its interruption, which led Rosine Lefort to speculate that, while the evidence is inconclusive, these conditions had perhaps been successfully met.

The role of play, gesture, and nonverbal behavior in the treatment of children has always led to the question whether such treatment can be properly called psychoanalysis, and the two cases presented here raise this issue in a stark form. At first sight, whereas psychoanalysis with adults takes place within the strict limits of speech between analyst and analysand, the introduction of nonverbal techniques and the treatment of children who, as here, are at the limits of language indicate that psychoanalysis with children is at the very least an adaptation of the technique with respect to adults. This would make child psychoanalysis, with its special technical and clinical expertise, a sub-specialization of psychoanalysis properly so-called. The position of Rosine Lefort and Robert Lefort on this issue is clear and unambiguous: the child in analysis is and remains a subject in his or her own right and in the full sense of the term. While the treatment may call, as here, for the presence of what Lacan called "the odd trifling object," the structure of the analytic relationship remains essentially the same—it is a framework within which the subject speaks to the analyst who occupies the position of the Other, as the vehicle of object *a*, cause of the subject's desire. That there is no difference between analysis with children or adults is consistent with Lacan's opposition to the developmental line of approach in psychoanalysis in which the child is seen as passing through a series of successive stages in his or her progression toward adulthood. Against this developmental approach Rosine Lefort and Robert Lefort argue that in the treatment of children—and the two cases presented here make this abundantly clear—the central issue concerns the binding or knotting together of the Real, the Symbolic, and the Imaginary. Their approach is consistent with the view that psychoanalytic theory does not describe the facts of actual development, but a structure that organizes and manifests itself within an individual's history without being reducible to developmental processes.

Can we say that Rosine Lefort adopts the position of analyst in these cases? Her own analysis had at the time not been long undertaken, she had no supervision for these cases, and on her own admission she lacked the conceptual and theoretical framework that her subsequent psychoanalytic training would provide her with. Indeed, she characterizes herself as a "note-taker," which would seem to imply that the observations recorded here constitute what the psychoanalyst calls the "clinical material." At first sight it would seem that this material is not psychoanalytic because it describes only the behavior of the child and reports nothing of the speech of the subject. But closer examination reveals that, first, the signifier is not absent from Rosine Lefort's sessions with Nadia and Marie-Françoise. Not only do the various objects have a signifying function in the treatment, they are also accompanied by the words and speech of both analyst and analysand. Indeed, at least in the case of Nadia, we find a description of the subject's emergence as what Lacan calls a *parlêtre*, speaking being, and, with this emergence, the entire structure of the subject is already given.

The second point that should be made is that the behavior occurs within the session and thus within the transference, which is a necessary condition for the behavior to be interpretable. Although necessary, this condition is not sufficient, however, since interpretation requires that the signifier and the signified also be distinct and separable. This is why it is crucial to note the signifying role played by the series of objects whose symbolic function emerges clearly in the transference relationship between Nadia and her analyst. The food—cookies, candy, cereal, rice pudding—that Rosine Lefort offers Nadia during the sessions takes on a signifying role as gift or as object of demand in the transference. The various objects that feature in the account of the sessions are the currency, at times oral, at times anal or phallic, of the exchanges between the child and her analyst. Indeed, as the account shows, the progress of the treatment is reflected in the increasingly symbolic function that these objects come to acquire, converting them into objects of exchange and thereby advancing from the impasse in which the child confronts the real of her body when the Other is absent.

The question of the transference is crucial when, as here, it concerns an analyst *avant la lettre*. Rosine Lefort is a young woman who is extremely attentive to the smallest details in the session, which she records faithfully and rigorously. It is obvious that her work is sustained by her own analysis and that it is therefore sustained by her own transference not only onto her young patients but also, via her own analysis, onto psychoanalysis itself. While it could be said that she adopts an extremely passive position, particularly with respect to the aggressiveness of her patients, in allowing herself to be smeared with cereal, slapped, bitten, hit with toys, and so on, at the same time she nevertheless constructs limits at the level of her response to the subject's demand where, refusing to satisfy needs, she facilitates the creation of the lack in the Other where the subject will come to locate her own lack.

In both his teaching and his clinical practice Lacan undertook a return to the first principles of psychoanalysis (this is the meaning of his "return to Freud") in order to overcome the pervasive conservatism in the psychoanalytic community that discouraged innovation and ritualized a technique generally misunderstood by its practitioners. We can therefore understand why Lacan gave his encouragement and support to the Leforts' ground-breaking work on psychoanalysis with children. We are fortunate that Lacan was insistent, since this turned out to be decisive for the authors' decision to write up and publish the case studies that appear here as *Birth of the Other*.

Translators' Note

Traduttore—tradittore, translator—traitor is an old pun. A would-be translator of psychoanalytic texts is doubly conscious of this delicate balance, and especially if he or she is also a psychoanalyst. Did not Freud regard the act of analysis as itself a translation, or deciphering, of what the subject is always inclined to betray—desire—by ignoring, forgetting, or dismissing what seems to be written in a foreign language, that of the unconscious? Just as it is the task of the psychoanalyst to recognize unique signifiers in spite of the transformation they undergo in the interval between perception and consciousness, written down as they are in memory in various layers, from signs of perception, through conceptual memories, to word representations, so the translator has to render something of the depth of resonance that each term harbors within itself by virtue of its etymological and actual place in the original language.

As psychoanalysts, our task was made easier by the fact that in both cases presented here, actual spoken signifiers were few and far between. Yet, in their simplicity, they already demonstrated the phonematic play of similarity and opposition that characterizes the structure of language, and as such, we have given them at least once in both the original form and in English.

As translators we could not avoid, despite the utmost fidelity to the original, standardizing certain aspects of 1950s French culture: the clothing Rosine Lefort wore in the institution, whether *blouse* or *tablier,* is here always a white coat. The daily fare of the infants, the ingredients of which are rarely specified, has become a generic cereal. Lefort's more homely terms for the bodily functions have been changed to their more neutral equivalents, though it is important to remember that the French *pipi,* urinating, turns up as a signifier with Marie-Françoise, just as *caca* does with Nadia. Generally, we have kept faithfully to the minutely prosaic but very precise descriptions of the sessions which Rosine Lefort counterpoints with her lucid theoretical account to form the unique analytical experience this book invites the reader to share.

But it is as translators of psychoanalytic concepts that we faced great difficulties, as their varied diffusion into English, which starting with selected translations of Lacan, has since then continued apace with a growing number of critical studies without uniform standards being agreed upon.

Lacan is famous for his use of "mathemes." Rather than formulas, he called them "little letters" with which, like the exact sciences, he not only tried to grasp something of the Real but also wished to transmit it integrally, regardless of how these ciphers, like formations of the unconscious, were subsequently to be deciphered, and necessarily so, according to the conventions of a particular tradition. For Lacan, transmission versus tradition was a dialectical couple of the same kind and importance as *traduttore—tradittore*.

We have therefore kept the conceptual distinction of the original between small other (Imaginary register) and big Other (Symbolic register) instead of relying on capital letters. It also differentiates it from ordinary language use of "other" and, in this context, emphasizes the difference between child and adult.

Although we could not keep the Lacanian play on the typographical identity of object *a* (which he often called object "small" *a*) and the first letter of small other (*autre*), with which he stressed a conceptual link—*a* as small other (or *i[a]*, image of the other, ego) is an imaginary version of *a* as object—we have everywhere tried to transmit Lacan's most important matheme, object *a*, integrally, by putting it into italic.

In the case of one such object we deferred to existing usage, though not without misgivings. It is the "look" rather than the "gaze" that comes closer to Lacan's idea of *regard* as object. It refers to a single moment, like a glance, something that is given or exchanged, and is in perfect opposition to seeing while yet referring to the object of vision, as in the "look" of fashion, or the insult "What are you looking at!" It is an object that has more to do, perhaps surprisingly, with the surprise implied in being caught looking than the possible eroticism of a burning gaze. Though "gaze" catches the important element of fascination, so would "stare," which at least has the advantage of not implying a strong intentional element of seeing, while "gaze" further connotes the kind of lengthy contemplation that is not consonant with an object that momentarily divides the subject against his or her will and cannot be seen in the mirror.

Just as nobody now follows Strachey in translating the Freudian *Trieb* as "instinct" rather than "drive," so his "fusion" of these partial drives has also been abandoned. We have chosen to render Lefort's *intrication* as "meshing" for two reasons: firstly, to keep the association with a net (or network, of the signifiers in which the drive is caught up from the start), and secondly, for its association with a gear mechanism, which reminds us that the drive, for Lacan, as for Freud, is a construct or montage of interlocking components.

We could not convey the economical French term *combler* without alternating between its three relevant meanings: to fulfill (a desire), to fill up (a hole in the body), and to complete (a lack in the Other).

Accoler and *décoller* proved troublesome. Rosine Lefort herself (in note 5 of the Conclusions) points to the etymological difference of these terms used to describe a specific relation between the subject and the Other in the form of an impossible attempt at fusion by means of the real body. For *accolement,* which can also mean embracing, we have used "sticking," occasionally "gluing" (implied in its opposite, *décoller*), and rarely "joining." For the loosening of this kind of attachment, *décoller,* we have reverted to "unsticking."

None of us are experts in topology, that branch of mathematics which Lacan began to use in the 1960s to articulate the Real with the Symbolic only, circumventing the mind's dependency on Imaginary pictorial supports for its thought. Rosine Lefort's dexterity in applying the concepts derived from this discipline speaks for itself; we can only hope mathematicians will not be alarmed at the possibility of encountering some technical term that does not fit their lexicon.

We cannot go into all the choices we had to make and naturally take full responsibility for all errors and liberties. However, we consider our job done if the reader of this book can judge for him or herself where we have translated, and where, may we be forgiven, betrayed.

Preface   *Rosine Lefort*

I carried out the treatments that constitute the subject matter of this book—as the treatments of Robert the Wolf Child and of Maryse, which form the material of two other books—between September 1951 and November 1952 at the Foundation Parent de Rosan, which was a part of the service directed by Jenny Aubry.*

This was an institution offering temporary asylum to children. It was part of the Assistance Publique, in the style of the institutions that still exist for very young children waiting to be placed or, as it occurs in the majority of cases, temporarily in institutional care for the duration of the illness of their mothers.

I carried out these treatments before receiving any theoretical training, and they are closely linked with my own analysis.

Nadia's treatment was the first chronologically. It will be shown how I started it. This treatment lasted approximately ten months, from October 1951 until July 1952.

By October 1951 I had been in analysis for eighteen months. My analysis had been imposed by the need to overcome a neurotic suffering, and for that reason it was very difficult for me. It was difficult to the point that during Nadia's treatment I felt, over a period of several months, that it was impossible for me to attend the sessions of my own analysis regularly.

The treatment of Nadia, and indeed of the other children, which I commenced successively in the course of the following three months, in some way performed the function, therefore, of a substitute in my own analytic process, within which it came to be inscribed.

---

* These treatments were carried out within the frame of a research project on the conditions and effects of the prolonged admission of young children (hospitalism). This research was carried out from 1948 until 1953 in the department directed by Jenny Aubry. It was initially subsidized by the National Institute of Hygiene and later, from the end of 1950 until 1953, by the Infancy International Center directed by Professor Robert Debré, in association with the research of the English team of the Tavistock Clinic under the direction of John Bowlby. The findings were published in the book by Jenny Aubry and her assistants, *Carence de soins maternels* (Paris: PUF, 1953), and published again in 1964 by Éditions de la Parole.

Note

The narrative of the sessions, marked by a vertical rule, is what I wrote in the years 1951 and 1952, in the evening after each session.

I conducted these treatments before acquiring any psychological or analytical theoretical training. Furthermore, I wrote these reports before Lacan gave his seminars, so that the terms of formulations I have used are those I had at my disposal then; they must be taken as such and bearing in mind those conditions.

PART 1 *Nadia or the Mirror*

1 / *The Small Other:* Invidia

Nadia arrived in the institution when she was thirteen and a half months old. She had known no other kind of establishment, as she had been separated from her mother, who had tuberculosis, at birth.

As often happens in such cases, she suffered from recurrent rhinopharyngeal infections, which meant it was impossible to place her in a foster home. Nadia was shuttled back and forth between nurseries and hospitals. We knew from the medical records that arrived with her that she had had her adenoids removed at two months. These problems had continued, accompanied by otitis and diarrhea. At five months she suffered double mastoiditis, which had to be treated by bilateral antrotomy. She spent three months in the hospital as a result of an abscess on the antrotomy scar.

When Nadia arrived at Parent de Rosan, she looked utterly wretched. Her general condition worsened a few days later as a result of chronic otorrhea and diarrhea.

At that time I was in Jenny Aubry's unit, responsible for looking after eight to ten children from one to three years old. When they arrived, they had to be put together in quarantine for a fortnight, to reduce the risk of spreading contagious childhood diseases. Nadia was one of this group, and even though she attracted my attention, she was by no means my sole concern. This should be borne in mind when considering the notes I took about her: the relations I had with her had nothing to do with individual psychotherapy at the beginning.

Nadia was very thin, with a yellowish complexion. Her face was emaciated; the striking feature was the big, dark-ringed eyes. The only lively thing about her was her look, which took in everything that went on around her.

Her growth was severely retarded: her weight was only eighteen pounds, and her length twenty-eight inches. In other words, she could have been taken for an eight-month-old baby.

The first thing that struck me when I saw her in her room was her immobility. She would sit for entire days on top of her pillow, both hands clutching the sides of the crib. She did not make the slightest movement to take a cookie that was held out to her. If she was picked up and put down on the floor, she would not budge; her expression would go dead, and she would rock violently. Even when she was sitting among the other children, she would not make any movement to attempt to pick up a toy. But if another child picked one up near her, she would cry out, throw herself forcefully backward, then sit up and start her rocking motion again.

This reaction to the appearance of another child in her field of perception, both at that time and later on, gives us a clue as to the nature of her relation to the small other.

The way she took hold of objects was very peculiar. She would move her skinny, long-fingered hands toward the object with spiderlike movements and just brush it with her fingertips. If she managed to grasp it, her hand would open almost immediately, as if some clockwork mechanism set off the motion of letting go of the object. There was not the faintest show of emotion involved in any of these movements.

Nadia had no spontaneous contact with adults. The staff put it down to her fear, but I did not see any evidence of that.

When Nadia's case was discussed, no diagnosis was put forward, because the lack of contact was not so extreme as to suggest any major pathology. Her detachment was far from complete; her lively look, always watching what was going on, supported this view.

When I first saw her, on 8 October, I realized that contact with her was a possibility; but she did not show it openly.

She was sitting in her crib, in her usual position, both hands clutching the sides, her body completely motionless. The few gestures she made showed a tendency to repetitiveness; the fixity of all her positions gave the impression of catatonia.

When I went back to see her on 12 October, she was in her crib in the dormitory. The possibility of contact with me was affirmed: she smiled and seemed delighted when I spoke to her. She went to sit on top of her pillow, smiling even more broadly.

I held out a rubber sailor to her; she took hold of it, squeezed it with both hands, but with clumsy movements and parasitic gestures, as I described above. She cradled the toy sailor, kissed it, licked it, threw it down, picked it up again, gave it back to me, then took it back again.

At that moment the nurse started feeding the other children. Each time Nadia saw her doing something for another child, she hit the toy sailor and threw it down, but without any visible sign of emotion.

When the nurse came to feed her, she seemed happy, but closed her mouth when she felt the spoon against her lips. Afterward she allowed herself to be filled up passively. The nurse said, "It's always like this with Nadia, but she ends up eating everything."

When I arrived on 13 October, she was sitting in her crib, very alert to what was going on around her. She had her thumb in her mouth, but was not sucking it; the thumb was well in her mouth, but there was no autoerotic pleasure.

As soon as I went up to her, a smile lit up her poor face with its dark-ringed eyes. She had a high temperature that day. She came into physical contact with me by playing with my hand, which I had rested on the side of the crib, and pulling at my fingers; she even went so far as to lick me.

She leaned quite far toward me, and I felt I could take her into my arms; but when I made to do so, her face set. Shortly afterward, she flashed a smile, but she turned away immediately and looked out of the window into the garden. When I put her back in her crib, however, she looked sullen.

I left her the toy sailor, as I moved away from her; and as I went up to another child, she looked at us and threw down the sailor. I gave it back to her; she turned her back on me and played with it, turning around every now and then, and trying every possible way—sighing, shrieking, laughing—to attract my attention.

She addressed her demand to me again on 15 October. She smiled when I approached her, then made little shrieking noises in my direction when I went up to another child under my care in the quarantine ward, and finally she started crying. Then she stopped, turned her back on me, put one thumb in her mouth, without sucking it, and put her other hand over it. She made a rocking movement with her hands, as if cradling herself.

When I went back to her, she parted her hands, looked at me, smiled, let go of her thumb, and went to sit on her pillow; she played with one of my hands. I held out a rubber sailor to her; she put out her hand several times to take it, then withdrew it; she decided to take it, but let it go immediately. This happened twice in a row; the third time she flung it to the end of the crib.

She refused to take the cracker the nurse held out to her; the nurse left it in the crib, but Nadia did not touch it at all.

She seemed, overall, less aware of her surroundings.

So this was the beginning, which in my mind was no more than an observation. At the time no one had ever dared to attempt treating such a young child. Shortly afterward, Nadia fell into a serious decline, and during the following days, her condition worsened steadily. She became paler and paler, completely withdrawn, miserable, refusing to take anything that was offered to her, not even a toy or a cracker, and she rocked incessantly. The look on her little old woman's face was pathetic and disconsolate. That was the look that followed me as I left her.

And it was that look which made me come back, which was the start of an analytic adventure for her and for me, and which made me an analyst.

At the time, having just arrived in Jenny Aubry's unit, there was no question of my "authorizing myself" to take the position of analyst. Nonetheless, what happened between Nadia and myself cannot be reduced to the straightforward transactions between an adult responsible for observation—and what sort of observation? was it a laboratory?—and an infant in distress. Fortunately I was in no way capable of any such observation.

Nadia's decline was what concerned me most, given the relation that had arisen between her and me. It was a relation that, for example, had nothing maternal about it. I did not offer myself to her as some kind of mother-substitute who would comfort her and satisfy her. I seemed to her to be completely different from the other adults she had known in her institutionalized life:

1. I did not get involved in the kind of physical handling she was subjected to by the nurses.

2. What is more, I did not involve myself in feeding her, in satisfying her oral need.

3. The relation between her and me was established only at the level of eye and voice: only at the level where something of her demand for love was bearable to her.

She told me in her own way, on 13 October, what was not acceptable to her, when I thought I could take her in my arms because she was leaning toward me. Her face set, and she turned away. So it was Nadia who imposed the limits on the relation between herself and myself. The pure Real of bodies made any relation impossible; but that was all she had known up to that point: being handled without being "spoken."

This notion of the "Real of the body" has at once to be situated in the context, and in the dialectic, which was to follow Nadia throughout her treatment. The Real, here, is posited only as register, in relation to two others—the Symbolic and the Imaginary—and particularly in relation to the Symbolic, to which Nadia showed that she had access right from the start of the treatment, even if only through the demand she addressed to me. What was Real for her was what failed to be symbolized in her relation to me, or rather, to my body. It was in this sense that the Real, as register, took on its value of impossibility.

The Symbolic is based on access to the signifier; it is there that the Real is waiting to be changed into a signifier through the word of the Other; an essential articulation, as we shall see. It was this Other who had failed to confer on Nadia the status of subject through the word, although she had known many Others in her varied existence. She was to find the status of subject through the treatment, in which I found myself in the place of Other.

I was only too sensitive to the limits she imposed on me, having myself suffered from neurosis. It had been through my body that I had experienced this suffering intensely; a body which, as always in such cases, I could only cope with by allowing it to become the object of care and attention. Nadia, for her part, only had her body insofar as it was the object of care and attention. The ambiguous solicitations of care givers, whether in the family or in an institution, can leave the subject in the totally derelict state of being physically manipulated in the real, without a single word to acknowledge his or her position as subject. As a result of this painful experience, I was reluctant to become a maternal figure for her, that is to say, to give her additional care and attention and, inconsiderately, to bring into play the Real of bodies, of the child's and mine.

Although I had ruled out a maternal relationship, at that time I had no preconceived idea of what I could give Nadia, except my attention and my availability, so that she could demand, or rather begin to make her demands, with all her reticence when it came to the question of physical contact.

I was far from having any trace of theoretical knowledge. My only knowledge was what could be considered an unconscious one, concerning the articulation of demand and the body.

Nadia established a relation with me into which she gradually reintroduced physical contact between bodies, hers and mine, in her roundabout way of expressing things to me or addressing me, whether with demands or refusals. In the analytic relation that established itself, Nadia put me in a position where she showed me the Real character of my body, while at the same time forcing me to renounce it. It was in this position that I was to let her challenge me, to listen to what she had to say, to let her speak death in order to live. From that position, she forced me to give up any idea of her well-being, she stripped me of any notion of trying to help her. I had to somehow tune it to her drama, I had to allow her to totter toward me as if toward an arena where her drama could be spoken and heard.

I was indeed a locus where she could express that the care that was provided for her was nothing but a prop that excluded her, leaving her empty, dead. She no longer had any object relations, except looking at the other child with the adult.

That was what she had shown me on 12 October when she saw the nurse feeding the other children: Nadia hit the toy sailor and threw it down. Even though there was no visible sign of emotion, it still revealed how she reacted when another child was the object of an adult's attention, in front of her. Outside this situation, the other child seemed not to exist for her. Even the understated nature of her reaction, which consisted merely in throwing down the object she was holding, or letting go of it with her usual mechanical movement, meant that nobody noticed what she was doing. It needed my presence and my acceptance of her gesture, by putting into words what she had done, in order for the sense of it to begin to emerge.

Would it be right in this context to mention jealousy, as the desire to have for herself something that the other obtained from the adult? That would be hard to justify; for what the nurse was giving the other children was food, and Nadia at first refused to accept it when it was her turn to be fed, and then swallowed the food without any pleasure. What was more, she did not enjoy being on an adult's lap; I occasionally saw her sitting there inert, like a lifeless object.

We can only conclude that it was "seeing" that was involved in Nadia's case: seeing an adult paying attention to another child. It was the most common visual experience for her in her institutionalized life. In the scene mentioned above, although it was in fact a question of food, it did not constitute an oral object for Nadia; it was a scopic object of envy. This inevitably brings to mind Lacan's passage on *invidia*.*

"*Invidia* comes from *videre*. The most exemplary case of *invidia* for us analysts is the one I found long ago in St. Augustine, and have

---

*Jacques Lacan, *Séminaire,* livre xi, *Les Quatre concepts fondamentaux de la psychanalyse* (Paris: Éditions du Seuil, 1967), 105-6.

given its due ever since, to wit the one of the little boy looking at his little brother hanging from the mother's breast, looking at him *amare conspectu,* with a bitter look, which decomposes him and has on him the effect of a poison.

"To understand what *invidia* is in its function of gaze, one should not confuse it with jealousy. What the little child or anyone else envies is not at all necessarily what the child might want (1), as is wrongly said. The boy who is looking at his younger brother, who is to say that he still needs to be at the breast? Everyone knows that envy is commonly provoked by the possession of goods which would, to the one who envies, be of no use and of which one does not suspect the true nature.

"Such is true envy. What makes the subject turn pale? The image of completeness closing on itself, and also because the *a,* the separated *a* from which the boy suspends himself, can be for another the possession that satisfies him, a *Befriedigung.*"

For Nadia, indeed, there was no question of an object as specific as the mother's breast, although this was to come up frequently later on. At that time it was merely a question of this apparently banal food, which was distributed at each mealtime to all the children in turn, to feed them and satisfy their needs. Nadia's reaction put this food into quite a different register from the Real of "filling up." Just as the little boy, watching his younger brother at the breast, would have been unable to accept the gift of the mother's breast, even if the mother had been moved by an excess of tenderness to offer it to him, so Nadia could not accept this food, which crushed her feelings of envy when confronted with what appeared to her a picture of completeness on the part of the other, and his satisfaction, rather than just a food-object as such. In this gap between the object and the image that aroused her envy, it was clear that Nadia had hung onto one dimension of her relation to the food-object that implicated not only the adult but also another child, with the Real of the object in brackets. This had occurred in spite of the fact that her demand had until then been permanently crushed, debased for the sake of satisfying her needs.

That is what properly defines *invidia,* which can only manifest itself in the scopic field, and it indicated the persistence of Nadia's desire. Her desire was in the specific relation to an object that aroused her covetousness only if it belonged to another child, and that in any case could not possibly satisfy her. Surely this object in relation to another, and which she had to keep at a distance, was none other than Lacan's object *a,* the object cause of desire.

This question of keeping the object at a distance appeared very clearly in Nadia's case, right from the initial tableau, with her hesitant way of grasping things, followed by the mechanical gesture of letting go. Surely she was showing that the object to which, in spite of herself, she was attracted was totally incapable of satisfying her. The only dimension of the object she had ever known was that of need, in other words, of the Real, of the thing, *das Ding,* which had failed to inscribe itself in the relation to the Other, which did not exist for her, so that she could not find satisfaction in it. She was reduced by it to completely withdrawing her demand and not being able to maintain her desire except in the gap of the object she had let go of, or in *invidia.*

The same process was involved where the body was concerned. Occasionally, an impulse of demand would escape from her, when she held out an arm to me or even both arms. But she could no more bear me to take her in my arms or touch her than she could bear her relation to the object, as if there was a danger that I might respond to her rudimentary demands. Real handling of her body, as she knew only too well, would cause her desire to disappear.

Such was the meaning of the limit she imposed on me and which I respected in our physical relations. It also explained the decline she fell into during these first few months. She found herself in an impasse, where she could not express her demand without finding that her desire was immediately canceled out by the Real of bodily contact: her desire that, in spite of everything, she managed to safeguard in the last bastion that remained for her—the scopic drive where *invidia* manifests itself.

Outside these situations, Nadia looked all around her, with an expression of curiosity that showed no sign of a sense of loss. It was as if this look protected her and carried within itself all the objects it saw. "What is specific about the scopic field," says Lacan, "is that the fall of the subject always goes unnoticed, because it is reduced to zero." Nadia took refuge in the scopic, which protected her from irremediable loss and from death: only her look was alive.

2/The Big Other: The Separable Object

The following days, alone with me, Nadia was shaken and very withdrawn. Even her smell evoked something of death, because of her permanent otorrhea and diarrhea.

All the same she was taken to the nursery. She was sitting on the floor like the other children, rocking herself, looking miserable. I went up to her but she seemed to be unaware of my presence. Her expression was lifeless.

I sat down behind her. When a child wanted to take the building block I had put beside her, she reacted as she always did: she cried out tearfully, threw herself backward against my legs, turned toward me and offered me an arm, but only one. This was her first true demand addressed to me, but it is worth noting that this demand was triggered by the surprise of the other's aggression.

On 23 October I sat down beside her on the floor. She was not doing anything; there was a block next to her. Her expression was lifeless and she looked terrible. I smiled at her but did not touch her. She did not respond and looked at me without a trace of feeling on her face. She seemed indifferent.

Another child came toward me. At that point Nadia held out her arms to me, hesitantly at first, then remained with arms outstretched. Her hands, however, were turned backward, the palms facing up. I took her onto my lap. She looked at me lingeringly, ventured a smile, then started to explore my mouth with her finger. After a while she smiled openly.

Again, another child came up to me and touched me. Nadia threw herself backward and showed great disgust at contact with this child. She tensed up and her face set. As soon as the child left she relaxed and returned to her exploration of my mouth, laughing all the while.

Later, at dinner, she was sitting in a little chair. She rocked violently, gripping the edge of the table with both hands. Eventually she slid herself under the table without touching the piece of cheese she had in front of her. As I came closer she did not take her eyes off me.

The next morning, 24 October, when she had demanded to come into my arms and was exploring my mouth, she babbled a little for the first time. I offered her a block, which she took. She hung onto it at first but let go, as soon as a child caught hold of my white coat, with the backing-off movement described earlier. At that moment she was overcome by a ticlike batting of the eyelids, which, however, did not return. I noted it because it was a valuable pointer; in her relation to me or to any adult, she would react violently against herself as soon as another child entered her field of perception: whether the child seized an object or came up to me, she could not bear to see it.

From 25 October on, she was no longer taken down to the nursery, first because she was ill, and second because the group situation only caused her stress, as her lifeless look and her rocking testified.

On 27 October the session took place, like all the others, in her dormitory, where there were eight cribs. Nadia smiled as soon as I came in and clearly recognized me. When she saw me taking a chair to sit beside her she laughed and babbled. She settled herself comfortably on top of her pillow, and, after some hesitation, leaned over to put her finger into my mouth.

She wanted me to take her onto my lap. But suddenly her face set and she tensed up as, without thinking, I put my hand on the neighboring crib, which was empty because all the other children were in the nursery. My suspicions were confirmed when I saw her smile as soon as I withdrew my hand. Once I had understood what was happening and stopped putting my hand on the edge of the other child's crib, Nadia became very active again and took a great deal of interest in me.

She took hold of the pencil jutting out from the pocket of my white coat, threw it on the floor, and turned her eyes toward it for me to pick it up. Then she burst out laughing, but had an attack of diarrhea at the same time. A nurse came to change her; Nadia cried and looked around to see where I was. She stopped doing this as soon as I was back beside her, then started the pencil game again, laughing loudly.

The next morning, 28 October, she continued her contact with me. The moment I was beside her, she began to fidget, shoved her finger into my mouth, then sucked it and put it back in, *before moving on to my hands, which she brushed with her long fingers. Then she took one of my fingers, shook it, and stopped suddenly as if she were disappointed that she could not do with it what she had done with the pencil:* to separate it from me and throw it down for me to pick up. She no longer knew what she was doing. She made movements that seemed to be asking me to pick her up, but as I held out my arms, her face tensed up and she turned away, putting her arms behind her. I withdrew my invitation so that she felt she could come back to explore my body around my mouth, while looking at me long and very anxiously.

The doctor arrived on his rounds and attracted her attention. Very rapidly she withdrew and put her thumb into her mouth and her other hand against her cheek, as if to cut herself off from me in the presence of a third party.

On 1 November she was in her crib with a temperature. She looked at my hands but could not bring herself to touch them. In place of them, one could say, she took hold of a toy, a rubber elephant, threw it down for me to pick up, and laughed. At one point she inadvertently hit herself with it and began to cry. She held out her arms to me and I took her onto my lap; at once, very anxiously, she explored my mouth. She pulled at my teeth as she had done with my finger. As if she could not find what she was looking for, she smacked me rather violently on the mouth and her face tensed up and set. Then a profound sorrow came over her and she put her head on my shoulder, both hands gripping my white coat.

Suddenly she returned to my mouth and put a finger into it, followed by her whole hand, looking away all the while. It was too much for her and she remained petrified.

On the morning of 3 November she had changed rooms. She seemed rather poorly to me; she looked terrible and seemed anxious. She held out her arms but turned her hands away. She sat on her pillow, legs crossed, and held one foot in her hand. She refused all contact.

When I arrived in the afternoon she smiled at me. I held out my hands and she leaned toward me.

For the first time I took her into another room, the one next door, following a decision taken on 31 October by the team: to entrust her to me to continue what appeared to be the preliminaries of an analytic treatment and not just an observation. Some of Nadia's reactions had certainly been reinforced by the conditions of observation. But in spite of these unfavorable circumstances, a relationship had been established between us, during the month of October, which enabled her to accept to come alone with me into this new room for the first truly individual session of her treatment. She was nevertheless still holding back as was shown by the way she kept her arms up with the palms turned outward as I carried her.

I put her in a crib with a rag doll and an animal made of waxed cloth. I sat down by the crib and brought the toys nearer to her. I had left the door open.

She picked up the animal, let it go, picked it up again, pressed it against my mouth, then against her own, babbling a little all the while. But she remained tense. The second time she put the toy to my mouth, I kissed it. She seemed surprised, put the animal to her own mouth, licked it, and then pressed it against mine again, first trying to force it in, then leaving it against my lips. I kissed it. Nadia's hand was so close that *the kiss was half on the toy and half on her hand.* She put the animal to her mouth, watching me anxiously at first, then with a smile. She played this game several times in succession.

At that moment a nurse arrived with her afternoon snack: it was cereal. Nadia obstinately closed her mouth against the spoon, watching me. When the nurse insisted, she allowed herself to be filled up, with an expressionless face and lowered eyes.

When the nurse had gone, *Nadia picked up the doll, which was within her reach, shook it a great deal, and put its hand into her mouth. She tried to tear off the hand with her teeth but could not do so; and, looking very tense and disgusted, she hit the doll and threw it to the foot of the crib.*

Then she wanted to come back onto my lap; she hit me on the mouth, that mouth she always returned to and that was, as we have seen, as much mine as hers.

Over the following days she continued to develop her relations with me, through the mediation of a fluffy toy chick, but always using it to examine my mouth and hers, each in turn, by pressing the object against them.

It seems that this game made the chick into an object that could be handled: not only did Nadia not let go of it with her habitual automatic movement of opening her hand while resolutely accomplishing her desire of making me kiss it, but she was also capable of separating from it and throwing it purposefully for me to pick up. She was so taken with her game that she was even capable, when I was picking up the chick for her and had my head down, of touching my hair, putting her finger in my ear, and then caressing my cheek with her hand for quite a long time. But then she tensed up and became anxious.

On 7 November, during a game with the same chick, she was able to touch my hands and guide the toy toward herself without anxiety: she laughed, full of joy, with a vivacious look, wriggling her legs. *The toy proved to be the intermediary she needed to accept having contact with me and to enjoy it.*

She threw down the chick, picked up a green car, and hit me on the mouth with it, babbling. In vain, she tried to push it into my mouth. She played a game of to-and-fro with the car, between her mouth and mine.

She threw the car away and turned her attention to *a doll that she picked up and put in my lap.* I stroked and cradled it. Nadia meanwhile, laughed and fidgeted. Then she took the doll away from me and inspected each arm in turn, as if she had to check that they were still there. After a while she copied what I had done to the doll, with a look of concentration: she stroked, cradled, and kissed it. Then she stopped, her face tense, tugged at the doll's dress to pull it over, and threw it down. At that moment she was very agitated and put her finger into my mouth as usual.

The following scene took place the evening of the same day, after dinner, when I went back to her room. Nadia smiled at me; I offered her the cracker that was her dessert. She took it and then let go of it immediately, twice in a row. She held out her arms; I picked her up. She was then able to keep the cracker and put it to my mouth. I bit off a corner of it.

I put her back into the crib; she vomited. But I should add that she did so when I had my back turned to go, and above all, when I spoke a few words to another child I knew.

I turned around and she smiled slightly, allowed a nurse to change her, still smiling, and, when I came up to her to say good-bye, she put her finger in my mouth, after furtively brushing her hand against my cheek.

During this period, between 16 and 27 October, it was through the small other that I came to exist for her. It was enough, indeed, that another child entered her field of perception and took the block I had put within her reach, without actually giving it to her, for her to turn toward me and hold out one of her arms. Or again, it was enough for another child to touch me: she who had seemed indifferent to my presence the moment before, held out her arms, both of them this time. Inversely, when she was in my arms exploring my mouth, she would throw herself backward and turn away from me as soon as another child came up to me and touched me. Or again, she would throw away the block I had given her as soon as a child clutched my apron.

So it was the other child who guided her toward the adult that I was for her; it was the other who led her to the Other: to the extent that this other could always come and take the object from this Other—from me, from my body—and be satisfied with it; something that would exclude her: for example, when the nurse fed another child in her presence, a scene that could appear before her eyes at any moment in her life in the institution. Her repeated batting of her eyelids on 24 October said enough about what she could not bear to see.

The scene of 27 October—when I pulled back my hand from the next crib, which was empty, would clarify the problem of the encumbering but fascinating presence of the other child. The test was in fact conclusive because she smiled when I withdrew my hand, that is, when I separated myself from the other. And since this small other was not in his crib, it was his trace that was at issue; a trace I erased when I withdrew my hand.

If we link this scene with the preceding one where the adult was feeding the child, where it was not food that provoked Nadia's covetousness but the relation of the child to the adult, her satisfaction in this instance derived from the fact that I separated myself not from a real child but from his trace. That put the other child in the same register as food: for Nadia the register of objects was already symbolic, such was her demand.

In this framework, to withdraw my hand from the neighboring crib had the value of an interpretation and put me in the foreground as an Other who could separate from an object, that is to say, who was marked by a lack. For the first time Nadia encountered an adult who could lack a small other. The other and the Other, who up till then had been scopically glued together for her, came apart.

It was the last time that Nadia felt herself destroyed and annihilated when faced with another child. She would no longer lose contact with me in the presence of another (with the exception of the session of 10 December).

As soon as she became active again, once I had withdrawn my hand from the neighboring crib, she would renew this operation of separation of objects from my body. She took out my pencil from the pocket of my white coat and threw it down for me to pick up. That made her laugh.

From 28 October on, the effect of this experience proved decisive in the refinding of her oral autoerotism. She stuck her finger into my mouth, sucked her finger, did it again, as if the erotic object taken from her own body could have this function only in relation to the hollow of my own mouth. The object-finger could not excite her mouth unless it was in the place of the object she took from me, that she made me lose: that is, the other child or the pencil.

The same session confirmed that what she was looking for was the separable nature as such of the object, for example, when she pulled my finger, shook it, and was disappointed that she could not do with it what she did with my pencil. It was the same "separability" that she looked for on 1 November, when, exploring my mouth, she pulled in vain at my teeth. After that she struck me on the mouth.

The object is erotic or autoerotic only if it is separable, barred; and this is true for all the different levels of the drive, excepting the scopic, where the separable aspect does not appear. To be "separable" from my body was what was necessary to make an object into an object of desire, an object cause of desire.

For Nadia this was not the case with food. She demonstrated this in the session on 3 November when she refused the cereal a nurse wanted to give her: she obstinately closed her mouth while watching me; she could accept this object only with an expressionless face and lowered eyes, without looking at me, passively. She became active again only after the nurse had left, when she tried to tear off one of the doll's hands with her teeth; she played out on the doll what food lacked in order to be an object of desire and satisfaction: to be an object that could be separated from the body of the Other. The object aimed at was not the food but the feeding hand.

Her relation to me had come to the forefront; she circled around my mouth as a place, a gap, found ready-made on my body; even if Nadia attempted to create other gaps herself, by pulling at my finger and at my teeth. But this mouth, this gap was not to be filled; and when, on the evening of 7 November, I bit off the corner of the cracker she had put into my mouth, it was she—in the transitivism at play between us—who vomited: as if she could not tolerate the least object filling the hollow of my mouth. That object I ate was again the irruption of a Real between her and me, which took her back one step, to the moment when I had put my hand on the neighboring crib. At that point, I was really completed, not by the small other, but by the object at play between the child and the adult in *invidia*. It was as if the object at issue between us had been unveiled. While it was she who vomited it was of course because she could not make me vomit; but the transitivism was evidence enough that identification was already at work between her body and mine, a primary form of identification before any search for an object on the body of the Other. What emerged was the necessity of a hole in the body of the Other, and Nadia, in transitivism, reestablished this.

She did not vomit, moreover, without the loss of my look, then given to another child, demonstrating the close link between eye and mouth. But she could not yet make this link; or rather, it could be established only in a relation of exclusion: either she looked at me and was unable to absorb nourishment, or she ate and withdrew her look from me and from the external world. As yet there was no meshing—or perhaps rather the opposite—between the scopic and the oral drives.

The drive object was not revealed in the gaze. Food uncovered it, but forbade the gaze when Nadia ate the cereal: and when she fed me with a piece of cracker, my gaze, which withdrew, revealed the object of the drive in the food while forbidding the oral dimension.

A double commandment emerged there: "Thou shalt not see the *a* any more than thou shalt eat it!" We could add: "Thou shalt eat thy food without knowing that, in thy gaze, thou carriest the *a* cause of thine own desire."

3/ The Scopic Drive:
"Getting Oneself Seen"

I put a crib in the room where the sessions took place, given the importance this object had for Nadia. Indeed, at the beginning, she had her most lively expression when she was in her crib. At the same time she could support herself by gripping the sides of her crib with her hands.

When I arrived in the dormitory on 9 November she was sleeping. She was lying on her back, her arms above her head, her hands open with the palms turned upward. Her poor little face made a profound impression on me, the rings around her eyes even darker in sleep: she made me think of death. I returned in the afternoon.

As soon as I put her in the crib she took a little green toy car; but she let it go with her usual mechanical hand movement several times in a row. Finally she took it and kept it, roaring with laughter; she put it to her mouth, then to mine, striking me quite hard with it, laughing all the time. Then she threw down the car and took the chick, playing the same game with that, putting it to her mouth, then to mine, pushing her hand against my mouth, *and gurgling joyfully.*

She then took the doll and held it out to me. I put the doll on my knee and cradled it. Nadia took it back, looked at it, threw it on her crib, and wanted to sit on my lap. She was a little anxious, then she babbled; for the first time, she looked lively and expressive. She put her finger in my mouth and inspected my white coat, pushing aside my collar slightly to scratch the base of my neck, looking serious and tense. She wanted to get back into her crib, where she picked up the doll again, and held it out to me. I cradled it; she took it back after getting me to kiss it and wanted to get back on my lap with the doll. She paid some attention to the doll, licked it, got me to cradle it again, then threw it down. She looked at me and tried to jump as if I were helping her jump up in my lap, roaring with laughter. So I helped her jump up; she was even happier; she leaned toward me and I kissed her, *while her head was pressing against my breast.* She did this several times, staying a little longer each time. However, she was always watchful of where my hands were in relation to her body; they were not allowed to touch her, and I only did what was absolutely necessary to keep her balance.

When I brought her back to her crib, she held out her arms to me, palms upward as usual, smiling shyly. She was uneasy and I felt a sense of shock in her when I left her, aware of how much she had held back though she wanted so much throughout the session.

On 10 November, while the nurse was changing her, she kept holding her hand up to me, smiling, but did not manage to take my hand, which I held out to her.

During the session, as soon as she was in her crib, she turned toward me and jumped up and down, laughing and looking at me. I put her on my lap: she wanted me to bounce her while she played with a fluffy chick.

I held out a cracker to her; she took it, after hesitating a great deal, then very quickly let go of it with her usual automatic movement. I picked it up and proceeded to give some of it to the doll. Nadia took it back and put it to my mouth; I ate a corner of it; she looked at it, then let it go again with the usual movement. I put it back on my knee, but she did not take any further notice of it. I felt she was tense and anxious; she took back the fluffy chick, smiling a little, huddling up to me very close for a few moments.

At this moment another little girl came into the room and Nadia took a great deal of interest in her, at the same time insisting that I should bounce her on my lap. She had no hesitation in touching the other child; she pulled her hair a little and touched her cheek with her hand. Between movements she looked at me while I continued to bounce her. At the same time she made a kissing sound with her mouth. I kissed her once, but she pushed me away. From that point on she became restless and anxious.

I took her back to her room, where she started rocking as I left.

On 12 November I learned that Nadia had spontaneously refused to take anything but a bottle for her breakfast that morning.

Her session started in her crib. She looked at the toys and jumped up and down for joy and looked at me. She threw the car, then the cracker down on the floor and held out her arms so I would put her on my lap. Once there, she wanted me to bounce her and kiss her; then she leaned over and took the toys from the crib one by one and threw them on the floor.

Then for the first time she wanted me to sit her on the floor where the toys and the cracker were. There she beamed, kicking her legs and watching me. She was very active, picked up the toys, and put them on a low chair that I had left in order to sit on the floor next to her. She even tried to crawl to get to the toys, which were quite far away. She was both in contact with me and happy to be sitting on the floor.

At the end of the session I asked the nurse to put Nadia with the other children for a little while, but to make sure she could bear it and not force her to stay if she became anxious.

These three sessions concerned the passage from *invidia* to the scopic drive in the strict sense of the word: "getting oneself seen"; from them we can glean the structural implications of such a passage.

In a first moment, Nadia used two objects in succession that she approached very differently and whose fate would be no less diverse: a small green car and a fluffy chick.

During the session of 9 November, the car appeared as an impossible object; this judgment is based simply on the fact that she was unable to pick it up without being forced to let it go with her automatic movement; it was only by confronting it with her mouth and then with mine that she felt able to keep it, while roaring with laughter. Then, at once, still laughing, she hit my mouth with it: from the impossible to the laugh, the car became another object, and she could playfully refuse to give it to me.

The fluffy chick was less alien since she pressed it against my cheek and then substituted herself for it, by pressing her hand in its place; and in this case she no longer hit me on the mouth but gurgled joyfully.

The difference between these two objects was to continue to develop; the car was always to be used to hit with, to make a noise and to be heard, as we shall see, while the chick was to retain its function as a mediator to approach or remove objects such as the bottle.

The next step Nadia made was with the doll, when she took it and held it out to me while she was in her crib. I responded by putting the doll on my lap and cradling it. Then Nadia took the same position on my lap, throwing down the doll into the crib she had just left. She gurgled.

In fact, she was taking the place of the void she had established by physically depriving me of something: the doll; that is to say, the small other she separated from me on 27 October, or rather from which I separated myself according to her wish, by withdrawing my hand from the edge of the crib.

One characteristic of the objects—car, chick, doll—began to emerge: they had nothing to do with a need, but very much to do with Nadia's *demand*. Their function as mediators conferred upon them a *signifying* dimension, which was shown again in the repetition they gave rise to in Nadia's relation to me.

This relation could not be reduced to a bringing into play of signifiers. Nadia was driven, in the sense of drive, to approach my body more directly, by a structural necessity that makes the object participate in both the signifier and in the body of the Other; she inspected my white coat, pushing the collar aside to scratch the base of my neck. At that moment she neither laughed nor gurgled, and she had to retreat. What was she retreating from, if not the Real of my body? What she was seeking on my body was an object that would be carried by it, that could be detached from it, like the small other and the pencil she had separated from it. The attempts she made on my fingers and my teeth underlined the separable nature of the object she was seeking.

One could say that from this point on such objects constituted something that Nadia never stopped coming up against. What was their status? Those objects were real because they were there on my body and she knew it. They were always in the same place, and whatever substitute objects she brought into her game, it was always to these objects that she would return. But they were also signifiers insofar as the impossibility of reaching them affected them with a bar, which meant that their status changed from the Real to that of the signifier: "The bar is one of the surest and shortest ways of raising the Real to the dignity of the signifier."*

Not yet being able to approach these objects that could be separated from my body, Nadia returned to the preceding object, the "doll-small-other," which she held out to me and took back in order to lick it, then threw down, before taking up her place on my lap once again, that is to say, always the place of the child on the adult's lap, where the two bodies are in contact. But a new element appeared in regard to the doll: she licked it after getting me to kiss it, that is, she had made it into an oral object.

*Jacques Lacan, "Les Formations de l'inconscient" (unpublished seminar of 23 April 1958).

From then on she became active: she tried to jump up in my lap; I helped her jump up and she burst out laughing. We shall see how important motor control was to become as the case developed. Motor activity, even at this early stage, was associated with the quest for the object on my body, which Nadia pursued by leaning her head against my breast, several times, and for a longer period each time.

She insisted that I should help her jump up. But she was always watchful of the position of my hands, which were not allowed to touch her, anymore than she allowed herself to touch me when I took her to her room (she always kept her palms in the air, turned outward). Surely that was a denial of what she was trying to take from my body and what I was not to know about.

It was during the session of 10 November that Nadia completed the transition from *invidia* to the scopic drive, when faced with another child. This other child fortuitously came into the room where I was sitting with Nadia on my lap. Nadia took an immediate interest in her, but only on condition that I bounce her up and down. Then, while bouncing, she looked at the other child, was able to touch her, to caress her, turning to look at me each time she made a gesture. At the same time she made a kissing sound with her lips.

The other ceased to be purely a scopic object, the object of *invidia* on the adult's lap. Now it was not only an object to touch and play with while I looked on but also an object linked with oral arousal, as witnessed by the kissing sound. Finally there was a clear link with muscular activity, since Nadia insisted throughout the whole scene on being bounced up and down on my lap. She had made the step from the purely scopic to the meshing of the drives as evidenced here, and she had done so, as we have seen, via the doll and the small other. Nadia had actively reconquered the entire gamut of *invidia*.

The active nature of the drives, as they gradually manifested themselves in Nadia, was in contradistinction to the passivity involved in the scopic, insofar as it always entails fascination with "seeing," which generates *invidia* and catatonia. Nadia passed from a situation where she was alone and passive when confronted with her sight to an activity that involved not only the object but also the Other that I was. It was as if she was saying to the other child, "Look at me being bounced up and down getting seen, how happy I am on the lap of the Other (seeing oneself), so I can look at you (seeing)."

It is a ruse to say that she said it to the other child, because clearly her discourse was directed at me: the other had become the medium for her discourse with the Other. This is the fundamental difference between *invidia* and the drive: the object is no longer an element of fascination but an element of discourse that necessarily implicates the Other, as a place of reference, even of inscription, in other words, of signification.

There is a further difference, insofar as new drives had come into play. Take, for example, the kissing sound she made with her mouth while looking at the other. But the circuit of the oral drive did not yet comprise all its three moments. Was the kissing sound aimed at the other child or at herself, since she did not kiss the other in reality? These two moments, kissing and kissing oneself, are both implicit in the sound of kissing; but one thing Nadia could not bear was my kissing her; this made her agitated and anxious.

She had just shown the same reticence with regard to touching. Even though touching the other and touching herself were combined in the caresses she gave to the other little girl, while I was looking, we have seen how careful she was that my hands should not touch her.

Being kissed, being touched, implicate the Other. She had just accepted it fully at the level of "being seen," but could not yet do so at the other levels; that is why she rocked when I left. She lost me in reality because she had not yet been able to accept me in her drive circuits as Other. The fact that she was unable to accept me should be brought in relation with the scopic dialectic of *invidia*, which was what she had known up to this point, in other words, that of a pure gaze without return, without the possibility of being looked at.

In the presence of the other child, she accepted being seen because I did not take any notice of the newcomer, but only of Nadia on my lap. She never stopped looking at her, and, moreover, she never stopped looking at me: she looked at her from the moment she "saw herself being seen" in my gaze.

This was not the case with touching; she was not able to find the active part since she could not reach the object I was carrying. Neither was it the case with the oral since, for the same reason, she could not eat the object of the Other. Also she could not bear to be kissed/eaten before herself eating. What was missing was the active part of the drive; but she was impelled to establish it on the morning of 12 November, by demanding to take her breakfast from the bottle. The fact that she demanded it outside the session was linked on the one hand with the impossible bodily object I carried and, on the other hand, with the absence of the bottle in the sessions. That was why I decided to introduce a bottle into the session the following day, as a dialectical object in the relationship between us.

The fact that she was able actively to consume this object represented a decisive step forward in the circuit of the drives: since, from 12 November on, after drinking up her bottle, it was she who demanded that I should kiss her, while bouncing her on my lap. In this very same session she moved the objects—toys and crackers—from her place—the crib she had left to come onto my lap—to my place, the chair I had left. It was not a question of objects as such for Nadia in her relation to me, but rather of their signifying, symbolic dimension. Through their mediation she found herself freed to such an extent from the real chain that the crib signified for her that I too, in the same process, being in the position of the Other, lost something of my presence insofar as it was too real.

The session culminated in a scene in which Nadia, happy to be sitting on the floor, showed herself to be beaming and gave in to the *jouissance* of letting herself be seen: kicking, crawling, very much in contact with me. She had now definitely passed from the relation to the other to that with the Other and, it is worth noting, had in the process acquired some narcissism.

Her activity and the mobility of her playing also show the degree to which she had moved toward an order other than the Real. Everything was organized here, in a succession that was a function of space, at a symbolic level of presence and absence; objects (toys) were promoted to the level of signifiers, when abolished as what they in fact were; it was very much a question of speaking.

In the course of the three sessions, it should be noted that I intervened actively rather than taking up the position of spectator. To summarize this activity I can say that I either followed Nadia very closely or barely preceded her; when I cradled the doll she held out to me or put on my lap; when I bit off a corner of the cracker I put in my mouth in spite of the previous experience that made her vomit. Most importantly, by my actions, while remaining attentive to her reactions, I was not passive; for it is clear that too much passivity, like too much activity, would have been in opposition to her experimentation at the level of the drives; a level where the aims—and not the pressure—are far from being unambiguous, whether active or passive.

I felt that the mobility of my own attitude would respond to her own mobility when, for example, on 12 November, I felt I should leave my chair to sit on the floor next to her.

Of course, in the same way that I did not remain passive, I did not remain silent, but without as such interpreting her behavior, and we shall see how important this "hearing" my voice was for Nadia.

4/The First Identification: The Transitive Relation to the Other

On 13 November, I decided to introduce a bottle of milk into the session, because Nadia had demanded a bottle for her breakfast.

I thought Nadia looked better. I put her straight down on the floor, which delighted her.

The first part of the session centered on the bottle. Her attention returned to it again and again. Using the fluffy chick, she pushed it over twice and then turned her back on it. Then she played at pressing the chick against my mouth and getting me to kiss her.

She then tried to stand up, using the chair to help her, but refused to let me help her, putting her feet at right angles if I did. She also tried to crawl.

She came onto my lap, got me to kiss her, grabbed the cracker, hesitated, then threw it down, turning her attention to the bottle, which she tried to grasp, all the while making loud and intense sucking noises. I gave it to her. When the nipple was eight inches away, she opened her mouth and held out her face. Sitting on one of my knees, *she drank the bottle greedily, as if filling a hole.* Her body was stiff and she did not look at me.

The second part of the session was spent in trying to stand up, propping herself against the end of the crib. She was delighted, and gurgled, looking at me without a trace of anxiety. Then she wanted me to bounce her; whenever I stopped, she became unhappy and even anxious.

When I took her back, I put her down on the floor, where the other children were. She clung to me for a moment, then let me put her down. Having checked that I was still there, she took a keen interest in the other children, with a mischievous look on her face. She looked at me every now and then, turning in all directions, and even went so far as to take a toy from the hands of another child and hold it out to me with a look of delight.

The nurse said she thought Nadia looked completely different.

During the night of 14 November Nadia suffered an acute attack of otitis, which necessitated a bilateral paracentesis.

She was happy when I came to collect her. When I put her down on the floor, she babbled contentedly. However, I felt she was tense and irritable. The chick was the only toy that brought her any joy. She used it violently to push aside the car and the doll; she seemed to have a great deal of animosity toward the latter.

She often looked at the bottle, but did not want it. She wanted to get on my lap, but then she was tense and anxious; she smiled briefly when she got me to kiss her. She wanted me to bounce her on my knee, but she quickly tensed up.

Then I took her back to her room and stayed by the crib for five minutes; my presence seemed to calm her down a little. She isolated herself with me, babbling and gurgling.

On 16 November I found her on the floor with the other children, with a toy in her hand. As soon as she saw me, she smiled broadly, *and for the first time, she tried to crawl toward me,* but she did not move very far. She held out her arms to me, with *her hands turned toward me;* I picked her up and carried her out, with her head pressed against my cheek.

From the very beginning of the session I felt she was anxious; nevertheless, she demanded various kinds of contact with me: to get up on my lap and *that I should take her in my arms for the first time.* She put her head against my cheek, one hand on my shoulder and one arm around my neck. She looked at me, smiling, got me to kiss her, *and patted my shoulder.*

Her face tensed up and she wanted to get back in my lap: arms up, the palms of her hands turned outward, she looked at where my hands were, tapping the one that was too near with one of the toys. I moved my hand away, and she smiled.

Her anxiety, which was always close to the surface, took over from time to time. She expressed it rather differently from the other times: she kept looking around the room, even behind her, periodically coming back to my face. So I took her back and put her on the floor, where almost immediately she started to take an interest in the other children.

That day's session made me realize that her anxiety showed itself in two different attitudes, depending on whether it was internal in origin or caused more directly by me. In the former case, Nadia looked at me intensely, with a frown. In the latter, she avoided my gaze, herself looking incessantly from one point to another in the room, her body tense and her face expressionless.

Unfortunately I was away for ten days. When I came back on 27 November, Nadia recognized me. She looked terrible; I heard that she had undergone another paracentesis while I was away. She was smiling much less and had reverted even more pronouncedly to the tic of holding her arms in their special position. She leaned toward me when I tried to pick her up, but kept her arms behind her with her palms facing backward.

The tone of the session was sad and uneasy; Nadia demanded nothing. She took the chick and spent a long time playing the old game, the back-and-forth between her mouth and mine. Then she noticed the bottle; her gaze rested on it more and more frequently, and she held out her arm toward it. I moved it toward her, but she turned away from it and started sucking the chick, watching me. I held the bottle close to her, but she turned away from it again and sucked the chick even harder, watching me all the while. So I sat Nadia on my lap and held the bottle! She hesitated a long time before moving her mouth toward it, moving her hand back and forth and making sucking noises. She took the nipple in her mouth and pushed it away with her tongue, watching me anxiously. I kissed her and hummed to her, and she drank greedily from the bottle. Finally, she rested her head against me, watching me anxiously; she also looked anxiously at the empty bottle.

When I took her back to her crib, she wanted me to take her in my arms for a moment. The only time she relaxed during this session was when she was drinking from the bottle, although even then one of her arms was tensed up behind her.

When I arrived to collect her on 28 November, she had just undergone a bilateral paracentesis. Her head was bandaged and her face was tense. She flashed a smile at me when she saw me, then her face tensed up again. When I went up to her crib, she raised her arms, but the palms were turned away, and when I held out my arms to pick her up, she did not lean toward me as she had done before my absence.

I took her to the room where we had the sessions. Sitting on the floor as usual, with her arms still up, motionless, staring fixedly at me, she was so tense that I took her on my lap. At first her expression became a little less tense, but then she reverted to the earlier one, keeping her arms up. As she seemed to be suffering physically, I rocked her gently, humming to her and talking about her pain. Little by little she relaxed, rested her head against me, and lowered her arms; but her hands and body remained tense. For a fleeting moment her body relaxed: Nadia almost lay in my arms and watched me intensely, making sucking noises. Several times she moved her hand near my face. Only after several attempts, however, did she put her hand to my mouth, without looking at me. I kissed her hand; she did not take it away. She pulled at my nose and my glasses and finally sat up. She spent a long time fingering the button of my white coat and smiled openly.

I offered her the chick; she laughed, grabbed it, and amused herself by throwing it down and picking it up again, stretching a long way in the process. She laughed more and more heartily; each time she repeated the game she looked at me, each time more relaxed. I could even say that she looked at me warmly.

When I took her back, she kept her arms behind her, but her face and eyes were smiling. Once she was back in her crib, she did not demand that I pick her up again; she looked at me anxiously and then relaxed. She did not take on the expression she had had at the beginning of the session; she smiled at me.

On 30 November, Nadia was perched on her pillow as I came in, and she smiled at me. I was struck by how ill she looked and by the dark rings around her eyes; however, her ears had stopped suppurating. As I was about to take her away for the session, she became serious and did not make a single gesture toward me; even though she gave a little cry of joy as I picked her up, her arms stayed up.

As usual, I sat her down. She remained motionless until I had sat down; she looked at me pathetically and started to suck her thumb. For a quarter of an hour she stayed tense, anxious, and afraid. She glanced at the toys from time to time without changing her expression; she was startled by any noises from outside. Not a smile, not a sound, not even a momentary relaxing of her expression. So I decided to take her back to her crib and stay with her for a while. But hardly had I picked her up when her attitude changed; she clung to me and smiled a little. When we arrived at the door of her room, she turned away violently and clung still harder to my white coat. So I took her back to the consulting room. There, she allowed one of her arms to rest on my shoulder and babbled a little.

She looked hard at her usual toys, so I sat on the floor and kept her in my lap. She laughed with contentment and her expression was truly relaxed. *She played a little with the button of my white coat,* then bent down to pick up the chick. She played at throwing it down and picking it up, laughing and looking at me; *she sucked it for longer and longer periods, looking furtively at the bottle.* I offered her the bottle; she dropped the chick, laughed, opened her mouth, and started to drink, her head resting against me. She took in only a few mouthfuls, then pushed away the nipple with her tongue; this was the only movement she made to show she did not want any more. I took away the bottle; she hesitated, wanted it back, took only one mouthful, and pushed it away again. Then she picked up the little green car.

She sat down, very erect, and played happily for a long time, making a noise by hitting the chair with the car. She was enchanted by the noise and kept looking at me, giving little shrieks of joy. Then her face became serious again; she went rigid and struck her head twice with the car. For two minutes, she alternately hit the chair, laughing, and struck her head, looking more concentrated and a little hesitant. At first I thought it was a game where she was trying to make different sounds, but when she struck her head, her face was very tense. She seemed to be wondering what it was doing to her, and there was a definite hesitation between the first and the second hit.

When I took her back to her crib, she smiled, but her face froze when I left the room.

On 1 December, she smiled as soon as I went into the room, and started to fidget. Once she was in my arms, she hesitated for a second, then put one arm on my shoulder, keeping the other one up, but without turning away the palm of her hand.

I sat her on my lap, which she seemed to prefer to being placed on the floor next to me. She looked at me for a moment, anxiously, both her arms in the air, then smiled, laughed, and bent down to pick up the green car. She struck the chair with it twice, delighted at the noise it made. She noticed the crackers, took one of them, put it to my mouth while making a sucking noise, then put it down on the floor—without either her mechanical movement or a throwing movement. She looked at it for a moment, then used the green car to push the cracker beyond the chair, out of reach.

For the next ten minutes she played at making noise with the car, hitting it against my chair. She watched me all the time, laughing, wriggling, and kicking her legs. During this game, she hit my leg twice with the car, laughing, and once she hit her head with her hand, looking very serious.

Then she leaned her head against me and put the car in my mouth. She sat up, saw the bottle, threw down the car, took the chick, and made sucking noises while trying to touch the bottle with the chick. She let go of the chick, watching me, and held out her hand toward the bottle, while stretching out in my arms and opening her mouth. She drank the complete bottleful, looking serious, watching me all the while, and her body was fairly relaxed. That took about ten minutes, and the quantity of milk did not seem to satisfy her.

She sat down and, right up to the end of the session, got me to bounce her on my lap; she was very excited and banged joyfully on the table. At regular intervals, she stretched out almost completely in my arms and looked at me; and I kissed her. That was what she wanted; but I sensed that these were only experiments on her part and that she would not be able to bear it if I tried to get her to stretch out further or to keep her in that position a moment longer than she wanted.

I put her back in her crib; she was thoroughly contented.

When I went into her room on 3 December, she started laughing and fidgeting straight away. Her ears were not running anymore and she looked better. When I took her in my arms, she withdrew hers at first, but she laughed.

She spent the first part of the session making a noise by hitting the car against the chair. She used the car to push crackers out of the way and got me to kiss her; she was very relaxed, but only briefly.

Then she became aggressive toward me, hitting my hands with the car and hitting my face with her hand, with a rather hostile expression. She kept pushing me away, except when she wanted me to kiss her. *Then she tried to push the whole car into my mouth,* with a great show of sucking.

At the end of the session, she drank the bottle; she had no hesitation in touching it, but did not dare to grasp it with her hand. She drank all the milk quite quickly, looking at me with a serious face. Her head was leaning against me, but her body did not relax; she remained sitting very erect.

Then she seemed to want to try to stand up.

Back in her own room, before I laid her down in her crib, *she pushed her finger into my mouth and made a curious sound: a sigh of contentment and relief, but quite clearly articulated.*

On 4 December, Nadia was on the floor with the other children when I arrived. She smiled at me contentedly and leaned toward me. While I was picking her up, the nurse said she was impressed by how happy Nadia looked and by her appetite.

As I picked Nadia up, she brushed her hand across my face briefly and babbled. Then she held her arms back, but smiled at the same time.

I did not sit her on my lap, as I normally did, but on the floor, as I had found her when I arrived. She looked at me with a serious face, then smiled and saw the crackers on the chair behind her. She managed to turn around and get one. She used it to push another one so that it fell on the floor, then amused herself for a few moments by making a noise, hitting the cracker she still had in her hand against the chair, watching me all the time, laughing and relaxed. For the first time, her look seemed to be saying, "I'm enjoying making a noise because you're near me."

Suddenly she leaned toward me, very deliberately, smiling and looking as if she was expecting something; so I put her on my lap, and she gave a great sigh of contentment. She was very relaxed.

She put the cracker to my mouth several times, then hit her head with it, but gently (and now she was tense again, but not anxious). She calmed down as she inspected my buttons, rubbing her hand quite hard on my white coat—on my breast—which made her anxious. Then she exchanged the cracker for the car *and hit me with it quite hard, with a distinct air of aggression;* but she was no longer anxious.

At that moment she heard a child crying in the next room. She sat up, her body tensed up, she glanced very anxiously around the room, then *twice she pulled me toward her by my white coat and pushed me away violently.* Then she pulled the little chair toward her and played at rocking it to and fro, which calmed her down. Gradually she started to smile at me and wanted me to bounce her on my lap; she burst out laughing. Several times, between bounces, she relaxed completely in my arms and smiled somewhat gravely when I kissed her.

Joyfully, she started to play her game with the chair again, then noticed the bottle, and pushed away the chair so she could try to reach it. I put it on the chair. She watched me rather tensely, touched the bottle several times, pushing it harder and harder. Then she stopped pushing away the bottle, but started to rock the chair *until the bottle fell down on the floor.* She leaned her body toward the bottle, but did not hold out her arms, and made sucking noises. I gave it to her and she drank, almost completely stretched out in my arms, with a serious smile; she wriggled her feet contentedly; both her arms were relaxed, but her left hand was clenched. Once she had finished, there was a minute's anxious

hesitation; then she babbled very joyfully, already in a fairly articulated way.

When I took her back she was smiling and radiant.

When I took her for the session on 5 December, she was smiling broadly and put her arms on my shoulders.

The first part of the session was almost identical with that of the
previous day's: making noise, babbling, playing at rocking the chair
to and fro, ending up with the bottle, which Nadia grabbed and
put down near my hand. She drank from it, very relaxed. When it
was empty, she looked at it for a long time, then *became aggressive with me* and hit me on the thigh, her face tense and a hostile
look in her eyes; then she hit me once on the mouth and her aggressivity disappeared.

Next, she tried something new: she looked at me, put both
hands on my breast, her hands quite tightly clenched, and babbled,
"mama-mama." Then she played her game of rocking the chair
again, laughing; after that she wanted me to sit her on my arm,
the way you carry a baby; but I did not understand this at first. I
did it; she smiled joyfully, babbling "ma-ma-ma," and caressed my
face, looked at me with satisfaction, put her arms around my neck,
and rested her head heavily against my cheek.

She took the cracker, pressed it against my mouth, then against
hers; she could not quite decide to eat it; she looked at the empty
bottle and made sucking sounds and movements.

She was not at all pleased when I took her back: I felt her tense
up against me as I was about to open the door of her room.

The 7 December session started badly, because Nadia had seen
me earlier when I went into her room to fetch a chair. She had
smiled at me and wriggled; I had spoken to her. When I came back,
I found her with the fixed expression she had had when she saw
me go away. Her face did not light up and she did not wriggle.
When I picked her up, she threw her arms back with her palms
facing outward. She gave a shadow of a smile and her fixed expression returned.

I sat her on the floor next to me. She did not take her eyes off
me for several minutes and looked very anxious; she sucked her
thumb without looking at anything in the room—not the toys, the
bottle, the cookies, or the chair.

So then I took her on my lap; she did not react at all, even her
expression remained the same. She put one of her fingers in my

mouth, while still sucking her other thumb. Her face was livened up a little by her sucking movements, but her look was still tense.

She put her head against me so I would kiss her, but her look was one of infinite sadness; her arms were held out in front of her, fists clenched. And yet her body was more relaxed than it had ever been. She could not bear me to express my affection in any other way than kissing her, and even my kisses were unbearable if they lasted longer than she wanted. If that was the case, she would sit up; her arms would become even tenser and she would bend the one nearer my body even more violently away from me.

At that moment I was called away to the telephone. I did not dare to leave Nadia alone in the room, so I put her back in her crib in her own room, where I left her dumbfounded and lost. When I went back to fetch her a few minutes later, she had not budged at all. She was very tense and urinated as I carried her back to the consulting room. Once we were there, she sat with a tense face, sucked her thumb, then picked up a piece of cracker that had fallen out of my pocket. She put it in my mouth, held it there, took it out, looked at it, put it to her own mouth; then, with a look of disgust, she broke it and threw it down. A few crumbs stuck to her hand: her disgust intensified, and she repeated her mechanical movement over and over again to get rid of them. That was the end of the session. She glanced at the bottle, then looked at the door.

As I carried her back, her hands tightened around my neck, and she rested her head against my cheek as we stood in front of the door to her room.

On 8 December, Nadia was less tense than on the previous day. She smiled at me, but she was still holding her arms behind her. *This session was to be the best one since we had started the treatment,* and Nadia was to be very active without showing anxiety.

She wanted to sit on my lap. She had a lively and joyful look. She put a cracker to my lips; I ate a corner of it, which seemed to cause her immense happiness; she did this several times; and at the end of the session she was to put the cracker in my mouth, then lick it herself, but not eat it. I noted that the movement with which she put the cracker to her mouth was not a hesitant one, and that it was free of anxiety.

During this session, she tried to crawl in order to reach what she wanted. She swiveled around, got up on one knee, and moved forward by fits and starts over a distance of almost a yard to reach the bottle. She took it, lifted it up, and turned toward me, but did not manage to carry it all the way back to me. I helped her and put her on my lap, placing the bottle on the floor within her reach. She leaned over and grabbed it.

She drank a few mouthfuls, lying in my arms; her body, and even her arms, were very relaxed. She pushed away the nipple with her tongue and then took back the bottle without drinking from it; she repeated this several times.

Afterward, she lay in my arms for a few moments, smiling and gurgling, looking happy. Then she wanted to make a noise with one of the toys. Throughout this session, during which she had been very active and independent of me, she had made sure I never stopped looking at her. There was a very dynamic feeling about her that day. As I carried her back, she had both arms around my neck.

Although I introduced the bottle into the 13 November session, after Nadia had demanded it herself outside the session the previous day, it was certainly not my intention to provide her with an object of consumption and satisfaction.

There were two aspects to this bottle. There was, on the one hand, the dimension of being an object of satisfaction of the need for sustenance: that was the function of "filling up" that Nadia experienced every day, as an integral part of the institutional regime she had lived under up to this time. On the other hand, the bottle was the object of Nadia's demand. It was really this demand she was exploring that came into play in the analysis and in the transference. For it was there—although I was not aware of it at the time, I had the strongest intuitive feeling—that the driving force of the transference was activated: in the irreducible repetition of this demand. It was indeed this second aspect, that of the demand for the bottle, which became an opening for Nadia; for what could one say of the other dimension, that of the Real, insofar as it was possible to isolate it? We will see in Marie-Françoise's case the impossible side of this stumbling block.

Demand, on the contrary, implies signification at the same time as repetition. Who is this demand addressed to, if not to an Other who does not respond because it does not speak in the true sense of the word? For Nadia, and in her gaze, this Other was always rigged out with an other; it lacked nothing, it had no desire—that was what she tried to dissociate herself from on 27 October. The signifier of the Other could not respond to the signifier implicated in her demand. What could respond was the milk in the bottle that was given to her and which she drank. The signifier of the Other, ultimately, was this milk; the milk was the Other. So there was no difference between Nadia and the Other when she drank the milk.

Does that mean that there was no Other for her? Certainly it does not. There was still the one whose demand she had to respond to by drinking the milk, or by allowing herself to be handled as her bodily needs were taken care of each day. It was only her sensitivity to another little counterpart being fed and cared for by the Other that triggered *invidia* in her. This bore witness to her own desire, which inscribed itself in the gap between her and this counterpart. In this case, the Other was merely the agent of the completeness of the small other; and, inversely, in Nadia's eyes, the small other was the image of the object of the completeness of the Other.

Where could she possibly be, under these conditions, alone with her demand, when the response of the Other became confused with the milk she drank? Did she want to be in the place of this small other that fulfilled the Other? We have seen that there was no question of this; indeed that was the very thing she feared most, to judge only from the way she drank from the bottle on 13 November, greedily, as if filling a hole, holding her body stiff and rigid, and without looking at me. There was no question of being some global metaphorical object responding to a supposed demand of the Other who was separated from her. The Other did not speak, did not have a separate existence; she drank it in with the milk.

So was this a question of the primary identification that Freud, in *The Ego and the Id*, spoke of as being related to the primitive oral phase of the subject, that "direct and immediate path" which precedes all object cathexes? Given that the dialectic of demand implicates the signifier as well as repetition, it would be hard to support that view. In fact, what Nadia repeated, and was forced to repeat whenever she drank the milk, was the denegation of my presence as Other. While she refused to be the metaphorical object that fulfilled the Other, she made of the milk a metaphorical object that represented me. I was no longer there, because of what she did, because of what she repeated, and yet I was there. She was caught in the trap of her past, which meant that in order to defend herself, she had to inscribe the Other in the milk she drank, and of which she made herself the container. But my presence betrayed the metaphorical signification of the milk, revealing the radical lack in the Other, of an Other who lacks speech. That was where the pain of the lack of hearing came in for Nadia, and her way of signifying the pain was the otitis, the price she paid for having drunk from the bottle. She had been familiar with physical pain for a long time, with her many attacks of otitis and the bilateral antrotomy she underwent at the age of five months.

The extremely high incidence of otitis in public nurseries is well known. This case calls into question traditional pediatric notions of its epidemiology and shows how inadequate they are. The relational element has been elided: the Other's being included in the object for the small subject, because it is not an external referent through the medium of speech.

This is what Lacan refers to as the coalescence, the holophrasis, of S_1 and S_2, which are respectively the signifier that represents the subject and the primordial signifier of the Other, that is the condition for any psychosomatic reaction.

In the sessions that were to follow, Nadia tried to articulate the bottle, which she drank over and over again, with my body, with the Other that I was. That was why she no longer suffered from otitis: by addressing my body, she was able to dissociate from the bottle this other order of objects, which were attached to me, and place me as a true Other: the carrier of signifying objects.

Each new demand she was to outline, or to address to me, pointed up the difference between the object and the Other. If she did return to the bottle, it was only after she had addressed objects I carried, as, for example, on 28 November, when she pulled at my nose and my glasses and fiddled with a button on my white coat: actions that delighted her. She was thus helping herself by substituting the breast, or what stood in its place, for the bottle.

The Other could not be established as separate without Nadia's attempting to fulfill it—filling my mouth with the cracker or the toy car. The image of the Other she wanted to fulfill was also her own image: the sucking noises she made when she put some object or other into my mouth were evidence of this. To fulfill me in order to fulfill herself—that was transitivism in action, which is at the basis of the most archaic form of identification, where it is not just a question of consuming the object in order to be fulfilled, but also of the Other not suffering and not losing anything in the process: refusal that the Other be barred.

Nadia expressed this in another way through her dismay when confronted with the empty bottle, which represented the hole she might have made in me; or even, through another effect of transitivism, as if she were accusing me of having emptied the bottle myself, of having drunk it all without leaving any for her; and so she hit me on the mouth. To sum up, then, what she refused was this separation that appeared between her and the Other. Drinking the bottle meant at the same time refusing to accept that it was empty and reproaching me with that; sometimes it would be a cracker that she put to my mouth, then to hers, or a finger she put in my mouth, while sucking her thumb.

But nothing could be done. From session to session, from 13 November onward, the difference between her and the Other that I was imposed itself on her. You could even say that it imposed itself by means of a kind of reversal of her desire that I should lack nothing: as a result I became the carrier of the object of her desire.

First it was the buttons on my white coat; on 4 December, she rubbed my breast with her hand—not without anxiety; finally, on 5 December, again leaning against my breast, she grasped my white coat with her hands. At that moment the signifier "mama" emerged from her mouth, putting the seal on the difference between her and me. That did not mean, however, that she would not continue to question this difference. She knew, nonetheless, that the emergence of the word "mama" introduced something altogether different into her relation to me, and she showed this in the joy with which she would let me hold her in my arms while she looked at my face or would put her arms around my neck and rest her head against my cheek, all the time repeating her "mama."

Her motor control improved considerably from the time she started to drink the milk on 12 November. On that day she showed herself to me in her motor activity and she experienced joy in so doing. This was not the case on 13 November, however, when, showing more bravado in her attempts, and even trying to stand up, she pushed me aside and refused my help. Possibly the presence of the bottle—in which I was included, as we have seen, in the capacity of Other—was behind this gesture of refusal of my help, which continued for a time.

Things were different in the sessions where she refused to drink from the bottle. In those cases, her activity was linked to my presence, whether she was demanding that I should bounce her on my lap or whether she was trying to crawl toward me. A link was established between my presence and her motor activity on several occasions, when she played the rocking game with the chair that I had got up from; it was even by rocking this chair that she made the bottle fall onto the floor on one occasion, as a prelude to demanding to drink it while lying stretched out in my arms.

Finally, on 8 December, her motor activity made it the best session we had had. In particular, Nadia established a link between the bottle, which she went to get, moving along on one knee, and my presence; she clung to my gaze the whole time.

There was a parallel development, from 30 November on, as regards "getting heard." At the beginning, Nadia had been uneasy and afraid every time there was a noise coming from outside the consulting room. As soon as she had drunk a few mouthfuls from the bottle, she was able to make the transition from the passive fear of what she heard to the activity of "getting heard" by hitting the toy car against my chair, accompanied by little shrieks of joy, and looking at me frequently. Clearly, the noise she made was addressed to me; this was confirmed by the number of times she looked at me. True, there was an element of aggressivity; it was my chair she was hitting, even if she only hit where I was not.

Such behavior included in itself the possibility of reversal: that was what she was exploring when she hit herself on the head with the toy car. It was a question of an exploration in order to "hear herself"—like a third moment in the auditory drive. It was not in any way a self-punishing, masochistic behavior, for it was not her aim to inflict pain on herself. "Getting heard" and "hearing oneself" comprise an active element that excludes the terror, the fear, the expectation linked to the "heard."

The "heard" had a definite relationship with my presence-absence. That was abundantly clear on 4 December, when, hearing another child crying, she alternated between grabbing my white coat, in order to pull me toward her, and pushing me violently away from her, and then reproduced the same game with my chair. The "heard" also played a part in waiting for the session; waiting for the "heard" of my footsteps and my voice in the corridor when I came to collect her.

This "getting heard" took on all its value as a drive in the passage toward activity, relative both to the passive "heard" and to her improved muscular activity. The "getting heard" addressed itself by its very nature to the Other that I was. The toy car, which was the instrument of this development, also served to express Nadia's aggression toward me, when she hit me or stuffed my mouth with it—without looking at me. Thus the toy car linked a number of drives.

Finally, during this period, the scopic drive in particular showed its primacy. After the sessions of 9 to 13 November, where the circuit of the scopic drive had completed itself, the introduction of the bottle had called the place of the object back into question.

Indeed, when Nadia drank the bottle on 13 November, it was without looking at me. As we have seen, at that time, the bottle included the Other and the other, as in the tableau of *invidia*. Only when she stopped drinking from the bottle was Nadia able to look at me and seek physical contact with me. But this look she gave me made her uneasy; for example, on November 16 she sat on my knee, looking all around her, even behind her, only returning to my face every now and then, just as her look had wandered at the beginning when she was propped up on her pillow; at that time the only lively thing about her had been that gaze. At other times, it was as if she had to turn away from the bottle to suck the chick; only then could she look at me. Or again, with the nipple in her mouth, she would push it out with her tongue while looking anxiously at me. The problem for her was that my presence and that of the bottle were linked in a relation of mutual exclusion.

But Nadia did not stop there. Passing progressively from the bottle to the other objects that were attached to me, she linked the bottle to my presence and drank while looking at me. Thus, from a relation of exclusion, she made the transition to one of inclusion by looking at me: I myself now included the bottle that had excluded me by including me.

This inclusion did not take place without her encountering a few snags, which meant that I became exterior to Nadia and the transitivism between herself and myself ceased to exist. That was what made her aggressive, at the risk of her acting as if the inclusion of the object in me had two meanings: she hit me on the mouth after looking for a long time at the empty bottle she had drunk from, as if it was I who had drunk from it, as if it was no longer me who was included in the bottle by her gaze, but the bottle that was included in me.

During this period, everything was moving toward one goal: to find an image, that of her fundamental fantasy, the unity of the A and the *a*, the cause of her desire. That was what would constitute the fascination of 10 December.

Before reaching that point, we cannot fail to discern at least two elements that, by their anticipatory character, gave a valuable indication of the opening they represented for Nadia: a precession of the path she was to find, and which was to culminate in this fascination, as we shall see. We already know the first moment: it was the emergence of the "mama, mama" when her hands were clenched on my breast and she then looked at me to show tenderness through newly acquired gestures. The second moment was also a breach opened in transitivism: on 7 December, she held a piece of cracker in my mouth, took it out, looked at it, put it to her own mouth, but felt nothing but disgust, to such an extent that she made several of her mechanical movements to try to get rid of the crumbs stuck to her hand. She knew that her disgust implied a difference between her and me since, after looking at the bottle, she looked at the door to bring the session to an end, to escape from this sad reality that there were two mouths, hers and mine, and that there were two of us. But she needed us not to be separated in order to find, in her look, her fundamental fantasy, a totalizing image of the adult and the child that was to fascinate her on 10 December, before she repressed it.

Such was the requirement of her analytic progress in the framework of the transference, combining two movements, as in any analysis: on the one hand, in the relation to the Other, the placing on the body of the Other of the object of desire, that is to say, the signifying dimension that implicates a loss; and on the other hand, the maintenance of transitivism, that is to say, the inclusion, by scopic sticking, of the big Other in herself: a maintenance that became refined down to the nodal point of her fundamental fantasy in the scopic field.

5 / The Fundamental Fantasy: Primary Repression

When I arrived on 10 December I found Nadia sitting in her crib completely absorbed in the spectacle of a nurse bouncing another child up and down on her lap.

This fascination was accompanied by noisy sucking movements. Nadia's body was fixed in the rigid posture she used to adopt at the start of the treatment. Yet now it was not only her look that was alive, but her mouth, too, was active.

I sat down behind her and called her several times by name before she turned around. She smiled briefly, but when I extended my arms, *she threw herself violently backward, her arms lifted and her fists clenched tight.*

She was so anxious that I could not take her for a session.

I nevertheless stayed a little while beside her. She got me to play with her feet and laughed a little; but her anxiety quickly regained the upper hand. Twice she tried to sit up, but then gave it up as if she were afraid, in sitting, of coming too close to me. She fingered my ring and, at one moment, her body tense, she hit my hand, *while babbling, only once, "ma-ma-ma";* now and then she mimicked sucking.

I left her. When I stood in the doorway she sat down and turned toward me, her face set and her expression tense.

That scene, which was exceptionally intense, was the logical and hallucinatory realization of Nadia's desire.

The logical aspect harks back to the debate of the preceding period where we saw the two movements that animated her: on the one hand, her transitivist relation to the Other that I was; and on the other hand, her relation to the Other as bearer of the signifier, by anticipation.

In the scene of 10 December, these two structures of the Other, between which Nadia had oscillated since the start of the treatment, were at play successively:

1. In a first moment, and on this day too, during her life in the institution, Nadia had known and knew only the image of the Other and the other coupled: A + *a*. That was what she always saw, it was

what was looking at her when, at feeding time, she had to wait for her bottle. It was an image that could not be separated into its two elements; and this was what she came back to in the scene of fascination, which throws light on what was involved: a purely scopic rapport, an image in which she found herself included.

2. The start of the treatment had as an immediate effect the dissociation of this totality: A + *a*, bringing in its wake the fall of Nadia and her distress.

I appeared to her as a separated Other, but prematurely; I separated myself and the small other was born. In the same movement, the small other became the one who deprived Nadia of the Other. It left her desperate and she encountered *invidia*. The other, in satisfying itself in some way by means of the Other, took Nadia's object, that which was part of her own body.

3. She vacillated in a movement that caused to appear at the same time both her demand to the Other and the questioning of the desire of this Other for the other. That was the scene of 27 October, where I had withdrawn my hand from the neighboring crib. There I proved to her that I could be separated from the small other, from my object; that I could have a hole. She confirmed this by taking my pencil, in wanting to pull off one of my fingers, in exploring my mouth more and more.

But at this very early stage she was not yet sufficiently separated from me, at least not to the point where, by means of transitivism, my loss was not also hers, except when, by vomiting, she refused what would fill up the hole of my mouth.

The true separation of A and *a* appeared clearly on 10 November, when Nadia succeeded in taking an interest in the other child, touching and caressing her, all the while making sure of her own link with my body by getting me to jump her up and down on my lap: at the same time, moreover, she made sure I took an interest in her rather than the small other.

At that point she was able to begin the quest for the object for herself: she demanded the bottle, on 12 November. Yet she did this outside the session; in the place where this bottle was only an object which was infinitely divisible, not yet linked specifically to the big Other, there where this big Other is itself inconsistent in its multiplicity.

4. Then, between 13 November and 8 December, there was the whole debate concerning the place of the object in relation to the big Other with its twofold nature. While Nadia at times indicated that the Other was the bearer of the object of desire, even to the point of

reaching, by anticipation, her first articulation of "mama" on 5 December, she remained on the whole much more attached to the primordial image, or to the primitive form of the Other, to which she was linked by transitivism. It was this latter that supported the logical irruption of the image on 10 December. She was fascinated and "the fascinated gaze is the subject itself" (Lacan).

For Nadia, in this fascination, the Other no longer had any being elsewhere than on her eye: the eye as privileged point of the envelope on which the Other was glued. The subject, that is to say, the whole surface of her skin, was concentrated in this privileged point.

In this first form of the Other there was as yet no question of loss: the subject produced her own object on her eye, glued to her eye without further need of a real Other; this real Other would in fact be separated and that was what Nadia had aggressively refused several times during the preceding period. In the image that fascinated her I was truly absent. Though I was also included in it to the extent that for Nadia, from the start until then, I had been the cause of an exacerbation of the question of the Other. It was in the transference, then, that she put me in this place of included object; an inclusion on a surface—we could say of an "envelope" if the metaphor did not risk suggesting the notion of a three-dimensional bag, whereas, as we shall see, it was a question of a pure surface structure.

The Other is included on the surface of the subject; that is the first form of identification through which the subject begins to constitute itself as such, a form that we could say is one of incorporation, on condition that we stress its logical mode, that is to say, a topology of the surface.

The sucking movements made during the scene were there to tell us that Nadia's hallucinatory realization—and it could only be hallucinatory—of her primordial desire was successful. The sucking movements were as successful in gluing the Other onto the surface of the body as the gaze in gluing the image onto the eye. They belonged to a level of drive satisfaction other than fascination, without there being a need to implicate more precisely the presence of an object. For presupposing an object would be to suppose it as separated (which was what Nadia encountered in the shape of the bottle on 13 November) and this separation would have been in logical contradiction to the relation of sticking that was at issue. In reality, the small other on the knees of the woman was part of the latter's body: it was her breast.

To sum up, the fundamental fantasy Nadia found there was *the one in which the subject itself was the envelope of the Other and all the ob-*

jects stuck to it, with a complete absence of separation. She could reach this ultimate point of regression only by means of the transference.

What happened when I called her several times by name, "Nadia"? She could obviously not renounce what fascinated her at once, but on the other hand, she was not captivated to such an extent that she was no longer sensitive to hearing her name, that she could not turn around and smile at me briefly; which is to say that she recognized me. However brief, this smile was the sign of the breach my call had made; Nadia was responsive to my presence and this presence had been introduced by the signifier of my call. The responsiveness she showed to it demonstrated that she was not irremediably enclosed in what fascinated her, even if she had difficulty giving it up. This smile addressed to me was evidence that Nadia was not psychotic.

She made the leap from the hallucinatory satisfaction of her desire to my presence as Other by means of my calling her name. It was too much, however, when I held out my arms to take her to a session, and I could not have taken her there in any case: confronted with my invitation she threw herself back into her crib, violently, her arms lifted and her fists clenched.

The meaning of the leap she had just made then appeared: from the Other stuck to her to the irruption of a real, separated Other. The identification that had stuck the Other onto her changed meaning; in a reversal, it passed to an identification by means of sticking of herself to the Other. That is what she encountered in a flash and against which she would fight: something that would make of her the real object that completed the Other. The inclusion of the Other had such an intensity in the transference that the exclusion which followed gave to my naming the weight of a demand, my own, to which she had to respond in reality.

It was this reversal that Nadia was going to face, both at the end of this session as later on in the analysis.

At first she tried to offer me a bit of her body, her foot, in place of the whole body, in a metonymic operation. If she laughed a little it was because this was successful, contrary to the metaphoric temptation to come into my arms or sit down in her crib, which would have provoked anxiety, the fear of coming too close to me, of fulfilling me. Then, at the end, she effected a reversal: she passed from her body to mine; she no longer offered me a part of her body, but fingered my ring, that is to say, an object stuck onto my body and separable, even though she hit my hand, which was not. In this reversal she discovered the metonymic object, both on her body and on mine; and she ended the session on a signifier "ma-ma-ma," as if it were an echo of my call. From the danger of the real of bodies, she went over to the path of significations, or rather, to signifying connections, metonymy.

She had shown that she knew this metonymic way previously, on 5 December, when, with her hands clenched on my breast, she had uttered her call "mama"; just as she did this day, in the new path of her desire. Between my naming and her "mama," metonymy had taken place, but it needed a long detour via metaphor, as we shall see, before she constituted her desire in it, at the moment of the first mirror.

The chief event of this session was the establishment in Nadia of the conditions in which metaphor and metonymy could operate.

This condition was the mutation of the Real, its promotion to a signifier at the level of image: fascinating as this image was, it became signifying in the very movement of repression it underwent because of my naming. It is indeed signification that founds metaphoric and metonymic structures: it is woven from them.

In this session, the precession in Nadia of metonymy over metaphor derived from the resistance to the return of the repressed. This return (that of the signifying image she had just repressed) would have accompanied the metaphor; while the metonymy of her call "mama," although connected with the repressed image, did not reveal it.

To illuminate this image and its function a little further we need to take up once more the structural effects of the intervention in which I called her by name three times in a row before she turned around.

I broke the spell of her fascination in disturbing her with her name: with a signifier. At that precise moment she detached the image from herself, never to find it again. My naming had the value of "the intimation which the Other proffers the subject with its discourse," according to Lacan's formulation, as well as a prohibition that had as consequence, for Nadia, a loss that destroyed the certainty of the image. It was as if I had told her that the Other was not there where she wanted to see it, in that image, but there where I was speaking from; and through that, I told her my desire. I was not for all that the agent of this loss. The agent was the signifier of her name by means of my voice; and in my position of analyst I was merely a witness of this loss. When I uttered the signifier "Nadia" I addressed myself to her as subject and I recognized her as such at the level of the signifier that represented her. I caused the image to disappear, I annulled it and caused her to repress it.

It was at that moment, if not before, that the image was promoted to the level of signifier. But was it really an image, that which, as Freud said concerning dream material, already partook of the signifier? Or was it something prior to any signification and that only becomes a signifier once repressed? Something Real, then, which undergoes a change into a signifier? What signifier?

It was obvious that Nadia could not expect any recognition of this image she produced in almost hallucinatory fashion; but, more than this, through my absence necessary for its production, I could not recognize her by means of it.

This image, taking its function of signifier of the woman and the child from an abolished Real, was not, however, subjected to a link with another signifier. This put it in the place of the nonrecognized, of the "impossible-to-recognize," which Lacan proposed to mark as primary repression. "The primary repressed is a signifier."*

We could link such a signifier to the ones Freud said supported the gap of the navel of the dream: they are free-standing signifiers, inaccessible to the secondary process, beyond the pleasure principle. This "beyond" could be put in relation with the very notion of primary repression:† "The repressed mnemic traces of the experiences lived in pre-history are not present in the subject in bound form, and are, in fact, to some extent unsuitable for the secondary process. It is also this absence of binding that endows them with the ability to form a fantasy of desire."

It is in this sense that A. Didier-Weill sees in a commandment like my nominal call to Nadia the emergence of an "archaic superego" whose effect would here correspond to a "you are Nadia, you are only Nadia, and you are not the image that fascinates you and which would contain me by making the sum of A + *a*."

My call, then, introduced through my voice the castration Nadia sought to evade in the image and thus, at the same time, the repression of this image. Nadia was compelled to repress it because I made myself present in the absence in which she maintained me during her fascination. She was no longer the "one who looks" but became the

---

*Lacan, *Les Quatre concepts fondamentaux de la psychanalyse,* seminar of 13 May 1964 and 17 June 1964: "the logical necessity of that moment in which the subject as X can only constitute itself from an *Urverdrängung,* from the necessary fall of that first signifier."

†We refer in several places in this commentary to the paper of Alain Didier-Weill given at the Congress on the Transmission of Psychoanalysis (Paris, July 1978), the text of which he has kindly given to us. We specifically borrowed the formula of Lacan on primary repression as well as the quotation from Freud, taken from an unpublished translation of *Beyond the Pleasure Principle.*

one looked at by me; no longer fascinated by the image but looked at by what imposed me on her in the Real, the signifier "Nadia."

At stake there was an articulation in the relation of the subject to the Other, an articulation that could bring about in any subject a "fertile moment" for entry into psychosis, if the subject were to remain fascinated with an image that would preclude the existence of an Other. The Other would remain at the level of an unbound signifier; it would not arrive at the point where it has to be the locus of all the other signifiers, and as such marked by a real dimension of being, which alone could form the basis of signification. This dimension only founds signification as a function of the repression of an original primary signifier that inaugurates the unconscious and makes this latter participate both in signification, by means of later repressions, and in the Real dimension of the Other, in its body.

We shall see in Marie-Françoise the illustration of such a fixation on the scopic level, with all its consequences; Nadia, on 10 December, turned around at my call and smiled.

She mirrored herself with pleasure in the totality of the image, in a perspective I deprived her of, yet she refused to be for the Other only that which she had always been in institutions, an object to be manipulated, available in the Real, excluding any form of signifying representation.

That was the place of the small institutionalized subjects who knew only this kind of life: there no Other came to account in a lasting fashion for a signifier that would have represented them. Luckily, whatever else is done, "it speaks" all the same in institutions, and the small subjects always have to deal with the signifier, even if only their names that they cannot fail to hear from numerous mouths, mouths from which they have perhaps to go and fetch, as Nadia so often did, the meaning of this naming. A vain search in which love, barely sketched, returned Nadia to the *jouissance* of a Real that was only a signifier in waiting and that only became one in the transference, at the moment when the image "dropped underneath."*

*Lacan, *Les Quatre concepts fondamentaux de la psychanalyse,* seminar of 12 February 1964: "Those radical points in the real that I call 'encounters,' which make us conceive of reality as something to be borne, as suffering which is there, waiting [*en souffrance*]; and the *Zwang*, the compulsion, which Freud defines as *Wiederholung*, commands the very detours of the Primary Process. This latter is nothing other than what I defined for you as the Unconscious. And it is our duty to seize it in its experience as rupture, between perception and consciousness, in that a-temporal place which forces us to posit what Freud called the 'other scene,' the 'between perception and consciousness.'"

The signifier she proffered had an essential function, a basis for the passage she effected then and which was to be the source of her debate until the mirror stage. It was the sign, in fact, that she had moved, in an instant, from the fear of being taken up again by the Other in a relation she had always known in hospital institutions and that would inevitably have returned her again to putting forward her protecting image, to her demand to the Other in the field of the signifier, the very coming into being of the subject.

That signifier had another implication that did not immediately appear and had to do with a beyond. It would have been enough, in fact, for the "mama" to have joined itself to some desire I might have had, to have stuck itself to the signification that might have emerged there, for it to have missed the cutting edge of the signifier, thus reducing analysis to mothering, returning Nadia to her totalizing image, even to psychosis. Moreover, she said so herself, just before, when she refused so pointedly to come into my arms: she showed that it was not me who was at stake, in the form of some mother substitute, but a beyond. In other words, beyond the signification of "mama" there was an irreducible signifying function. One cannot help thinking of the function of the signifier "trimethylamine" that unknotted Freud's guilt in the dream of Irma's injection, after he had seen the unbearable image of her infected throat. The baby that Nadia was had no other signifier at her disposal than "mama," which could well have enticed me if I had taken it literally.

It could just as easily have been the signifier "papa," the one all children utter first, and in front of whom? Their mother. Like Nadia, except that they say it more clearly; they indicate that their call is addressed beyond the mother, beyond her real body, of which the signifier in question frees them, just as the "mama" inaugurated Nadia's deliverance.

Beyond the demand that passed by way of the signifier, there was rooted, in dissatisfaction, the desire of what had fallen for Nadia, on 10 December, and that would always remain repressed: the image of the woman and child, A + a. At the same time, I became the big A for her, carrier of objects a that she could not take; hence her clenched fists. My intervention in the scene had as effect the separation of A and a.

Initially, my calling her by name framed her in her S_1, signifier of her body, waiting for the signifier of the body of the Other. In a second moment, her "mama," which addressed itself to something beyond me, and beyond her too, beyond any knowledge between her and me, founded the S_2, that is, the signifier of the body of the Other, and put in brackets what linked itself between the "mama" and the Other. S_1 could then link itself with the beyond of that signifier, with the S_2 inaccessible to any knowledge, of which I became the support.* That was where she inaugurated her relation of subject in the treatment and realized the conciseness of the Lacanian formulation: "a subject is represented by one signifier for another signifier."

*Lacan, *Les Quatre concepts fondamentaux de la psychanalyse*, reference to the seminar of 17 February 1964.

Lacan has defined the articulations in the relation between two fields, that of the "Ich" and that of the Other, as being alienation and separation. He there defines separation as the intersection between two sets of which one represents the subject and one the big Other, where sense is produced. The lenticular overlapping of the two circles represents the overlapping of two lacks and constitutes the place of non-sense where the subject of the unconscious realizes itself.

Alienation is represented by the "vel" which, in the case of Nadia, could be stated as "the image of the woman and the child or death." Interpretation, in only taking it in the movement of the session as a whole, aims not so much at sense as at the reduction of the signifiers in their non-sense, which has allowed, in a priviliged moment, the summary of the determinants of Nadia's structure.

My desire as analyst here appears as an essential function in its relation with the desire of Nadia where "something of alienation is preserved, not with the S_1 and S_2 of the first pair of signifiers—from which the formula of the subject's alienation is deduced—but, on the one hand, with what constituted itself on the basis of primary repression, from the fall of the binary signifier; and, on the other hand, with what appears first as lack, in what is signified by the pair of signifiers, in the interval which links them, to wit, the desire of the Other."

6/The Pre-Specular: Ambivalence

On 11 December I could not take her for a morning session because she was sleeping. That evening she was up and dressed; when she saw me she smiled but in a fleeting manner. She seemed anxious.

On the way to the consulting room, in my arms, she kept one arm back and the other on my shoulder.

As soon as she had sat down she took a cracker and put it into my mouth. I ate a corner and she burst out laughing, repeating the game several times; then she pushed the cracker away from her.

She tried to play with the chair, then stopped, looked at me, and sucked her thumb while completely hiding her mouth with the other hand. Now and then she would stop a few seconds to babble and shake her hand as if she were about to hit me, but it struck the void; at the same time she would turn her head from right to left as if she were saying "no-no-no."

She looked so anxious and reacted so tensely to noises coming from the corridor that I took her back, walking up and down the corridor with her for a short while. Her arms were relaxed but she put them back when I entered her room.

Sitting on the floor among the other children, her anxious interest was divided between me and the nurse.

When I arrived on 12 December, the night nurse told me: "Nadia's tongue is out all the time, she keeps licking everything!"

I found Nadia up and dressed, a toy in her hand. When I stooped to pick her up, she did not lean forward but *neither did she push back her arms; for the first time she extended them to me in the normal position* of a child who is waiting to be picked up. However, as always, her face tensed up between the moment she felt my arms around her and the moment she was sitting in my arms; then she smiled and babbled.

In the session, she put the cracker to my mouth but I did not eat it; in any case, Nadia only touched my mouth with it, pulling it back quickly with a laugh. She did not insist and, with the help of this first cracker, pushed the other one off the chair with an expression of delight. She moved over in order to pick it up and began her game again. Then she threw the one she was holding and several times made the gesture of hitting me, but in the void, babbling in a guttural fashion while making movements of denial with her head. She looked at me intensely but without anxiety.

For the first time *she gripped my white coat* so that I might put her on my lap. From there, she looked at the toys; but her attention was turned in on herself, to find out what she desired. She looked at me fixedly for some seconds, fingering the button of my white coat, then pulled on it so I would sit her on my arm. I responded and she smiled at me; though her face was tense, her body was less of a dead weight and more of a presence in my arms. There was an attempt at closer contact; but a brief time sufficed: she wanted to pick up a toy from the floor; doing this, she noticed the bottle, toward which she displayed the usual hesitant approach. She gave it to me, came back on my lap, and for the first time, *drank from it while lying completely stretched out in my arms,* looking into my eyes. *When she had finished drinking she remained in the same position, sucking her thumb while giving me a look that was searching, serious, and relaxed. For the first time I felt she truly enjoyed this contact she had wanted.*

I took her back with her arms around my neck; she babbled a great deal.

When I had put her back down on the floor with the other children, she looked at me, ignored the toy I had put next to her, and went to another child to take a piece of cardboard she was playing with. Despite the little girl's cries, Nadia succeeded in wrenching it away from her and gave me a triumphant look.

On 14 December Nadia gave me a radiant smile and wriggled as soon as I entered the room. I took her into my arms and she sighed contentedly, then babbled joyously: *for the first time she at once put both her arms on my shoulders* and leaned her head against my cheek. On the way to the session, she babbled and smiled incessantly, but I noticed that her diaper was dirty before I took her: I handed her over to a nurse for changing. While she was being changed she did not cry as before but neither did she let me out of her sight; she held out one of her arms to me while waving it around. She gave a deep sigh of contentment when I took her back into my arms.

When I wanted to put her on the floor, she clung to me and did not let go of me when I sat down. She looked at me for some minutes, smiling, passive, but very relaxed.

This session had several characteristics:

1. Nadia was very active without a trace of inhibition.

2. Often, she would stretch out against me, giving me a tender look before resuming her activity; she did not want more.

3. *She showed considerable aggressivity toward the bottle and other toys, which she pushed away from her without anxiety.*

She started with the crackers: she used them to make noise with, shook them, and ended up pushing them away, even using her feet. Not a trace of anxiety.

Then it was the bottle's turn as she pulled it toward her. She lay down in my arms to drink two mouthfuls and, after inspecting the nipple, pushed it away. It was not enough that it was on the floor *but she also had to pick it up so that she could throw it down violently* and did not give up, using both her hands and her feet until it had been dispatched beneath the radiator. She did the same with the toys. This aggressivity was still without anxiety.

After that, she turned toward me, brandishing her arm above my leg. Then she fingered the buttons of my white coat, got me to kiss her and bounce her up and down, while babbling joyously "ma-ma-ma," "da-da-da." Her look at that moment was full of life and mischief.

As she bounced up and down on my lap, she made a curious blowing sound with her nose, which she screwed up, her face tense, her mouth distorted in a grimace; all this while she looked at me intensely. I did not understand.

At the end of the session, she showed herself to be aggressive. She took a piece of paper from the breast pocket of my white coat: she made a noise with it, shook it, tore it, got excited, and from time to time put it into her mouth while looking at the bottle under the radiator, even making the gesture of giving it a kick. She took the piece of paper out of her mouth rather violently and put it into mine, pulling it out with even greater violence before tearing it to shreds; all this without anxiety.

Taking her back posed no problems, but toward the toy I placed in her crib she showed the same negative behavior as in the session: she threw it on the floor while looking at me.

I noticed a great change in motor activity during the last two sessions: not in quantity but in quality. The movements were the same as in the sessions of the week before, but without inhibition; she translated her emotions at once into actions that contrasted with the clumsy and automatic movements of the beginning of the treatment, two months before. She was no longer trying out her legs; she moved them spontaneously. To express her aggressivity toward me, she needed an intermediary, the paper, just as in the earlier sessions she had made use of the chick in her attempts at contact with me.

On 15 December I found her trying to put a large doll on a chair. I called her, she turned around, smiled, and tried again to sit the doll down before giving it to me. I took her into my arms together with the doll.

As soon as we were sitting down, Nadia on my lap, she did the same things as the day before: aggressivity against the crackers and the toys, which she pushed aside violently; furtive glances in the direction of the bottle, which she would not touch; the same absence of inhibition with respect to motor activity; a strongly articulated babble, especially "ma-ma-ma" while looking at me or fingering the buttons of my white coat. She was openly aggressive toward me, since she struck me on the leg without the piece of paper as intermediary. She took the paper at one point to finger it joyfully and put it back in my pocket. I noticed that her face did not tense up when she hit me; she was not inhibited; she was happy.

Twice she pushed me away with her arms while shaking her head and almost saying "no-no."

The active phase of the session was at an end.

Two new incidents succeeded each other.

First, she contemplated my face at length: eyes, hair, nose, mouth, while now and then leaning her head against me. Once she even threw back her head and looked at me upside down. Then she sat up again, intrigued, to look at me the right way up, laughed, and with a mischievous look, put her head back and again looked at me for a long time.

She sat up, her face became serious. She had diarrhea. She lay down in my arms, sucked her thumb, and looked at me with a serious expression; she was very quiet. I cuddled her but then felt she was uneasy. I took her to have her changed: while she was being changed her eyes did not leave me; she remained joyful.

Back in the consulting room, she wanted to sit in my arms, then on my lap, so she could get hold of a toy. She was active again. At that moment a child yelled in the adjoining room. She stopped, looked at me anxiously, pressed her head against me, and sucked her thumb after lying down in my arms. She plugged one of her ears with her hand so as not to hear the cries. I took her back to her room.

On 17 December, sitting in her crib, she smiled at me but did not lean toward me. Yet, once I was carrying her, she put her arms on my shoulder.

Initially, her attention was focused on the cracker: she shook it, used it to make a noise, put it in my mouth, then in hers. She violently struck the table with it, then the base of my neck. After a game of to-and-fro between her mouth and mine, she went for the cracker and sent it flying. She then turned toward me *to inspect the buttons of my white coat at length, babbling "mama" and not "ma-ma-ma"; then she struck my breast with her hand.* After that she let me cuddle her, sitting in my arms.

After the aggressivity against the cracker, it was the bottle's turn: she shook it and hit it so hard on the floor that it cracked and the milk squirted: she was delighted. The bottle ended up underneath the radiator. She took the paper from my pocket, waved it around, and drenched it in the spilled milk so that only a few dirty shreds remained. She came back to my arms and took my glasses; she threw them behind her, leaned backward a long way to pick them up, and managed to do so.

The nurse told me that Nadia had been standing up on her legs in her crib and was very lively. She even wanted to show me at the end of the session, and I had no time to tell her not to. Under my gaze, in fact, Nadia refused completely to stand up and gave me an anxious look.

On 18 December the *session was an explosion of joyous activity.* Nadia first stayed five minutes on my lap, made a noise with the cracker, laughed, babbled, banged her hands on the chair. Then she wanted me to sit her on the floor, but as she looked at me anxiously, I sat her against me. She gave me a radiant smile.

She launched into a great deal of activity, full of joy and excitement at the discovery of what her arms and legs were capable of. To take back the objects she had thrown away, she used two modes of locomotion: either she crawled backward on her belly, turning around now and then to see where she was going, or, with her right leg folded underneath her, she almost hoisted herself up on it and fell back in a sitting position, slightly to the left of her course, her right arm stretched out toward the object; she also managed to swivel around. Each new movement set her off laughing and caused her to agitate her arms and legs a great deal. She seemed to derive intense enjoyment from the activity of her limbs and looked at me delightedly after each new attempt.

Apart from this explosion of activity that absorbed her attention, the following salient features were present in the session: (1) she showed aggressivity toward the bottle, which she grasped, shook, struck against the floor, and hit with a toy and then pushed away from her with her hands and her feet; (2) she fingered the buttons of my white coat and she wanted to return to my lap in order to do this, a fingering accompanied by frequent "mamas" and hitting of my breast and legs; (3) she turned to me without ambivalence when she was afraid: when she was scared by the noise of the chair she threw down, she moved, gripped my white coat, and tried to hoist herself onto my lap; I helped her up, she got me to kiss her, then climbed down to continue her activities.

I noted how for the first time the entry of another person into the room did not completely monopolize her attention: she had a look and then looked at me and immediately continued what she was doing, even though the nurse was still in the room.

When I took Nadia back, the nurse told me she was demanding more food. Nadia did not seem happy that the session was over.

On 19 December I found Nadia standing up supported by a nurse. When I took her away she was delighted.

The whole session was devoted to the joys of movement. She made a noise with the cracker, with the paper, and then sent them flying; she did the same with the car, the doll, and the chick. She crawled to pick up the objects and threw them even further. She crawled from my lap to the window, came back to my lap, and tried to climb up so that I would kiss her. She then went to the radiator and banged on it with intense joy. When she crawled, she used one knee and two arms: in other words, she was almost on all fours.

When I took her back, she was hugging a toy that she had brought from the consulting room, and, when another child wanted to take it away from her, she crawled right up to her crib.

I should point out that I had forgotten my glasses that day. Nadia noticed and, intrigued, came over to finger my eyes. She scratched the bridge of my nose, where she normally took hold of my glasses to pull them off.

On 21 December, as soon as she was on the floor, she became very active and directed an aggressivity tinged with violence toward me. She hit me several times, either with her hand or with a toy, but only after she had hit herself quite hard on her head with a toy. This state of violence, tension, and excitability lasted for ten minutes. She calmed herself by hitting the bottle, knocking it over, spilling milk on the floor, and spreading the splashes with her hand; eventually, she threw the bottle underneath the radiator. She turned her aggressivity, which by now had diminished, against my glasses. She could not bear to see me with them on, tore them off me, and threw them down.

She crawled a lot, but would only set off after I smiled. Each time she returned, she wanted me to cuddle her. She gripped my white coat, then held out her arms and smiled. Sitting in my arms, she caressed my face with an adoring expression, only to set off again almost at once to explore.

At the end of the session, she crawled over to pick up the bottle from underneath the radiator. She hit the bottle quite hard against the radiator and hurled it across the room. She scattered the toys around. Then she tried to stand up by gripping the windowsill and came back to my arms.

When she was back in her crib, she walked along it from head to foot under my gaze. Dinner had started and she seemed very hungry. She was aggressive toward me and struck my breast: in my joy at seeing her walk I had taken her back into my arms. Then she became tender, pressed her mouth hard against my cheek, without kissing, and wrapped her arms tightly around my neck.

On 22 December, Nadia stood up when I came to fetch her.

As soon as I put her down, there was a violent scene: she pushed away the crackers, breaking one by throwing it on the floor; she hit her head once with the doll, struck me on the leg, and grabbed my glasses, which she then threw away. She did not show any interest in the bottle.

Then she spent twenty-five minutes exploring the room. At the far end, she noticed a sweater on the floor and went over to it almost on all fours; she stopped halfway to look at me and babbled with some degree of articulation and modulation: she seemed to be explaining something. She set off again and picked up the sweater, which from then on she dragged along with her everywhere. She started by rubbing her face with it, laughing and babbling with delight; she shook it, stamped her feet, and trailed it in her wake over to the door, where she picked up a piece of cracker, threw it down again. Then she came back to me for a cuddle and pulled off my glasses.

Still trailing her sweater, she set off for the same corner of the room where she had picked it up; there she had seen a broken toy:

three wheels, a flat piece of wood, and a piece of string. She took it, handled it, shook it, inspected the wheels, and above all the hole where the wheel was missing. Then she threw it away from her but pulled it back toward her with the string.

When she was back in her crib, she stood up and *walked toward me* and grasped my white coat.

On 24 December she showed anxiety when I went to fetch her in the morning; she made no movement toward me, did not smile, but she did not put her arms back either. She had had diarrhea the day before. She relaxed a little in my arms and smiled during the walk to the consulting room.

This session was different from the preceding ones because (1) Nadia was anxious; (2) she was far less active; (3) she kept demanding to be taken into my arms and then reacted violently to my mouth.

She began by throwing down the crackers, the doll, and the car; then she set upon my glasses, which I could no longer put back on during the session. After she had knocked the bottle over and had paid it no further attention, she set off with my glasses, throwing them further and further, hitting them with the car. She then used the same car to hit herself on the head and then me on the mouth. She was tense and violent.

She looked around her, saw the sweater and the piece of wood with three wheels from the previous day, but did not go for them. Instead, she came back so that I would take her into my arms. She clambered down for a few moments and went and shook the doll on the chair, then came back to my arms, smiled with a happy expression, and caressed my face. It was the only moment of joy in that day's session; all the rest was shot through with violence.

Then she fingered the buttons on my white coat and *touched my skin by chance:* she stopped short, very anxious, and wanted to go back down on to the floor though she was still touching me. She broke up a cracker and wanted me to hold her again. Once there she began to finger the buttons, taking care not to touch my skin. She hiccupped, which intrigued her for a moment before she forgot about it. She then set upon my mouth, her face tense and hostile: she struck my mouth with her hand, scratched it, and pulled at my lips. Then she pushed back my head violently, with her hand on my mouth, and kept me there. When it looked as if I was going to raise my head again, she pushed harder and became even more hostile. With the other hand she scratched my neck, sinking her fingers into my skin and pulling it. She was truly in the grip of a strangely intense emotion—she still had hiccups—to the point where I decided to take her to the window to calm her down a little. Her attention was distracted by the arrival of a group of children whom she wanted to watch; she was uneasy rather than tense.

As I carried her back, she smiled at me and was quite calm; back in her crib, she tapped me with her hand, without anxiety, and smiled a little, with a knowing expression. At that moment two nurses arrived; Nadia turned toward me, smiling, stamping with joy while tapping me, as if she was making of me her thing under the gaze of others.

But the violence of the scene that had taken place left her uneasy; and I later heard that after I left she defecated, smeared the excrement all over herself right up to her face, and even ate some of it.

On 25 December, Christmas day, there was a lot of crying in the hospital: there were fewer nurses and the older children were not taken down to the nursery. Nadia was rocking herself in her crib, but stopped as soon as she saw me. She got up and walked toward me, up to the foot of the crib.

She was still rather violent that day. The first thing she did was pull my glasses off: she set upon them for a long time and tried as hard as she could to break them. I could not put them back on for the rest of the session. Then it was the bottle's turn; she knocked it over, emptied it partially on the floor, and threw it beneath the window. She used the chick to spread the puddles of milk and then sent it flying. She picked up the bottle again and threw it under the radiator; this made her laugh.

She wanted me to hold her and to bounce her up and down. Then for a minute she buried her head on my shoulder, hugging me tightly with both her arms; she sat up again with a delighted expression, giving me a tender look.

When I put her down on the floor she became aggressive and violent toward herself. She would either move away from me or would want me to hold her.

On the whole, the session was an expression of great violence toward (1) objects, against which she held herself in check all the same, exploding brutally but then calming down again; (2) myself, through my glasses, but also, more directly, my mouth, as in the previous session; (3) herself, when she hit herself on the head.

When she was back in her crib, she was uneasy about the atmosphere in the room and wanted me to hold her briefly.

On 26 December, I found her standing up at the foot of her crib with a very lively expression. She was radiant when I took her away.

She began the session by pulling off my glasses, then she threw them down and hit them aggressively. This went on for five minutes. Then she fell upon the crackers with violence and scattered them. Next she turned on the bottle, which she knocked over then emptied partially onto the floor. As she threw it away from her underneath her leg, a little milk dripped on her foot; she stopped in midgesture and became furious. She struck the bottle against my leg, hit it with my glasses, touched the milk on her foot and then the splashes on the floor. She sucked her finger, which was wet with milk, once, then struck the puddle quite hard with her hand. When she had calmed down somewhat, she picked up the bottle, which was still against my leg; she then *tried to bring the nipple to her lips* but missed. She was not at all happy and threw the bottle away with a definitive gesture.

She took some paper from my pocket, then waved it and sucked it a lot. She wanted to sit in my arms but her violence and anger were such that I thought it best to put her back in the session crib. She did not calm down, hit me, and again pushed back my head while holding her hand over my mouth. She was so anxious that I took her back to her room. When I put her down in the crib, she pulled off my glasses once more and went over to the far end of the crib.

Maryse, another child I had in treatment, and whose crib was in the same dormitory, had a cold. When she called me, I saw Nadia's face set and the rings under her eyes darken. The nurse took her to be changed and left her for a moment with her bottom exposed. Nadia crawled toward her crib, very fast, and pretended she could not hear me when I called her.

On 28 December, I learned that on the day after the previous session, she had smeared herself with excrement. She had taken it from her diaper with both hands, had put it in her hair, her ears, all over her face and legs; she had even stuffed her mouth full of it.

When I arrived that morning, she was standing up at the foot of her crib. She wriggled and smiled. Nevertheless, she was going to be uneasy and anxious during the session. She began by pulling off my glasses and throwing the crackers around. Twice she wanted to attack the bottle but ended up not doing so. She wanted me to hold her, pressing herself against me. Once in my arms, she seemed torn by emotions and very unstable. *She was continually switching from committing acts of aggression toward my mouth, neck, and white coat* to aiming similar gestures at the railings of the crib I was leaning against.

She picked up a cracker and put it in my mouth. I simply closed my lips for a second: *she then pulled it out, looked at it, and scratched my tongue with her nail to see if there was anything there.* She put the cracker back into my mouth and I bit off a tiny piece, which she in turn took out with her finger. A third time I bit off a piece, which she took out. *She looked at it, drooled copiously, and then threw it down in disgust.*

She next tried to take some paper from my pocket. Because she could not do it and was on the point of crying, I gave it to her. She threw it down, picked it up again, and put it into her mouth, drooling copiously.

She came back onto my lap so I could cuddle her, but she was tense, anxious, and kept shifting position. She looked at me anxiously. One minute she stretched out in my arms and the next she wanted to get back down onto the floor, but leaning her head against my body. Helping herself by means of the crib railings, she managed to get up on her feet three times, standing up straight. Each time she looked at me timidly and sat down for a few seconds on my knee before trying again (I was still sitting on the floor).

She sat down and leaned against me again, but she was so anxious, as her darkly ringed eyes showed, that she no longer seemed to know which was the more painful, to remain quiet or to express her violence. I took her back to her crib.

In her crib, she hit a toy and looked at me. Then, while she smiled at me, she urinated.

On 29 December I found Nadia standing up at the foot of her crib. She was very lively but was looking poorly. The nurse told me she was never satisfied and was fidgety.

On the way to the consulting room she pulled off my glasses and, in the session, set upon them; but there was a new element: twice she held them against my eyes and waited for me to put them back so as to have the pleasure of pulling them off again. She threw down the crackers and one of them broke in two. Nadia was taken aback at first, then furious. She eyed the bottle, which was a long way away, but felt no urge to crawl toward it; *this was the*

*second session in a row in which she hardly moved about in the room,
preferring instead to be on my lap or close against me.*

She attacked a piece of cracker once again and put it to my
mouth, but would let only her fingers go inside it. *She took them
out quickly and brought up a considerable amount of food. Her expression changed to one of disgust:* some of the regurgitated food had
dropped on her foot and she tried to shake it off. But at the same
time she voluptuously spread with her finger what had fallen on
the floor and then put her finger to her mouth.

She wanted to come onto my lap, but, as in the previous session, she was constantly changing position, now sitting, now standing, and she was aggressive toward my mouth. At times she
stretched out for a short interval, relaxed, and was so given over
that I hummed softly. She looked at me intensely and, when I had
finished, answered: there is no other word to describe her babbling
at that moment: very articulated, slow, modulated, pregnant with
meaning, like language.

Now and then she explored a screw in the crib with her finger.

At the end of the session, she was sucking the paper taken from
my pocket, then tore it and scattered the pieces, when she had another attack of vomiting. Then she urinated.

She often sucked the arms of my glasses and would keep on
making sucking movements.

On the way back she was tense and wanted to be put in her crib
at once. From there she laughed and hit me.

On 30 December, she wriggled as soon as she saw me. She was
very intrigued when I began putting socks on her; she trampled
with joy. On the whole the session was going to be full of smiles.
She would only show anxiety when she was sitting on the floor.
The session was therefore conducted on my lap, except for the
scene with my glasses at the start and the aggressivity toward the
bottle at the end.

Nadia pulled off my glasses, but did not set about them; she
wanted to come back onto my lap. From there she picked up a
cracker. She threw it down and picked it up several times. Then
she put it into my mouth and left it there. *A large part of this cracker stuck out from my mouth; she hit it to make it fall and then burst
out laughing.* She repeated this twice more, and it was always with
a certain violence that she stuffed the cracker into my mouth. Her
face was tense with effort. Then she flung the crackers away, in
disgust and fury.

She wanted to take the paper from my pocket, but flew into a rage when she did not succeed: she hit me on the breast. In doing this, she happened to touch my skin and stopped short. Then she scratched my skin a little. *She opened my white coat and thrust in her head to take a closer look.* This lasted only a few seconds. She sat up straight, furious, and hit me again even harder on the breast with both hands.

She wanted to get off my lap to knock over the bottle, pursued it underneath the radiator, banged the bottle against it, spilled the milk, and sent the bottle flying. Then she calmed down, relaxed, and smiled; she wanted to be in my arms. There she played with the crib railings. She put my hand on a railing and used it to stand up. Then she lay down in my arms so that I might kiss her. It seemed that she did not like my humming.

In the session *she urinated in her diaper;* when I put her back into her crib, she hit me a little and smiled.

On 31 December I found Nadia sitting on the floor, holding a rubber doll, and looking very alert. As soon as I picked her up, she snatched off my glasses and threw them down.

For the first time she was wearing shoes, and throughout the session she enjoyed enormously discovering the noise she could make by stamping with them. She was to do it a great deal during the session, laughing out loud, looking at her shoes and then at mine.

Since our usual room was being used, we were in a different one. She looked all around, then looked at me, threw the crackers around, pushed over the bottle, shook my glasses, *put them to her own eyes, then to mine,* and then threw them out of her reach and came onto my knee.

She took the piece of paper out of my pocket; turning around, she noticed a big rubber ball under the crib. She got down and went to get it, moving along on her behind with one leg folded under her. She came back onto my lap, bringing the ball with her. She sucked it, drooling copiously, and picked it up each time it fell down. She let it go and got me to kiss her, hiding her face in my breast.

Getting up again, *she pulled at my lips while poking out her own tongue. She looked for mine with her finger, and when she found it, pushed it back inside with a look of disgust and closed her mouth. Again, she poked out her tongue and tried to find mine; she scraped it with her fingernail, making a lot of movements with her mouth and her tongue.* After all that, her nose was running a great deal; she rubbed it for some time with her hand, which she then shoved violently into my mouth. She pulled out her hand with a smile and took no further notice of my mouth.

She got down from my lap and sent the bottle flying even further away; but she did not hit it and came straight back to my arms. There, she stood up several times over, holding onto the crib and looking at me delightedly, getting me to kiss her and looking at me tenderly.

During the whole of this session she was full of joy and very relaxed. The incident with the mouth, although important, had been less violent and quite brief.

I took her back and sat her on the floor with the other children. She picked up a toy and sat in front of me; but then she saw another child hold out a toy to me, which I took, and so she started to crawl toward me, changed her mind, went away, and sat down, with her back to me. Then she changed her mind again, came back toward me, holding out her arms to me; but she put them down again quickly. I picked her up and she pulled off my glasses.

The nurse told me Nadia had eaten her own excrement again but that she never ate what came out of her nose.

On 1 January I found Nadia dressed, but with bare feet. So I put on her shoes and socks for her. She kicked her legs for joy and laughed.

As usual, she pulled off my glasses, hit them against the chair, and sent them flying; the same with the crackers. She wanted to do the same with the bottle, but did not manage to and was completely nonplussed, so that although she seemed to have a faint desire to try again during the session, she did not do so. She just looked at it, fascinated.

She came back onto my lap and got me to kiss her, then got down to fetch my glasses. She held them against my eyes; I put them on and she burst out laughing and pulled them off. This happened three times in a row, but the third time she did not give them back to me and threw them down after hitting me on the breast. Then she touched a button on my white coat and pushed her head in between my white coat and my blouse for a few moments. Then she shoved a piece of cracker violently into my mouth, quickly pulled it out, and threw it down.

After that, she wanted to sit in my arms, hid her head on my shoulder, then got down, made for the door, and came back, holding out her arms and looking mischievous, tender, and not at all anxious.

On 2 January, she kicked her legs joyfully while I put on her shoes and socks.

During this session she was very active in the room; she did not come and sit on my lap, but came as far as my knees and then went off in the opposite direction, laughing and *saying once, "no-no."* She was babbling the whole time and in such an articulated way that I felt sure she would soon start talking.

She pulled off my glasses, pushed over the bottle, and spread out the pools of milk. She put a cracker into my mouth and used her finger to push off the piece that had stayed stuck to my tongue. Then she sucked that finger. *She hit me on the breast and hit herself a great deal with the toys.* She did not show any anxiety.

On 3 January, I found her standing up in her crib. She was hanging onto one side and banging her behind against the other. She stopped as soon as she saw me and smiled. I sat down to put her shoes on, which made her very happy. She pressed her cheek to mine as I carried her to the consulting room.

As on the previous day, she moved about a great deal, trying to walk on all fours; and even though she did not quite manage it, she got up on her knees to get hold of things.

She pulled off my glasses, sent them flying; she did the same with the crackers, then had a moment's hesitation in front of the bottle and gave up the idea.

She noticed some wastepaper and cardboard at the other end of the room and maneuvered around my legs to get at it. She sucked a piece of paper, hit the cardboard on the floor, without aggressivity, and twice tried to come back toward me, but halfway there turned back toward the cardboard. Still maneuvering around my legs, she came back and sat down near me and pushed over the bottle with the doll. The bottle ended up beneath the window. She sent all the toys flying a long way away from her. Then she came close to me and tenderly *snuggled her head on my breast.*

She put a cracker into my mouth; I bit off a little corner; she threw down the cracker and used her finger to scrape off the pieces that were stuck to my tongue, as if to make sure there was nothing left on it. There was no sign of the disgust she had shown on the previous day. Then she came into my arms and got me to kiss her, gave me a tender look, and got down again. She babbled a great deal, right up to the end of the session.

She shook the chick violently, hit my leg with it twice, and then sat down opposite me; she blew a long raspberry at me *and turned toward the bottle, shook it, banged it, sent it flying, and made big puddles of milk with her hand.*

I took her back; she was in very good shape.

Nadia had lost the image of the totality "A + *a*" that, by virtue of my calling her by her name, had been detached from her eye. Due to the preponderance of the scopic drive, which functioned in two dimensions, she had been able to achieve metaphorically the negation of all loss by juxtaposing in her eyes the image of the Other and the other; the other was the object *a* for Nadia, since the Other, the woman, carried this object, which was the cause of Nadia's desire, on her body. This other, object *a* on the body of the Other, was, as we have seen, the breast.

On 10 December, my calling her by her name had an effect of separation: she lost the inclusion through the eye, found my real body, and encountered in it the two sides of her true relation to me: that she could take in it the place of the metaphoric object, that is to say, the object that had fallen from it; or, by reversal, by Nadia's calling me "mama," she could put this body at a signifying distance. In concrete terms, this metaphor was the horror of being stuck to me, of being a part of my body, of being my breast; the metonymy, the signifying distance, was her foot that she held out to me, my hand that she took, her "mama" that she sent out as an echo of my calling her by her name.

From then on, the body of the Other that I was, was to be at the center of this pre-specular phase in two ways. On the one hand it was an object of contemplation; on the other, it was the carrier of objects *a*. In it, she was seeking both love and the drive object. She oscillated incessantly between her unconditional demand for love and the aggressivity that sought to take away the object from my body. This oscillation can be described as *ambivalence;* her search for love put her in the position of making herself my object, a metaphorical position, and her quest for the object introduced her into the register of this very object on my body, the signifier, the metonymic position.

This oscillation was to remain external to Nadia until, in a final transition, on 16 January, as we shall see, she made of herself my metaphorical object, fallen at my feet: an untenable position that was to drive her to seek metonymy, that of the image of her own body in the mirror. On 10 December she had already anticipated the way she would escape from this metaphor.

In this debate on her relation to the body of the Other, we can see the persistence of what was already present in her relation to the image stuck to her eye, in other words a topological structure of surface: of skin, whether it was that of the Other where Nadia looked for the hole or her own, in which the Other had to stop up the hole by gluing itself to it.

The session of 12 December was a prime example of the way Nadia entered into this debate. Her ambivalence was clear: after putting up her arms in the normal way so that I would pick her up (and later she would also put them around my neck), she pretended to hit me, but not without moving her head in such a way as to deny it. In the session, she ignored all the usual objects and looked for an object on my body by playing with the buttons on my white coat.

This was the one and only time she attained the metaphoric realization of the image of 10 December, as she drank from the bottle, lying in my arms and looking at me. The desire she had realized through her hallucination was now realized in a real contact between her body and mine, and she found pleasure in it, if not *jouissance*. She looked overjoyed, her eyes looking into mine, and even showed autoerotism, as she sucked her thumb after she had finished drinking, lying in my arms.

Thus she had passed from the hallucinatory realization of her primordial fantasy (10 December) to the realization of her desire in relation to the Real of the body of the Other. It was as if she had to establish her debate, to let it take root, in the Real, something she had probably never done before. It was one single instance, which was never to be repeated again to such a complete extent; she was never to find it again, and yet she would go on looking for it incessantly. On this occasion there was also an element of primary repression, which in some way was a complement to the real roots of the relation to the Other.

At the end of this scene she showed no anxiety. She might well have become anxious if, in the context of the transference, my *jouissance* as Other who had given her the bottle had made her my metaphorical object. Indeed, as we saw on 10 December, Nadia could not bear to be in that position; she made a metonymic opening by taking a piece of cardboard from another child and showing it to me triumphantly. It is true that I had spontaneously put her back among the other children rather than taking her back to her crib, which might have been experienced as a closure of the dual relation between her and me. Indeed she had defended herself against this, and not without anxiety, in the second part of the 10 December session, by taking refuge, if we can put it that way, in metonymy.

In the two sessions that followed, she confirmed her rejection of the metaphor and her accession to metonymy by both clarifying their meanings and showing their relations to signifiers and to loss.

On 14 December, for example, even though she relaxed for a few moments in my arms to take the bottle, she pushed it away after a couple of mouthfuls. It was the first time she pushed it away violently, using her hands and feet to send it to the other end of the room, where it landed under the radiator. On the other hand, she then turned her attention to the buttons on my white coat, babbling joyfully "ma-ma-ma, da-da-da," her face full of joy and mischief. Moving from the metaphoric object to the metonymic, she thus showed that the former was linked to violence and destruction and the latter to discourse: her oscillation between these two types of object was to continue right up to the mirror phase.

This opposition between the two types of object appeared again at the end of the 14 December session, and not without an attempt by Nadia to overcome it. She took a piece of paper out of my breast pocket; and she was to use this for almost a month, right up to the mirror phase, to express not only the nature of the object but also its relation to my body.

This piece of paper was a separable, metonymic object, which she took as she had taken the piece of cardboard from the other child; it took part initially in her relation to the crackers, the bottle, and speech. She put it into my mouth, took it out, and destroyed it, in order to deprive me of it, just as she did with the crackers. As with the bottle, she put it in her mouth (looking at the bottle all the while). As with speech, she made it audible, when she screwed it up and tore it up. All this she did without anxiety because, unlike the metaphoric object, the piece of paper did not reveal itself for what it represented.

The metaphoric object, on the other hand, had a clearly recognizable substitutive connection with my body. Take, for example, the big doll that she was trying to sit in a chair when I arrived on 15 December. She brought it with her to the session, but immediately substituted it for the metonymic objects stuck to my body: the buttons of my white coat, which she played with while babbling, and the piece of paper she took out of my pocket. She could not, however, stop herself from returning to my body and experiencing its ambivalence; she oscillated between tenderness and hostility, hitting me quite playfully and pushing me away with movements of her head that indicated denial of her hostility, and almost saying "no-no."

The return to her tender mood brought her to contemplate my face in detail. She even turned her head upside down to look at me the wrong way up, laughing, just the way she had looked at me when she drank the bottle as she lay in my arms. But in this case the bottle was absent, and her mode of contemplation was closer to that of 10 December, when the image was glued to her eye. From that time on, the Real of my presence took on the role of a command; she could no longer include me in herself by attaching me to her; I was irremediably external to her. The primordial repression (of 10 December) had intimated this loss to her that manifested itself in her body immediately: she sat up with a serious face and had an attack of diarrhea. Her excrement appeared for the first time in her relation to the Other, inasmuch as it was an object that represented a loss, the severance from the Other.

From the following day onward, Nadia subjected me to this loss, which was that of the primordial image: she snatched off my glasses and went on doing so in almost every session, sometimes several times over, right up to the first part of the mirror phase. She was even to attack them so hard that she broke them. In this pre-specular phase, the transitivism that still linked Nadia to the Other that I was gave these glasses the role of representing the image that had come unstuck from her eye. It was as if this same image was glued to mine and that she had to unstick it completely and destroy it. There was a very active side to what Nadia was doing, as we could see from her rapid progress in the realm of motor activity. For example, on 19 December she was not satisfied with establishing that I did not have my glasses on just for any old reason; she was intrigued and scratched the bridge of my nose, the place where she had put on my glasses so that she could take them off again. It was as if what counted was not that I was lacking them, but that in taking them off me, she had unstuck an image that would be negativized and yet present, if we can put it that way, in this form. A gap appeared between the glasses and the image and situated the glasses at the level of metonymy, which put Nadia completely at ease when she pulled them off, while at the same time confirming the image that had to be unstuck in its status of signifier.

Thus, up to 24 December, she made the transition from a metaphorical object like the bottle to metonymic objects, such as the paper and my glasses, and even, on 22 December, an old sweater she rubbed her face with, while babbling and stamping for joy.

If we take a metaphorical object like the bottle, she had to destroy it, whether she hit it violently on the floor to the point where it cracked and the milk spurted out or whether she tipped it over, emptied the milk out of it, and spread the milk out in bigger puddles with her hand. At this point the phenomenon of spreading things out appeared, whether it was the milk or other objects in relation to the structures of surface. This surface was the surface of bodies, mine and hers: this element predominated in the entire session of 24 December.

On that day, Nadia encountered something that was to have considerable consequences for her. While she was taking an interest in the buttons of my white coat, she touched my skin underneath. She stopped short and fled. Back on the floor, she broke a cracker into pieces. A moment later, she wanted to come back into my arms so she could play with the buttons again, but she approached them cautiously, not wanting to touch my skin. Then she went for my mouth, hit me, pulled at my lips, and scratched me, with a hostile look on her face. Then she pushed my head back violently with one hand and clawed at my neck with the other one, digging her fingers into my skin, pinching and pulling it. She was so violent that I picked her up and took her to the window to try to distract her. She calmed down a little. But the violence of the scene, which had followed on from the encounter with my skin, left her feeling very uneasy, and I later heard that after I left she not only had an attack of diarrhea but also daubed herself with it all the way up to her face and even ate some of it.

Thus she passed from my skin, which she could not bear insofar as it was a closed surface, without holes, to her own; and, by smearing it with excrement, up to and including her mouth, she was saying that it was her skin that had to be a surface without faults or holes, all of a piece, without exterior or interior. This was the translation, onto her skin, of the image of 10 December. At that point where the eye had failed, as a result of my intervening and calling her by her name, the skin was to answer for the totality of A + *a*. And that happened as soon as I left, that is to say, as soon as I was no longer there, just as I had not been there on 10 December.

Something came to light here about what my body and hers, mutually joined together, had to be for her: my body had to be a surface with holes, because of the objects she wanted to get from it, so that the holes in the surface of her own body could be filled by them. So she was overwhelmed by passion when she encountered my skin, which was the Real of the absence of the hole. Thus she had wanted, quite obviously, to cut open this surface without a hole, by digging her finger into my neck. The hole in the surface of my body was the guarantee that the object of my body would be a part of hers.

And thus, when I left, she metaphorically substituted for my presence, and for the object of my body, this object from her own body, not only on her skin but also in her mouth. She showed that there was continuity between the exterior and the interior of her body, in other words, that her body was only one surface with only one side. It was after I left that she did this: my absence as Other meant that the signifier was replaced by the Real.

That was the first time she smeared herself with excrement during the treatment; she was to do it two or three times more, always in my absence, always outside the sessions.

If such a structure of the surface of the body was arrived at with Nadia, a structure that topologically corresponded to the Möbius strip, it was because she had sought the relation of bodies between herself and myself—in the place of the Other—as if driven ineluctably in a relation of inclusion, initially by attachment to the eye and later to the entire skin.

On the contrary, the limit, even the impossibility, she encountered in achieving such a relation of bodies by inclusion provoked an aggressivity in her that developed in two moments: as soon as she had touched my skin, she went for my mouth, or rather, my lips, before she stopped up this mouth with her hand and turned, in a second moment, to my neck to try to make a hole in it with her finger.

Here we find once more the transitivism between her body and mine; for was she not expressing a certain absence of the hole in my mouth, which she would then have to recreate—she, for whom, nevertheless, the exploration of my body had started with the hole of this mouth? The meaning of her refusal of this mouth could well be interpreted as a refusal at the level of her own: she had no mouth; her mouth did not exist as long as she could not be filled up by the sticking on of the Other or the object that the Other carried. That was what allowed her excrement, in my absence, and within this transitivistic dimension, to be stuck to her and complete not only her skin but also her mouth.

On 25 December this dual transitivistic movement appeared again; when, after hiding her head on my shoulder, she squeezed me tight in her arms, with a tender look, it was very difficult to decide, between her and me, who was completing whom. In any case, on that day she could not bear to be physically separated from me; that was what made her violent, and she confirmed this by becoming aggressive toward herself. When she came back into my arms, she turned her aggressiveness toward my neck again. This violence against me was to continue during the subsequent sessions, right up to 30 December. She also turned her violence against herself, and on several occasions, in my absence, she smeared herself with excrement, as she had done the first time.

The transitivism connected with the mouth regained the intensity it had had at the beginning, when I had bitten off a corner of the cracker and she had vomited. Early on, on 28 December, she had put a cracker into my mouth, taken it out, examined it, and then scraped my tongue with her fingernail. She put it back into my mouth and got me to bite off a little piece, but only to take it out again with her finger and throw it down in disgust. In the following session, she failed even to get a piece of cracker into my mouth; only her fingers found their way in, and she took them out quickly, simultaneously bringing up a great deal of the food she had eaten. Then she showed the same kind of disgust as on the previous day; but this time it was not directed at an object that had come out of my mouth or out of hers; because a small quantity of the food she had brought up had landed on her foot, she shook it to make it fall off.

She was to show this disgust another time (31 December), while busying herself with my mouth; on that day it was not a question of my mouth's hole, but of my tongue. At the beginning, she pushed it back in and closed her own mouth symmetrically. Then, in a second moment, it was her own tongue she poked out, while looking for mine. A complete game was established between her tongue and mine; her disgust was aroused by this metaphorical discovery of the organ that revealed, still transitively, an oral fantasy via the encounter with the Real. If this encounter with the real organ provoked her disgust, it was because it conflicted with the effect of prohibition, structurally linked with the signifier.

This scene could be resolved only when Nadia rubbed her hand under her nose, which had been running a great deal, rammed her whole hand into my mouth quite violently, and then took it out with a smile and took no further notice of my mouth. It was as if she had reestablished the hole in its wholeness.

From these episodes onward, in which she encountered disgust, we can discern the articulation of metaphor and metonymy. Metaphor, closer to the Real, in a substitutive effect reinforced by transitivism, here revealed what had been repressed. Metonymy, closer to the signifier, by its own effect, released Nadia from this transitivism and from too close a proximity to the Real of our bodies. This stage was reached, as we saw, from the second part of the 10 December session. The transition from metaphor to metonymy was already present in the fear she exhibited of being too close, even glued to me, and that was why, metonymically, she held out only one foot to me before she called out her "mama" to me.

The entire debate that was going on within her during this prespecular phase resulted from her being driven toward the inclusion of the Other by sticking to it and from the fact that she could not bring herself to reveal it to me, as I was the agent of interdiction because I called her by her name and spoke to her.

She had two ways out of this impasse: reversal and the veil.

Reversal was what she resorted to when, on finding my tongue, she not only hid her own, but also pushed mine out of sight with her hand covered in what had come out of her nose. It was as if she was putting back onto me what had run onto her skin; she gave what was on her skin (her excrement) back to me as my responsibility; and in any case she would not smear herself with excrement again after this. After she had pushed my metaphorical tongue-object back into my throat, is it not true to say that she turned around the metaphor, to the point where she made the transition from "sticking me to her" to "sticking herself onto me" in my mouth? Pulling off my glasses gave rise to a similar reversal, when, for example, on 29 December, after attacking them, she twice held them to my eyes and waited for me to put them back on so she could take them off again; in other words, she turned the pulling off into a game and thus attenuated the sense of unsticking of the image. At the end of this session, when she brought up her food, smeared it around with her finger, and then sucked her finger, she repeatedly sucked the arms of my glasses, making an equation between what she had lost and what she had caused me to lose. It was a question of effacing any hole that appeared in the surface, whether it was her surface or mine.

If we turn to the question of the veil, she encountered it rather than giving it a function on 30 December. In that session she put a cracker into my mouth and knocked off the corner that was sticking out, which made her laugh a great deal. On the other hand, she did not manage to take out the piece of paper and hit me on the breast. In doing that, she came into contact with my skin and stopped short, as she had done on 24 December. This time, however, she returned to it, scratching my skin with her finger, and then impulsively pushed aside my white coat and put her head down inside it for a few moments to have a look. She sat up again, furious, and hit me on the breast. What had she seen? Nothing but my blouse under my white coat. Why, then, this sudden anger? Because the object she was seeking remained veiled, and the veil confirmed that she had to do with the forbidden, that is to say, the inclusion of the object of the Other, through her look, onto her eye. So she resorted to a reversal: she stretched out in my arms, embracing me in order to get me to kiss her, as if once again, not being able to include what belonged to the Other, she made herself into the object of the Other. This was a metaphoric step that was to reach its culmination, as we shall see, on 16 January.

She did not give up the search for the object on my body, for during this scene she had urinated in her diaper, under the veil of her diaper, introducing through her urination, in other words, the Real of her body, another lacking object. This was an aggressive reaction to her disappointment, just as in the preceding two sessions.

Three times she was to start again to bury her head inside my white coat for a few seconds, until 3 January. Each time it was to achieve the same metaphoric result: because her look was unable to take the metonymic and veiled object, in other words my breast, from my body, she made herself into my object, in my arms, stuck to me, and not without a certain tenderness.

Another object took the center stage in her relation to me: her feet. It was the first bodily object that she had held out to me once she had emerged from her fascination of 10 December. On 30 December, what gave her the greatest enjoyment was not that I was concerned with her feet, but that I put her socks on, in other words, that I veiled them. From that time on she always had something on her feet when we had a session, and on the following day she wore shoes for the first time in her life. She was overjoyed and looked at me with peals of laughter, not only because of these veiled objects but also because of the noise she could make with them when she stamped. It was "getting heard" by means of this object that neither she nor I could see and that was situated at the level of hearing, to which Nadia was extremely sensitive. From then on, each session would begin under the sign of the shoes and socks: as soon as she saw me take them out, her fixed expression would disappear, her face would light up with a joyful smile, and she would even kick her legs.

On 31 December the shoes appeared to take on the fullness of their dialectical function. Certainly, they were metonymic, insofar as they did not reveal their relation to the fundamental fantasy of the desire to be stuck to the Other; but more than that, they acquired the dimension of being beyond all knowledge, when Nadia showed great joy in looking alternately at her shoes and mine, during the session. Their obvious function of "unary trait" allowed her to reach the level of identification, in an anticipation that was successful in comparison with her current debate, which was still very much linked to the first form of identification by sticking, something that left her in an impasse of transitivism.

While the holes in the surface of her body revealed themselves for what they were—always to be stopped up—for the first time, with the shoes, she could assume metonymically a hole that was beyond the surface, without revealing a loss, either mine or hers, that is to say, without the Other's knowing about the loss; it meant she could anticipate the existence of the interior of an envelope. The beyond of the hole in the envelope explained Nadia's joy and made a gap in her anxiety at seeing me arrive for the session. The metaphor of my presence was overtaken by the metonymy of the shoes, which foreshadowed the structure of bodies she was to find in the mirror: the toric structure.

7 / The Small Other—The Doll: The Metaphorical Place of the Subject

On 4 January, there was a Christmas tree in the institution. I was still holding onto an illusion, because I took Nadia to see it when there was no one else around. I had had to wrap her up in a blanket; she was very agitated, dejected, and tense. She looked at the tree a little, but was much more interested in what I had in my pocket. I took her back up to her room.

That afternoon, when I went to collect her for the session, she was in very good shape and brought along the ball she had got at the Christmas tree.

She sat on the floor, sucking and biting the ball, then put it down a moment to throw the crackers around violently. She got up on my lap, sucking and biting the ball again; then she noticed an old, deflated balloon at the other end of the room and went to get it. She sucked it as she had done her own ball, then came back toward me, pushing it in front of her. It rolled, and as she followed after it, she accidentally knocked over the bottle of milk with her foot. She stopped short, looked at the bottle, which remained balanced on her shoe, took it and shook it violently, banged it on the floor, and made big semicircles, rubbing the milk into the floor. The milk spurted all around, and the toys went all over the place. Then she sent the bottle itself flying. The whole scene was violent, and her face was tense.

Once she had sent the bottle flying, she looked at me and burst out laughing, tapping her shoes on the floor, and got back on my lap, delighted; she wanted me to bounce her, but not for long, as she was overexcited.

She got down again, and at that point she pulled off my glasses; she gave them back to me just so that she could pull them off again.

She took the piece of paper from my pocket, rubbed it in the pools of milk, and then rubbed my face with it, smiling all the time. Then she picked up a cracker that was soaking in a pool of milk, licked it several times, threw it violently away from her, and grabbed the doll, which she sprinkled with milk from the bottle. She pulled off the doll's hat, hit its head very hard on the floor, made big semicircles with it on the floor, and then threw it far away from her. She hit me with it once, but not until she had hit herself on the head with the toy car. She did all this while babbling in a very articulated and mischievous way.

When I put her back on the floor with the others, her main interest was in grabbing the toys away from them, and she would move over quite long distances to do this. Her mood remained exuberant, and she kept in contact with me, but she went away when another child clung onto me.

During the session she had started to walk on all fours.

On 5 January, she had just been changed and had her face washed when I arrived; she seemed frightened. Her expression of fear transformed into one of anguish when she saw me, and she recoiled perceptibly. I talked to her a little, to calm her, but her expression did not alter. I got out her shoes and socks to see if she wanted after all to come to the session, and before I had even managed to get hold of them from under her mattress, she was kicking with joy; she laughed as she looked at me and tried to pull my glasses off.

In the session, she did pull them off; she broke the crackers and threw them around; she sucked my glasses energetically. Several times in a row she put a cracker in my mouth; each time I bit off a little corner. *She would then throw it down and take out what remained on my tongue with her finger,* with a look of disgust.

She threw around the toys, the doll, and the crackers, using her arms and legs; her expression was tense. She hesitated in front of the milk bottle, gave it a little tap, with the intention of knocking it over, but she was too diffident, and the bottle remained upright. She came into my arms and smiled at me. She got down again, as she had done during the previous session, *and accidentally knocked over the bottle. She became furious with it,* hit it, and made the milk spurt all over the place. She stopped to lick the nipple a little and then flung the bottle away and took no more notice of it.

She then came over to me and licked my sleeve; I had the impression she would have liked to eat me; I told her so. She hit me once with her hand and appeared anxious. She wanted me to take her in my arms again; once she was there, she relaxed and laughed.

I took her back and put her down on the floor. She moved around the room on all fours, looking at me frequently and laughing.

Throughout this session, apart from the few brief moments when I was holding her in my arms, she was rather anxious and inhibited both in her motor activity and in her babbling. At the end of the session she kept touching her diaper between her legs.

On 6 January she seemed tense again; she did not smile at me straight away; but, as on the previous day, as soon as she saw me getting out her shoes and socks, she kicked her legs and laughed; she was pleased, but there was an undertone of violence. I was told she had been suffering from diarrhea since the previous day.

The great innovation in this session was that she started to walk; but her walking was tinged with aggressivity toward me.

She began the session with the usual scenario with the crackers: she threw one down, it broke, she took no more notice of it. The second one, however, did not break and she attacked it with my glasses; she threw them down in fury when she found she could not manage to break it. So she took back the cracker and forced the whole thing violently into my mouth, not letting go of it with her fingers. She took it out and looked at it, furious at finding it still intact. Disgusted, she threw it far away from her and gave a loud fart.

She tipped over the bottle, making the milk spurt all over the place, then flung the bottle aside. She sucked her finger, which she had dipped in a puddle of milk, then she rubbed her whole hand, still quite tightly clenched, in the same puddle.

She came back into my arms for a second, refused to stay there, and went to pick up the recalcitrant cracker. She licked it, then threw it hard into the puddle of milk. Finally it broke, but she was not truly satisfied until she had broken it apart into little pieces.

Then she got onto my lap and smiled; for the first time she appeared to be relaxed.

She got down again to pick up my glasses, which she gave back to me, only to pull them off again and suck them. *She took the paper out of my pocket and moved quite a long way away from me with it; from there, she looked at me and put it in her mouth.* She came back quickly toward me, frowning, and with a look that made me think she wanted to eat me. But before she got to me, she turned around and went back, supporting herself on her feet by holding onto the bars of the crib, after throwing down the piece of paper.

During the last ten minutes of the session she walked along the side of the crib, hanging onto the bars, back and forth between me and the opposite end, babbling vociferously all the time "ga-ga-da-da." Her face was tense and she looked furious with me and with herself.

When I picked her up to take her back, she laughed contentedly and put her arms around my neck, but only briefly; once we were out in the corridor, she pushed me away.

Back in her room, she wanted me to put her on the floor straight away. She picked up a toy that made a noise and whirled it around above her head. When I walked across the room to leave, she followed me quickly on all fours. When I turned around, she went to fetch the toy, demanded that I should pick her up, and hit me on the head with the toy, laughing. Moreover, she had hit her own head on the crib as she got up, and, not at all happy about this, had hit the crib.

Throughout the session Nadia had had hiccups; they stopped as soon as she was back in her own room.

On 8 January I found Nadia with the same expression of fear; as on the previous occasions, her look changed only when she saw me get out her shoes and socks; she kicked her legs joyfully and babbled.

At the beginning of the session she was not happy because the doctor and a nurse were in the room. She was able to take the crackers while they were still in the room, but only after they had left could she throw them around.

During the first part of the session she was angry but did not show any anxiety. She was throwing everything around; she tried to push over the bottle with her hand, but when she did not succeed gave it a mighty blow with the fluffy chick. Once it had been tipped over, she did not attack it; she did not even touch it and spent some time contemplating it in silence with a tense look on her face.

Having spread out the pool of milk, she went for the doll, hitting its head hard on the floor, then whirling it round. She snatched off my glasses and used the doll to send them flying as far as she could.

She gave up on the doll after she hit her hand in the process of whirling it around. Then she hit herself once on the head with her hand and got me to pick her up, smiled happily, and got me to kiss her for quite some time.

Just as in the previous session, she took great delight in walking along the side of the crib, babbling a great deal and looking at me without interruption, as if I was to share her joy.

Then she noticed a broom near the door; she very much wanted to get to it. She shook the crib violently so that it gradually moved toward the broom; but she refused my help when she tried to leave the crib to get right up to the broom. She could not reach it, so had to abandon her plan, and came toward me with a great show of tenderness, caressing my shoulder, looking at me from close up. Then she licked my cheek and babbled with joy.

She went off again to pick up the paper she had taken from me and thrown away earlier; she came back and hit me on the back with the paper, laughing; then, letting go of it, hit me with her hand. She laughed, picked up the paper again, put it in her mouth, and walked on all fours, with a tense look. She came back to me; I happened to have my hand on the fluffy chick. *She lifted my hand and put it down a little further away,* so she could take her chick. When I took her back to her room, she wriggled so that I would put her down on the floor. She wasted no time in trying to grab a toy from another child; when she failed to do so, she looked at me with annoyance and moved quickly to pick up a shoe that was lying around near her.

On 9 January I found Nadia in tears, sitting on the floor among the other children. She raised her arms expectantly when she saw me, but the movement was incomplete. She relaxed only when she was in my arms. The nurse told me Nadia was crying because she was jealous and she could not bear to see the nurse cuddling another child.

In the session she snatched off my glasses, attacked them, put them into my hand, took them away again, then gave them back. She did this several times over, with normal movements and without her old mechanical gesture. Eventually she left them in my hand and went to pick up a cracker, which she put to her mouth. I thought she had bitten off a little piece, but there was no sign of this on the one she took out of her mouth. She examined it attentively, unhurriedly, and showed no sign of disgust. She licked it, then threw it well away from her. She pushed over the bottle, but did not touch it.

Then she babbled with joy in my arms, licked my shoulder, and groped at my arms; she stood on the floor and walked around the crib for a while. She was not keen to move very far away from me and kept coming back either to sit on my lap or to stand in front of me, leaning on my shoulders. She had a very tender look on her face.

After some hesitation, she went to spread out the pools of milk, looking all the while at the bottle, but not touching it.

She became extremely violent toward the doll, then struck herself on the head, and laughed as she hit me. She stood up again, delighted.

When I took her back to her room she was full of joy, carrying a piece of cracker.

Since I was told that evening that Nadia found it very difficult to bear the time in between the sessions, that she became withdrawn and it was impossible to distract her, I decided to give her another session that same day.

Her face was quite expressionless when I went to fetch her.

During the session, she put the crackers on the floor, came to take the pencil out of my pocket, put it into my mouth, then into hers, then looked at it for a long time, and threw it down. After that she came and stood next to me and cuddled up to me, smiling tenderly, and babbling almost in a sing-song.

She opened her mouth and put it to mine for a second, drooling and making a sucking movement, smiling and happy; then she patted my neck tenderly.

She noticed the potty, which now became an object of interest for her. She went toward it, but came back to pick up the pencil and sat down some way away from the potty. She let go of the pencil and went on all fours to *have a look inside the potty.* Then she went back to get *the pencil to poke around in the potty before she plunged it in for a long time, several times in a row.* She babbled joyfully and came back into my arms.

I took her back to her crib.

When I went back past her room later on, I saw Nadia in her crib, with an inert look on her face, lying on her side and sucking her thumb.

On 10 January I arrived later than usual and Nadia was already in her crib. She was sucking her thumb, almost asleep, but she quickly woke up when I got out her shoes. I felt she was tense.

In the session, she broke the crackers, took my glasses, gave them back to me, then sent them flying. She pushed the bottle gently, but it did not fall over, and she did not pursue the matter.

She came into my arms, fingered my skin, licked my cheek, and moved her mouth toward mine; nothing more. She noticed the potty and looked at me with a laugh.

I had to take her back to her crib for her evening meal.

She had had diarrhea since 6 January.

I was surprised to find her lying on the floor on 11 January. The nurse had put her there to change her. She was tense and did not relax until I picked her up.

In the session *she took a cracker and bit off a tiny piece, inspect-ed it again, and sent it flying.* Then she stuffed her finger into my mouth *and scraped my tongue* as if it were me who had eaten the piece of cracker.

Right away she wanted to push over the bottle, but did not dare to, either with her hand or with the chick. She went to pick up a ball from under one of the cribs, but remembering she had banged her head against this crib in a previous session, she hit it twice before venturing underneath it. She sucked the ball, and each time it rolled further away she would go to fetch it. While she was do-ing this, her foot caught the bottle, making it fall over. So she abandoned the ball, picked up the bottle, shook it at the floor to get some milk to come out, then sent the bottle flying. She was tense and aggressive.

She picked up the doll so she could throw it a good distance away from herself. Then she struck herself on the head and came back into my arms. She licked my shoulder, stood up by support-ing herself on the crib, took a couple of steps, and came back to me for a cuddle. I kissed her, and she stood up and went for my mouth, pulling at my lips, pushing my head back, holding it there, groping at my neck. Each time I made to put my head forward again, she would push it back, with a furious look.

She got down and went toward the door, and I had the impres-sion she wanted to walk, but not in the consulting room. I picked her up and opened the door to see what it was she wanted. She leaned toward the corridor and babbled. So I took her back to her room; at first she wanted to sit on the floor like the others. She hit another child, who tried to take away the car she had had in her hand since the session; she came back to me and held out her arms to me. What she wanted was to walk, with me supporting her. As her dia-per had slipped when she started to walk, I gave her to a nurse to change her. Nadia cried. I took her back in my arms; she refused to let me put her down on the floor, but wanted me to take her into the corridor, then into the next room. In there, she wanted to walk; she went to a box of toys and took out a rubber sailor.

On 12 January she did not walk much; she wanted above all to be in my arms, *where she could attack my mouth; she showed renewed interest in the buttons of my white coat.*

When I took her back to her room, she was aggressive toward the other children and wanted to walk.

On 13 January, she held out her right foot to me so I could put on her shoe, but refused to let me put on the left one; she grabbed it from me and threw it down. The nurse put it on for her without the slightest difficulty.

She was very aggressive throughout the session, particularly after she had gone to hit the potty with the car. After that she did not dare go near the potty, but moved around it, throwing the car aggressively in front of her, picking it up, and throwing it down again.

She frequently came into my arms and showed considerable violence toward my mouth; she hit it once very hard with the car, after I had said to her, as she was pulling aggressively at my lips, that she was cross with the mouth because she had not had everything she wanted from it. She stopped short for a moment, in front of my white coat, on a level with my breasts, and started to throw the toys over her shoulder; she hit herself with the car before throwing that as well.

She got down and started to walk from one crib to another, babbling as if she was hurling insults.

Back in her room, she wanted to walk around in order to snatch things from the other children, but the overall impression she gave was of not knowing what she wanted. The father of one of the other children arrived; Nadia was terrified and took refuge in my arms, watching the stranger intently.

On 14 January she again refused to let me put on her left shoe, and again the nurse had no trouble in putting it on her.

On that day there was a feeling that she was refusing the sessions and she showed a distinct preference for walking, in her own room to start with.

When I shut the door of the consulting room, she hit it and showed interest in the electric switch. Although she was still throwing the crackers around, she was far less aggressive toward them. She wanted to get one that had fallen behind the little armchair, but the bottle was standing in her way. She touched it cautiously and backed away; she went back and forth, trying to find a way around without touching the bottle. Nonetheless, she was not able to avoid pushing it over, and she pushed it away. It got stuck against my foot; she pushed it further away, under a chair, and took no further notice of it.

So she picked up the cracker and touched the heating pipe with it. She dropped the cracker and touched the pipe with her hand; she was fascinated by the heat and shook her hand, looking at her palm.

I took her in my arms and she pulled off my glasses, gave them back to me with a laugh, then put them up to my eyes. I put them back on; she had been expecting me to do this, with a mischievous look on her face. She pulled them off again. She got down to pick up her cracker again and went up to the potty; after going around the potty a few times, she hit the edge with the cracker and then hit inside it.

She came back toward me and got me to eat a corner of the cracker, which she then took out of my mouth with her finger. I told her what she was doing; she smiled at me, carried on, and then threw down the cracker.

From that moment on she was tense and aggressive. She wanted to go up to the potty, but kept going around it, and then went away from it. She came back to me and hid her head on my breast, looking at me tenderly. She went and maltreated the doll a little, then came and took the piece of paper away from me and threw it over her head.

Again she put her head lovingly on my breast; then she stood herself up with the help of the bars of the crib, got me to admire her, to kiss her, and then started the procedure again.

At the end of the session she no longer knew what she was doing or what she wanted: whether to get away from me or to climb into my arms. She kept alternating between the two; in both cases the action was incomplete, hesitant. She would give up one to start the other one again, babbling in a modulated way, either violently, as if hurling insults, or in a tender sing-song.

I took her back to her room, where she wanted to walk toward me without any support. Since she did not manage to do this, she got me to cuddle her and then wanted me to put her down on the floor so she could crawl toward the next room, where she could hear other children playing. If another child cried, she would become anxious and stop immediately, coming back into my arms to find security before going off again.

On 16 January I found her lying on the table, in tears because the nurse had just cleaned out her ears; they had spontaneously drained themselves. She must have been crying a great deal, as her eyes were very red.

When she saw me she stopped crying but did not hold out her arms to me. I picked her up; she sobbed briefly, put her arms around my neck, and clung onto me. She trampled discreetly, pulled back a little, but only so that she could look intently at my face, then she smiled and leaned her arms on my shoulders.

She was pleased to go into the consulting room. She held out one arm toward some new toys; there was a Noah's ark with various wooden animals and a rubber sailor. I decided I would not sit on the floor anymore, but on a low chair, now that she was able to stand up if she had something to hold onto. Because of the state she was in that morning, however, I had to go down to her level on two occasions.

The emotional tone of this session was dominated by an overwhelming desire to be cuddled and by a violent negativism that forced Nadia to push me away as soon as she had let herself go a little. She did not babble at all.

Straight away she moved toward the ark and started to take out the toys. *Her movements were very clumsy again, and there was a return of the tic of opening her hand when she let go of a toy.* This automatic movement, however, was different from the one she had made at the beginning: when she had let go of the toy, she would look at it, inert, but would keep her hand clenched above the toy.

She put back the toys she had taken out of the ark, and the only things that retained her interest were a little celluloid boat, the rubber sailor, and later on, a lead soldier. She took the sailor and made several of her mechanical movements before flinging it away. That was the last of the tics. She kicked a building block under one of the cribs. She threw down the boat several times and then abandoned it and came toward me. She pushed herself against my breast very hard, three times, but her hands stayed clenched and she sat up quickly and pushed me away with her arms.

She discovered that she could walk, pushing the little armchair in front of her. *She stopped in the middle of doing this, began to cry,* took refuge in my arms, and clung to me. Twice she wanted to get back down, but sobbed briefly and clung to me again before she finally decided to get down.

From this moment on, she made sucking noises. She went to get the lead soldier and sucked its gun while looking at the bottle. Then she put it down in different positions near the bottle, which she did not dare to touch. She picked up the soldier again, sucked it again, still looking at the bottle. I told her she was sucking it instead of the bottle; so she dropped it, made sucking noises, picked up the boat, sucked it once, and threw it violently away, then started sucking the sailor. She dropped it and came into my arms, above all to stand up against me, propping herself up on my shoulders. That was the only point during this session that she looked at me tenderly; after that *she bit my chin, very close to my mouth, without aggressivity, and with a hint of a weak sucking movement.*

Then, as she sat in my arms, she pulled off my glasses, threw them down, and went off to pick up the sailor, which she sucked energetically. She did not let it go. *She came back toward me, holding the sailor in her hand, and lay down on the floor* at my feet, laughing, playing with her feet, turning around and around contentedly.

This went on for five minutes. Nadia tried to get up, but could not. She demanded my help, with a tense look.

When I took her back to her room, still holding the sailor, she noticed her reflection in a mirror while I was carrying her in my arms. I should add that we passed by this mirror every day when I took her for the sessions. It was a big mirror above a fireplace and there was a changing table in front of it. *On that particular day, when she saw herself in it, she wanted me to stand her up on the table in front of the mirror. Her expression was fixed, almost anxious, and eventually she turned her head away violently.*

I left her standing in front of a little armchair. She was still holding her sailor.

A few moments later, I heard crying and found her in tears, without the sailor, sitting by a crib. She grabbed hold of my white coat; I picked her up, and she calmed down in my arms, but I did not give her back the sailor. I put her back in her crib; she lay down flat on her back on her mattress and started crying silently, mournfully, when I closed the door, in a way I had never seen her cry before.

Although this period, from 4 to 16 January, was a part of the pre-specular phase, it deserves to be treated separately. This is because Nadia had reintroduced an element of her scopic fantasy she had given up on 9 November: the doll. This doll gave rise to such a strong accentuation of the metaphorical relation to the Other that Nadia ended up by being blocked by it, on 16 January, just before the mirror. The doll was the small other sitting on the knee of the big Other: it was like a return of the repressed image of 10 December. However, the developments in Nadia's relation to me allowed her to show herself to be very active and aggressive, whether toward the doll or toward the doll with me, even to the point where the sadistic fantasy of destruction that lurked beneath this aggressivity made her afraid.

From 5 January onward, indeed, when I arrived I found her frightened. She would only calm down when she saw me getting out her shoes and socks, whose metonymic importance we have seen: they were the only objects that guaranteed she would not dissolve in my body and in the other. She could not bear her own internal tension, either in the sessions or in her everyday life, and she cried very easily—for example when she saw another child sitting on a nurse's lap. Moreover, during the sessions all her violence toward the doll turned against herself, and she hit herself on the head, not without hitting me afterward, which did not make things any better. Also, she regularly wanted me to cuddle her and kiss her after this kind of scene; but this embrace only threw her from Charybdis to Scylla. That is why at the end of this period I noted that she no longer knew where she was or what she wanted. At the same time she could hardly bear the time in between the sessions and she was withdrawn.

In spite of the impasse she encountered along the pathway of metaphor, she continued ineluctably to make her way along it. This was a result of the nature of her relation to the Other, a relation which, subject to repression, was, for that reason, subject to the return of the repressed. On 13 January she even refused to resort to the metonymy of the shoe.

A special relation emerged toward me with regard to her mouth. Early on, she had not succeeded in attaining what could properly be described as oral behavior; both in drinking the bottle and in eating the crackers, she confined herself to a licking game. She only licked the nipple of the bottle, without drinking; she licked the sleeve of my white coat or licked my cheek. If she put a cracker into her mouth, it was only to take it out again, to examine it and check that she had not left any trace of herself on it, to lick it once—as she licked me—and to throw it away.

On 9 January, during the second session of the day, she went so far as to put her open mouth to mine for a moment, drooling copiously and making some sucking movements. She appeared very happy and loving, as if in doing this she had achieved an exemplary relationship of surfaces, where the hole would be stopped, both for her and for me: a relationship freed from all desire for devouring between herself and me. The preceding days she had shown a hint of such desire; but she had given it up as if it were imperative that I should know nothing of it. This necessity of not-knowing in the Other, which appeared as such in the pre-specular phase, was linked on the one hand to the maintenance of the small subject's sadistic desire, but was at the same time what repressed this desire (the metaphorical structure, reinforced by transitivism, played a predominant role in this repression, as we have seen). Also, once I had unmasked to her her desire to devour me when she was licking me, she hit me with her hand and looked anxious. Subsequently she wanted to come up into my arms, that is to say, to stick herself to me in order to annul this desire and also to hide it from me.

On the same day she had put her open mouth to mine, another hole in the surface of her body gave a sign to her, in the form of the potty. As I noted, this was a new element in her field of interest; but it was new only in the context of the sessions, because it is well known that in institutions the collective ceremony of the potty takes place several times a day. But, as with the bottle, what could she possibly know at that level where she had been left, strictly in the realm of needs? Rather than being a question of a demand of the Other that inscribed itself in a real relation to the Other, it was a question of the stopping of an orifice: the mouth in the scene just described, and here, it was the potty that stopped up the anal orifice, a hole in the surface of her body. The inscription of this phenomenon of surface was confirmed once more the following day, when she fingered my skin, licked my cheek, put her mouth close to mine, but without actually touching it, saw the potty, and turned to look at me, laughing.

Certainly, what she did on 9 January, when she used my pencil to explore this potty, plunging it in at length, might have pointed to the exploration of contents, if the whole context of bodily structure had not undermined this interpretation. Furthermore, the potty had initially been the object of her gaze, that is to say, of an exploration of its surface. It was only secondarily that she went to get the pencil she had taken from me, in order to feel the potty, before plunging it in, as if it was necessary for an object taken from my body to come and stop up the hole in the potty that was also the orifice in her body. We cannot ignore, either, the comparison between this pencil and the thermometer, which she had been given anally twice a day since birth.

Insofar as it was an object linked to the surface of her body, the potty she explored was clearly, by displacement, identical to the other orifice of the hole in her body, her mouth (being, of course, together with the anus, the orifices of one and the same hole in the body). She had glued her mouth to mine; now she treated the potty as if it were something that stuck itself to a part of her skin. She showed this identity on 14 January, when she took a cracker, went around the potty, hit the edge of it with the cracker, and hit inside the potty before getting me to eat a little corner of the cracker, which she then took out of my mouth with her finger. I told her what she was doing; she smiled, but became tense and aggressive; she wanted to go up to the potty again, but did not manage to do so. She returned to press her body to mine and confirmed her defeat by taking the piece of paper from my pocket for the last time and throwing it over her head. The metonymic value of this piece of paper in this instance gave the space for the joining of bodies, whose metaphorical nature we have already seen. (This was a process she had begun the day before, when she threw the toys aggressively behind her.)

This choice of the metaphorical was a return of the repressed, and it led her even further, since, at the end of the 14 January session, when she did detach herself from me, it was so she could stand up in front of me and get me to admire her. This foreshadowed what she would do in front of the mirror to discover the integral outline of her body. But while I took the place of the mirror, as a real mirror, all I could reflect back to her was her place as metaphorical object.

It was at that moment that I noted again that she did not know what she was doing or what she wanted. Did she want to get away from me or come into my arms? She alternated between attempts at the two movements, babbling tenderly or violently as if hurling insults.

The session of 16 January was the last in this pre-specular phase and ended with the first encounter with the mirror.

Nadia could not take any more. She returned overwhelmingly to the metaphorical position she had been pushed to seek out and which she had yet refused there and then, on 10 December (in the second part of the session, immediately after the repression of the image), as if to rediscover the repressed image. She reverted to the behavior and the symptoms she had had at the beginning, notably the tic of opening her hand and letting go of an object she had just grasped.

Her ambivalence became more marked, too, between the desire to be cuddled and a violent negativity. Even though she clenched her hands on my breasts on that day, there was no call of "mama"; she had not said it for more than a month; on the contrary, she was obliged to reject me. Moreover, not a single articulated sound emerged from her mouth during that session. She tried to rediscover something of the muscular satisfaction of movement, but her heart was not in it and she burst into tears at the first setback.

The rubber sailor, which appeared on 11 January, held a privileged position. She found it again on 16 January, in the ark, and it aroused a great deal of interest in her; but she was unable to pick it up without her tic of letting it go. So, after several attempts, she eventually threw it away. The tic did not reappear at all during the rest of the session; it was as if the automatism was linked to the prohibition of taking the object, an object she had to lose.

She was, however, able to pick up the sailor again, but not until she had sucked the gun of the lead soldier, making sucking noises and looking at the bottle. When I told her she was sucking the gun instead of the bottle, her response was immediate: she dropped the soldier, looked away from the bottle, picked up the sailor, and started sucking it while looking at me. Her rapid changes from one object to another showed what a state of indecisiveness she was in. The true metonymic object, the soldier's gun, came to an abrupt halt and sent her back to the substitutive object, the bottle. She even abandoned the metaphorical object, the sailor, in order to come into my arms. Once again, as in the 14 January session, she wanted to stand up against me, looking at me, holding onto my shoulders and looking lovingly at me, as if she was reflecting herself briefly in my eyes, making herself into my object, standing erect on my lap. But in contrast to 14 January, the closeness of our bodies precipitated her toward inclusion by sticking onto my body; she bit my chin near my mouth and made a feeble sucking movement.

From then on she attempted the impossible unraveling in the metaphoric field, initially by taking care to pull off my glasses, in other words, to unstick something from my eyes, so that I would not be able to see what she did immediately afterward: she went to pick up the sailor and sucked it energetically. But she came back toward me. The sailor, like the soldier's gun, had a metonymic dimension at the beginning, but Nadia dropped it to come and stick herself to me, to suck me and bite me, to initiate through the sailor her entry into metaphor. It was by using an object such as this that, having symbolically deprived me of my gaze, she was able to come back and make of herself my object fallen at my feet. What did she want? She told me what it was when, looking tense, she demanded that I should help her stand up: that I should pick up the metaphoric object she had made of herself for me, for the Other, while still keeping her own metaphoric object, the sailor.

In this scene, she refused to acknowledge her own loss as much as mine, still completely attached to the image of 10 December. Two elements came into play at this juncture: her own desire to be in the place of the other and my supposed desire, by reversal, to pick her up and put her onto myself, the last realization of her fundamental fantasy. But this realization no longer had the qualities of the image, where the scopic masked every loss, above all in my absence. Because in this scene, just as I when had called to her on 10 December, I was present; and it was no longer a question for her of losing herself in the "seeing" of the object, but in having and sucking it. Not being able to prevent me from knowing it, she paid the price of having, by making herself my object, throwing herself at my feet, so that I had to pick her up as she had picked up hers. If, however, she was happy, it was in a similar way to her *jouissance* at having drunk the bottle in my arms on 12 December. Just as on that occasion, her happiness indicated that her relation to the Other in the Real was starting to take root. On 12 December she had found a way out by holding out a piece of cardboard to me, a metonymic object she had taken from another child. This time, she was herself entirely in the place of the metaphoric object she gave to me. The only way out for her, at the end of this session, was by the promotion of the metonymic object *par excellence:* the image of the totality of her body in the mirror.*

*Cf. the commentary on this first encounter with the mirror on 16 January.

8 / The Mirror 1—Our Image: From Metaphor to Metonymy

The following day, 17 January, Nadia was much better. She had not had diarrhea since the previous session, for the first time in about ten days. I found her sitting in her crib, *sucking her thumb,* and smiling, which was something she had not done for some time. She grasped my white coat so that I would pick her up. I asked a nurse to put on her socks and shoes; during this procedure, Nadia held out her arms to me, kicking impatiently.

Everyone agreed that she looked different since the previous day, when she had had her first encounter with the mirror—although at the time I did not make the connection. *She had lost her little old woman look, her face had become that of a child,* and a child of her age.

I took her off for the session; she was delighted. I sat on the low chair; Nadia looked uneasy as she checked my position in relation to her own. She seemed reassured and went to get the toys out of the ark, one after the other. On that day her movements were less clumsy, more direct, and her tic had disappeared. She took a great deal of interest in a little cup from a doll's tea set; the whole session was to center on this. She threw it down, then picked it up and examined it. I told her it was a cup to drink from, just as I had named all the toys as she took them out of the ark.

She put the cup to her mouth and sucked it, but she was looking at the bottle; she threw down the cup, tried to push over the bottle with her hand, did not dare to do so, and tried to reach it with a wooden post she had taken out of the ark and had been sucking before approaching the bottle with it. She still could not bring herself to touch the bottle; she threw the post closer and closer, but it never quite reached it. She managed to push the bottle over only by swinging the ark around sharply. Then she grabbed the bottle and threw it violently at the wall. It ricocheted and came to rest against my leg. She looked at it for a moment, then went to pick up the cup and brought it with her into my arms. She got me to kiss her, threw down the cup, went to pick it up, but came back into my arms without it. Once again she got me to kiss her, put her arms lovingly around my neck, leaned her head against my cheek, and pressed herself against me, babbling tenderly. It was the first time *she expressed her tenderness like a child of her age.*

She introduced the game of throwing down the cup and picking it up before climbing back on my lap. After the third or fourth time, she threw it in the crib rather than on the floor, so that she could reach it from my lap just by leaning forward. Before grasping it, she would suck and lick the bar of the crib with obvious delight. Eventually, she threw the cup down on the floor and wanted to get down herself so that she could get hold of *the bottle, which she threw violently into a corner of the room as if it were a ball—for the first time she had picked it up—*after hitting it several times with the cup and babbling "a-pa, a-pa."

A nurse opened the door a crack to put some steel wool on the floor by the door and left. Nadia immediately made toward it as fast as she could to see what it was, full of curiosity; but when she had almost reached her goal, she stopped, stood up, looked at me lovingly, and came back onto my lap.

I took her back to her room. She did not want me to leave her just yet, and, well ensconced on my arm, with one hand on my shoulder, she watched what was going on, looking alert, and poking out the tip of her tongue. Hardly had I put her back in her crib when a trainee went up to her and held out her arms to her, while I was still near her crib. Nadia lay down flat on her pillow, with her arms behind her, as she had always used to do. But her expression was not the same: her attitude was of refusal of the unknown, because I was there, but not one of anxiety; her gaze moved from the trainee to me. I took her back into my arms for a moment; she clung to me, then started to look relaxed and interested, as she had been just before. When I left, I felt I could put her into the trainee's arms; but this was too much for Nadia. Her look became anxious, her face fell; she looked like a little old woman again.

When I arrived on 18 January, Nadia was sleeping flat on her stomach, like a frog, and she was snoring. The nurse woke her up. Nadia saw her first and put her head back on the pillow to go back to sleep. I called to her, she turned her head, saw me, smiled, shook herself, sat up, and got up so I could take her, still a little sleepy, in my arms. While the nurse was changing her and putting on her shoes, she kept holding out her arms to me. Eventually she got impatient and hit me on the breast, poking out her tongue.

She was no longer suffering from diarrhea, was putting on

weight, eating well, and moving incessantly. She had a mischievous look when I took her off, smiling and poking out the tip of her tongue.

She started the session by taking a rubber doll (not the sailor) out of the ark and throwing it down. She did the same with the building blocks, which she enjoyed taking out of the ark and putting back again; she had the interested air of a child who feels free and secure. The ark tipped over, taking with it the bottle, which rolled beneath the window. She looked at it and then lost interest in it, but not before she had hit herself on the head with a toy.

The ark had landed on its side. She tried at first to get at the toys through the bars that formed one side of it. She became obstinate and shook the ark in fury. Then very quickly she realized she could get at them through the lid, which was now on one side.

Inside the ark she found a little dish from a doll's tea set and spent some time examining it. I told her it was a dish; she put it back inside the ark. She looked at me and came over to pull off my glasses, then gave them back to me almost immediately, laughing. She went back to get the dish from the ark; but the dish had got stuck, and Nadia gave a little groan. She managed to get it, sucked it, threw it down, picked it up, and held it out to me. When I held out my hand to take it, she withdrew it, sucked it, threw it down, and wanted to come into my arms. From there, she played the same game with the dish as she had done with the cup on the previous day, throwing it down, going to pick it up; she did this twice.

Pushing away the crackers, she took a sugar lump and put it in the dish, then threw it out. She did this twice over. She came back into my arms, bringing the dish with her, and started to play the previous game again: throwing it down and picking it up. This was accompanied by varied and articulated babbling: "a-pa, a-pou, a-té, a-da, a-ca"; and she looked at me tenderly.

During this game, as on 16 January, Nadia lay down on the floor, kicking her legs, playing with her feet, getting me to admire her movements. On this day, she managed to get herself upright all on her own. Although her face was tense while she was making the effort, as soon as she was sitting up she turned to me with a triumphant look.

I took her back, smiling, still holding the dish. She did not want me to put her down on the floor just yet, and from her position in my arms watched what was going on around her, with an impudent expression and the tip of her tongue poking out. She threw the dish down into a crib and wanted to be stood up by the crib so that she could pick it up again and then come back into my arms.

I put her into the trainee's arms. She did not look as anxious as she had on the previous day.

When I arrived on 19 January I found Nadia repeatedly hitting two children with a wooden doll. She had cornered them against the window, with the help of a crib, and they were very afraid. When she saw me she became even more violent, lashing out at the children, the window, and the crib. I took her away, still holding the wooden doll. Her face was tense and she was breathing noisily.

During the first part of the session, she turned toward me to see how I had accepted this violence—against which I later felt I needed to protect her. She was trying to break everything, hitting the toys on the floor, and thus making a great deal of noise. She pursued the toys avidly, throwing them as far away as she could, as if they had somehow hurt her. First she focused on the ark and the toys in it, then on the dish, after sucking it. After that she turned her attention to a piece of cloth; after she had given it to me and come to me for a cuddle, she leaned against me and tried to tear it up.

There was such a strong element of autodestruction as a result of lack that I told her so. Whether she understood or not, I have no idea, but she stopped and babbled: "a-ga, a-poum" (like when something falls).

She went straight over to the bottle, turned it nipple down, and started banging it on the floor so hard that it cracked. Then she sent it flying with her feet and subjected the doll to the same fate.

When I took her back, she was calmer; she wanted to walk for a while, and then I put her into the arms of one of the nurses.

The following day, 20 January, after this somewhat explosive session, Nadia had a temperature, with a painful ear and a suppurating fingernail. I found her in her crib; she did not appear to be suffering. She was watching what was going on in the room with great interest. She got up and held out her arms to me. She seemed very pleased with the dressing that had been put on. During the time I went away to get her shoes, she refused her snack.

In the session, she was violent *and expressed real aggressivity toward me.* She started by throwing around the entire contents of the ark and the ark itself. She kept the dish and teased me with a mischievous look: she held it out to me, then held herself toward me, as if she wanted me to pick her up, but then refused to let me, laughing.

She threw down the crackers, climbed onto my lap to pull off my glasses, and babbled a great deal. Still on my lap, she threw the doll into the crib, further and further away, then she too wanted to be put into the crib. Looking very much at ease, she took possession of the crib as if it were a battlefield she had conquered and looked at me triumphantly.

She threw the doll out of the crib and followed it with a piece of cloth. With a satisfied look, she stood up, came toward me, and gently, *with her mouth open, tried to eat my cheek.* She sat down again and acted toward me first excitedly and then aggressively punctuating the blows she directed at me with exclamations that appeared to mean something like, "There you are! Take that!" *Holding me by the hair, she pulled my head down,* and keeping me in that position, *hit me with her other hand.* Then, *pulling my head up by the hair, she hit me on the cheeks and mouth with both her hands.* Her violence culminated in wanting to poke her finger in my eye. All this violence was periodically interrupted by very brief caresses, punctuated by little cries of "ma-ma-ma."

I took her back, and she wanted to walk for a little while.

I heard that she was in very good shape in the evening, had eaten well, and did not seem to be in pain.

When I arrived on 21 January, I heard that Nadia had a great deal of pain in her ear. She smiled at me and stood up as soon as I came closer. I could not find her shoes, and while I was waiting for a nurse to bring them, I sat down next to her. She was very disappointed. She sat down again, watching me with a fixed expression, and stretched out her arms behind her with an anxious look. I held out my arms to her; she briefly stretched her arms out even more behind her and then sat up again and leaned toward me, smiling at first with her eyes and then more openly as I picked her up. She was very excited while the nurse was changing her and putting on her shoes, but I noticed that if I started to move away, she became inert.

I learned that an ENT examination had revealed that it was a ganglion, and not her ear, that was giving her pain; but there had been no evidence in the sessions, and nor was there this time, that she was suffering from it.

In the session, she stayed on my lap for a moment, completely relaxed, looking at what was on the floor. Then she demanded that I put her down.

She took the toys out of the ark violently, apart from two objects: the *piece of cloth,* which she played with, put down, and picked up several times before pushing it away; and the dish, which she played with and put down before pushing this away, too. This dish triggered a bout of aggressivity against the bottle that she did not dare to express; she turned toward me so that I would put her in the crib. She made herself comfortable in it, looking at me delightedly and babbling joyfully. She came toward me to lick the bar of the crib and then my arm. After several attempts, she managed to stand up by herself and got me to admire her, face toward me, leaning on my shoulders. She put her open mouth on one of them for some time, drooling copiously. She wanted to get back on my lap, where she looked me in the eyes with a joyful expression and then got back down. There, she played with *a cracker, which she put into my hand, and then grabbed from me, watching me and laughing* and kicking her legs several times. As this scene unfolded, I told her that she was doing to me what had been done to her; and that by eating she was learning to love, to be loved, and to love life. Then she wanted me to put her back in the crib; she lay down, her face turned toward me, with an expression of happiness. She was only able to let herself enjoy this for a few moments; she then sat up and put one hand on my shoulder.

When I took her back, she demanded that I should help her walk. She went toward another room, where she appeared very interested in somebody sweeping up. By the evening, her temperature was back to normal and her finger was better.

On 22 January, she had a bandage around her head because of the ganglion, but she did not have a temperature and seemed to be in good shape. She reacted in her usual excited way as I approached her crib.

The nurse put on Nadia's shoes for her on the small table in front of the mirror. Once she had assured herself that I was nearby, *Nadia showed a great deal of interest in her reflection, and then in mine,* when I moved so that I was visible. *Her gaze moved from her reflection to mine and from mine to my real face.*

As on the previous day, she started the session by staying on my lap for a few minutes, very relaxed. She took the piece of paper from my pocket and threw it down; she tried to take the pencil but failed the first time and so gave up trying and wanted me to put her down on the floor.

She took several objects out of the ark, among them the dish. Then, for the first time she put some of the objects back into the ark. Holding the dish in one hand, she pushed the bottle over without hesitation. She picked it up, shook it, then threw it far away, watched to see where it ended up, turned her back on it, and picked up and sucked the piece of paper. I then told her she did not want anything to do with the bottle, because it reminded her of bad things, and that she was sucking the piece of paper that had come from my pocket.

She climbed into my arms and put her mouth tenderly on my shoulder, pulled off my glasses, threw them down, licked the bar of the crib, and wanted to get into the latter. As on the day before, she lay down in it and looked at me, excited and smiling. She sat up and put her face very close to mine, looking delighted. She leaned over even further and put her arms around my neck, after licking my shoulder, then got back onto my lap and relaxed for a moment before getting down onto the floor.

Quite aggressively, she threw out of the ark the objects she had put back into it, then sent the ark flying. Similarly, she put a cracker into my hand and grabbed it back, twice in succession. She noticed that the piece of paper she had just sucked and thrown down was on the other side of the crib; she quickly made toward it, but stopped on the way to pick up a cracker, which she threw behind her, and then the dish, which she kept. Then she stretched out on the floor, kicking her legs for joy and looking at me.

Then she threw down the dish and followed after it, herself rolling along on the floor. To pick it up, she got onto all fours and then sat up; she made all these movements without any help, but she needed a certain amount of determination to carry them out, as evidenced by the little cries that punctuated her efforts.

She came back to my feet, hesitated to give me the dish, did not give it to me, and got onto my lap so she could get into the crib. She stretched out again, very relaxed, with her head turned toward me. She wanted me to put my face near her, and she caressed it with both her hands, chuckling happily. Then *she wanted me to pick her up and take her out of the crib, holding her under her arms while she was still stretched out: she pressed her whole body against mine, put her arms around my neck, and put her open mouth on my cheek; she was drooling and her mouth slid down to mine.* There was no attempt at biting or sucking. She gave little muffled cries of joy, and her face was radiant as she looked at me afterwards from very close up, with one hand resting on my cheek.

After this display of tenderness, *I had the impression that she was reborn*, and I said so to her. She moved slowly and seriously around the room, finding her interest in the external world once more.

When I took her back to her room, it was in a terrible mess: there was a heap of dust in the middle and the cribs were facing in all different directions. There was no nurse. I hesitated a moment, then I put Nadia into her crib, as I was in a hurry. But the indefinable look that came across her face reminded me that someone who has just been reborn in such circumstances should not be put back into a crib; for her, it was a symbol of the dereliction that had made this rebirth necessary in the first place. I took her back into my arms. She hugged me around the neck, then wanted to get down and walk. She poked around in the pile of dust and found an old piece of bread, which she sucked and held out to another child.

Then a nurse arrived. I put Nadia into her arms; she commented that Nadia looked radiant. Nadia looked at her and smiled, then held out her arms to me, leaning out so I would take her back. She put her cheek next to mine, very tenderly. Knowing very well that it was not me who took care of her all the time, and accepting that without anxiety or fear, she held out her arms to the nurse and I left.

On 23 January, Nadia was with the other children, standing up. As soon as she saw me, she became very aggressive toward the others. She grabbed my white coat and I took her away; she was delighted. She was carrying a doll that served as a weapon against the others. For the last two weeks, whenever I had come to fetch Nadia and she had had to wait, either to be changed or to have her shoes put on, she would hit herself on the mouth and pull her lips, playfully.

She started the session on my lap, still holding the doll. She looked to see if the piece of paper was in my pocket, but did not take it. She threw down the doll and wanted to be put in the crib. She looked at me radiantly, caressed my face, *and became agitated; she had just soiled her diaper* but she did not have diarrhea. She wanted me to put her down on the floor. She shook the ark quite violently and threw the dish across the room. She sat down, holding a cracker, which she then threw away, and lifted her pinafore, putting her hand on her dirty diaper and looking at me. She was pleased when I took her away to be changed. As soon as the soiled diaper had been taken off, Nadia looked at me, kicking and babbling.

When we were back in the consulting room, she got onto the crib and licked my shoulder. Then she became violent. She wanted to get down; *she stamped on the dish and kicked it across the room.* She wanted to pick the dish up again, and as she went to do so, she leaned on my arm, *which she bit in passing.* Then she took a cracker, and for the first time she ate a piece. She held the cracker out to me, snatched it back, bit off another piece, threw down the rest, and came into my arms. She got back into the crib, then pulled off my glasses and threw them down. Then she lay down on my lap, her head hanging off the end, so that I would sit her up several times in a row. Back into the crib, back on my lap; then *she hit me on the mouth and bit my chin violently.* She calmed down.

When I took her back, she was still aggressive, but no longer tense. I left her in the nurse's arms.

On 24 January, I walked past Nadia's room several times before I went in to collect her. I found her hitting her backside very hard against one of the sides of the crib, hanging on to the opposite side. She cheered up only very gradually; once she was in my arms, she laughed.

In the session she remained very aggressive. She pulled off my glasses and threw them away, threw around everything that was in the ark, and *tipped over the bottle by pulling on the cloth she had covered it with.* She looked at it and then picked up the arm of my glasses and sucked it, turning toward me.

She came into my arms for the same exercise as on the previous day, and this relaxed her. When she got down again, *she bit my arm;* back on the floor, she got up on her legs almost unaided and had me admire her.

When I took her back, dinner had already started, and Nadia threw herself down on her pillow with a hostile expression. After I left, I heard her crying because the nurse was taking too long to bring her a second dish of cereal.

On 25 January I found Nadia crying, avidly defending a cracker that another child was trying to take away from her. As soon as she saw me, she hit the other child hard and she was smiling as I took her away.

This session was much more relaxed than the previous one. Although she started by getting into the crib, she got out again immediately and turned her attention to the ark. She spent almost the entire session on her feet; from my chair, I helped her to stay upright. Each time she moved away, and I got up so she could continue walking, she would come back toward me and climb up on my lap or into the crib; she did not want me to leave my chair. If she absolutely wanted to move away from me, she would go on her behind.

She took everything out of the ark, without a trace of violence, and when the ark was empty she did not send it flying. She took off my glasses and threw them down, picked them up, and wanted to be put back into the crib. She kept holding onto the glasses, caressed my face with her other hand, then drooled on my cheek. She got down again and *shook my glasses; one of the arms broke off. She looked at me, intrigued, then at the two pieces of the glasses. Then she put the arm of the glasses into the ark for a second, took it out again, and held onto it for the rest of the session.* (The nurse gave it back to me after the session.) She got down, threw the crackers around, sucked the arm of the glasses, and then bit me gently on the wrist.

I took her back to her room and asked the nurse to keep the second course of Nadia's dinner so that I could come and feed her myself. I felt it was time to build a bridge between, on the one hand, what happened in the sessions when she expressed her aggression against all the usual objects connected with feeding (the dish, the bottle) and rejected them, and against my body, whether it was by hitting my mouth, biting my chin or my wrist, or licking my shoulder or my cheek; and, on the other hand, the food she received at mealtimes, which she demanded very strongly and which I had deprived her of the previous day because we had come back from the session in the middle of the meal; and the reproach she had addressed to me had been full of anxiety.

So I returned an hour later. I found Nadia sitting up in her crib; she was sucking her thumb, whimpering as she saw the nurse feeding another child. I picked up her dish, sat down on the crib next to hers, and started feeding her with spoonfuls of the puree. At first she was most intrigued; she looked at me, looked at the nurse, then at the dish, and started to eat. Then she became very excited that it was I who was feeding her; she threw herself down on her stomach, with her head turned to one side so she could see me. She was smiling, happy, full of life, kicking her legs gently. Twice, she stretched out on her back, waiting joyfully in this position for me to give her a couple more mouthfuls.

Then she wanted to eat her dessert, sitting on my lap; but after eating a few mouthfuls, facing me, and not taking her eyes off me, she started to eat it with her finger.

When she had finished, I put the dish and the spoon on the pillow of the neighboring crib and *her objective then became to grab hold of the spoon;* it was like a battle she had to win. In fact, it took her three attempts *followed by three of her automatic letting-go movements* before she succeeded in getting hold of the spoon properly. The nurse wanted her to drink an infusion of lime flowers; Nadia refused, tipped it into her dish, picked up the mug, and threw it down on the floor. She picked up the spoon again and hit the dish with it. Then she brushed her hand across the dish, then across my face, and licked the inside of the dish. *Now Nadia was clutching the spoon triumphantly.* She showed it to me enthusiastically; and she did not let go of it from then on. She went off to explore the whole floor, walking and holding her spoon victoriously. She met the doctor *and hit him with her spoon; then she used it to touch all the objects she encountered on her way.*

She walked all the way back to her crib. When I put her back in her crib, still holding her spoon, she wanted me to take her back into my arms. The doctor came in; if he came too near, she would hit him with the spoon.

On 26 January, I found Nadia walking in the corridor, exploring. As on the previous day, she wanted to stand up all through the session and did not want me to get up out of my chair.

She went over to the ark, took out the cloth, but *saw the bottle* and went *without hesitation to push it over with her hand,* turning around toward me afterward with a satisfied look.

Then she came into my arms, hesitated about taking out the piece of paper, gave up the idea, and returned to the ark; she took out a cup and a dish from the tea set. She threw down the cup; it was mainly the dish that interested her; I called the dish by its name, because she knew the word very well. *She scraped the inside with her finger* and wanted to get into the crib, where she played with the dish, but not without a number of her automatic letting-go movements. She ended up throwing it down and turned toward me to take off my glasses. Once again, she shook them so hard, babbling all the time, that she broke one of the arms. As she got down to pick it up, she bit my wrist in passing. She pushed away *the glasses and sucked the arm*. Finally, she went and used it to hit the side of the potty, and then the inside, then she exchanged the arm of the glasses for the dish.

She started playing her game with the dish again, throwing it down and picking it up four times in a row; but on one occasion the dish fell upside down and she had some trouble in picking it up. As she was straining to grasp it, it slid against her diaper, and she lifted her pinafore right up so she could see it. She muttered to herself, spun around, and managed to grab it. She did not suck this dish anymore, but scraped the inside of it repeatedly; she held it out to me twice but without giving it to me; she did not actually give it to me until a little later.

At one moment, she caught sight of a lollipop stick under one of the cribs; she went to get it, sucked it, threw it away, and then, after all, gave it to me.

At the end of this session, I decided to put a dish of cereal and a spoon in the room the following day. I thought that Nadia needed to rid herself of a great deal of violent negativism against food. I predicted that she would smear cereal over herself and me.

On 27 January, in the session, she sat on my lap for a moment and looked at the toys and the other objects on the floor; it took her several moments to notice the dish of cereal. She climbed down and stopped for a second in front of the ark, but that did not interest her; then she went and sat in front of the dish. She took the spoon, licked it a little, then threw it down. She plunged her hand into the cereal, and the first time licked her hand completely clean. She plunged her hand in a second time, hardly licked it at all, and, clearly not very happy, tried to wipe it off on the floor.

Then she tipped over the dish, went to pick up the spoon again, managed to grasp it after several of her mechanical letting-go movements, and came onto my lap; once there, she threw down the spoon, as well as a pencil she had taken from my pocket, and my glasses. She got down to pick up the spoon, climbed into the crib, and played with the spoon, smiling all the time. Then she threw it down again, showed me her shoe, and climbed down again.

She went to get the spoon, *picked up the doll, looked at it intensely, and put the spoon to its mouth*, but immediately *smacked the doll violently against the floor*, then held it out to me. She watched with delight as I put it on my lap, but then took it and hit it; she wanted to get up on my lap with the doll, and finally to get into the crib, the doll in one hand and the spoon in the other. Then she threw down the doll and *became aggressive against the spoon:* she stood up *to trample on it.* She picked it up, threw it away, picked it up again, lay down with it, and *put it into my mouth, which increased her aggressivity* against the spoon.

She got me to take off one of her shoes and one sock, which she sent flying out of the crib, and then carried on manipulating the spoon. She did so with such dexterity that it made me think of a cat playing with a ball of yarn. Her face was very lively, and she looked at me from time to time with the same deeply moved expression she had had when I gave her her dinner.

Throughout this scene, I kept telling her that she wanted to feed herself, the doll, or me, but that I could not feed her during the sessions because it would be unbearable for her, because she both wanted me to feed her and not to feed her, and she felt this with violence and aggressivity because that was what she had lacked.

Then she got up, clung onto my shoulder, and hit me in the face with the spoon, hit me on the mouth with her hand, and bit my shoulder. Then she returned to her game with the spoon, babbling delightedly.

Going back to her room, spoon in hand, set off some strong reactions. Another child took it away from her, very pleased with himself, while Nadia screamed. A nurse who witnessed the scene only verbalized the other child's pleasure at taking the spoon. A few minutes later, after I had left, Nadia was violently attacked by Robert the Wolf Child and cried frenetically. I went back and took her in my arms to calm her down, but she started howling again when I had to go.

On 28 January, I found Nadia smiling, but she needed changing: she had soiled her diaper. She cried while she was being changed, because the nurse told her off for not having wanted to use the potty that morning. Her dress had to be changed, too, and she resisted tearfully.

In the session, she went straight up to the ark to take out the cloth, picked it up, threw it down, picked it up again, held it out to me; she snatched it away from me, only to put it on my lap, babbling a great deal. She went over to the dish of cereal, *took the spoon, licked it and threw it down without her mechanical gesture, then plunged her hand into the cereal, took it out, and licked it;* all that was done in a rather aggressive manner. She went to look for the spoon and hit the crackers with it.

As in previous sessions, she made sure I did not leave my chair to help her when she wanted to go to the other end of the room to pick up a piece of paper. Since she could not walk there unaided, and not wanting to slide along on her behind, she trampled with impatience, then gave up the idea, and climbed onto my lap to do some gymnastic exercises, which made her laugh. After that, she got me to put her down on the floor, where she lay on her back, kicking her legs joyfully and playing with the spoon.

She came back into my arms to get into the crib; there, she stood up, shook the crib, *went to touch the wall,* and came back onto my knees, where she also stood upright, holding onto my shoulders; she drooled down one of them and put one of her fingers into my mouth. Finally, she got down *to hit the spoon against the wall, babbling all the time.* When I left her, she was playing with her spoon in her crib.

On 29 January, the atmosphere in the room was very tense; several of the children were crying and the nurse was taking no notice. I took Nadia out; her face lit up as soon as we left the room.

She stamped her feet joyously as we went into the consulting room and went straight to take *the cloth out of the ark. She wanted to put it on my lap* but did not do it well and it fell off. *So she trampled on it, then gave it to me, only to snatch it away again,* and took no further notice of it.

She made for the dish, but before she grabbed the spoon, she pushed over the bottle slowly, deliberately, consciously, and without violence—I was supporting her; when it fell over, she did not touch it and returned to the dish.

She took the spoon, licked it, then licked her hand, after dunking it in the cereal. This immediately triggered all her aggressivity against anything to do with food: she turned the dish over and over, hit it with the spoon; she jabbered furiously, then plaintively when she could not manage to put the dish back in the right place. *She also used this spoon to hit the crackers, the floor, the wall, and the crib;* at first she was beaming with satisfaction; then she climbed back onto my knee to hit me on the mouth with her spoon, pull off my glasses, and touch my eyes. Then she did some gymnastics on my knees, her head thrown back, as in the previous session.

She went to the ark and took out the dog and a building block and threw them down. She took the cup and sucked it aggressively, looking at the dish. I said to her that she would really like me to feed her, but that her desire made her violent because she was always disappointed by food, because the person she would have liked to be there to feed her was not there. So she did not want to eat at all, and yet she had been forced to. She knew that I would not force her to eat; and now she would like me to force her, but that would hurt her. I would not give her anything to eat unless she demanded it of me; for then, she would like it.

At the same time, Nadia enacted exactly what I was saying to her, in the order I said it. She took up the cup and held it out to me, waiting anxiously for my reaction. I put a little cereal into it. She climbed on my lap, looking tense and breathing noisily. I held the cup in front of her without moving it toward her mouth—which in any case she did not open—as I talked to her. She dipped her fingers into it and licked them: that made her even more anxious.

She wanted to get into the crib, took the cup from me, and tipped it over my hand. She picked up her spoon and, anxiously, grasped my shoulders in order to get up onto my lap. Once she was there, her face lit up as I told her she knew why I did not feed her; she could not yet accept it, because she still wanted to express her violence toward this food that she had been forced to take without having anyone to love. She beamed at me and licked my chin. I said to her again that it was me she really wanted to eat.

I took her back, holding her spoon in her hand, but I had to stay with her a long time before I felt I could leave her. She walked around, turned away from the nurse, went to touch the door, and looked at me, as if waiting. I opened the door; she went out straight away and walked all over the place; but she turned away as she passed the door to her own room.

At the end, she was still anxious, and I put her into the arms of one of the nurses whom she knew well, because she did not want me to put her on the floor with the other children.

On 30 January I found Nadia in her crib because she had been vaccinated. She was very anxious because she did not like the nurse who prepared her for the session.

She went into the consulting room looking delighted and went to get the toys out of the ark; then she lined them up next to her but did not throw them around. This was so she could get the dish and the cup. I had noted that she showed violence only toward things that had to do with food and toward the doll. In the preceding few sessions, she had not systematically thrown around all the contents of the *ark,* and had actually been *able to put back* the objects she had taken out of it, and *even to put my glasses into it.*

Standing in front of the dish, she licked the spoon and then her hand, which she had dipped in the cereal. She thought it was good and did it twice more. *But, quite visibly, finding that this food was good triggered her violence.* She stuck the spoon back into the cereal, shook it violently over the floor, and spread out and wiped away spots of cereal with her other hand. She dipped the spoon in again and climbed up onto my knees while licking it. She stood up and, holding onto one of my shoulders, she shook the spoon quite hard, over my cheeks and my hair, without actually hitting me. She got into the crib, sat opposite me, put the spoon into my mouth, and left it there expectantly. I licked it a little bit, and she beamed at me, put her arms around my neck, and got back down onto the floor.

But the violence started up again. Nadia was still holding her spoon; she picked up the little cup, shook it, and threw it far away; then she did the same with the little dish. She pulled off my glasses and threw them under the crib. She picked up the dish, licked it, then looked at me and threw it down in fury.

As this scene unfolded, I explained what she was doing in relation to me, telling her again what I had told her in the previous session.

Then she got back onto my lap, bringing the spoon with her. She went straight into the crib and sat down. *Sitting comfortably, she gave me the spoon, showed me the dish of cereal, and waited.*

I filled the spoon and leaned my hand, holding the spoon, beside her on the crib, telling her she could do whatever she wanted and that she knew I understood. Absolutely radiant, she took the spoon, licked it rapturously, and clearly thought it was very good. She held it out to me again, so I could lick it, too. She held it out a third time; but this time, she knocked it out of my hand so that it fell on the floor and she looked at me, rather pleased. She had not knocked it down aggressively or anxiously. I could feel very clearly that she needed to express her old rancor toward food. Seeing her pleased expression, I told her it was good to be able to express it and still feel secure in the knowledge that I understood how important it is to fill oneself with good and nice things, near to someone whose presence makes you feel good about it, and that this was what she had lacked. The food she had been forced to eat had made her feel disgusted with everybody. She listened attentively and got me to pick up the spoon and fill it three times. In the reverse order of the previous time, the first two times she pushed the spoon out of my hand and the third time she took it, licked it delightedly, and held out her arms to me.

Sitting on my knee, she pressed her cheek to mine, then tried to push the spoon between the opening of my white coat, and then she licked my chin. I said to her that her great desire was for food that came from me, for an incorporation of me into her, and reciprocally, of her into me.

I took her back full of joy, but going back into her room was difficult. I had to take her in my arms again, because she started to cry when she saw I was leaving. She wanted to go out again; I took her out just for a moment, saying I would come back the next day, as I always did.

On 31 January, in the morning, she held onto my finger while the nurse was cleaning her face, ears, and nose; then her diaper was changed: she loathed having a dirty diaper, and she had had diarrhea for the preceding three days.

As soon as the session started, she went to the ark, took out the cup and little dish, and threw them down before climbing onto my lap. There, she stood up and hit my hair and forehead with two spoons, but without violence. She had picked up these two spoons from the table where the nurse had changed her.

Then she sucked the end of my nose, nibbling at it a little and drooling copiously, as if she wanted to absorb me. I said this to her and added that she realized she could not do this because her body and mine were two, not one. I also said that if she was not pleased with the cup and the dish, that is to say, with external food that was not me, since I was in the sessions with her every day, she could still find, as she had done the day before, that the cereal was good, and it was good to fill herself up with it while I was close by. While I was talking, she went up to the ark, put the little dish back into it, then stood still for a moment in front of the dish of cereal. She sat down; she was also near to the bottle, but took no more interest in it at all.

She dipped a spoon into the cereal, licked it, and for some time seemed to be wondering whether it was good enough to eat and give up on the rest. She started again and decided it was very good indeed, after smearing it all around her mouth; she looked at me, babbling and licking her lips. *She then used the spoon to eat just over half of the cereal, looking at me frequently and smiling.*

Finally, she shook the spoon, clearly wanting to splatter the cereal over the floor, then spread the drops out with her hand. Then she turned over the dish and dragged it along to make a long trail; then she hit the bottom of the dish with her two spoons, delightedly, stamping, looking at me, and babbling.

At this point she was more excited than aggressive and started to play a game. She wanted to come back into my arms; she was full of joy, put her arms around my neck, and rubbed her cheek against mine; I found I was besmeared just as much as she was.

When she wanted to get down, I took her back to her room. She was not pleased about that. She walked a little and went toward the table in front of the mirror and wanted to get up on it. *She stood up in front of the mirror, smiling, and looked at my reflection in it; the smile disappeared from her face.*

Was this in connection with what I had said to her in the session about there being two of us? This possibility occurred to me only later, but I think it was the case, because her expression was that of someone who has just come face to face with a reality that is not pleasant, and who turns away from it.

She came back into my arms and did not want to leave. I spoke to her gently, saying that I was there, that she was in my arms, and she would be there again the next day for the session. I left her fighting back her tears.

I had the impression that she had come out of her earlier confusion, which had led her to look in my mouth for what she herself had eaten. This realization that we were two distinct people— that neither was she in me, nor I in her—had brought on the bout of diarrhea.

Being reborn was difficult, disturbing, and full of insecurity, especially given her original experience.

On 16 January, it was Nadia who had demanded to be stood up in front of the mirror on the way back from the session. There she herself had made the leap from being my metaphorical object, fallen at my feet, to her own metonymical object: her specular image. But let us go back to the concrete circumstances of the encounter with this image, from Nadia's point of view and from mine.

Nadia already knew this mirror. There was no way she could not have had some experience of it, given on the one hand that it was just above the changing table, and on the other the habit the nurses had of holding the babies up in front of the mirror and getting them to look at themselves together with the nurse.

On this subject, we can say that the mirror privileges a moment of pleasure for the adult who is quite happy to share it with the child, gazing on the latter's image with a more tender eye than on the real child being cared for. The adult's pleasure is of the kind that remains attached to the specular image for everyone, and is further reinforced by the inverted trace of the primordial experience of the mirror that the adult in question had and that is revived when, next to his or her image, the adult sees in the mirror the image of a small child—any small other that takes the place of narcissistic completeness.

Although the child is not yet aware of the actual specular dimension of such experiences, he or she does not escape the summons of that which prefigures the specular in the pre-specular phase: the image of the Other.

We saw how Nadia looked narcissistically at her reflection, in the fascinating image of 10 December. Was it a return to this image, insofar as it was repressed, that she was attempting on 16 January, when she demanded that I should stand her up in front of the mirror? Perhaps; but in any case, she failed, as her immediate expression of anxiety showed. She turned away her head immediately and took refuge in my arms. What she saw in the mirror had nothing to do with the totality of the fascinating image; for at the very moment when she actively demanded that I put her in front of the mirror, she saw herself alone, without a glance at my reflection, or even at that of the sailor she was still carrying. We will come back to the role of this sailor.

As for me, I should point out that at this turning point of Nadia's, all I could do was follow her. If I look back at the account I wrote of the 16 January session, I find that I actually wrote at the end of the session: "I forgot to say that Nadia demanded that I stand her up in front of the mirror." In other words, at the time, this mirror was in no way linked with any theoretical knowledge—knowledge of which I had no inkling whatsoever, as I have already mentioned. It was far more a question of my own relation to the mirror and to my own specular image, a relation that raised a question; and in this way I can say that Nadia's treatment, in the full sense of the word, was a part of my own analysis, since it was with and through her that I was to come to grips with my own specular image, or rather with its relations with the Other. It was an exemplary illustration of, on the one hand, the place of the analyst as the one who is taught by the analysand; but, much more than teaching, it was a question of the essential unconscious passage that this baby-analysand was to cause me to make. After treating Nadia, standing in front of a mirror was quite a different experience for me.

For Nadia, everything in the passage from metaphor to metonymy was played out within the framework structured by the signifier, which in turn sprang from a change in the relation of the Real of our bodies.

For the first time on 16 January, Nadia made of herself, of her whole body, my metaphorical object, fallen at my feet; and also for the first time, in front of the mirror, she made herself into her own metonymic object. The passage from metaphor to metonymy did not become absolute until she brought her own body into play as a global metaphorical and metonymic object.

The metaphor was the partial object she had wanted to take from my body; now it was the relation to the Other in the form of a sticking to a surface; it was the investigation of the hole in the body of the Other, which could represent its desire in the form of a lack that was already signifying—that is what founded and established the desire of the Other, which Nadia had to respond to in order to gain its love. This was transference love, which existed entirely in the realm of metaphor. But metaphor still retained its links with the Real; from then on, this transference love aimed to include the Other, by sticking to it. When it proved impossible to do this, because of the resistance of the Real of bodies, the subject offered herself for inclusion in the Other. It was on 16 January that Nadia arrived at this ultimate point, at my feet.

This step brought into play both the Real of our bodies—and how!—and that which, of this Real, had been transformed into signifiers. The symptom displayed itself in the field of the metaphor. As such, it had to do with the Real, in other words, with the attempt to include the Other and with the signifier that forbade such an attempt. The truth that was linked to it was this aim of inclusion, which appeared to Nadia through the Real of bodies; and that was where a contradiction erupted, since the order of the signifier deemed the realization of it, the Real, to be impossible. The repression that was linked to my calling her by her name, on 10 December, caused two things to happen concurrently: it caused the Real of the fascinating image to topple and it imposed a prohibition in the form of the signifier.

In this fundamental experience, we can discern what makes the transition from metaphor to metonymy in relation to the Other: the image of the Other had been included, by sticking on Nadia's eye, and retained a dimension of the Real before I called her by her name. The prohibition which that action imposed caused the image to fall, and for Nadia excluded any sticking of the Other—which I was—onto her body. Metonymy arose, in anticipation of what would be the exclusion of the Other at the time of the first mirror: at that point, indeed, I would be completely excluded as image. At that crucial moment at the end of the January 16 session, an articulation was made between the body included metaphorically on the Other, and the exclusion of the Other by the relation of the subject to another image, that of herself in the mirror.

Thus the metaphor appeared as a structure of inclusion, aimed at bodies, where the signifier held the memory of the Real that promoted it. As Nadia showed us, metonymy excluded the image of the Other as a place on which to stick. That which the Other had been transitively as real image fell; its function as real mirror broke down in the subject's encounter with her own image. The loss became real as a result, on the one hand, of the impossibility of sticking to a virtual image; and on the other hand, at the level of the sailor, which symbolized her loss when she sucked it while I watched her, as she already apprehended the impossibility of including the Other that I was. It is true that the discovery of this sailor on 11 January, outside the consulting room, already indicated the exteriority of this object in relation to the Other; it was this sailor that represented the twin loss of the Other and the object, at the time of the first mirror.

Although I say now that Nadia did not look at the sailor in the mirror at all, it is only with hindsight; at the time I did not see it, either. I did not credit it with any greater degree of existence when I came back after the session because Nadia was crying; I picked her up, her alone, and put her back into her crib, realizing at that moment, however, that she was crying because the sailor had been taken away from her. So again, it is only after the event that I can say that if I did take in Nadia's loss of the sailor, that loss was also mine, since I spontaneously did not take any notice of it. At that moment, at least, if she suffered this loss, I was once again slightly ahead of her, by means of a certain unconscious knowledge: the knowledge that it was not up to me to shield her from her loss.

Following her in this way, did I not make this loss my own? Was it not mine, too? What blithe ignorance, to put the sailor in brackets and reduce it to the mere object of a loss.

That is where the fundamental difference arose between metaphor, which did not efface the object even if it substituted another, and metonymy, which untied this relation by effacing the object and affecting it with a sign (−). My own ignorance lay in, conditioned, the part I had to play in this transition, going ahead in it, even taking Nadia's place. There is nothing to indicate, after the event, that this was not countertransference love that was guiding me when I saw only Nadia in the mirror. It is one of the mysteries of analysis, since one can certainly say that it would have sufficed that I had been less personally involved and more available to apprehend objectively Nadia's relation to the sailor, in order to have been tempted to give the sailor back to her and shield her from a loss. What would have been the consequence of that?

If the sailor had not also represented a loss for me, I could have been sensitive to how important that object was to her and have given it back to her to comfort her. But in that case, and in the light of everything that had gone before concerning Nadia's relation to objects, would I not have been doing something I had never done, namely imposing an object on her so that she would not lack anything? Through the intermediary of such an object, the bottle, for example, I would have offered myself as a substitute for the object she had lacked in reality. It is an attitude that is not uncommon in the treatment of very young children when the analyst, rather than being sensitive to the register of lack in which object relations are deployed, veers off toward prejudices about the good or bad object.

Over a long period of time Nadia had prepared me to understand that the good object was not the object of need, by showing me how inhibited she was when faced with oral objects, whether it was the bottle or the object I carried (my breast); it showed that object relations comprise many more elements in the circuit of the drives than a mere approximation of the object to the satisfaction of a need.

If we consider the intensity of the reaction she showed toward the sailor, as well as the sailor's distance from an oral object as such and its link with both the scopic and the oral level, and finally, the parallel with the scene of 10 December, we can see that all this implies quite another debate: that of an object really filling a lack, both hers and mine really.

Filling my lack was what she had brought into question when she lay down at my feet and got me to pick her up. In other words, by reversal, she herself took the position in relation to me that she had given to the sailor in relation to herself. But this position was ambiguous, because it was connected with the real object that Nadia would have liked to take from me. It was an object like the one she had encountered on 10 December, as her sucking movements indicated; but I was radically excluded from it, and she came up against the prohibition of my death.

Was she seeking to change this when she went toward the mirror to find the specular image of the sailor, which would make of it an object quite other than a real one: a symbolic object, a phallic object, like that which the obsessional subject may bring into play, at the price of making his desire impossible, himself taking the place of the phallus that symbolically fulfills the desire of the mother?

This place of the phallic object was not without some connection to that of two other objects that had recently appeared: on the one hand, the pencil in the session of 9 January, which Nadia had used to explore my mouth and which she had then sucked and used to explore the potty; and on the other hand, on 12 and 14 January, her left shoe, which she had not allowed me to put on for her at the beginning of the session.

There is another hypothesis that could bring us a step further forward, this time along the path where Nadia's lack would have been filled by means of identification; that is to say, the path of perversion. Indeed, whatever interest I might have shown in the sailor could have led her not to take the place of the sailor, as in the preceding case, but to grant it to herself according to the model I would have provided her with: that is to say, by presenting myself to her as a phallic woman, in reality.

This is not an unusual occurrence, either, if the analyst is not careful; if the analyst confuses the fantasy of the phallic mother necessary for the child, with letting the child believe in the real existence of this phallus. In *Little Hans,* Freud clearly drew the line between fantasy and reality in this respect, when he got the father to say quite unambiguously that the mother did not have the phallus. That was what was to save Hans from perversion: encouraging him not to take his mother's drawers for the desired object, or at least, not to take any interest in them except when she was wearing them, in other words, to reduce them to a veil behind which the phallic fantasy could preserve its dialectical role, without an effect of closure resulting from denial of the lack.

A third hypothesis is mentioned here only as a reminder: that the sailor could have been a transitional object, in other words, it would have belonged neither to Nadia nor to me. But we can see clearly that this hypothesis does not hold up; for if I had taken the kind of interest that an adult normally takes in such an object, taking care to give it back in order to comfort the child, we would unavoidably have been led back to one of the two preceding eventualities.

There is another hypothesis that has far greater importance, insofar as it concerns the toppling over into psychosis.

Let us imagine that at the moment when Nadia turned violently away from her image in the mirror and hid in my arms I had in reality not been there, my place had been empty. What would have been left for her? It would no longer have been the hallucinated object of

10 December, it would have been a real object, the sailor in her hand. She had linked it so intimately with me, through the gaze and the mouth, that it would have been unthinkable that she could have relegated it to the rank of interchangeable and indifferent objects. So she would have become fixated on this sailor, riveted to it, and she would have reincorporated it through her eyes and her mouth, infinitely, incessantly, to fill the gap left by my disappearance.

As we shall see with Marie-Françoise, that is the case with the psychotic object, which remains as real witness to the Other that has been radically lost.

The evidence that Nadia herself showed regarding the failure of her attempt to go and find the image of her completeness by means of the sailor was that the mirror did not reflect it back to her and she turned away from it toward me, in anxiety.

Within the transference, at that juncture where she had arrived with me along her path, she was at the point of articulating her search for the object and the presence of the Other. It was only hanging by a thread, at this point, whether the small subject would turn toward the Other or would be sent into an impasse up against the wall of an object that would cut her off from the presence of the Other forever, which would have left the Other's place empty at the precise moment when the Other was invoked. It would be a most fertile moment for entry into psychosis, if the Other either did not respond or did not make itself available. Thus it is that psychosis, paradoxically, is more likely to arise as a result of the breaking off of the relation to an Other from whom the child expects and obtains a great deal—whether it is the mother or a therapist—than from the breaking off of a more neutral relation, which may leave the child with unfulfilled expectations, though not without causing irreversible damage if this situation is prolonged.

With Nadia, this marked the difference between the hallucinated object and the sailor: the former could function as a cut and a defense against an Other who was indifferent, or as good as. Nadia did not ask herself, in her relations with the nurses, in which too little had been invested and which were not privileged relations, the question about the relaying of the object via the gaze of the Other. The latter, the sailor, caused her to weigh up the prohibition of the death of the Other, insofar as the Other was already there.

I had been there before 10 December, and it had been my death that was the risk on that day. It was by way of my death that she had introduced me into her life, throughout her whole debate, during the pre-specular phase.

Only this latter hypothesis takes account of something deeper in this debate: the relation to the Other, in which the subject runs the risk of psychosis. In other cases, neuroses or perversions, the Other is there and is not radically called into question.

Either the object or the Other has to be lost. Nadia had shown that it was the object that had to be lost when she let go of something with her automatic hand movement; indeed, she had returned to it as a limit until just before the first mirror. We shall see that Marie-Françoise had remained fixated on this object, with the ultimate defense against her loss that she had encountered in scopic fascination and the phenomenon of the double, but at the price of the annulment of the Other—in other words, psychosis.

So what was the consequence of my not giving back the sailor to Nadia? I instituted an irremediable loss for her on the level of the Real; and, by following her anxious attitude in the mirror, I confirmed the failure she had encountered in her attempt to compensate for this loss.

In this first encounter with the mirror, an essential path was cleared. This was possible only through what was played out between Nadia and myself with the sailor. Nadia had lost this object, but she knew that I did not have it. Thus she was able to turn the corner from seeking the real object on my body, in spite of the impossibility she encountered there, to a questioning of the lack.

From that point on it was no longer the Real that was in question, but rather the Imaginary and the Symbolic that opened up the relation to the lack of an object and that would find their privileged arena in the mirror.

The sailor, insofar as it was the object of Nadia's loss, and insofar as it was not given back to her, by me, was her object *a*. I confirmed it in this position, because, at the moment of Nadia's encounter with the mirror, the image of the sailor, "*i(a)*,"* which she had in her hands, did not appear; it had no specular image.

The Real of the sailor, excluded from the mirror, was to give consistency to the Imaginary for Nadia.

Besides the registers implicated, a certain mathematical model is likely to give us an account of the clinical evidence.

If we go back to the 16 January session, just before the mirror, we find Nadia—for the first time—on my lap, her mouth stuck to my face, trying to absorb me: attempting the one: $1 + 1 = 1$.

---

*Translators' note: Lacan's matheme for the image of the small other.

Then—the second moment—she got down in front of me, picked up her sailor, and sucked it energetically: on the one hand, me plus my eye = 2; on the other hand, her plus her sailor = 2. The situation ceased to develop as if $2 + 2 = 0$, in other words, in each of the two sides of the equation, a third term was lacking: the Symbolic.

The following situation caused the possibility of a loss to appear, when Nadia presented herself as having fallen at my feet: she showed herself to me as the object of my loss = -1. I was 2; $2 - 1 = 3$, insofar as this loss could be accounted for as a third element with the two others: my image + my eye. It should be pointed out that my image here was not a specular one; that was not to occur until the third mirror; rather, at this point, it was the one Nadia had known from the beginning, in which she could admire herself: pre-specular and to do with primary narcissism.

This third moment, comprising such an image, a real element, my eye, and a loss, opened the way for the fourth moment, that of the mirror.

After $2 + 2 = 0$, $2 - 1 = 3$, Nadia tried at her own level in the mirror to make $2 + 1 = 3$. But in the mirror she saw neither my image nor that of the sailor, since the encounter with her own image made her turn away immediately. Instead of $2 + 1$, she encountered only $2 - 2$, herself and her image on the one hand, and myself and the sailor on the other.

In this sequence, we have to concede that the logical movement of the end of the January 16 session, which propelled Nadia toward the mirror, somehow ineluctably, was a search that aimed to find again what she experienced at my feet when I picked her up; in other words, the $2 - 1 = 3$, which would give the $2 + 1$ through symmetry in the mirror. I had picked up my object *a* lying at my feet. She went to look for hers in the mirror. But the symmetry did not work, because nothing was yet specularizable; neither the object, to be sure, nor myself. So she could not promote me to the rank of somebody else, of a "new subject," because she eliminated not my gaze but my eye, insofar as it was the carrier of object *a*. She also eliminated the sailor, which she did not even look at. She was to experience the real loss of the sailor when I did not give it back to her; it became nonspecularizable for all time. At the same time, I comforted her by picking her up a second time and putting her back into her crib. But then I went away. She lost me at that point where I could still have belonged to the image of 10 December, which her eye had contained. The scales fell from her eyes: the (sailor – other) and (me – real Other [unbarred]). She was no longer blind: this was clear from the gaze she addressed to me as I went out the door, a pathetic gaze, but which truly existed as a gaze, a gaze that was to come into play even in the field of the specular, later on; even if at this moment her eyes were still full of despair.

From the following day on, the effect was clear: she finally had the face of a child of her age.

Nadia was not to return to the mirror until 22 January. Between 17 and 22 January, while her face showed that the spectacular effect persisted, as a result of her encounter with her image in the mirror coupled with the loss of the sailor, it was still only the very first moment of the mirror phase: where the small subject found her own image but had not yet encountered that of the Other. And, during the following five sessions, through her violence and somatization, Nadia was to demonstrate the radical inadequacy of this first moment in the mirror phase. There were three aspects that became manifest: in her relation to the object, in her relation to my body, and in her relation to her own body.

In Nadia's relation to the object, the effect of her encounter with her own image was clear, with regard to the possibility of separation. She no longer needed her mechanical movement to separate herself from an object. She was very active and deliberate when, from 17 January onward, she would, for example, take the bottle and hit it before sending it flying, punctuating her action with a very clear signifier, for the first time: "a-pa, a-pa." During the following days, however, the signifier was missing when she was faced with the bottle and her violence increased. Nonetheless she managed actively to express her desire to destroy the bottle the following day when she hit it so hard on the floor that it cracked. Then she kicked it across the room, as she had done in the pre-specular phase (on 17 December, for example).

When she addressed herself to me, she was able to do it in a more nuanced way, using the cracker that she kept putting in and out of the dish, babbling "a-pa, a-pou, a-té, a-ca" while looking at me. For the first time at that moment, the signifier was enriched by the dimension of the signified; all we need to do is to double up the final syllables to give us "papa," "tété" (breast), and "caca"; "pou" has to do with "poum" (bang), which for her meant "to fall." We could define the "a" that preceded the syllables as privative, denoting what was in the Other that I was and to whom she addressed herself.

Since Nadia's loss of the sailor, this Other was the agent of privation, and at the same time the place of a signification in which the disappearance and appearance of the object could inscribe itself, in a process that was symbolic with regard to register and metaphorical with regard to the signifier. Immediately afterward, moreover, in the same session, she made herself into my object fallen at my feet, as on 16 January, but this time it was a game and she got up herself. On 20 January she emphasized the metaphorical playful aspect when she held out the dish to me and teased me by taking it back again before offering her whole body to me, as if she wanted me to take her, and then refused, laughingly, to let me.

At other times during this period, she herself took the role of agent of privation, which was my role: she held out a cracker only to snatch it away from me immediately, with a laugh.

All these elements certainly bore witness to a far greater mastery of objects, whether she was destroying them or refusing to let me have them. Yet everything remained in a relation that was too much imbued with the Real, which generated violence, not to mention the destructive explosion. It was even more distinct in her relations to other children or to the doll. Thus, on 19 January, I found her repeatedly hitting two children and watching me to see whether I would accept her violence; another example was when she sent the doll flying after cracking the bottle.

All these scenes were obviously inscribed in her relation to me. It was certainly no longer the metaphorical relation of before the mirror, where she had blocked herself when confronted with her desire to take something from my body or when she had offered herself to complete my body. The experience of the mirror, where she found the unified image of her body at the price of a loss, led her to wish to force my body to submit to the same privation. Such aggressivity, which she expressed not only against objects but also against me—which actually comes down to the same thing, for those objects were only those she deprived me of—was also indicative of the change that had taken place since she acquired her image; a change that, as we have seen, was inscribed on her face. Now, at the price of a loss, she was truly Nadia, but she was driven ineluctably to put me in the same position, marked by a loss—to put the "bar" through the "A" ($\bar{A}$) and no longer to make herself my object. Metaphor had been to do with the completeness of the Other, which came from the image generative of *invidia*. Metonymy, born at the moment of Nadia's encounter with her image, had to do with the unity of her body; but in her quest, she could be sure of this unity only if I passed along the same path, that of a loss that would produce it for me as it had done for her.

Before the second mirror, Nadia's quest stumbled over the apprehension of the real register of my loss, which generated violence and destructive explosions and put Nadia herself in danger; for if I was not marked by this loss, it must be that I had kept on my eye the image she had lost on 10 December. So that was where she sought to find it, as if the image that had been significant for her at the moment when she lost it still maintained a trace of the Real on the surface of my eye.

Metaphor was not to give way completely to metonymy except through the exclusively signifying value of the image on my eye: the wiping away of its trace and repression. This loss, which had to affect me under these circumstances, was necessary in order for a true metonymic relation to be established between Nadia and myself.

In passing, we can grasp what is at stake for small subjects who have actually encountered their image in the mirror, but have not been able to encounter that of the Other, which leaves them prey to a psychotic destructiveness.

There is another danger, which Nadia's behavior evinced on 20 January, when she walked toward me and gently tried to eat my cheek, to absorb me. It was as if, rather than discovering my unity metonymically, she was making me into her metaphorical object, reversing the situation of 16 January. But there she encountered the impossible, that of the Real, and this unleashed her violence: she held me by the hair, pulled my head down, kept me in this position, and hit me with her other hand. Her violence culminated when she wanted to poke her finger into my eye; in other words, to find or destroy on me the image of 10 December.

We will find another example of this kind of scene in the very first session with Marie-Françoise, where she confirmed the necessity of creating a hole in the Other. Nadia would succeed in doing this at the time of the second mirror, but Marie-Françoise failed, with the result that she remained psychotic. It is true that Nadia, in an ambivalence that was still not far off, interspersed her violence with caresses punctuated with "ma-ma-ma," in other words, with the signifier of the (future) metonymic place of the Other.

However, just as in the pre-specular phase, in the approach Nadia made to my body in her quest, she was not sufficiently sure of the separateness of her body and mine; she paid the price somatically with her painful ear and her suppurating whitlow. This reaction of her body testified to her malaise but also indicated which field her drama was being played out in: it was the field of the signifier, where her body and mine were at stake, not only in the Real but also in the primordial pair of signifiers (S_1 and S_2) that represented them. We can say this on the basis of the fact that there are hardly ever any such reactions in the case of psychotic children, precisely because their drama does not develop in the field of the signifier.

Nadia was running after my S_2; she was to find it in my specular image at the time of the second mirror, making me move from the position of a metaphorical object to a metonymic position, necessary for the relation between signifiers. It was a logical, ineluctable proceeding, but it was also veiled. She herself had introduced this very veil for the first time, in the form of the cloth, on 19 January.

On 22 January, Nadia had her second encounter with the mirror, at the beginning of the session, while the nurse was putting her shoes and socks on for her on the little table at the foot of the mirror. There, she showed her full interest in both reflections, hers and mine. On this occasion, she was able to look properly at her own, while I was beside her, and she was able to compare mine with my real body.

The whole of the ensuing session was adorned with physical effusions of tenderness: she caressed my face, pushed her body up against mine, vertically, with her arms around my neck, her open mouth against my cheek, giving little shrieks of joy, gazing into my eyes. I had the impression that she was being "reborn," and I said so to her. In other words, she had realized that what I had said to her the day before constituted a difference between her body and mine: "By eating you learn to love, to be loved, and to love life."

At that moment, she was a long way from the conflictual love of the transference, marked with metaphor, where, in the pre-specular phase her body had had to be for me, and where, since the first mirror, my body had had to be for her.

When we returned from the session, Nadia held out her arms to the nurse for the first time and the nurse was struck by how radiant she looked. Nadia also gave a piece of bread to another child. In relation to the woman, in relation to the child, something had momentarily loosened up, in this metaphorical bond that shackled her; metonymy allowed her access to the freedom of signification, through the medium of my speech.

But, from the following day, whatever parts of her ego and of her love did not have to do with the drives were wiped out by a massive return of the Real of the body; not, this time, at the scopic level, but at the level of digestion. This opened the way for us to take up once more the oral debate, which was not to be truly, intrinsically resolved until the end of Nadia's treatment, as we shall see.

Indeed, on 23 January, while she was caressing my face, involved as she was in trying to keep up her effusive tenderness of the previous day, she defecated in her diaper. Immediately she bit my arm and my chin and hit me on the mouth. The Real of her body had made its return, together with the drives. The love she had just encountered, and the drives, are not the same thing, as Freud pointed out.

From this point on, the drives would appear by way of her attempts to devour me or to take an object from me: my glasses, of which she broke off one of the arms several times and then sucked it, making the link between the oral and the scopic. This link was to persist for some time, since for Nadia the scopic supplemented the oral, which appeared more and more as a limit point. It is probable that this dead end was what she knew before she took refuge in the scopic; she rediscovered it very rapidly after the second mirror in the form of the desire to absorb me, while at the same time she became more and more hungry at the table. The return of orality to the forefront threw her back into the quest she had been involved in before the mirror, that is, the inclusion of the Other, whose orality was clearly the prototype at the level of the drives.

So she was once more to go around a loop that would last about ten days and would end with the true separation between her and me, between her and the Other. But at the time, I had the impression that, by means of this orality, the massive return of the Real of the body, or rather, of metaphor, would mean that Nadia ran the risk of becoming locked in such an impasse that the metonymy of the specular would be eclipsed. At the time, intuitively, I was trying to reinscribe this orality into something more livable, something less directly connected with my body. That is why I decided, on 25 January, to return an hour after the session to give her the last course of her dinner, outside the session and outside the analytic space. In my mind, it was a question of moderating the rigidity of the oral limit, which was ineluctable when she addressed herself to my body during the sessions, by enlarging the oral relation through the ritual of meals that Nadia was familiar with and through the implements that were linked with it: the dish, the spoon, and the mug. Was I led to do this because of what Nadia had already indicated to me, with regard to the importance of what happened outside the sessions, outside the analytic space, when she had fetched the rubber sailor from another room, on January 11, and on January 16 had made it at the same time into an oral object that she sucked while looking at me and the object of her loss at the time of the first mirror, immediately afterward? What I could not have foreseen was the way she promoted one particular object, the spoon, to the forefront on 25 January, when I gave her the last course of her dinner, and the way she was to use it from then on to serve as mediator in her oral debate with me.

We should recall that this spoon had appeared right at the start of the treatment, for the first time on 12 October, and for the second on 3 November, when the nurse had wanted to give Nadia her snack with a spoon, in my presence. But at that time, the spoon had not in any way been a particularly important object, and Nadia's refusal of food concerned her relation to the Other under my gaze; the spoon was not yet able to serve as a mediator.

When I went to give her the second course of her dinner, things happened as I had anticipated: the ritual of the meal saved her from her former inhibitions. Although she was not very interested at first, she soon started to smile and expressed her joy that it was me who was feeding her, within the framework and the time of her meal among the other children. It is true that the unsticking of the metaphorical image had already taken place, even if Nadia had problems accepting it. On this day, the metaphor of the sticking together of bodies was able to give way to the spoon; we now need to define what its function was.

1. When I arrived, I found Nadia sitting in her crib, sucking her thumb, whimpering, in front of a tableau of a nurse feeding another child with a spoon. To be sure, it was no longer the fascinating image, which had been repressed; but there was a remnant of oral autoerotism, which had formerly elicited sucking movements when she was confronted with this kind of scene. At that time it had been her tongue that gave her pleasure, while now it was her thumb. Formerly, the object had been included, stuck to her eye; now it was external. The pleasure was no longer so primary as it had been, and she was whimpering in front of this new reality. Reality for her was that there was an Other, an Other who gave an object-supposed-to-satisfy—food—to another small counterpart. This object she was expecting to get from the Other had assumed more importance now, in reality, than her autoerotic satisfaction, which she was only using as a last resort while she waited her turn.

2. Further, as we have seen, she accepted that I should feed her within the habitual framework of the satisfaction of her needs; the pleasure she showed while I was feeding her testified that it was a question of something other than need and that her autoerotism lacked the Other. Also, in the position of the Other that I was, the question of her relation to me could not fail to arise immediately. Moreover, her satisfied need left the problem of her desire completely

unresolved, a desire that remained thwarted with regard to the food-object. Besides, it was not a demand for more food that she addressed to me, and she was to go and find the object linked both to her body and to mine. The spoon fitted this definition particularly well, insofar as I had used it to feed her, and at the same time it was a focus of both Nadia's oral and scopic drives, if we think back to the preceding scene that had made her whimper as she sucked her thumb.

This spoon was an extension of my body; I put it with the dish on the pillow of the next crib, and Nadia immediately wanted to go and retrieve it, or rather, had to conquer it.

3. In fact, what happened at this time showed that for Nadia it was not merely a question of grabbing an object but rather of endowing it with an essential and logical position in her bodily relation to me. Also, when she wanted to pick it up, it took her no less than three attempts, followed by three of her mechanical movements, before she could really take hold of it. This was proof that the spoon was still infiltrated by its status of bodily object, this object she had wanted to take from me throughout all the preceding phases; the imprint of reality it bore inhibited her action.

4. Once she had really taken hold of it, it was the lime-flower infusion she refused to take; when the nurse wanted her to drink from the mug, she tipped it into the dish and threw it on the floor, then hit the dish with the spoon. The position of the dish now counterpointed that of the spoon, with regard to the relation to my body; we will come back to this when we discuss the session of 26 January.

5. The whole of the end of the session of 25 January shows the transformation Nadia had forced the spoon to make. It was no longer a real object: she got hold of it. It was no longer a metaphorical object linked to my body: the trace of this link had been so completely wiped out that she could use the spoon as an extension of her own body, as she had used it to extend mine. We can see clearly enough the new position the spoon had taken up, if we remember the triumphant way she brandished it, her enthusiasm as she showed it to me, and the flurry of activity as she went off victoriously to touch all the objects with it. But what exactly was this position?

The obliteration of its metaphorical character made it into a pure signifying object, disengaged from the substitutive dimension of a bodily object she had taken from me. As such, she could now deprive me of it without revealing the lack with which she affected me, anymore than her desire to "have something from my body" was revealed. My lack, and her having it, marked by her own lack, as we shall see, remained misrecognized at the level of the spoon, via the signifying, metonymic promotion of this object. This promotion was the secret behind the explosion of her power over the external world. We could say that the spoon became the signifier of lack: that is to say, structurally, the phallus she deprived me of, without my knowing, to her mind, that I lacked one. And she herself did not know the status of this object, as she used it only to impose a mark on all the other objects, including the doctor who came up to her. She did not want to know what it was she had, any more than I was to know what she had taken away from me—she was so focused on the external world: such was the dimension of her own lack. The spoon served her to baptize the world, which in the process lost its excess of Real. The baptism was "in the name of . . . ," in the name of the Other, well beyond myself, who only represented him: the mythical father.

As often happens in analysis, Nadia boldly anticipated the metonymic character of the spoon. It was not the first time she had anticipated the point she was to arrive at; we saw it when she held out her foot to me after I had called her by her name, on 10 December, before she entered into the long debate of the pre-specular phase.

From the next day, 26 January, it was no longer the spoon that was the center of her attention, but the dish, in the form of the little dish from the doll's tea set, which she had taken out of the ark. She returned to the dish as if she was returning to the interrogation of my body. And besides, almost immediately dropping the dish, she pulled off my glasses, and as she babbled, shook them so violently that one of the arms broke off. It was this arm that she was to suck, but not until she had bitten me on the wrist, thus underlining her return to the relation to the body linked with orality. But that was not all; she was also to use the broken arm of my glasses to hit the edge of the potty and then its inside. It was no longer a question of a metonymic object, but of the object of loss: whether it was the image she wanted to get back from me or the stool she passed while I was holding her in my arms on 23 January.

Then she dropped the arm of my glasses and picked up the dish. She sat on the floor and played a symbolic game of loss and refinding with the dish, a game in which the object showed through when the dish slipped between her legs against her diaper and she muttered and raised her pinafore to get it, giving a sign of another place of lack on her body. This she confirmed when she abandoned the dish and went to fetch the lollipop stick she had noticed under one of the cribs; she sucked it and wanted to give it to me, but not without hesitation, as she had thrown it down and then picked it up again.

Throughout this scene, the object made a move back toward the imaginary debate. It was not a question of the spoon as a metonymic signifier of lack, driving Nadia toward action in the enthusiasm of something unknown, but once again, of a knowledge: it was an insoluble question, to know which of us two, her or me, was affected by the lack. If it was her, she could only be aggressive against me; and if it was me, and if she knew I knew it, she could only give it up.

At the end of this session, I decided to bring a dish of cereal and a spoon into the material of the session. The reason for this was that I had been struck by the massive return of her orality as an impasse, the same situation as before I had given her her dinner. I thought I had failed to put at her disposal that which she had just managed to conquer on my body, in the form of the spoon; I also thought, and I noted it at the time, that the cereal, in the sessions, might acquire a dimension other than that of pure nourishment: explicitly, that of Nadia's smearing of herself and me, which did not fail to happen.

Nadia did not hesitate when faced with the spoon and the dish of cereal. She licked the spoon once and ate the cereal with her hand. But she quickly returned to the spoon, which no longer had its triumphal character of 25 January.

In a first moment, she arrived at a signification of the object of loss, initially her object, because she threw it down. But she also threw down my pencil, which she had taken from my pocket, and my glasses, joining together her loss and mine.

On the other hand, immediately afterward when she picked up the spoon again and played with it, smiling at first, she threw it down again in order to show me just one of her shoes. Was it to deny her own loss in front of me? We know how important these shoes had been for Nadia when, during the entire pre-specular phase, which had been so difficult for her, her face had lit up, not at the sight of me, but when I had brought her shoes at the beginning of a session. Was this already the representative of the object she wanted to take away from me? It is highly improbable, given her inhibition with regard to one particular object on my body, or its pure representative.

Rather, we encountered here the masked, unknown character, both to herself and to me, which meant that on that day an object such as the spoon could fulfill its metonymic role.

Once again, something was defining itself, to do with these objects, regarding the fundamental difference between metaphor and metonymy.

With metaphor, the psychical representative of the object, even though it was on the path toward signification, could send the subject back toward a return to the Real of bodies, in spite of the sense that was arising in the subject or perhaps because of the sense revealed in the subject. This happened by crossing the bar that separated the signifiers present in metaphorical substitution. This return of the Real of bodies was the return to the dual situation.

Metonymy introduced a supplementary dimension that Freud summed up in the term that causes so much difficulty in translation: *Vorstellungsrepräsentanz,* ideational representative, a kind of doubling of the mechanism in question, where the *Vorstellung,* "representation," does not define a unique phenomenon concerning a given object, but rather, a field. This field of representation is the signifier; and it is in this field that the "representative" of the object, the *Repräsentanz,* can inscribe itself as a signifier and, as such, according to the logic of the signifier, can enter into a connection with the other signifiers in the chain. That is what excluded the possibility of the imaginary, or even the real, return of bodies. The non-known effaced any direct capturing of signification, and, to take up Freud's terminology, it was there that energy, whose quantum is that of affect, was bound. Thence came the liberating and triumphal character of the spoon.

The metonymic character of the object-spoon remained transitory, however. Was it the poverty of the signifying chain, normal at Nadia's age, which meant that there were so few connections? Or was it the continuing possibility of a return toward metaphor by way of the loss of an object, whether she no longer had it, or whether it was taken away from her, or even whether she deprived herself of it?

The difficulty that characterizes orality can, by its very nature, draw the subject back into the impasse of the consumption of the body. So it was that Nadia endowed the spoon once again with its character of pure representative of the oral object when she put it to the doll's mouth; but, making explicit the prohibition linked to the signifier from 10 December onward, she followed at once by punishing the doll, hitting it violently on the floor.

The prohibition then passed from the doll to the spoon, after Nadia got into the crib with the doll in one hand and the spoon in the other; this time it was the turn of the spoon to be subjected to her aggressivity, and she trampled on it. Like Nadia, like the doll, I had no right to the spoon, since, when she put it into my mouth, she unleashed her fury once more against the spoon. It has to be said that her aggression was not directed against me; it was against this object-spoon that had betrayed her by coming to represent the object of loss. And she herself realized this loss by getting one of her shoes and one of her socks taken off, which she then sent flying. Once she had paid this price, she was able to find the spoon again for a brief moment, in its old place, and she played with it, babbling, with a delighted look. However, when I interpreted for her the difficulty she had in bearing my feeding her during the sessions, she attacked me with the spoon and bit my shoulder.

At this time, she never let go of her spoon when she went back after the sessions. But there was always a risk that another child would take it away from her, and this made her howl. I gave it back to her, in such cases, unlike the sailor, showing her—and this was only too clear—that it was not the object of a loss, even if, as we saw, it may have appeared to be one in Nadia's debate with me. What I gave back to her was not an object, in order to shield her from a loss, but the object she had managed to promote, on 25 January, to the status of *Vorstellungsrepräsentanz*.

The spoon could not prevent her, however, from being ineluctably led back to her relation with the food-object in the form of the cereal. It was that which dominated the entire debate of the four following sessions, between 28 and 31 January, and which culminated in the third mirror.

After the explosive anticipation of the metonymic role of the spoon on 25 January, Nadia made a complete loop in these four sessions, questioning her own relation to the food-object. For sure, she was helped by the spoon's role as instrument, even as mediator, as much in its relation to food as such as in its bodily relation to me. But the importance she conferred on this object showed that she remembered the metonymic dimension it had suddenly acquired. In fact, the spoon served, more than just for eating, to set a mark both on food and on my body, and even on the consulting room.

The spoon gave Nadia a way of approaching food, with which she had such a difficult relation. On 29 January, holding the spoon in one hand, she plunged her other hand into the cereal, licked her hand, and then unleashed her aggressivity against everything that was food: the bottle, which she pushed aside with a slow gesture, consciously and deliberately, the dish, which she turned upside down and then hit with the spoon, and then the crackers. She then repeated the imposition of this mark with the spoon, hitting the floor, the wall, the crib, and not without satisfaction. Coming back onto my lap, she hit my mouth. Thus she continued with what I called her "baptism of the external world," but this time it was not without ambiguity and there was no air of victory as there had been the time before.

Imposing the mark of the spoon retained a trace of the conflict that linked Nadia to the objects she was "baptizing." The energy she expended in so doing, and her tension, bespoke the resistance of the Real she had to force.

This Real was above all that of her bodily relation to me, in which the spoon played a pivotal role. In a first moment, on 27 January, as we saw, she had wanted to put it into my mouth, having licked it herself at the beginning of the session. There she rediscovered the transitivistic dimension that had prevailed at the beginning of the treatment, when her mouth was confused with mine.

On 30 January, she tried to push the spoon into the opening of my white coat, going back to her quest of the pre-specular phase that aimed at that object on my body. But this time it was no longer her head she pushed inside my white coat. Moreover, it was to be the last time she tried to seek out the breast; the spoon had "de-realized" it.

From then on, the spoon was to serve her to recover what, in the pre-specular phase, had had to do with the topology of the surface of our bodies. Although she did use it a little to eat with, she used it primarily to spread out the cereal, initially on the floor, where she would even try to wipe out the splashes she had made there; but above all, she used it on me, when, on 30 January, she shook the spoonful of cereal over my cheeks and my hair. On 29 January she had pulled off my glasses and probed the surface of my eyes, in a return to the scopic via the organ of the eye, which defines the relation of bodies in two dimensions: the topological relation of surface.

On 31 January, there was the same preoccupation with the surface of the body. I said to her, at the beginning of the session, when she was sucking the tip of my nose, nibbling at me, and drooling copiously, that she wanted to absorb me, but that it was impossible because her body and mine were two, not one. I added that she was not pleased with any external food that was not me, but that she could enjoy the cereal, as she had done, because she could fill herself up with it while I was near her. Her reply was to eat half of her cereal with the spoon, looking at me, babbling, and licking her lips, thus giving to the cereal a role of metaphor of my body, in contradistinction to my real body, which was the impossible I had just told her of. So then she spread out the rest of the cereal on the floor, first with the spoon, then with her hand, and finally turned the dish over and pulled it along, making a long trail of cereal. It was not a question of ingestion, but of spreading out; spreading out on the skin, hers and mine, when, all covered in cereal, she wanted to climb up into my arms and rub her cheek against mine, looking joyful.

She had already encountered this spreading out in the course of the analysis, on 24 December, after she had touched my skin. After that experience, she had smeared her skin with her own excrement. On this day, she was no longer representing me as an object on her skin by an object of her body, for now the spoon played the role of mediator, a representative signifier of bodies, to the point where she had doubled up on it at the beginning of the session; by this I mean that Nadia arrived with two spoons she had picked up from the changing table, one for her and one for me. Her spoon and mine, these metonymic objects, made it possible for us to cover each other with the cereal and opened up the metonymic pathway of our bodies. Thus Nadia was able to demand the mirror for the third time.

The only thing she looked at in it this time was my reflection. It made the smile disappear from her face; she came back into my arms and did not want to leave. Had the mirror revealed to her my own loss, the loss she felt in seeing my reflection at a distance and without seeing herself? Put another way, metaphor, which was active in the sticking together of our cheeks, gave way to the metonymic image of my body, which was what she was seeking without knowing it. It was an experience symmetrical with the first mirror, where she had seen herself alone, without seeing either my image or that of the sailor; but the consequences of this had been decisive for her.

The third mirror, like the first, was to be decisive for her. We shall see this in the course of the three days that followed, when there were to be no less than six more encounters with the mirror.

To conclude, then, the three first mirrors appear, after the event, as a liquidation of the past for Nadia and brought about the destruction of her pathology through the creation of a structure elaborated in the analysis.

After my calling her by her name brought about the repression of the image "A + *a*," which she carried on her eye, thus inaugurating her subjectivity, she tended to occupy the metaphorical position of my object *a* throughout the pre-specular phase. It was the metonymic image of her body that she discovered at the time of the first mirror that liberated and transformed her.

But she could not find me at the time of the first mirror, because in her pathology, either I was a part of the image or I bore it on the surface of my eye (as she did, too) and she tried several times over to find it by pulling off my glasses and poking at my eyes. In both cases, in my status of Other, I was not affected by any loss.

At the time of her second encounter with the mirror, she put the image that fascinated her through it. It was indeed the return of the repressed, since both of us entered into it with a perspective that aimed at the exclusion of any loss: a nonsymbolized loss that arose once more in the Real the day after the second mirror. It was the leftover of the pathology she had had before the analysis, centering on transitivism, although Nadia had, as we have seen, come to grips with metaphorical structure in her pre-specular debate. At this point this was the only signifier that could allow us to speak of structure.

Whatever was revealed of Nadia's position as object a in metaphor gave way to metonymy, initially to her advantage, at the time of her encounter with her reflection in the mirror; then it was to mine, at the time of the encounter with my reflection in the third mirror, as we shall see.

From the metaphor that reproduced the image "A + a" in the field of signification, Nadia made herself into my a, fallen at my feet, so with the knowledge of the one and the Other, she passed on to metonymy, as a creation of signification unbeknown to the subject, by means of connection between the signifiers. The unknown took over from the repressed, that is to say, that part of the image that had become unconscious and that, at every moment, was trying to push its way back, to return.

In these first three mirrors, while the promotion of signification was decisive in Nadia's development, paradoxically each mirror revealed a loss, which she acknowledged and at first perceived in the immediacy of the encounter. It is easy to see that it was this that cut short any jubilation. These losses—the sailor at the time of the first mirror, the stool the day after the second, and myself as a real body at the time of the third, indicate the pathological nature of the constructions Nadia had made, perhaps on the borders of psychosis.

But we can also measure the considerable gain she had made from the time of the encounter with the mirror; in her case, it was even more evident than can generally be observed with children. Through her analysis, she created her structure in the field of the signifier, and the mirror was the keystone in the decisive passage from metaphor to metonymy, from the metaphor of the inclusion of surfaces to the metonymic sublimation of the surface of the body by means of the surface of the mirror. At that point, she was able to reach the paradigmatic role the mirror plays for each subject.

9/The Mirror 2—The Turning Around: From Surface to Space

On 1 February Nadia began the session on my lap, looking intensely at my face, babbling "ma-ma-ma." She then took my glasses, returned them to me, took them back again, and threw them under the crib. She threw the cloth from the ark, took the small cup, sucked it before throwing it away, and did the same to the small dish. She came back onto my lap and touched both of my eyes lingeringly. She then *put her arms around my neck and nibbled my chin while drooling profusely.* I told her the same thing as in the previous session.

She then went to the dish of cereal, started by dipping her spoon into it, licked it, then dipped in her hand, licking it and smearing her face. She turned around to show me, and that seemed to give her pleasure. Still holding her spoon, *she took hold of the edge of the dish, knocked over the cereal by pulling the dish toward her in order to lengthen the trail, and put the dish back in its place.* She then lay down her spoon, rubbed her hands in the expanse of cereal, sucked each hand in turn, picked up her spoon again, and came toward me.

She stood herself up, using my knees to help her, touched my eyes, and looked for my glasses. Having spotted them near the door she set off toward them. Stopping halfway, she babbled a lot—as she had been doing from the start of the session—then came back into my arms and went from there into the crib. Standing upright, facing me, she hugged me tightly around the neck with both arms, put her mouth to my shoulder, drooling copiously, and wanted me to get her out of the crib in this position, in which she remained on my lap for quite a long time.

She got down, *went to explore the wall,* babbling away, and reached the window. She looked out and then came back into my arms.

When we returned to her room she did not want me to put her back in her crib, but led me, walking, to the table, which was in front of the mirror, and demanded to be lifted up. She looked at herself, looked at my reflection and my reality, returned to her image, trampling as she touched it. *She shook the mirror, touched my reflection cautiously, and turned around at once to be in my arms.*

She hugged me very tightly around the neck as if to assure herself of my presence and cast a quick look at the mirror to see this different image.

She then wanted to explore the whole building, including the kitchen on the first floor, where the meowing of a cat mesmerized her. She touched all the objects with curiosity: electric switches, doorknobs, extinguisher . . . She touched them truly, seeking to feel them properly.

When we came back to her room she wanted to return to the mirror. There she played the same scene as before, *but less long and with less tension; she smiled faintly* while I kept an arm around her.

I handed her back to a nurse while repeating to her that I would be there tomorrow. She held her arms out to me; I took her back for a minute in order to explain again and she accepted the inevitable, with resignation.

This session, composed of two such different parts, gave me the impression that Nadia was aware that there were two of us. While this was disappointing and full of risks of insecurity, against which she could fight only by awakening her interest in the outside world, she dared to set off because I was there in spite of everything. It would be less disappointing than wanting to eat me, as the last scene before the mirror proved, where Nadia was even smiling.

On 2 February, as soon as Nadia saw me, she got up and stamped her feet. A nurse changed her and dressed her for the session. Nadia did not take her eyes off me. She babbled, kicked her legs, tried to catch hold of the mirror in front of which she was being changed, then took one of my fingers and would not let go. Before leaving she wanted to remain a few moments in front of the mirror; but this gave her no pleasure.

During the whole of the session, Nadia was very relaxed and excited, without anxiety or violence. She used a varied and articulated babble, reserving for me the "ma-ma-ma" that became "mama-mama."

She started by throwing the cloth out of the ark, so she could grab and throw the little dish and cup, after having licked the latter. She returned to my arms and, standing up on my lap, tore off my glasses, touching my eyes lingeringly. She hugged my neck, *bit and sucked my chin,* without either aggression or true suction: it was in the register of a kiss.

She got down to sit in front of the dish of pudding—it was tapioca. She took the spoon, dunked it, licked it, and *made me lick it*. Then it was the turn of her hand; she smeared herself a great deal. She threw the contents of the dish onto the floor, put the dish back in its place, *then scooped up the tapioca she had spilled with both hands and ate some, smearing herself* even more. Picking up the spoon, she came back to my lap, where she remained upright and put her arms around my neck, rubbing her smeared face against mine, cheerfully babbling "mama-mama."

She got down, explored the wall, excited, babbling away; she came to the window and looked out, enchanted. She threw down the crackers then picked one up and ate a corner of it; she made me eat some too.

I took her back in great shape. She wanted to go back to *the mirror. She looked at her reflection, then mine, then looked at me myself while putting her head tenderly against mine and, without changing position, looked at this new reflection of the two of us together. She beamed, then tapped on the surface of the mirror with a building block, excited but not violent.*

On 3 February, while the nurse was changing and dressing her, I twice had to leave the room for a short time. Each time I returned, I found Nadia crying, distressed; she calmed down as soon as she saw me. When we passed *the mirror she turned away from it.*

In the session she began by throwing out of the ark whatever prevented her from reaching the cup and the little dish. She picked them up and threw them away. She did not empty the ark completely but shook it a lot, babbling imperiously. She was *rather violent but without anxiety or inhibition.* She came back to my lap to tear off and throw down my glasses; she pressed herself against me a moment, put the spoon into my mouth, then got down to sit in front of the dish of pudding.

She tasted the tapioca and smeared it on herself with her hand, but only briefly because she *knocked over the bottle. This bottle would become the center of her interest,* except for three short interludes during which, successively, she threw the toys out of the ark and put the spoon back into it, then ate the pudding with both hands, smearing her face, and lastly came to my lap and to the crib, showing tenderness and babbling: "mama-mama." As for the bottle, she handled it with aggressivity: sent it rolling, shook it so that milk spurted onto the floor, *crushed the nipple between her hands, enchanted when milk spurted out, or else pushed it back into the neck of the bottle. She intensely enjoyed these aggressive manipulations.* She did this for a long period, babbling imperiously and, twice, came to hide between my knees, saying "mama-mama." She looked at me from time to time. I felt she was free.

At the end of the session she sucked the toys that had fallen into the pudding, threw the crackers, and explored the wall, interested in the paper stuck on it and in the electric switch.

When I took her back to her room she did not want to stay there. She wanted to explore the whole floor again, showing great interest in all sorts of things, especially the bathtub in which she was washed each morning. In the course of this exploration she wanted to feel everything; now and again she put her smeared cheek against mine.

When we returned, *she turned toward the mirror,* as we passed in front of it. She remained in my arms, *looked at each of us,* squeezed my neck, *put her cheek against mine, smiling with emotion and following the whole scene in the mirror. Then she turned around and buried her head in my neck.*

She led me to the window to look outside. I handed her back to the nurse; she accepted this but her expression was sad as I closed the door and left.

On 4 February, Nadia was radiant and babbled as soon as she was in my arms, still in the room, whereas up to then the babbling had started only once we were in the consulting room.

When we arrived there, she said "mama-mama" to me, her cheek against mine. Then she wanted to get down and go to the ark, from which she took out the cloth and the little sailor, which she found once more with joy, recognizing it: it was not the one of 16 January and the first mirror, but another I used to bring along right at the start, when I first came to see her.

On her little chair she noticed at once that there was *a piece of chocolate* as well as the crackers. *She could not put it to her mouth without two of her automatic letting-go movements, but then she came to eat it on my lap,* putting her head against me tenderly and *giving the impression that at that moment she knew the feeling of plenitude* of a baby fed on the bottle or at the breast. She had an ecstatic expression, which she would keep to the end of the session.

She took little interest in the cereal, merely licking her spoon, then her hand, just once.

She came into my arms, tearing off and throwing down my glasses, *touching one of my eyes lingeringly; she then went into the crib but only so that I would take her out again* and so that she could remain pressed against me for a few seconds. This happened several times.

After throwing down the crackers with the spoon, she came back to the ark, emptied it completely, felt the bottom, and put the spoon in it. *Then she looked at the doll, picked it up, seemed to hesitate, and then tried to put it to bed in the ark* after having taken out the spoon. As the doll would not go in at once, she laid it down across the ark and left it for a few seconds to come and lean against my knees. She then picked it up and *put the spoon back in the ark* in its place.

Then she took the bottle, knocked it over, squeezed the nipple once between her fingers while babbling, *lifted it very briefly to her mouth, threw it down,* and lost all interest in it.

After a cuddle of five minutes during which she let me bounce her on my knees and kiss her, she began a joyful exploration of the wall and the window.

She was not happy to be taken back to her room.

The next morning, 5 February, the doctor was at the foot of her crib when I arrived. She looked at me, then at him, then at me again, and began to fidget, lay down flat on her stomach, kicking her legs, looking at me laughing, very moved. She stood up and gripped my white coat so I would take her in my arms. She gave herself over to a great show of tenderness, hugging me around the neck with both arms, putting her mouth to my nose, then my cheek, lingeringly. They changed her and put her shoes on. She had not had diarrhea for two days.

In the consulting room, there was by chance, in a corner, a children's table; she noticed it at once and was henceforth interested only in this table. She took possession of it with great joy, hitting it with a spatula she had picked up while being changed. She did this with delectation, babbling imperiously, happily.

I dragged the table over to the other toys. She continued to stand in front of it, using the spatula to scrape some pieces of wafer stuck to it. She also licked them, then seemed to want to sit in the little chair: I came closer and *she stuck out her bottom* to sit down. She sat down after a second of inspection of her new position, looked at me, delighted, then banged on the table again.

She wanted to come into my arms, pressed herself against me while saying "mama-mama"; then she went into the crib, where she played and made me play with *the spatula,* which she even held out to me for a moment, saying *"Here!"*

She wanted me to sit her down again in front of the table, delighted, then left to explore the wall and the window, babbling. There, she wanted to be in my arms to look outside; she was *extremely interested in the coal-carriers* taking their sacks to the cellar. This spectacle absorbed her for five minutes.

Back in her room, she refused to go into the arms of a nurse she did not know. She pressed herself pathetically against me, her cheek against mine. I reassured her and put her back into the arms of a nurse she knew: she was sad about my departure, but accepted it, as if she knew, with this nurse, that I would return.

On 6 February, Nadia babbled as soon as she saw me. It was the first time she had done this before she was in my arms. The nurse changing her then complained that she would not stop moving and scolded her; yet, she said, while watching Nadia hold out her arms to me, that after a month's absence she no longer recognized this Nadia who previously had passed unnoticed because she was so still and silent.

In the session Nadia remained a few seconds in my arms, embracing my neck, pressing her cheek against mine and saying "mama-mama."

She went to the ark, took out the cloth, and put it back; I could see she was thinking of something else. In fact she was looking for the little table of the day before, which I could not find this morning. Her eyes sought it in every corner and she seemed disappointed.

She went and threw some crackers around and came back to me with the chocolate. She sucked a piece of it, then let it go. She went up close to the dish, licked the spoon several times, and tipped out a little cereal. Then she turned toward the bottle, which she knocked down with an imperious "a-ga," and pressed herself against the pane, which she happily rapped with the spoon.

She came back to my lap to wrench off my glasses and throw them down before returning to the ark. She threw out the cloth and the rubber sailor, took back the cloth, hesitated in bringing it to her mouth after looking at it for a long while, then *tried to tear it with her teeth*. She cast it away and ignored it thereafter, but I had the impression it represented something specific for her.

Then, she emptied the ark completely, throwing out all the toys, and picked up the cup and small dish again, aggressively. The ark was now empty and, *lifting it with one hand, she made sure with the other that it was truly empty*. She put it down and looked for something: she was seeking *my glasses, which she picked up and put into the ark.* She lifted it again and with her free hand, fingered my glasses in the bottom, then put the ark back on the floor.

She became interested in the doll, looked at it for quite a long time, shook it gently by one arm, without aggressivity. I did not know what she wanted but I had the impression that she did not either, as if she did not know what to do with this doll. Then she moved on to the bottle, which she gently knocked over.

She went back to the ark and checked that my glasses were still inside. At once, *she went to look for her spoon, which she laid down beside my glasses,* then she lifted up the ark, pressed it against her, looked inside, put it down, and went to play with the small dish close to the wall. She came back to the ark, took out my glasses and her spoon, felt the empty bottom, and put back the two objects again. All the while she babbled a great deal and came now and then to lean against me.

Eventually, she climbed back into my arms, very happy, and wanted to explore the room.

I took her back to her room. She walked a little. It took a long time for her to accept going into the arms of a nurse. I spoke to her softly until she accepted.

I asked for her to be put in contact with one or two older children playing in a neighboring room. But in the absence of any nurse, the experience turned sour: I heard her crying later, distressed, calling: "mama-mama."

The next morning, 7 February, I unfortunately arrived too late for her to have a true session. But for a short while I took her to the consulting room, where she showed herself to be very dynamic, babbling nonstop, exploring the wall and window: everything interested her.

Supper had started when I took her back. I put her back in her crib, but she could not tolerate waiting her turn and started to cry, holding out her arms. I put her back in her crib only when it was her turn. The nurse, seated on the edge of the next crib, fed her: Nadia ate quickly and well. As she looked at me and as I felt that she wanted me to stay close to her, I did so, speaking to her or speaking about her to the nurse. She did not demand that I should feed her myself, but ended her supper with the small piece of chocolate she had brought back from the session.

On 8 February I took Nadia for the first time to the consulting room in which I used to treat children and which was in the other building.

She was rather tense during the walk there and, once we were in the room, I kept her sitting on my lap. Though she remained tense, she looked at everything there was to see in the room and did not lose herself in the objects taken from my pocket, as she had done when I had taken her to see the Christmas tree. She decided to take the crackers, which she threw down, and the chocolate, which she kept and licked. Nevertheless, her expression remained rigid. She wanted to be put down on the ground, took two steps, and held out her arms while looking toward the door.

So I took her back to her room. Her rigid expression disappeared. Under a crib she noticed a mug that another child had dropped. She took it, sat down, and made as if she wanted to drink.

She led me onto the landing and noticed other mugs on a table. She wanted me to stand her up on that table, and she took a mug from it. She thus had two of them: with one she banged on a dish, harder and harder, and with the other she banged on the wall. I sensed a violence that needed to come out and I thought a session of five minutes in the usual room might be good, so that she could express herself, because the new experience had been trying.

So I put her into a nurse's arms while I went to prepare the consulting room. Though I told her I would be back at once, she began to sob. When I returned five minutes later, she was still crying and stretched out her arms as soon as she saw me.

I carried her into the usual room. Once there, she immediately expressed the violence that the anxiety had triggered: she threw everything around and shook the ark, while babbling and walking.

After ten minutes, when I felt she was relaxed, I took her back, but she found it hard to let me go.

We said that what was decisive in the third mirror with respect to the encounter with my reflection, even if this was no more patent at that moment than during the first mirror, would find its full significance during the three days following, 1, 2, and 3 February. That is indeed what happened with regard to the metonymic role of the specular image, that of Nadia and I, in the oral and scopic registers.

If we limit ourselves to the dominant facts of the session of 1 February which preceded the fourth and fifth mirrors, we can note:

1. Nadia's intense look at my face, accompanied by "ma-ma-ma," that is, the coupling of the scopic with the signifier.

2. The return to the scopic object of which I would be the bearer, when, having snatched off my glasses, she pressed both of my eyes for a long while.

3. The passage to orality when, again, she nibbled my chin while drooling. I told her then again that she could not absorb me and that there were two of us.

4. Her response was, moreover, the same as the day before, at least in the way she smeared her face with her hands drenched in cereal.

5. Again, she touched my eyes and looked for my glasses as if she wanted to return them to me, a movement she started but that was stopped halfway, while she babbled intensely.

In these five points Nadia had shown, if this was still necessary, the persistent relation between the image included, if we could say so, on the surface of my eyes and the substitutive equivalent she made for it with the cereal she smeared herself with. The oral object was thus only a surface object and brought her satisfaction, as she showed me when smeared with it, only on the level of the "being seen" or the "getting herself seen" by me, on that day.

Just as she had done the previous day, before going to the mirror, she hugged me tightly around the neck with both arms, which brought her smeared cheek against mine, and furthermore, put her mouth to my shoulder while drooling. Thus our bodily relations were not only on the surface; the hole of her mouth participated actively, making the synthesis between the two preceding moments of nibbling and smearing.

It was the same structure that Nadia projected in her relation to the consulting room when, babbling nonstop, she went to explore the opaque surface of the wall as far as the hole of the window through which her look was directed toward the outside. This introduced for the first time, just as clearly, a beyond of the pure surface, that is, a third dimension that founded an exterior and an interior, not only of the room, but of her body. It was like the look that could not emerge from the surface of the eye unless it could pass through what represented a hole in that surface.

On the way back she led me to the table in front of the mirror: it was the fourth mirror. All inhibition had disappeared with respect to the look she gave her own reflection, and mine, before turning around toward me, toward my real presence as a body. For the first time, touching would concern the specular image as it had up to that time concerned the surface of my eyes. It is true that here too it was a question of surface, that of the mirror.

If Nadia stamped her feet and shook the mirror when touching her image, it was because she had just made a considerable leap forward in relation to the previous experience of the succession of wall and window. Here the surface and the hole were conjoined; the hole lost its Real character because it now corresponded to the surface of the mirror. That is why she shook it, as if to test the disappearance of the real hole and the appearance of her image in a hole that was not a hole, which placed her image in a derealized plane, where its unitary meaningfulness—its function of gathering together—led Nadia to the true conclusion of her trajectory since the first mirror: the metonymic function of her image. That is to say, it did not have a substitutive function, but a function of connection between this image and her.

If proof were needed of her approach toward her own image it would lie in her attitude toward mine. Indeed, the caution with which she touched my reflection was a sign of the fear she had that my image was perhaps my substitute, my double, whose Real dimension would deprive her of me. At once she snuggled herself into my arms to escape this metaphoric substitution that still conjoined, as we can see, the image and a certain Real. But she was strong enough from her own experience of the relation of her real body and her image, from her experience of previous mirrors, notably the second, to make me enter into the mirror and tinge the Real of my body with it, when she stole a glance, however rapid, toward it in order to see our image.

That the dialectic of the Real and the signifier was in question when Nadia wanted to explore the whole building and feel the consistency of all the objects she encountered follows from the fact that it was no longer a question of the derealization of the objects she baptized with the spoon when the Real of those objects bothered her and when she could, with the help of a metonymic object, diminish their consistency. It was a question of an opposite movement here; that is, starting from the ex-sistence of the image, Nadia wanted to refind the consistency of objects. One could add that the ex-sistence of the image, when Nadia shook the mirror, did not go without a need to control its per-sistence. She verified this when she asked to return for the fifth time in front of the mirror, where she repeated the same scene as before the fourth mirror a quarter of an hour earlier. She was less tense and smiled more—it is true that I kept my arm around her—and followed in the mirror her movement of seeking the status of her reflection. What was at issue was what corresponded to the existence of this image, as if this latter could only persist against the background of the consistency of the external world; as if the signifier could not articulate itself in its metonymic connections other than with the consistency of a world of real objects, whose only quality is to consist.

The spoon allowed her, in its role of metonymic signifier, to eliminate a too-much of consistency from the objects; the mirror pushed her to reestablish a consistency of objects, which the ex-sistence of her reflection and mine risked contaminating, abolishing even.

On 2 February Nadia followed the same circuit as on the day before, between the surface of my eyes that she touched lingeringly and a surface of skin, hers and mine, united in smearing. Similarly, she explored the wall of the room up to the hole of the window. For the first time she addressed me not in an invoking "ma-ma-ma" but in a "mama" that designated me.

The seventh mirror concerned above all the image of us together, which she had hardly looked at during the fourth and fifth mirrors. Though she smiled cheerfully, she still questioned the surface of the mirror by hitting it with a building block, with an excited expression, as if on the surface of the mirror she was making the same attempt to separate the image as transitivism had imposed on her: what was on her eye was necessarily on mine too.

During the eighth mirror, which began the session of 8 February, Nadia made an inverse attempt concerning the importance of the Real of my body and my image: as I really had to go out twice while she was being prepared, she frankly turned away from the mirror when we passed in front of it. What she lost when I absented myself prevented her from re-experiencing the same loss in front of the mirror.

There followed a return backward, during the session, when Nadia came back to the bottle. To be sure, her interest in the bottle was no longer in what it was as an object to be consumed or not: here it was only the object of destruction. All the while she was babbling imperiously and, twice, came to hide between my knees, saying "mama, mama." Because of my absences at the beginning, which she had tolerated so badly, the bottle became a luring and deceiving object. It was as such that she actively rejected it and eliminated oral access to it, pushing the nipple into the neck. No question any more of sucking what deceived.

Her distress turned into violence against the object representing me; the repetition of a violence that was not so distant and that she knew between the first and second mirrors when her destructive bent was a consequence of the absence of my reflection in the mirror. That violence was in any case itself a repetition of the pre-specular violence that appeared after Nadia drank from the bottle on 12 December. It was, then, not surprising that it was this same object that was substitution and metaphor of the Other in its insufficiency. In the dynamism that animated Nadia at that moment, it was not a question of her turning this substitutive object into the center of a regret where she would seek refuge by fixing herself there; she only expressed her very understandable violence against me by means of it, and that is why the displacement onto the bottle was here only the occasion of a turning point without any symptom formation. Furthermore, the relay of this metaphorical object, simultaneous and not successive, was taken up, as we have seen, by the spoon: Nadia did not fail, indeed, to eat the pudding with both hands, smearing herself copiously with it, reserving for me the empty spoon which she put into my mouth—a lure for me this time—before putting it away, for future use, in the ark.

Following which, again, as between the fourth and fifth mirrors, she wanted to explore the building and feel the consistency of all the objects; and she recognized the bathtub. Each time she touched an object she laughed and looked at me: that is to say, that through me she made sure of another order, not the one of objects, but of the signifiers in the Other that I was.

These are the premises of what she would look for during the ninth mirror. She fully accepted our reflection there, finding herself in my arms, and experienced the pressing of her cheek against mine, without, however, forgetting in the end, a more direct relation of bodies where she buried her head in my neck.

It is true that something of that order remained to be articulated, because she subsequently took me to the window to look outside. Was that telling me that it concerned the aftereffects of that violence which prevented her, during the eighth mirror, from accepting the specular image and forced her to return to objects?

She would now no longer demand the mirror until 9 February. What dominated the five following sessions—perhaps it was in relation to the fragility, for Nadia, of the specular image, mine above all, which she experienced on 31 January, during the third mirror—was a certain return to the spoon and its metonymic function.

To start with, the spoon, as signifier that represented her, was coupled with the doll, a more figurative representation of herself. This doll, on 4 February, was to have replaced the spoon at the bottom of the ark; but as Nadia did not succeed in getting the doll inside, she put back the spoon.

This substitution, even if it failed, indicated clearly the passage, which is always possible, from a metonymic to a metaphoric representation, indeed, even the possibility for a subject of affecting a metonymic representative with a metaphoric dimension. The remainder of the session demonstrated that such an attempt was indeed at issue. Nadia came back for an instant to the bottle, which she even briefly lifted to her lips before throwing it down. Then she had me bounce her on my knees, refinding the bodily pleasure of the start of the analysis. Then she moved on to the exploration of the wall, then the window from which she looked at the outside world—something she would do several times in the course of these sessions: that is to say, that she came back to what she was doing, on 1 February, before the fourth mirror, before the moment when the hole was integrated into the plane of the mirror, as if she wanted to refind behind the pane the Real of objects. What is the status of the pane in relation to the mirror? That is a question that was to come into its own in the treatment of Marie-Françoise.

But Nadia's dynamism and her aura of freedom already bore witness to the fact that it was more a case of questioning than of regression. She said so, in any case, on 6 February, when, after pushing over the bottle and letting forth an imperious "a-ga," she leaned on the pane and tapped it happily with her spoon. The continuation of her babbling, her "mamas" accompanied by tenderness in my arms, or as a distress call when she was afraid of the older children after the session of 6 February, showed that her trajectory was following its course, preparing other mirrors.

Other mirrors, for the mirror became the only locus of her image: for the last time, on 4 February, she snatched my glasses and, for the last time, she touched only one of my eyes lingeringly. The question had already been posed for Nadia—concerning the foot she extended to me on 10 December and the shoe afterward—of the sense of this doubling, or rather, the reduction of a bodily object that is double to a unity when it enters discourse as a signifier, and when it loses its character of bodily attribute, of the body as bearer of objects or images. It would thus be the last time that she would touch the surface of my eyes, or rather, of my eye: this singular was a linguistic reference.

Furthermore, my glasses would now change status and become a signifier representing me. It was, indeed, on 6 February that she made a clear demonstration of this when she deposited my glasses and her spoon side by side, in the ark she had emptied, finding again what she had already attained by anticipation at the end of the 10 December session, that is, that a signifier represents a subject for another signifier. For her, the ark containing my glasses and her spoon was also a treasure she would hold close to her heart.

This signifying realization created the space in which she would situate herself, that is, a closed three-dimensional space, with a bottom she assured herself of by feeling it. If those objects lost all (identifiable) character of what they represented metonymically qua signifiers (the field of *Vorstellung*), the link yet remained between them and what they were as representatives (*Repräsentanzen*), through the intermediary of this spatial dimension; for it was also that of the room in which we both found ourselves, and which she then wanted to explore with obvious delight.

10 / The Mirror 3—The Third Term: The Name-of-the-Father; the Ego Ideal

On 9 February, I found Nadia standing up, holding onto a crib. As soon as she saw me, she shook herself violently, then shook the crib. I felt she was in a violent mood. I went over to her; she continued to shake herself and looked at me furiously. She had it in for me, both because of the day before and because she had heard me talking in the corridor to another child I was treating.

I had heard the nurse say to her, "You're not to go out!" and close the door again. When I went in, a child was crying: it was Nadia. I said to her that she had heard me, but the door was closed, and I could understand that she was disappointed.

She carried on shaking the crib for a moment, then held out her arms to me, but still looked furious.

She was violent throughout the entire session. It was not the same quality of violence as she had shown a month before, which had been directed at objects and at the external world; at that time, she had been relaxed whenever I was involved and showed a violent negativism toward everything that was not me: she was able to wipe out some of her past thanks to the bond that had been established. *This particular day's violence was directed at me;* I was the cause of it. Even though she still expressed her violence through the medium of objects, it was no longer with the same tonality; it was addressed specifically to me, in her face and in her body language. I had caused her to be born: she had emotions again; and I was making her suffer.

She grabbed a little plastic container from the ark. She threw it down once; from then on she did not let go of it until the end of the session. She sucked it, nibbled it, pretended to drink out of it, and kept putting her hand into it. She took the little dish and the cup out of the ark, but threw them down and took no further notice of them.

She came onto my lap, got down again, stamped her feet, licked the spoon from the dish of cereal, threw down the chocolate, and came back onto my lap with a cracker. She ate a little piece, got me to eat some of it, ate a little more herself, and got down again, still holding onto it.

Then she took the sailor out of the ark, put it back again, and threw the blocks around. She sat down with her little plastic container, put her hand in it, and then pretended to drink out of it; she was not happy. I told her it was empty, just like the little cup and the little dish, but that there was milk in the bottle and cereal in the dish. By way of reply, she took the bottle, tipped it upside down, and shook it so that milk would spurt onto the floor; then she turned it the right way up and held it up by the nipple.

She came back into my arms and stretched out, still furious; then she climbed down next to the ark so she could take out *a little car, which she wanted to put into the little container.* She managed to get it in, but as she pulled her hand out she turned the container upside down, so the car fell out; twice, however, she held the container the right way up and delightedly rattled it with the car inside; she then took the car out with her hand.

She wanted to get into the crib; she threw down the container and put her arms around my neck, hugging me tightly, so that I would take her out of the crib, and then she stayed in my arms.

I took her back to her room. She was in my arms and wanted me to stop *in front of the mirror. She put her cheek to my mouth and watched intently in the mirror as I kissed her. Then she turned her head, put her mouth to my cheek, and imitated the long, slow kiss she had felt me give her as she watched it in the mirror.* It was an astonishing scene, above all because of the deep emotion that marked her expression.

After that, the separation was very difficult, the more so because Nadia had seen another child crying on the lap of one of the nurses and had turned away abruptly from this spectacle, hugging me tightly around the neck with one arm and showing me the door with the other. I calmed her down somewhat, but she was still crying as I left.

On 10 February, I put Nadia's shoes and socks on for her; there was no nurse. She did not throw down her shoes and held out her feet to me, babbling a great deal.

In the session she threw the cloth out of the ark, so that she could get the little plastic container; she took it with her and stopped next to the dish of pudding, licking and nibbling the container, while her gaze rested on the pudding; she babbled. She put her other hand to her mouth, and I noticed that she had brought with her from her own room a crust of bread, which she now ate.

She pushed her hand into the container and babbled imperiously as she took note of its emptiness. I said to her that yes, it was empty, but that there was milk, pudding, crackers, and chocolate. She licked the little container again, moving her gaze from me to the dish. I said to her that maybe she wanted some pudding in her container: she held it out to me, I put a little in it for her, and gave it back to her. She took it, babbling fast and imperiously, looked inside, and emptied it out onto the floor: she looked intensely satisfied with herself.

She came onto my lap and stretched out, very relaxed, chuckling gently. She played with her feet a little and then got down again.

She threw the little dish and cup out of the ark and took out a transparent ball that contained water and three ducks. She brought the ball with her as she climbed back onto my lap. She shook the ball, looked at it, tried to catch one of the ducks, and *made sure I took part in the game.* Finally, she played with the ball, as she almost lay in my arms.

She threw the ball down, got down herself, rolled it along on the floor like a regular ball, went to explore the wall and the windowpane, and came back every now and then to stretch out for a minute on my lap.

As I took her back, I had to stand her up *in front of the mirror. She started playing the previous day's kissing game again, with the same degree of intensity; she tapped the mirror excitedly but not aggressively. While looking in the mirror, she noticed a nurse she knew; she looked at her image with great interest, and without the slightest hesitation or caution, she turned her head to see the nurse in reality. She laughed at her discovery, wrapped her arms around my neck, and put her cheek next to mine. I did not feel this time that she was seeking refuge with me, but that she was getting me to share in her joy in this discovery, in this progress toward life.*

She was very happy, and this was the big event of the session.

On 12 February Nadia had been moved back into her old room. I found her rocking quite violently, hitting her back against the side of the crib. She did not look well, and she had dark rings around her eyes as if she were about to have an attack of otitis.

In the session, she took the cloth out of the ark and *babbled,* "*pa-pa-pa.*" It was the first time I had heard her say this, and yet it is usually the first thing a child says. She could say a number of other things, always with the same structure, beginning with "a-": "a-ga, a-poum, a-da, a-ca," as well as "ma-ma-ma" and "mama."

She put a corner of the cloth into her mouth, then threw it down and picked up the little plastic container, which she licked as she sat on my lap. She got down and pushed over everything that was on the little table: the dish of cereal, the chocolate, and the crackers. She spilled some of the cereal on the table and the rest on the floor. She hung onto the spoon and used her hand to spread the pool of cereal all over the table; she licked her hand only once, and then just barely. She walked around the crib a little, then went to put the cloth back into the ark; at the same time she took out the sailor and the ball with the ducks inside. She got ready to play with the ball on my lap, but it slipped out of her grasp; she babbled furiously. She climbed down to pick it up, put it back in the ark, emptied everything else out of the latter, and then put her spoon next to the ball.

She wanted to get into the crib, but once there, she felt ill at ease, as she did wherever she went that day. She put her arms around my neck and her cheek to mine; I took her out of the crib, and she stayed in this position for some minutes. Then she went to fetch her spoon from the ark, but she put it back right away: she had just noticed a file of temperature charts on the radiator, and she wanted me to give it to her. I put it on the floor; she inspected it from all sides and enjoyed opening and closing the mechanism; she put her foot inside it. She ended up sitting down, as she had slipped on her shoes; she tried to pull them off, but I had to do it for her. She pulled off her socks herself, babbling intensely. She took one sock in each hand, waved them in all directions, babbling all the while, and then hit her shoes on the floor. She wanted to put them into the ark with the ball with the ducks inside. Then she picked up the ark and held it close, delightedly. She put it down gently and used her socks to hit the puddle of pudding, babbling; she was both excited and dissatisfied.

I took her back to her room and gave her to one of the nurses. I picked her up once more because she was crying and then I left. But I heard her crying inconsolably, so I went back and picked her up again. She cried a little, wrapping her arms tightly around my neck. At that moment the trainee came back, and Nadia held out her arms to her; but when the trainee made to pick her up, she hugged me even tighter. Then she wanted to go *in front of the mirror.*

She looked at all three of us, herself, me, and the trainee. She turned away as if from something unpleasant, *kissed my cheek, and bit my chin.*

Eventually she agreed to let me put her into the trainee's arms.

On 13 February, she was still suffering the effects of a mild attack of otitis, very much on edge.

In the session, she would touch neither the dish of cereal nor the chocolate. *It was only empty receptacles for food that would transiently arouse her violence.* As on the previous day, she was very ill at ease.

She started by inspecting a toy rabbit made of rags. She took the sailor out of the ark and put it into my hand; she looked at it and then put it back into the ark. She took out the ball with the ducks inside and licked it; then she put it down and took out the cloth. Underneath the cloth, she discovered a pink doll's tea set; she picked it up and threw it on the floor. She became very angry with it, trampling on it and hitting it with a building block.

She came and relaxed on my lap. She walked around the crib a little and came back to sit at my feet and put the sailor and some wooden animals back into the ark. She did this several times in succession, simply for the joy of taking things out and putting them back in, or putting things outside and then inside. She babbled profusely.

She remained fidgety and *did not settle down except briefly in my arms.* She wanted to play with the file of temperature charts, then I felt she was looking for something that was not there.

I took her back to her room and realized *it was the mirror she had been looking for.* She wanted me to stand her up in front of it. *She looked at us in it, laughed, got me to kiss her, shook the mirror, got me to kiss her again, looking attentively in the mirror, and turned around to kiss me. She did not try to kiss the image in the mirror.*

Then she noticed the trainee in *the mirror, smiled at her image, as she recognized her, and turned around toward her.* The trainee held out her arms to her, but Nadia clung onto my neck. I spoke to her gently and handed her to the trainee; but when I had got as far as the door, she changed her mind and held out her arms to me.

Nevertheless, I went away for a few minutes; when I came back, I found Nadia looking radiant, walking around, holding the trainee's hand. She went back and forth twice in front of me, looking at me and babbling. She clung onto me, hugged me around the neck, licked me, kissed me, and buried her head in my shoulder. I carried her around for a moment, then told her she was going to go back to the trainee. She watched me as I was speaking, then leaned toward the trainee, who held out her arms to her; but Nadia's face was sad. I left.

One of the nurses said to me that Nadia was full of life, and affectionate. She told me that Nadia had been able to reach the *drawer* of a table, by shaking her crib, and *had opened it, taken everything out, and put it in her crib;* she had shown particular interest in a piece of glass.

The following day, 14 February, Nadia had a high temperature and had to have another paracentesis, on one side only. I stayed with her for a while, but could not take her away for a session.

On 15 February she was much better, but had lost about two pounds and had diarrhea.

In the session, she started by taking the cloth out of the ark; she got me to admire it, prodded it a great deal, put it on my lap, without letting go of it, and returned to put it back in the ark. While she was doing this, she discovered a little Russian box and picked it up. She threw it down, then set it upright on the floor; she seemed delighted at the way it balanced. She walked around a little, holding the box, babbled a great deal, articulating several syllables, especially "a-poum-ca-da," joined together as if they were a word. She came back and sat on my lap; there, she *played with the little box, pushed her index finger into it, and made a stirring movement with it, saying "ca-ca-ca"; she also put her tongue into it. Then she put the box into my mouth,* but without letting go of it. She even tried to put my glasses into it, but when she realized this was not possible, she threw them down violently.

She took practically everything out of the ark, especially the doll's tea set, but was not interested in it. Then she took out the sailor, put my glasses into the ark, and put back the sailor. She came back onto my lap and relaxed completely; leaning against me, she played with the little box for some time, then got down again and went over to the ark to get out and put back the ball with the ducks inside. At that moment, one of her shoes came off, and she sent it flying. Then she threw the little box high up against the wall and walked over to pick it up.

Now she wanted to get into the crib with the little box and the cloth, which she had taken out of the ark as she went past. She babbled a great deal, waving the cloth in all directions, without violence, the way you wave a handkerchief; she was looking at me and smiling. Once she threw it down and got me to pick it up, then she waved it again. Finally, she stood up, came into my arms, and put hers around my neck.

I took her back; she turned away from the door of her room and hit me on the shoulder, babbling discontentedly as I opened the door. But when she saw the trainee in the room, she gave her a lovely smile and held out her arms to her. As soon as the trainee came close, she drew back, burst out laughing, and waved her cloth. As the trainee kept trying, Nadia hugged me tightly around the neck, nestled her head on my shoulder, and kissed me with a slight sucking motion. *She enjoyed this game immensely: to pretend she was going into the trainee's arms and then to nestle up to me: that made her burst out laughing.*

Then she turned toward the mirror and stood up in front of it. In addition to our two reflections, *she saw the trainee's; she laughed at this new image and turned around quickly to laugh at the reality of the person.* The trainee held out her arms to her, but Nadia clung to me, laughing. She looked at both of us for a long time—the trainee and me—in the mirror, then came back into my arms to give me a kiss, but without any sucking motion.

She stood up on the table again to pick up a spoon, then another one after she had come back into my arms. I started to prepare her for my departure. The trainee held out her arms to her. Nadia went to her without crying, still turned toward me; her whole body indicated her rejection of the trainee.

At dinner time, I heard a child crying in distress. I thought it was Nadia; a nurse told me I was right. As she must have heard me, I went to see. The nurse had started to serve the dinner in such a way that Nadia would be the last. She was crying with one fist pushed into her mouth. As soon as she saw me, she stood up and held out her arms to me, in supplication. She snuggled up to me energetically and immediately her crying stopped. In a few minutes she was smiling again and had rediscovered her interest in something other than food. She showed a great deal of interest in the garden, which was covered in snow, and babbled. She wanted to go out of the room, but then her turn came to be fed.

As I could neither leave her nor feed her, I kept her on my lap, sitting on the edge of her crib, while the nurse quickly pushed the food into her. The whole time, she leaned her head against me, wriggling her feet and legs and looking at me frequently.

When her dinner was finished, she wanted to sit in my arms again and then to go up to *the mirror. In front of the mirror, she got me to kiss her, kissed me herself, and smiled rapturously at me as she looked at my reflection.* She bent down to pick up a spoon and put it into my mouth. Before picking up another one, she used her hand to pick up some food that was left in a dish and ate it. She came back into my arms, bringing the two spoons with her. When I said some words to her, she repeated *"cuillère"* (spoon) for the first time and looked at me very proudly.

A child started crying at that moment and Nadia snuggled up close to me, anxious as ever when she heard anyone crying.

I calmed her down and gave her back to one of the nurses.

When I arrived on 16 February, Nadia had shaken her crib so much that it was up against the one next to it. She had a rather grumpy expression, but looked better and no longer had a temperature. I took her away barefoot, because she threw down her socks and shoes, and there was no nurse to put them on for her; she clearly was not going to allow me to do it.

She noticed immediately that there was something new in the ark: there were two nesting boxes. She picked them up and did not let them go for the next ten minutes. When she took them out of the ark, they came apart; she took one in each hand. She probed inside them, licked the smaller one a little, and walked across the room, still holding them and babbling. She put the smaller one back inside the other, but could not manage to take it out again. She became irritated, stamped her foot, and jabbered furiously; she threw them down violently, which made them separate; she looked at them for a moment, dumbfounded, then quickly turned her back on them, walked right behind the crib, and bent down to look underneath; that meant she could see the boxes again, and she babbled joyfully and looked at me with a happy expression. She walked off again and picked up one in each hand. *It was a little like a game of hide-and-seek,* and she did it again. Earlier, she had taken the sailor out of the ark, put it back inside, and had come to hide her head on my shoulder. As she got down, she felt my stocking on my knee, put her open mouth to it, and slowly closed it a little.

After this scene, she went to the table, licked the spoon, used it to knock down the chocolate and a cracker, and then put the spoon into the ark. She took it out again and came onto my lap; on the way, she knocked over the bottle. Then she licked the spoon and got me to lick it. She went back down onto the floor, and for several minutes played at throwing the spoon from the other side of the ark and leaning over to pick it up. She started babbling joyfully again, smiling with a teasing look: "ca-da, a-poum-ca-da!"

She went back to the little table and put the spoon in the dish. She turned around, pointing her behind at me, looked at my knees, and waited. I sat her on my lap and she tried to pull the table toward her; I helped her to do it and she looked at me delightedly. She made herself comfortable, rested her head against my breast for a few moments, looked at me tenderly, then *sat up at the table*. Bringing the dish toward her with one hand, *she clumsily filled the spoon with squashed banana and ate it*. She seemed to be wondering whether it was good or not; then she put the spoon down on the table and *got me to join her in eating* almost all of what was left in the dish. At the beginning, her face was tense, because in the process quite a lot of banana was falling onto her diaper, her legs, and my white coat. Then she relaxed and started to find it funny. Eventually, she *slowly tipped out what was left in the dish onto the table* and threw the dish on the floor. *She got down and stood on the upside-down dish with both feet. Then she stamped each foot in turn on the bottom of the dish*, with the attitude, expression, and babbling of someone who has taken possession of something they dearly wanted. Then she turned to me with a radiant and triumphant expression.

She came back onto my lap and spread the banana over the table with her hand, eating a little of it from time to time.

When I took her back she was in very good shape. She looked as well as she had done before the attack of otitis.

She wanted to go *in front of the mirror. She looked at us in it, keeping her eyes fixed on this image; she leaned her head against my cheek, then against my mouth. I kissed her, she smiled at me in the mirror, then turned around to kiss me*, after putting her arms around my neck.

It was easier to persuade her to go into the arms of one of the nurses when I left.

The next day, 17 February, I found Nadia standing, holding herself up with one hand on the lap of one of the nurses; with the other hand she was hitting the child who was sitting on the nurse's lap. The nurse told her, with a laugh, that she was getting too jealous.

In the room, she walked around a great deal, joyfully; she tipped over a dish of stewed fruit, but kept the spoon.

She wanted to go out, and she explored the whole building, including the kitchen, where she demanded *some jam*, which she usually refused to eat. But on this day, *she ate it from a spoon, demanded some more,* and kept the spoon, which she licked while I carried her back to her room.

On the landing we met Robert the Wolf Child, who followed us. He held out a little Christmas tree decoration to her, which she took delightedly; she looked at me and wriggled her legs for joy. After Robert had gone, another little boy held out a cracker to her; her face shone, and she wriggled her legs even more.

Getting away was to prove difficult.

On 18 February, Nadia was in her crib when I arrived; she had shaken it all the way over to the window, so that she could see out. I tried again—as I had on 8 February—to take her to the *room where I usually held the sessions,* given that she liked a change of environment and a chance to explore. She was breathing more heavily as I carried her there, but she was not holding herself rigid. She was a little afraid, and her reflex was to hold on to me tightly, particularly during the brief moment when we passed from one building to the other; at that moment she pressed her forehead so hard against my cheek, it felt as if she wanted to get inside it.

She sat on my lap as always and looked at everything in the new room. She picked up a piece of chocolate-covered rice and sucked it. Then she noticed a box I had filled with sand—I had thought it would be more appropriate for her than the big sandbox—and *she babbled "ca-da"* and got down and plunged her hand into *the sand.* Then she put her hand to her mouth, which was sticky, so that some sand stuck to it; she grimaced, started to cry, and came onto my lap. I wiped her mouth for her and she got down again, babbling "ca-da." She looked at the ark and her usual toys, but did not touch them.

She got back onto my lap and pulled the dish over toward her. She opened her mouth and looked alternately at me and the rice, leaning toward the rice and waiting. "Do you want some?" She smiled and pushed her dish toward my hand. I gave her a spoonful; *she wanted me to feed her about half of the rice; eventually she ate it herself, first with the spoon, and then with her hand.*

While I was feeding her or she was feeding herself, she kicked her legs for joy, her face lit up, and she looked at me radiantly.

She got down from my lap to have a look at what was inside the ark; although she did not throw around the doll's tea set, she held onto one of the little cups.

She came back to the table and used the spoon to push the chocolate and the crackers onto the floor and then moved toward the door.

I took her back to her room; she wanted me to take her out again to walk around. I stayed with her for another quarter of an hour and I found it hard to leave her.

Up until 1 March, when I went to collect her, she would do with me whatever I did with her: I would arrive and leave; *so she started off by leaving so that she could then come into my arms.* In those sessions, she expressed her annoyance with me for not being there all the time; in parallel, she became attached to a nurse who showed some affection toward her, or rather, whom she had seduced, for this nurse had not particularly liked her—one could even say she was rather a hard person—but now she was teaching Nadia a great deal.

Nadia would have liked a lot from me. I could feel her keenness, but she was quite capable of exploiting this keenness with others apart from me, especially when she was feeling resentful toward me.

On 22 February, she would have liked to go to the new consulting room, but I did not dare take her from one building to another, as it was very cold.

She stayed in my arms by the window; she looked out into the garden and watched the people who were out there. She babbled in a special way; she would concentrate hard before articulating something: *she was not babbling anymore; she was on the verge of speech.*

She took me out into the corridor and into another room. She examined everything, including the children, but always referred back to me. She took me back into the room to eat some pudding. *She ate half of it and tipped out the rest, while pushing away my mouth.*

She did not want to go back to her own room and took me to the bathroom.

On 23 February, we were still in the old consulting room. First she threw down the nesting boxes, then she walked around, making sucking noises. She took the toys out of the ark, babbling a great deal, and looking very alert.

Twice in a row she took me to the door, turned around, took three steps inside the room, and wanted to come into my arms.

She got down and tipped over the bottle, then sat on my lap, pulled the dish of squashed banana toward her, ate some of it, tipped it onto the floor, and used the spoon to knock off the crackers and the chocolate as well.

Then she took me into the other rooms and into the bathroom, but this time it was not just to explore—it was to show me what her everyday world looked like.

On 27 February it was warm enough to go to the other building and use the new consulting room. I found Nadia playing with another child; when she saw me, she threw away her toy and held out her arms to me. Her right ear was suppurating again and she was teething.

In the session, she looked at everything, touched the sand, and threw down the crackers and chocolate. She came onto my lap to take the spoon and ate just a little; she was more interested in sucking the spoon.

On 1 March she was standing up when I arrived, having cornered a little boy whom she wanted to stop from going away. When she saw me, she babbled: "heug-gheu!" in a deep and loud voice. She hit the other child and came to settle herself in my arms with a radiant smile.

As soon as she was in the new consulting room, as in the preceding session, she looked at everything there was, laughing, and *walked toward the door babbling "ca-ca-ca," "po-po-po."* Since I knew that she was put on the potty twice a day, and that she did it without any difficulty, I said to her that maybe she wanted us to go find a potty. She walked to the staircase. I picked her up to go find the potty, and then we went back into the consulting room. I put the potty down by the crib.

I sat down, and Nadia got down to fetch the potty. She was almost delirious with joy with the potty; she fingered it, put it down, picked it up again, and held it to her. I told her how happy she was to have the potty for herself, and to do with it whatever she wanted, because she knew I would not ask anything of her, she could do as she pleased, and that made her happy.

She put her hand *inside the potty* and fingered the edges. Then she took off my glasses and put them into it, headed for the door, went out, and *walked triumphantly in the corridor, still carrying her potty;* eventually my glasses fell out.

She went from room to room with her potty, just as she had

done the first time she had grabbed and held her spoon so triumphantly. She babbled a great deal; every now and then she would get me to carry her, still holding onto her potty. She kept looking at me in a way that was both tender and slightly comical.

When she put the potty down for a moment, she would either walk around it, babbling intensely, or she would go off into another room, only to come back very quickly, find her potty again, and pick it up.

She walked all the way back from the session, *still holding her potty*. She came into my arms and wanted to be stood up *in front of the mirror. Clearly, she wanted to see herself in it, carrying her potty in both her hands. She laughed delightedly and shook the mirror a little, very excited; she leaned the potty against it for a moment in order to hold it even closer to her.*

She came back into my arms, still holding the potty, and *noticed a key on a cupboard. She wanted to pick it up and put it in the potty.* She got me to sit down on the floor and sat on my lap so that she could play with the key in the potty. She wanted me to help her defend the potty if another child tried to take it away.

On that day, she was almost speaking.

This third phase consisted of seven mirrors, between 9 and 16 February. Plus one: 1 March would be Nadia's last explicit reference to the mirror.

On 9 February, from the start, Nadia introduced jealousy proper into her relationship with me. It was no longer the *invidia* she had shown at the beginning, the state of being completely focused on the other supposed to be satisfied by what the Other has bestowed. Now the violent and aggressive reproach was addressed to me, apparently at least.

Does that mean that the passage from *invidia* to jealousy would be the passage from the relation to the other to the relation to the Other? We cannot answer this question without taking up again the points of structure inherent in the situations of *invidia* and jealousy, which takes us directly, as we shall see, to the introduction of the third term in the mirror.

The *invidia* at the beginning of the treatment manifested itself only (exclusively) in my presence. I was necessary to it as a unique and real presence. It did not seem that Nadia showed any signs of it in my absence, judging only from the nurses' report of her state of amorphous collapse. So we had present in this first tableau a unique Other, not interchangeable, present in the Real, and an other, whoever it might be, who was interchangeable: it was necessary and sufficient that this other came close to or attracted the attention of the Other.

The tableau of jealousy is structurally rather different. There, the Other is no longer unique; I did not need to be present in reality. The nurses testified to this when they spoke of Nadia "really getting too jealous." The Other had become interchangeable, even if, within the transference, it was to me more particularly that Nadia expressed her intolerance of seeing or hearing me giving attention to another child. From *invidia* to jealousy, the status of the Other had changed: for Nadia it had acquired its specular image. More than that, it was on course—and this would happen during the last mirrors—for taking a place which, far from being unique, entered into relations with other Others. Of course this did not mean that they would occupy the place of Other of the Other—which would have referred Nadia back to that multiplicity of Others she had always known, without any possible relationship with one of them. If a relationship was possible for her, it was because the Other had acquired its signifying dimension, metonymic to her own desire, and so able to establish links with other signifiers—this was the case with my glasses and her spoon. The Other had lost its exclusively Real dimension, exterior to her, and thereby gained the possibility of being represented by other adults.

Only, the other did not follow the same path; it remained still in the state of an object partaking too much of the Real, and, as such, it attracted Nadia's aggressivity and destructive violence—which she had evinced for example on 19 January when I found her engaged in hitting two children again and again, only looking at me to see how I accepted her violence. She reserved the same fate for the doll. Certainly, this dimension of the Real of the other was blunted in the play of the relation to the Other, acquiring a signifying imprint in the form of its place as possible metaphorical object for the Other. But what it would not acquire was a specular image—she would never look at it in the mirror. In this sense it retained a nonspecularizable character that placed it on the level of object a: from the start of the treatment the small other had always had this role of object a of the Other for Nadia.

Thus, this jealousy was chiefly concerned with the Other, with the questioning by the subject of the lack of the Other, which, we may recall, Nadia started doing from 27 October on, in anticipation, when I took away my hand from the neighboring child's crib.

Jealousy is the question the subject puts to the Other concerning what the subject itself is for this Other, and no longer, as in *invidia,* the question of the object of the Other that satisfies the other.

The place of the Other would evolve with the succeeding mirrors. On 9 February, having expressed her jealousy at the start of the session and her aggressivity against me later on, it was from the mirror, at the end of the session, that Nadia asked for confirmation that she was truly my object, by putting her cheek to my lips and following the kisses I gave her intently in the mirror. To be my object, but not just any object: my oral object. As a prior condition to this she had to have stripped it of any dimension of devoration, and in the most radical fashion, by pretending to drink from a small empty container, even confirming its emptiness by plunging her hand into it before throwing it away and taking no further notice of it. The oral object in question was a "nothing": any Real it had had was banished from it, only the signifier remained, so that it became the metaphorical object in the true sense: separated from the Real. There remained only the profound emotion Nadia showed in front of the mirror at taking the place of such an object for me.

It was the same game she repeated the following day when, with great satisfaction, she emptied onto the floor the bit of pudding she had asked me to put into the little container; all this before going in front of the mirror, where she played the same scene as the day before. During this eleventh mirror, she knocked on the surface with an excited expression that was not aggressive, as if she was rather feeling this surface, a surface that also had to do with a space. She had indeed just had an experience of space in the session, when she found the transparent ball half filled with water and ducks in the ark. She did not fail, to be sure, to explore the surface of this ball, but also to try to catch one of the ducks, in vain, and, moreover, without insistence, before playing with the ball as a regular ball by rolling it on the floor. Just as her experience of space with the ark, in which she had put my glasses and her spoon on 6 February, had incited her to explore the room we were in with some pleasure, so she went, after her game with the ball with the ducks, to feel the wall, and even the windowpane, that is, what separated her from the outside world. The consulting room became the ball; she placed herself, in her playing, as much outside with respect to the ball as on the inside of a container, with me, with respect to the room in the same manner as when she had placed us metonymically inside the ark. But here, the ducks were beyond any grasp, just as the reflection in the mirror was. The bottom of the ark, which she felt when handling my glasses, which themselves still had a real density, was replaced by the surface of the mirror, in front of the objects she saw in it.

The decisive step she made in this eleventh mirror was when she saw the reflection of a nurse she knew. She stopped short and turned without hesitation toward the nurse, laughing and pressing her cheek to mine. A decisive step, to be sure, which required still more of her, since the mirror was radically different from the windowpane and the bottom of the ark. It was there that the world of images truly founded itself; specifically, the image of the Other, which lost its unique character with the blotting out of the Real of its body by the specular. Yet it was a characteristic of the Other that Nadia was not keen to lose, even though, as always, by anticipation—it was not the first time—she showed only the joy of discovery on this first encounter with the third term in the mirror. It was a joy that was far from counterbalancing the loss she underwent since, from the following morning on, she looked as unhealthy as when she was on the point of having an episode of otitis, which she would indeed end up having on 14 February.

The loss she suffered with this encounter of the third term in the mirror was something she had not yet known in my arms in front of this mirror, because she had always immediately compensated the loss included in the specular image by taking refuge against the Real of the consistency of my body: indeed, she had only appeared in front of the mirror when her cheek could be glued to mine. Whatever joy Nadia experienced in finding the nurse's image again in reality, it left her helpless because it was impossible to glue herself to the body of the Other. Her gaze, here, truly "made her eye despair."

Between 12 and 16 February Nadia performed a veritable working through in order to situate the Other as a third term. Her first means was a signifier she uttered for the first time and that designates the third term for any child: "pa-pa-pa." Until then all her phonemes began with a privative "a": "a-pa," "a-ga," "a-poum," "a-da," "a-ca," with the exception of "ma-ma-ma." This signifier "pa-pa" is thrown at the mother, even before the mirror, as an echo of her desire, by children who have not known the destitution of this signifier. For Nadia, it was the point she would arrive at in the sequence that followed but which she had put at the start here. She linked it directly with the cloth she took out of the ark at the same time that she said "pa-pa-pa."

This cloth was not a new element and we saw the veiling dimension Nadia gave it on 24 January when she knocked over the bottle she had veiled with it, by pulling on the cloth without touching the bottle. Similarly, she linked it qua veil with the diaper that veiled her body and to my body that she veiled by putting it on my knees and leaving it there. On 29 January she put it on my knees only in order to pull it off again almost at once, as if she did not know whether she wanted it to play its role of veil or not to be there at all. On 6 February she tried to tear it with her teeth.

The fact that, on 12 February, she took it out of the ark while babbling "pa-pa" linked it to the signifier as veil. She put it back into the ark and took out the sailor and the ball with ducks, metonymic objects, of which the ark had become the site. She then confirmed this by emptying the ark of all toys in order to put back the ball with ducks, her spoon, and finally her shoes, before hugging the ark with a look of delight: it was the reconstituted treasure of her signifiers (ark of the covenant!).

Back from that session, she started a game of peek-a-boo with the trainee, to whom she extended her arms, only to take refuge in mine as soon as the trainee attempted to pick her up. During the twelfth mirror she was confronted with our three reflections. There, her game stopped at once; for if she attempted to tame the image of the third term by means of her game of peek-a-boo, in the Real, here she could only turn from the reflection in the mirror to glue herself to me, her cheek against mine, and nibble at my chin. Exactly as she did on 23 January when, during a scene of tenderness, she passed a stool and her tenderness changed into aggressivity toward me. This aggressivity was due to the loss she suffered in her body, while now she suffered a loss in her gaze before the image of the trainee. Renewal of the loss of the image of 10 December stuck on her eye.

The following day, 13 February, she still had slight otitis and the unease persisted. Nadia lifted the cloth and unveiled a pink doll's tea set; she proceeded to set about the unveiled object with a building block. At the end of that short session she seemed to be looking for something that was not there. What she was looking for was the mirror: she told me so by leading me to it. What she then played in front of it, not without pleasure since she laughed, was the persistence of our reflections: she let herself be kissed, shook the mirror, kissed me while looking at us in the mirror. I noted at that moment that she never once tried to kiss an image in the mirror, either hers or mine: she clearly separated the specular and the Real.

Then she noticed the image of the trainee in the mirror, smiled at the reflection, and turned toward the trainee; but she would truly agree to go into her arms only when I spoke to her: that is, when I gave her my word so that she might accept this Other that the trainee was. Nadia was then going to busy herself actively with accepting this latter, not in the passive mode of sticking herself to her, but in the active mode of walking the length of the room while holding onto the trainee with one hand only.

It seems that, at bottom, her joy was not unmixed, since on 14 February she had an episode of otitis and a high temperature, and, the day after, she not only had diarrhea but also lost two pounds.

She then became very interested in containers, whether it was the drawer she emptied into her crib or, in the session, a little Russian box she found in the ark. She stuck her index finger into it, saying "ca-ca-ca," anticipating what she would say later when she requested the potty during the session, fifteen days later. She then stuck her tongue into it and wanted to put the little box into my mouth, indicating for the first time the structure of the body, as container holed from mouth to anus. The first of all containers had been the ark, with metonymic objects; she wanted to make another one of the Russian box when she tried to put my glasses into it; but, as she failed, she went back to the ark, put my glasses into it, then, successively, the sailor and the ball with ducks. The ark thus kept its role as reserve of signifiers, before the consulting room crib took over this role. This time she herself would climb into it, with the little box and the cloth that she waved like a handkerchief.

She would use the cloth again, on her return, to veil the trainee: then she held out her arms, only to withdraw her offer, laughing loudly. In the mirror that followed, the fourteenth, she would accept the image of the trainee a little better, comparing it with the reality, as she had done for me, in the beginning, in front of the mirror. But if then my real body had been a refuge against the image, here the Real of the trainee provoked nothing but a refusal in Nadia. Between my image and my body she chose my body; between the image and the body of the trainee, one could say she chose the image. It was as if, in the dimension of the Real of the Other, there could only have been one of them—the initial *invidia*—and the presence of any other Other had to pass by way of the image, while awaiting the last dimension, of the signifier. It was the one Nadia would find just after the fifteenth mirror.

She had demanded this mirror after I had come back at dinnertime because I heard her cry with impatience and above all because I thought she had heard me speak to a nurse. She held out her arms, I picked her up, she calmed down, not because I fed her, but because, in my arms, she forgot the food she seemed to be waiting for and looked out through the window at the garden under the snow. When she subsequently wanted to go in front of the mirror, it was to comfort herself by having herself kissed and kissing me, all the while looking at our reflection.

Now, what could not have taken place in this mirror, the third term, was no longer the trainee, but the spoon. That spoon was no longer hers only, but also mine, since she put it into my mouth; and, what is more, she picked up another—one for her and one for me. It was probable that the only reason this game of spoons could proceed in a signifying sense was because, during her dinner, it was not me who fed her and because, during that time, I spoke to her. She demonstrated this separation between food and spoon when, having picked up the second spoon, she ate what remained in the dish with her hand. She came back into my arms with both spoons and there repeated the word "cuillère" very proudly, giving to this signifier the accomplishment of an articulated naming.

She closed the circuit of the third term between the "pa-pa-pa" of 12 February and the "cuillère" of 15 February. What we perceived of the third term in the "pa-pa-pa" had been illustrated and demonstrated between the eleventh and fifteenth mirrors: from the articulation of the image in relation to the Real of the Other's body—as third and as metaphorical place of the lack in the specular image—to the naming of the spoon as signifier of that lack, at the same time annulling the bothersome Real of this third term. After the questioning of the specular image, the naming liberated Nadia, just as my naming allowed her to emerge from her fascination on 10 December. There she had found the signifier that represented her (S_1): here she had again completed a circuit that brought her to the metonymic signifier of the Other (S_2), which was also that of the mythical father.

From the very next day, the spoon fell from this role of signifier that referred Nadia to the primordial signifier of the Other; it was now only an object with use-value. So Nadia stuck it into the dish of rice, asked to be seated at the table, and began to eat with the spoon.

As for the sixteenth encounter with the mirror, the last of this series—because the seventeenth would not take place until two weeks later—Nadia drew a conclusion regarding the status of the image. This time she experimented smilingly with it before agreeing to go into the arms of a nurse when I left, as if the third term was no longer a problem.

The course Nadia followed now appeared clearly as a serial putting into place of the primordial signifiers: "Nadia," "mama," "pa-pa-pa." The spoon, as long as Nadia had not named it, had come to take the place of the object of lack, that is, a place within the field of the signifier, what Nadia could not say, burdened as she was by the Real of my body that she both knew she had to lose but could not accept losing. The naming of the spoon restored the lack to "pa-pa-pa," the existence of which she had first posed by means of the signifier, and the spoon to Nadia, for her to really make use of. What was necessary, in a way, was for her to posit the place of lack, in order to say it with a metonymic representative, that which the mirror could not really give her because she oscillated between the image and the Real body. It was this dimension of appeasement that appeared in outline in the sixteenth mirror; that is why it was practically the last, like a full stop.

In the two weeks that followed, Nadia changed a great deal; these changes were but the effects of what she had conquered in a month with respect to her structure.

Her relations with the external world of objects were marked by the greatest curiosity. It was possible to try a change of consulting rooms once again. Far from being lost, as she was the first time, in those new surroundings, she discovered new things in it, particularly the sand. At that time too, she liked to walk around in the building; in the kitchen, she began to taste the jam she had until then refused to eat in her room.

Toward the end of February, she started to forge richer social links with adults, in particular with a nurse who had become fond of her, or rather, whom she had seduced, which moderated her avidity for me somewhat. In any case, she did to me what I did to her with my alternation of absence and presence: when I arrived, she began by leaving, before returning to my arms.

In relation to the other children, she was prey to a definite jealousy that made her hit them uninhibitedly. She was also able to play with them, even to receive some presents from them.

1 March was a turning point, because of the appearance in center stage, right from the start, of the signifiers "ca-ca-ca" and "po-po-po."

While this was not the first time she had dealt with the potty in a session, since she had already shown an interest between 9 and 14 January, there was now no trace of inhibition whatsoever, which was not the case at the beginning of January. On 1 February she had also evoked the potty by sticking her finger in the little Russian box, saying "ca-ca-ca."

When she took the potty she seemed particularly delighted to notice that the receptacle had a rim and an interior: a very paradox-ical discovery for an infant who, for a long time, had been familiar with this object at least twice a day. But it was truly a discovery, as if the potty had not had a proper existence until then, that it had formed part of her body on the analogy of the breast, part of the small sub-ject's body, corking, in the beginning, the orifice of the mouth. The potty had corked her anal orifice and been part of her skin.

It was the mirror, in which she demanded explicitly to see herself carrying the potty with both hands, which gave to this object, as to any object, a license to exist and which gave her, Nadia, another or-ifice to her body. Then, she laughed, enchanted, shaking the mirror as if to test the persistence of the image. She also pressed the potty against the mirror, that limit of space that marks all real human ob-jects with a beyond of virtuality. As it had done for her body, the mirror created for the potty an interior, an exterior, a rim, a bottom, and a lack also: it was the key of the cupboard she put into it that symbolized this object of lack.

It was the last time that Nadia brought the mirror explicitly into play.

That day she had arrived at the borders of speech. She was nine-teen months old.

11 / *The Holed and Toric Body*

When I arrived on 4 March, Nadia was standing beside a crib but was not leaning on it in any way. She babbled when she saw me and walked toward me; but she was furious that I did not take her into my arms at once: I first had to pick up the blanket. She stepped back, babbled, and, in my arms, grabbed my glasses and threw them down: I asked her why she did this.

As soon as she was upstairs, in the new consulting room, *she picked up the potty and threw it down three times, babbling energetically all the while.*

She stopped in front of the sandbox, mesmerized: she neither babbled nor moved; then she left it again without having done anything with it.

She then set off to explore outside of the room. When she came back she ate one spoonful of pudding, then gave some to me to eat before handing me the spoon, opening her mouth, and waiting. She wanted me to feed all of it to her.

When she had finished, she took the mug, put her hand into it, and did not seem pleased to find it empty. She took the bottle, put it to her mouth, then back on the table long enough to clamber onto my lap before picking it up again to give to me. She fingered the nipple for a while, babbling "ga-ga-ga" and put it into her mouth, but not in order to drink. Taking back the bottle from me and holding it by the nipple, she climbed down and put the bottle down, still holding it in the same way. It fell over when she tried to take hold of the ball with ducks; she then sent it flying. She played a little with it as if it were a regular ball. Then she set off into the corridor, mug in hand. She came back into the room only to exchange the mug for two crackers and went off with one in each hand.

I told her the session was over; not happy, she threw down one cracker but kept the other and started nibbling it as she went down the stairs.

Back in her own room, she wanted to go back out again and return to the consulting room. So I stayed with her for ten minutes to prepare her for that day's difficult separation, aggravated by the crying of a child whose ears were being attended to. A nurse came up to Nadia, who was still in my arms, to inspect her ears;

Nadia clung to me still closer and began to cry. But she did not need ear care; I calmed her down and handed her over to the nurse, who put her in her crib, so that Nadia might be quite certain that she would not need to receive the dreaded ear treatment.

On 5 March I had to dress her and put on her shoes myself since there was no nurse. She was really happy and stretched out her feet for me to put her shoes on.

Because Nadia liked to go for a walk, come and go, ferret everywhere, I left the door of the consulting room open. She began by throwing some candy around and then ate nearly an entire cracker, while walking, happily, from the landing to the room. She demanded that I carry her around so that she could continue ferreting everywhere; she babbled intensely, especially when she discovered a new object. She came back into the room, laughing, took the spoon, and twice fed me some stewed fruit. She laughed when she had finished, saw the sand, touched it briefly, and then went to push over the potty with a certain degree of aggressivity: she threw it down several times in a row, stamping her feet and babbling vigorously "heugh-gheu!"

She settled on my lap and demanded that I give her all the stewed fruit to eat. She was very relaxed, kicking her feet with pleasure, leaning her head against me, or looking at me. She even wanted me to scrape the dish at the end.

She climbed down from my lap to pick up the spoon, and, delighted, brandished it as she walked out. She came back and stuck the spoon into the sand, scooping some of it onto the floor; but, remembering her first experience, she did not put the spoon to her mouth.

I told her the session was over and she left in my arms, having exchanged the spoon for the last remaining cracker. But she would have liked to go back and, as soon as we arrived in her room, she led me back to the stairs.

On 7 March, it was already too late to take her for a session because supper had started. She had had her soup and was waiting for the stewed fruit. When I arrived I saw her moving from her crib into the neighboring child's. I would not have shown myself if she had not begun to cry when the nurse told her to get back into her own crib. When I came to her, she held out her arms, stopped crying, and began to laugh. She wanted me to walk her and forgot her supper for a quarter of an hour. I took her back for the end of supper.

Nadia ate the stewed fruit the nurse was feeding her, looked at me, and babbled between spoonfuls. She also smiled at the nurse with whom she had by now established a bond, something that would make the cut of a session's end less dramatic. I noticed, however, during this scene, that as soon as I came close to another child, Nadia would throw down the spoon in fury.

She wanted to go walking again at the end, but returned without difficulty to the arms of the nurse, who gave her a banana.

On 9 March, when I came to fetch her, Nadia made me feel that she had not had a real session since 5 March. When she saw me, she made a scene: babbling furiously, looking daggers at me, and banging on the floor. Laughing, I told her that she was not very pleased with me because she had not seen me for several days and thought I was abandoning her. I laughed as I said this, because even though she was aggressive, she was without anxiety. Then she laughed and held out her arms; nestling against my neck, she clucked with pleasure, babbled, and laughed all the way to the consulting room on the second floor of the other building.

She walked right up to the door but came back into my arms to open it.

She threw the candy around, made me lick the spoon, and took a cracker, which she ate as she walked; then she came back for the other cracker, which she left when she saw the potty. She took hold of it joyfully, saying "caca." Then she put it down by the sandbox, contemplated the latter, and set off to explore the landing, babbling and laughing all the while.

She came back into the room, threw down the toys from a shelf, and went out again, sucking a rubber doll. While she was sucking her doll as if it were food, and looking at the dish, I told her that if she did not want to eat, it was because she believed I had abandoned her and therefore that I did not want her to eat. I added that the food was there for her to do with as she pleased. Her answer was to turn, laughing, to my chair, taking possession of it as if it were a table, laying both her hands flat upon it; she wanted me to put the dish on it and *demanded that I feed her with the spoon; at one point she took it back from me in order to feed me from it.* At the end she looked at me while handing back the spoon, laughing softly and babbling, as if to say, "Wasn't that good?" I told her that she found good what she had demanded of me to make her eat, just as I found good what she gave me to eat. She then wanted to drink from the spoon some of the milk from the bottle, which she had made me pour into the dish.

She picked up the doll, put it into the sandbox, then took it back in order to throw it down. She stuck her hand into a box containing some sand. I had to wipe her when it was time to go back; she was delighted.

I was now seeing her on average four times a week; I had stopped seeing her every day.

On 11 March Nadia's face was set and I felt she was ill at ease, for some reason unknown to me.

She fell upon *the bottle, which she drank up completely* in my arms. Her expression became very confident; she relaxed and soon became dynamic and active again.

On 12 March she walked a little without support, which gave her great joy. In the first part of the session she ate some tapioca and drank from the bottle. In the second part she played aggressive and dynamic games with the potty and wanted to eat tapioca with the help of my glasses.

She showed some interest in the sand and water and walked a great deal, with and *without my help.*

On 14 and 15 March, I had to see her in her room because she had a high temperature. But she was not cast down and could not understand why I could not take her to the session. She did not accept it and hit me, without anxiety, however. She was capable of very tender behavior the next minute.

On 17 March, I found her in the back room, alone with a blind child. Her crib had been moved there because she kept getting into the other cribs, one little boy's in particular. She was standing beside her crib, stamping; she did not look too good, and her ear was running.

She began the session sitting on my lap. She sucked the spoon she had dipped into the tapioca and made me suck it. She threw it down to take a cracker, then set off to explore, babbling.

She came back to take a little train, which she sucked while looking at the dish. I interpreted her desire for food and her inhibition; I told her that she believed I had withdrawn her food because I had not taken her to sessions the last two times. I added that she had an earache and that I did not want her to be ill.

She then let go of the train, gave me the spoon, and opened her mouth. *I gave her three spoonfuls before she took the spoon and threw it down in order to eat with her hand.* She ate the spoonfuls I gave her *with satisfaction* and babbled. To that extent she could be *aggressive without anxiety*. She then became extremely dynamic.

She came down from my lap and, for a quarter of an hour, went back and forth between the landing and the room saying "caca . . . potty . . . potty . . . mama . . . mama!" At first she ignored the potty, which was, as ever, in the corner of the room. Then she stopped before it, farted audibly a few times, and left again. Finally, she squatted at some distance from it, but not on it.

I told her that she had the desire to give me this present, but that she also was not feeling happy with me that day. I added that one can only give what one is sure is properly one's own and that the game with the potty assured her that I acknowledged her property and her independence. I thought while telling her this of how she had always been put on the potty twice a day.

I took her back to her room; she was feeling much better than at the beginning of the session.

On 19 March she looked well. The whole session was dominated by her joy in walking unaided and without support, a game she started over and over again, coming to snuggle against my neck in between attempts.

She ate, fed me, and ignored the potty. But for the first time she seemed to become aware of the doll in the cradle; she looked at it without moving, then came back, very dynamic. She looked at the sand, but that was all she wanted to do.

When I took her back, she wanted to go out again because the nurse did not take care of her immediately; she was quite aggressive when she looked at me, but I did not open the door for her.

On 21 March for the first time she helped me to dress her.

She began the session on my lap, ate a corner of each cracker before throwing them down. The new rhythm of the sessions triggered her aggressivity.

She took the spoon, made me lick it, filled it up once for herself, ate from it, and then threw it away. She got off my lap, put the mug to her mouth, and made the gesture of drinking as if there were something to drink. Then she held it out toward the bottle and waited. I poured some milk into it; *she looked at this milk, then emptied it conscientiously on the floor with a look of delight.*

Once back on my lap, *she began to eat and to feed me, scooping the tapioca with her hand.* She seemed to experience profound pleasure in *feeding me this way and thus in making me lick her fingers,* which she would lick herself immediately afterward. *Then she made me dip my finger in the tapioca and sucked it voluptuously; I told her it was another way of suckling.*

She set off, very active, to explore the nurse's room, stopping to eye the passing people. She came back and took the mug, which served as a shovel in the sand. She emptied a box containing some sand, then examined it with her hands.

Then she picked up a cracker, which she wanted to throw down into the crib, which she was trying to get into.

I took her back to her room to put her to bed. She clung to me, then held out her arms to the nurse, who began to undress her.

On 22 March, I found Nadia crouched on the scales, surrounded by soiled diapers (caca). She held out her arms and hugged me around the neck.

She began the session on my lap, put the spoon into my mouth to *feed me three spoonfuls, then threw down the spoon.* She *dipped her finger* in the cereal, *made me suck it,* and waited for me to dip my finger so that she could suck it. I told her she was not happy with the spoon because she really wanted the breast, which would truly fill her up. She babbled and I continued *that I was not her mommy, that it was only my finger,* and that she knew this, that that is why she would like at times to throw everything around.

She then got off my lap and *became very violent* against the baby doll, the mattress, the pillow. Then she went to walk outside the room.

Having come back into my arms to nestle tenderly against my neck and suck her thumb, she took the bottle, drank all the milk, went to play with the potty, and used the mug as a shovel in the sand.

I took her back to her room.

On 23 March, when I went to fetch her, she looked at me and at the nurse with a certain air of well-being.

In the session, on my lap, she made me suck the spoon that was in the stewed fruit, sucked it herself, but preferred to eat and get me to eat some small pieces of banana with her hands.

She took a wooden animal with a removable head. She picked up the strip of wood that joined the head to the body, dipped it into the stewed fruit, and sucked it; but she was not satisfied. So she dipped her finger and sucked it, and next, my finger, which she made me dip before sucking it. I did it once, telling her it was not that which she wanted, that sucking the finger would not re- place the mother's breast. She flung the toy far away.

The emotional tone of the scene changed: Nadia became dynam- ic, babbled her aggressivity, and seemed to accept very actively the frustration she was subjected to. She stood up by herself to throw the baby doll, the mattress, and the pillow out of the cradle.

She came back beside me to eat a bit of cracker and then went to fetch the potty, which she shook and threw down several times into the sand; it was me who had to pick it up and give it back to her each time.

Excited, she went to walk on the landing and came back to throw herself onto my lap, babbling lovingly.

I put her back into her room where I found out that that very morning she had walked the length of the room unaided.

On 25 March she had started her supper when I arrived. I took her into my arms for a moment and left to prepare the room. When I came back a little later, she was delighted and did not, for the first time, display any distress or aggressivity, even though she had seen me and I had deferred the start of the session. She was in great shape and babbled a great deal.

She spent the entire session standing in front of the little table. She ate all the pudding, in various steps and ways: she made me eat with the spoon and I had to do the same for her; then she threw down the spoon, ate with her hands, and made me dip in my finger so she could suck it in the intervals. She walked as far as the crib and from there to the chair, threw down some toys and picked them up again, sat down to finger the sailor, and then went to take the mug from the shelf and threw it down; it fell into the washba- sin. That left Nadia abashed.

She then went to fetch a chair and wanted me to stand her on top of it, so she could press the electric switch: she succeeded in switching the light on and off.

With respect to food, she urinated twice into her diaper. I took her back in great shape, and, for the first time since the session of 22 January, when I had said she was being born again, I was able to put her back into her crib.

On 29 March—she had not had a session for four days—it was late: Nadia was sitting, smiling, in her crib; she got up and tram- pled while looking at me, and her face lit up when I held out my arms. She rubbed against my neck, cooed, tapped my shoulders and my cheek, but not without making me feel her reproach for having left her so long without seeing her.

I dressed her in rompers. She was very intrigued.

The session was short because she seemed to me to be anxious. She ate, knocked the bottle over, and played with the potty.

On the way back, she demanded—for the first time in a long while—to go in front of *the mirror: she stroked her reflection, had me kiss her, and turned around to kiss me.*

On 5 April, supper was late; I found her lying on her side, sucking her thumb, seemingly asleep. I took her away but I was wrong to do so: she had been waiting for supper and was not very happy.

She demonstrated this to me in the session by throwing everything on the floor. I took her back to her room quite quickly and remained beside her until the nurse started to give her her supper.

On 6 April I hesitated before taking her to a session because she had otitis again, but she pulled me toward the door.

With great interest she watched me clean up the room, which was very dirty from a previous session with Robert the Wolf Child.

It was a short session. Nadia was very dynamic, babbling and roguish. She pushed the bottle over and played at asking me for stewed fruit, only in order to say "no-no" with her head and a comical guttural babble. She discovered a cracker box, turned it over, and fingered the bottom with great interest. She put a rubber bird into it, then pulled out the ribbed paper lining the box and played with it: she folded it, shook it, and would put an object into the paper and take it out again.

She was not at all happy when I took her back.

On 8 April I was told that Nadia had been crying a lot that day. I found her stretched out on the floor, in tears. She had a blue stain of methylene under her nose and had just had her ears attended to: they were still running.

As soon as she was in my arms she smiled at me and leaned her body toward the door.

It was to be an excellent session. She showed that she had really conquered the room; she seemed as much at ease there as in the room we had been using for the sessions only three weeks before. During our walk there she knew where she was going and babbled with joy, wriggling her legs.

She began by licking the spoon, making me lick it, and demanding of me to give her some stewed fruit. She threw down the rabbit and the bird, babbling and laughing all the while. Then she noticed, in the crib, the bottle I had forgotten to take away after another child's session. Before taking hold of it, *she played with the nipple, alternately pulling on it and pushing it in;* then she sat down on the floor with the bottle, shaking it to let some milk spurt, and finally abandoned it.

Having asked me for two spoonfuls of cereal and having noticed that I had put her crackers and candy in the box from the previous session, she went to put a small salad bowl into the crib. She crunched a little bit of cracker, turned the box over, picked up the salad bowl, and sat down with it beside the box. There, she tried to get two little wooden animals out of the bowl; she succeeded, put them back, took them out again, then put them back definitively after having put them in the box for a moment.

Babbling with pleasure, she sucked a piece of candy and made me suck another while she held it. She continued to suck them both on my lap.

She got down again to demand some cereal, knocked over the mug of milk, put the toys out on the floor, and sat down in the middle of them. She played a long time at changing the contents of the nesting boxes, turning them over in all directions. She found some building blocks, which she joyously struck together, examined a truck while clapping her hands and looking at me. Then she walked back upright to the table and demanded the rest of the stewed fruit.

She went toward the sand and she passed a stool, laughing: she had, moreover, said "caca" two minutes earlier. I sensed that she was ill at ease; *I took her back to the room where I changed her diaper for the first time; she seemed very happy.* Then I put her back on the floor and for ten minutes she walked from one room to another; I had only to follow her.

She put two toys into another child's crib, but this was not a gift: as soon as he took hold of them, she pulled on them as well, so that the stronger one won, now him, now her. This game was addressed to me and she seemed very much at ease.

On 9 April, I found Nadia walking on all fours and I noticed how much better she did this since she had learned to walk upright. There was an explosion of babbling and stamping of feet as soon as we arrived at the door of the consulting room.

She began by licking the spoon and making me lick it. Then she gave it to me so that I could feed her. She noticed the crackers in the box on the floor; she went to take them out and put them back in, and then got up looking rather embarrassed. I observed that her diaper was dirty. Given her joy the day before when I changed her, I told her I would fetch another one and come back. I left the door open; she did not seem uneasy, which meant that she had understood. On my return, she babbled joyously when she saw me holding a diaper. *I changed her in the crib.* She laughed and wriggled her legs in the process and when I put her back on the floor she seemed profoundly happy; she looked at me with an expression that combined joy, gratitude, and affection. She leaned against my knees to tell me so and then continued her activities in the room, babbling joyously.

Having looked at the bottle, *she took hold of the sailor and sucked it, turning her back on the bottle.* As soon as I told her that she was sucking it in place of the bottle, she threw the toys down from the shelf and crouched to put the building blocks into two boxes.

She put a piece of candy into a metal box and vainly tried to get the wrapper off another piece. I did it for her and gave it back to her. She sat down with her treasures by the shelf, sucked, and made me suck the piece of candy before putting it into the box, which she shook to make a noise; she was enchanted. She took a wrapped piece of candy from the box and handed it to me to unwrap; she put candy and wrapper back into the box. She amused herself for a long time with pulling them out and putting them back in, demanding my help when they stuck to her hand. Now and then she would say "caca," beaming, and *finally put a piece of candy into the potty. She took it back, sucked it, and sent the potty flying.* Then she crunched the other piece of candy.

She walked about the room, often going to lean her back against the crib to look at me, with the same happy expression as when I changed her. Still holding onto her box, *she went over to the sandbox,* in which she saw an old mug serving as bucket. She looked from the mug to me, then she decided to take the mug in order to throw it down on the floor and put the box in its place. She ignored it from then on.

She put a pebble to her mouth; I had to prevent her from eating it. She played with the electric switch. She came back to the table, joyously knocked over the mug of milk, drank the remaining drop, and came onto my lap so that I would give her three spoonfuls of stewed fruit. She climbed down to pick up a cracker and kept hold of it as I took her back to her room.

On 11 April I found Nadia stretched out on a table being attended to (though it was found that neither of her ears had been running). She cried and struggled; I stayed close beside her, talking to her to calm her. I had stayed on so that she might afterward be able to express in relation to me the aggressivity triggered by the pain. It was an aggressivity she would express from the moment she was secure in my arms, out of the room, until I had changed her diaper.

I held out my arms as soon as it was finished; she curled up in them as in a refuge, until we had left the room. From that point on she ostensibly turned away her head but pressed herself against me as soon as we passed someone. When I wanted to kiss her she withdrew her head, but not her body. I spoke to her of all this.

In the session, she began by licking the spoon and making me lick it, then demanded a few spoonfuls of food. But, still unhappy about my nonintervention while her ears were being attended to, she threw down the bird and the metal box, fitted and unpacked some nesting boxes, and put into her mouth a wrapped piece of candy, which annoyed her. I took off the wrapping; she crunched the candy and sucked it, apparently finding it good.

I had taken her for the session with a dirty diaper and she seemed really uncomfortable. *I put her in the crib to change her; this brought her the same joy as before.* But, more than that, it caused her resentment about the ear treatment to vanish and I was myself surprised at the happiness it brought her; *she seemed like another child:* free, happy, teasing, without the least trace of anxiety.

Back on the floor, she demanded a few spoonfuls of food and came back to my lap to have herself rocked; she let herself go completely and accompanied my humming. After a while, she went down to examine some building blocks, hitting them together, babbling energetically. She took *the baby doll* out of the cradle, let it go, sat down on the floor, *and wanted to put it to bed in the truck.* She was furious to find she could not do so, and sent both flying. She then took the sailor and sucked it, looking at me and wriggling her feet. She came back to the blocks. I *built a tower with three of them,* which made her furious; *she knocked it down* and sent the blocks flying, babbling energetically and without anxiety.

She then amused herself by throwing down the cup and saucer and picking them up in order to suck them. Spying an empty roll of sticking-plaster, she picked it up and sucked it and looked at the bottle. I told her what she was doing and she came to my lap and carried on. I then told her that perhaps she wanted me to give her the bottle but that she should give it to me herself for me to be quite sure that she really wanted to drink it; otherwise it would do her more harm than good. At once, she went to sit on the floor, annoyed, turning her back on me, playing agitatedly on her own with a block, *looking just like a sulky child*.

I spoke to her softly, laughing, because it was rather comical and not at all disagreeable. Then she held out her arms and, stretching out in mine, she held out her arm *toward the bottle*. I gave it to her; she only drank a little from it, but with real pleasure. She was truly delighted and gently wriggled her feet.

Then she began a game: she wanted me to give her the bottle; then she would laughingly turn away her head. She enjoyed this teasing immensely. It came down to telling me: "I am happy, it was good because of you, but I do not want any more today because I waited a long time for you; I can play and tease you with the bottle because I know I will find it again and that it will be good."

She then played the same game with the stewed fruit. I took her back in great shape, and she held out her arms to the nurse, looking at me with a malicious expression.

On 15 April, when I arrived, the other children were playing on the floor and Nadia avoided me as she always did when I had not seen her for several days. Then she turned around, smiled, and held out her arms. The moment we left the room her face lit up; and when we went into the consulting room, she was delighted.

The main characteristic of this session was the complete ease she felt with me. She remained for long periods in my arms, her body completely relaxed, playing with blocks and parts of the doll's tea set.

I was not going to change her diaper. She ate the entire dish of stewed fruit with her fingers, giving me some from time to time, and likewise with me giving some to her in the same way, by hand. She would often look at the sand, but would not touch it.

On 17 April Nadia was sucking her thumb when I arrived. She held out her arms, smiling broadly, and got me to kiss her many times during the walk to the consulting room.

She started the session on my lap, looking with a smile at the dish of stewed fruit. Nevertheless, she seemed to be waiting for something before she could go to the dish. I had brought her to the room with a wet diaper, so I asked her if she wanted me to change her. She stretched out her hand toward the diaper and I changed her in the crib. While I was doing this, she babbled ceaselessly, wriggled her legs, and played with a rabbit she had picked up from the table.

As soon as she was back on the floor, she ate a spoonful of fruit, offered me the spoon, threw down the box and the bird, and climbed onto my lap; that is where she wanted me to feed her, either sitting or lying down; she was smiling. This time she ate only half the dishful; she would eat the rest later.

She went to fetch the pieces of candy from the box, was not happy that they were not unwrapped, and would only demand that I take the wrappers off after ten minutes of expressing her annoyance: she threw toys, climbed onto my lap, demanded the stewed fruit in order to refuse it, babbled as if she were swearing at me, banged the blocks together. At last she decided to give me *one piece of candy* to unwrap, and as soon as she thus had two pieces, one in each hand, she sucked each of them alternately, delighted. *She even climbed back onto my lap immediately afterward to make me suck them.* As I was unable to give her the breast, to suck what I had sucked was the only substitute that gave her the impression of absorbing me as food.

I took her back. She was fine but seemed unhappy that the session was over. Her ears were cured and she had no diarrhea.

On 18 April, when I came to fetch her, she first walked away from me, then, arriving at the wall, she turned around toward me and came back holding out her arms. Her diaper was very dirty, but I took her as she was and would change her in the session.

So I began by changing her in the crib, something that always gave her the same joy. Then she came onto my lap for me to give her some cereal. She ate just a little then went down to take *some candy;* she sucked each piece in turn, then *sucked them again after having dipped them in the cereal.* She seemed to appreciate very much this way of eating it; that is why *she made me eat some in the same way,* making a lot of mess over me. At the end she came onto my lap for me to cuddle her: her body was completely relaxed, her expression was one of calm happiness; from time to time she sucked her candy and made me suck it immediately afterward.

She went back to the dish, but she looked at the mug rather than the dish. Before making up her mind to do something with it, she farted noisily, something that seemed to intrigue her, because she looked at me taken aback. Then she looked from me to the mug, stamping impatiently: she found that I did not understand her desire quickly enough. I then picked up *the mug;* she immediately leaned forward, her mouth open: *she drank half the milk.* I had to put the mug down because she wanted to climb onto my lap, where she relaxed for a few minutes, before going down to *take the mug with both hands and drinking nearly all the rest of the milk: then she gave it to me so that I could give her the last few sips.*

She ended the session playing with some boxes and blocks, all the while leaning against my knees. She even came into my arms to continue her game.

On 19 April I found Nadia smiling, sitting on the edge of her crib. It was the first time that I found her with a lively and gay expression that had clearly been there even before I arrived. She noticed the little white coat I put on her and which was new to her. She looked at it with a great deal of interest and seemed to find it to her liking.

The session was short because it was late but also because Nadia gave herself over to me, making herself very dependent.

She ate all the cereal and, the rest of the time, got me to cuddle her, feeding herself visibly, not only on cereal, but on affection and trust; *her body was completely relaxed in my arms.* At last she could receive fully; but I thought it *unwise to prolong this experience in case she reacted with anxiety,* which would make it more difficult for her to receive in the following sessions. And she had a great need to receive.

Though she was clean, she wanted to be changed by me for the sheer pleasure of physical handling; the rest of the time, lying in my arms, she played with her hands and stroked my face, babbling affectionately.

On 22 April I had been asked to fetch Nadia only at quarter to seven, once supper was over. But when I arrived, it had not yet started. Nadia was sucking her thumb and, when she saw me, held out her arms. I dressed her and took her with me, but the session would be short because of supper.

She spent her time lying in my arms, letting herself be fed in a state of bliss. She did not try to walk and I took her back just when supper was starting.

It was interesting to note that Nadia would not experience as a frustration by me—as she had done before—the fact of taking her back only when supper had started. I put her to bed; she was smil-

ing, and I undressed her myself in order not to make her wait longer. In all of this she seemed to have no problems, but the next day's
session was to show what was going on.

On 23 April, the children were not yet up and the atmosphere
in the room was dreary. Nadia's face brightened when she saw
me. She helped me a great deal when I dressed her: she gave me
one foot after the other when I put her socks and shoes on, laughing all the while. She touched my glasses but did not pull them
off.

Sitting on my lap, she began by demanding two spoonfuls of
pudding, then she took the clean diaper—which had become part
of the material ever since she asked me to change her during the
session—and waited. I changed her in the crib; I did not put the
rompers back on because she did not like them.

Then she remained a moment lying in my arms, happy, asked
again for some pudding, and I put down the spoon when she said
"no." *Then she started to put her thumb to her mouth, but let her
hand drop back before it reached her mouth,* as if she realized that
there was no need for it since I was there, as well as all kinds of
food she might want. I told her so. She laughed, touched my
cheek, and went to get the pieces of candy to suck them and make
me suck them as she sat on my lap. She was very joyous throughout the game, as if she had now accepted a substitute for the breast
as nourishment. This would be confirmed by the substitutive game
played around "caca" that followed immediately afterward.

On the shelf she discovered a mug *with beads inside.* For a quarter of an hour *she played with them, saying "ca-ca-ca"* and laughing. During this game she took a picture book, put it on my lap,
laughing and very interested, *and looked at and caressed the picture
of a cat.* She seemed to recognize it: it was the only animal she had
been able to see in the institution. She did not react at all to the
dog next to it.

She started again to play her bead game, which consisted in taking them out of the mug, putting them back, strewing some on
the floor to make me pick them up, being delighted when I put
them back into the mug.

At the end, *she held one between two fingers, made me hold out
my hand, and feigned to give it to me before laughingly putting it
back into the mug.* The whole game was jolly, excited, and punctuated by energetic "cacas." She was in great shape when I took
her back.

This period, following on the last mirror, was quite long; it lasted nearly two months, running from 4 March to 29 April. During the latter half I saw Nadia only three times a week as opposed to every day.

The dominant tone was still oral, but the orality she encountered now had nothing to do with what she had come up against earlier. During all these sessions orality manifested itself only as a waiting for something else in her relation to me: something that came to the fore only in the session of 23 April. What was being awaited was something anal, which was already transparent at each moment in Nadia's interests. What she was waiting for was my demand, the passage of her demand of me toward my demand of her, that is, the connecting of the anal to the Other. Such a connection can be made only:

1. If the small subject has a sense of its body as including an exterior and an interior, with the inscription in the field of the Other of the inferior orifice of the body's hole—it being understood that this hole goes from mouth to anus.

2. If the subject experiences its body as autonomous from the point of view of motor activity. During the period following the mirror, orality had to do with a three-dimensional body having an inside and an outside. Food was no longer a problem, whether it concerned consumption or the gift Nadia could make me of it, already in a perspective of exchange. That is because in a mirror my body, as much as hers, already entailed an inside.

On 5 March, for example, she amused herself by making me taste the fruit with the spoon, then gave me the spoon in order for me to feed her the whole dish, and even insisting at the end that I scrape the dish clean. That scene had a very different atmosphere from the previous one: on the one hand, the spoon was stripped of its purely signifying or representative function, as soon as she had named it, at the time of the fifteenth mirror on 15 February; the spoon was reduced to its use-value. That is the reason why I noted that Nadia "amused herself"; the question of food was sufficiently lightened for it to gain a dimension of play, so that Nadia was cheerful and laughed a great deal. This happened in the best possible way, that is, food had the value of a metonymic object between her and me.

It was not always so; for a month, from 9 March on, Nadia would oscillate between a metonymic value assigned to food and the attempt to find again in it an object that was a metaphor of the body. That was where my interpretations came in, with the limits I had to impose.

On 9 March, for example, Nadia sucked a rubber doll while looking at the dish. As she had not had a session for several days I told her that she felt I had abandoned her and that I therefore did not want her to eat. She understood very well, since she was then able to ask me to feed her with the spoon, and even once to feed me with it.

In the following sessions, however, this exchange of food between us stopped abruptly; she fell back on the demand for food she had addressed to me; and this was indeed a regression, since it was the bottle she then asked me for on several occasions. Of course, this latter did not have the quality it had in December, because our relationship had passed through the mirror stage in the meantime; that is what allowed her to be relaxed and dynamic after having drunk from the bottle in my arms, as on 11 March. It was nevertheless symptomatic of a demand that she would make much more precise, a demand addressed to my body and that would remain metaphorical of the object of her lack.

Between 21 and 29 March, though she persisted in her demand for the bottle, she was clear about the fact that this bottle no longer had the value of a bodily object, for other objects had taken over: her fingers and one of mine, whose effect of metaphorical signification was perfectly clear. It was as if the bottle had only given her the pleasure of sucking but missed, from the point of view of the body, its metaphorical effect. Had it, then, only become a container of milk, pure food? Was she saying that this was not the thing in question when she emptied onto the floor the little bit of milk she had demanded I pour into the mug? By contrast, immediately afterward, she dipped her hand into the tapioca, licked it and made me lick it, licking her fingers immediately after I had licked them, and above all, making me dip my finger into it for her to suck voluptuously: another way of suckling, I told her.

It was this same game she started again the following day, 22 March. I interpreted that I was not her mother, that it was only my finger, that she knew this, and that that was why she wanted to throw everything around sometimes. Then she ran wild against the representative of the other, the baby doll in the cradle—the baby doll and the cradle being new objects in a new consulting room, where she ascertained that other children came with me.

She did not accept this limit I imposed on her, because the next day she began again to suck and make me suck her fingers, followed by one of mine after she had made me dip it into the cereal.

On 25 March she confirmed again that she refused my interpretation and persisted in metaphor, when, during the finger sucking game, she urinated twice. This urination shed light on what was at issue concerning the object she sought on my body: I had told her that my finger was not the maternal breast; she responded by indicating that her search for the breast was also one for the imaginary phallus. The finger-object she wanted to find symmetrically on her and me was the equivalent of a denegation of lack. What I refused her was to let her believe that she could possess metaphorically the object of her oral desire, with a bit of my body as the substitute, and moreover, in the field of metaphor, to let her believe in the symmetrical montage it operated: that it would be sufficient to make me suck her fingers for her to be satisfied in sucking mine, a new transitivism that passed by way of a metaphorical inscription aimed at canceling the loss she encountered in the mirror.

All of the foregoing could be considered as the outline of a perverse side, as denial of castration; an outline cut short by my interpretation of my own limit and lack, my refusal to return to metaphor.

Nadia then came to a conclusion on 29 March, when she went back, once only, in front of the mirror. The fact that she caressed her image, had got me to kiss her, and turned around to kiss me indicated—beyond the narcissistic comfort needed after four days without sessions—a return to the specular image, to its metonymic implication that went together with the giving up of the preceding metaphoric object. That renunciation was not accomplished without tension, since, on the days following, Nadia had otitis and she would take about fifteen days to find a metonymic object, in the form of the candy she sucked and made me suck, something that did not concern the bodily relation from the oral point of view.

At the start of April, following her failure to fill her lack by means of a metaphorical body object, she was driven to approach another field more directly, that of the anal pole of her body. There were two reasons for this: on the one hand, her acquisition of a three-dimensional structure in relation to her body and the possibility she had of questioning the object expelled from it; and on the other hand, her growing motor autonomy.

As always Nadia had already introduced this questioning of a new pole of her body by way of anticipation on 1 March, in the form of the potty in the mirror, which had separated this object from the surface of her skin. But she was not yet ready to bring this lower orifice of the hole of her body into a relation with the Other that I was.

During all the sessions of March she remained at the level of a dubitative and very inhibited questioning of the metaphorical objects classically linked to the anal pole: the potty, the sand, the boxes. As far as her own relation, properly speaking, to her body was concerned, only the growing importance of motor exercise and her progress in it was in evidence. That allowed her to experience, not only her body as independent, autonomous, and as such as a source of pleasure, but also the consulting room as an inside related to an outside. She did not abstain from going out, or walking in the corridor or from room to room, rummaging everywhere, or coming and going between the room and the landing, or wanting to go for a walk holding my hand, and always, during all these activities, she was babbling, laughing, re-joicing in her motor progress: whether she was walking more and more without support or whether she started walking properly on all fours. This great activity in each session was both the backdrop and the means of her debate, which she pursued by passing ceaselessly from food to the potty and to the sand.

Where the sand was concerned, she showed herself very inhibited most of the time. Her first experience of it had been unfortunate. When, on 18 February, in the new consulting room, she had encoun-tered it without knowing what it was, having never in her life been into a garden, she had dipped in her sticky hand and then sucked it, which had made her cry. So, in front of the sand, she remained motionless, did not touch it, or hardly touched it. When at the beginning of March she dipped her hand in it she made me wipe it immediately.

As for the potty, she began to attack it in the session at the begin-ning of March. On the seventeenth she posed the problem in the following terms: coming and going between the room and the land-ing, she babbled: "caca . . . potty . . . potty . . . mama . . . mama," while passing the potty and ignoring it. She only stopped in front of it after that to fart a few times, going on to squat on the floor fur-ther on, but not on the potty. On the nineteenth, she ate some food and fed me, but ignored the potty. On the twenty-third she took the potty and threw it down into the sand three times for me to pick up. On the twenty-ninth, she established a very clear link between the bottle she pushed over after having eaten some cereal and the potty she was aggressive toward, immediately afterward. It was a case of: "Neither the bottle nor the potty."

This oscillation between food and the potty showed to what ex-tent Nadia found the same problems when confronted with the lat-ter as she did with the former, especially the bottle. Everything she could have debated, displaced, resolved even, during the analysis, with respect to the bottle was reactivated here in connection with the potty.

There were two reasons for this. On the one hand, the problem of the oral could not be resolved by means of a relation becoming good because of a bottle becoming good. On the contrary, throughout her trajectory, Nadia had proved that the real issue was not the object itself but its lack, its central lack, the unique condition for the transformation of the Real into a signifier, in which the subject must constitute itself. Hence each time that Nadia came across an object as important in the small subject's relation to the world as the bottle or the potty, the same debate was provoked and always found its privileged field, not in some relation to the object, but in relation to the Other.

On the other hand, one could say that for the subject there will always be an object that functions as a sign of its relation to the lack, even when the primordial objects of early life will have ceased to be those drive objects with which the development of the subject has been only too neatly partitioned into stages, whereas from one object to another, there runs a thread that can be observed very precociously: the one of castration, of relation to the lack.

That is how, as in the case of Nadia, what concerns the oral and what concerns the anal is meshed; and also, as we have seen, the phallus as signifier of lack. On 6 April Nadia evoked the phallus in a game with a cracker box she knocked down, and then, feeling the inside of the empty box with interest, deposited a little rubber bird in it. She played at making noise by crumpling and shaking the ribbed paper lining the box: it was the "heard" of the bird, in expectation of its song, which would come later.

During this period, Nadia was very interested in boxes, not only in order to feel their three dimensions, inside, outside, and bottom or side, but above all because of the decanting of objects they made possible: to make of them containers with a content and to transfer this content from one box to another, something that gave her great enjoyment. On 8 April, she even clapped her hands afterward, making a triumphant gesture while looking at me.

That day, at the end of the session, she moved to the sand, dirtied her diaper, laughed, but felt uncomfortable. I took her back to her room and changed her myself for the first time. It was the first of a whole series of changes at my hands, almost each session, for a month.

More than one question raised itself regarding the diaper; first of all: why that day and not before?

It was obviously not the first time she had passed a stool in a session. I will only recall the one on 23 January to mark the difference of meaning between the two.

We may recall that on 23 January she passed a stool while she stroked my face with great affection, the morning after the second mirror. We were then able to invoke the return of the Real of her body, that stool having been a part of her body. So it was excluded, under those conditions, that in my place of Other I could have busied myself with it, enclosing in the Real what only demanded to be let out of it.

On 8 April the context in which Nadia soiled her diaper was completely different. Rather than a part of her body, what was at issue was a container, boxes, and a content, interchangeable. It was a question of the body's interior, of the body as container, which cannot be destroyed by the loss of the content.

When at last I changed her she was very happy and walked for ten minutes from one room to another, from one container to another, we could say. Her contentment, her dynamism, allow us to conclude, retroactively, about her demand to be changed by me. I was now the Other of this anal object for her.

In the following sessions her demand became completely transparent: she wanted me to change her, in the consulting room crib at first, and displayed great joy. While I was changing her, she was laughing, wriggling her legs, and then demonstrated her affection. In the beginning she wanted me to change her dirty diaper; but quite soon, she wanted me to change her diaper when it was simply wet. On 19 April she even wanted me to change a clean diaper, for "nothing," for the pleasure of it. Finally, on 23 April, she took her clean diaper, which I had put in the room, and gave it to me to change her with.

She articulated the meaning of this changing in the session of 9 April, both on the oral level with the candy and on the anal level with the potty. The piece of candy, like her, had "to be changed," that is, unwrapped, before she put it into a box that she shook to make a noise. But before this she had sucked it and made me suck it with obvious pleasure. That was the oral level. I had to unwrap a second piece of candy that was in the box and she put both candy and wrapper back into it, taking them out and putting them back several times while saying "caca." She ended up by putting the piece of candy into the potty, taking it out to suck it, and sending the potty flying. The oral object had become the anal object, without losing its former nature. In this double attribution it made the link between the two orifices of the body's hole, mouth and anus. It was more a question of the orifices of the body than of the object, just as in the beginning it was a question of the hole of the mouth rather than the oral object. If the real lower orifice of the body's hole could not be at play, the hole of the potty stood in for it, and the unwrapping of the candy stood in for the unveiling of this hole, like the changing she asked of me and that she enjoyed—unveiling but also blocking of the hole by the diaper. She could obviously only enjoy it through me as Other, beyond the Real of her body and of mine, in a structuring metonymy.

The final session of this period, on 23 April, brought a new link, not between the oral and the anal, but, from a structural point of view, in the relation to the Other.

The evening before, almost as if to conclude a short session, Nadia had spent her time in my arms pleasurably, being fed. Neither the food nor having to wait for supper on her return was a problem for her; her smile did not leave her when she let me undress her before supper, as if this undressing had to do with changing. She could let herself be seen without fear of losing a part of her body under the look of the Other, indeed through the hands of the Other.

On 23 April she began the session by offering me her feet—a reminder of the session of 10 December—laughingly, for me to put on her socks and shoes. Though it was far from being the first time, this time it was without fear or tension; she specified the link with my look when I veiled her feet: she touched my glasses but did not pull them off.

In the session, she ate two spoonfuls of pudding, handed me her clean diaper, waited for me to change her, and remained lying in my arms with a happy expression. Though she ate a few more spoonfuls of pudding, she soon put down the spoon, telling me "no." That is when a scene of joyous play took place, with the oral object exchanged between her and me. Having put down the spoon she sketched a movement: that of putting her thumb to her mouth and letting her hand drop before it had reached her mouth. I told her she was aware of my being there, as well as the food, that being the reason she had given up her thumb. Then she laughed, touched my cheek, and went to take some pieces of candy. She came back onto my lap alternately to suck them and have me suck them.

There was no question there of a metaphorical substitute for the object of the body, of sucking a finger, or even her own thumb, but of a metonymical object between her and me. Such an object, the candy, even constituted an unary trait for Nadia, which was not the first—the shoes also had this function, for example, when on 31 December she got them for the first time and alternately looked from hers to mine. Nevertheless, this was her first questioning of my oral desire as analogous to hers. She responded to it with a bi-univocal identification, where she made me leave the place of the Other as bearer of the object and marked me as lacking. Exchange of object, exchange of lack.

Soon afterward she would pursue the same dialectic of the lacking object with the beads. She went to the shelf and discovered, or rather went to get from where she knew they would be, some beads in a mug. Her game was to last a quarter of an hour: she took the beads from the mug, put them back in, scattered some on the floor, and wanted me to pick them up and put them back, something which delighted her. The game was quite gay, excited, and punctuated by energetic "cacas." At the end she took one between her fingers, got me to hold out my hand, and played at giving it to me before laughingly putting it back into the mug. By making me hold out my hand, she was really making sure, as with the piece of candy, that I would ask her for the bead; but what gave her enjoyment was to refuse it to me—perhaps to make me lack?

It was obviously no longer the same thing as the cracker she had so often given me to bite before searching for a piece of it on my tongue with her finger, sometimes even with a reaction of disgust indicating its Real dimension. Then it was a question of a lack on the body, of hers looking for the object on mine, of mine having to lack it.

Now it was laughter that fused, for we were in the field of the joke, after the mirror, the mirror that made me lose my real body and barred me as an "A." What made her laugh was to recognize this, to grasp it victoriously, and to be able to recognize herself in it, as in the mirror, beyond a real loss, for her as for me.

The same metonymic questioning emerged when, in the middle of the game, she took a picture book, put it on my knees, and lingered on the image of the cat, the only animal she really knew, in order to stroke it laughingly. Her laugh indicated that the Real of the cat she had experienced had become an image; that, as in the mirror, a loss had occurred somewhere, but that whatever there was to be communicated to me of the cat was in this image.

It was the articulation of the Real and the image, and the lack that can inscribe itself there as a watermark, which was important. It cannot inscribe itself if one of the terms is absent: she was not interested in the picture of the dog because she had never seen a real one.

This does not exhaust the problem of the image and the representation of the object since there are objects that cannot be specularized, the loss of which cannot be inscribed between the Real and the image, since they have no image: they have to remain veiled.

To summarize, between 4 March and 23 April Nadia structurally established the hole of her body; the result was the toric structure of this body.

For the body's hole to be established, the lower orifice of this hole must be constituted and it would seem there is only one way of doing this: the inscription of the orifice in the field of the Other. She had only the previous reference of the upper orifice, the mouth, to guide her. This first orifice had to pass through all the vicissitudes of transitivism to establish itself: firstly that of the search for the bodily object that could block it; secondly, in ambivalence. It found its status only in the mirror, through the metonymy of an exchange of kisses and the emergence of the third term articulated in the "pa-pa-pa."

The lower orifice of the bodily hole can establish itself only on bases already acquired through the confrontation of images, hers and mine, in the mirror. The Real has already been sent off from the hole. Only a metaphorical object remains in the attempt to block it, my finger as imaginary phallus; a neurotic, even a perverse perspective to which my interpretation put a stop, allowing Nadia to resume her dialectic of inscribing the orifice in the field of the Other. She did this through the reintroduction of a metonymical object, the piece of candy, which could form a link between the upper oral orifice and the lower anal one; this latter being itself linked, no less metonymically, through its hole and edges, to the potty. The object was no longer filling, either orally or anally; the upper and lower orifices of the hole in the body inscribed themselves metonymically beyond the object.

The unique, necessary, and sufficient condition for this inscription is the specular image. It is unique and necessary because the image of the Other, outside of the mirror, can only be fascination and transitivism, or at best, metaphor, with, on the horizon, the Other's *jouissance* in which the Symbolic falls down. It is sufficient because the mirror leads the subject back to the lack in the Other, veiled by its image, and for which another object takes responsibility, an object outside of the mirror, the third term, the signifier of the Name-of-the-Father.

12 / The Exchange

On 25 April I arrived after dinner; Nadia was getting out of her crib. The nurse told me that this was the great innovation of the last few days, and she added: "As soon as you turn your back, Nadia gets out."

She "helped" a lot while I was dressing her, but she did not like my dressing her in rompers.

She started the session by taking the pieces of candy; she got me to unwrap them, but would only suck them once I had sucked them myself. She climbed onto my lap, sucked the pieces of candy, got me to suck them again, and indicated that she wanted a few spoonfuls of pudding.

She got down from my lap and went to the shelf with a very definite aim: to get the beads. Plunging her hand into *the mug full of beads,* she turned around to me with a smile and babbled; then she started the same game she had played in the preceding session; but on this day, *she gave me one of the beads* to start the game. She became excited very quickly, babbled incessantly *"caca-caca,"* threw down the beads, picked them up, and put them back into the mug, which she put down provisionally on the shelf. Then she picked up *the little train, which she put into the potty.* Several times in a row *she put this toy into the potty, which she then tipped over so that the train fell out, babbling all the time.* Eventually, she hit the potty, flung it away, and turned her attention back to the beads.

I realized at that point that she had soiled her diaper, and I said so to her. Until the moment when she demanded that I should change her, she was quite violent: *she scattered the beads around, saying "caca" with her back turned to me.* Then she went and put the train into the crib and took the baby doll out of the latter, picking it up by its diaper, but she was afraid of it and wanted me to remove it from the shelf where she had left it. Then she got onto my lap, bringing the crackers with her. She got me to eat some, and ate some herself, then got down and put them back into the box, picked up the clean diaper, and held it out to me. So I changed her; she expressed the same joy as before; and I did not put the rompers back on her.

I took her back to her room, undressed her, and put her back into her crib, something she now loved me to do for her.

On 26 April, I found Nadia with a sorry little face; her nose was bleeding because they had removed some scabs; they had put on some methylene blue. This smearing of red and blue had disfigured her. She helped a lot as I dressed her. I did not put on the rompers.

As soon as we were in the consulting room, she took the pieces of candy, which she sucked after she had made me suck them. She came back onto my lap so that I would give her a few spoonfuls of semolina, then went over to the shelf; that day she was far less interested in the beads (she fingered them for a short while, gave one to me, and took no further notice of them) than in the train. She sat down and moved it back and forth without letting go of it; her whole body followed this movement, which was evocative of rocking. Nadia was smiling, and her expression showed that she was very much involved in what she was doing. She pushed the train toward me; I sent it back to her and she burst out laughing.

Next she came up to me and ate some semolina, then she brought a book over to me. She was looking in it for her favorite picture, the cat, because she could recognize it. She put the book back on the shelf, making sucking noises—it was a noise she often made when I came to collect her before supper.

She took *a little dish from the pink doll's tea set and held it in her mouth between her teeth,* like an African woman with a tray. She came toward me like this, with sparkling eyes. Since her look shifted from me to the box of crackers, I put one cracker in the little dish. She took it off the dish, threw the dish down, took the cracker, ate half of it, and threw away the rest.

Then she wanted me to give her what was left of the semolina. In between, she would push the objects off the edge of the table and go to pick them up. Not only did she pick them up, she also put them into the nesting box, looking at me triumphantly.

Supper had already started when I took her back, but this did not upset her.

On 29 April, when I arrived at the institution, I heard all about Nadia's pranks. She kept getting out of her crib, either to get into other children's or to go out into the corridor. Indeed, when I went to collect her, I found her out on the balcony: the window was wide open and she was watching with great interest the children playing in the garden. She looked radiant as I took her away; she helped me a great deal as I dressed her, and she was babbling and humming.

In the session, she first got me to suck the pieces of candy, but this time she did not suck them herself. She sat on my lap to eat some rice pudding, then got down and knocked the train and the nesting box off the table, at the same time demanding a few more spoonfuls. She picked up the train and the box, then went to fetch *the book* and put it on my lap. Today, however, even though she showed me the picture of the cat in particular, she also showed interest in the picture of a little calf next to a pail of milk. Afterward, she put the book back on the shelf.

Next, she wanted me to change her wet diaper; but this time, she wanted to be changed on my lap and not in the crib.

As soon as I put her back down on the floor, she demanded some rice pudding and then went to fetch the beads. From this moment, right up to the end of the session, in other words, for twenty-five minutes—for she refused to allow the session to end—*she was to play with the beads and exhibit an astonishing degree of dynamism* and freedom and an extraordinarily wide range of emotions. The game was now joyful, now angry. Either the beads were given to me or they were scattered around for me to pick up; or again, she would take them for herself and try to juggle with them. She moved them from one receptacle to another: she put them into the little truck and not into the mug. When she had scattered them around, she would go and pick them up, either standing up or on all fours, babbling passionately: "caca . . . cou . . . caca . . . cou."

In the middle of this game, she had a brief moment of *anger:* after she had scattered the beads over a wide area, *she urinated while standing up.* I changed her again, and she went back to her beads.

Every now and then she would stop briefly in the middle of her game, either to get me to give her some of the rice pudding or to snuggle up between my knees, babbling tenderly.

When I finally managed to take her back after a forty-five-minute session, she stretched out toward the room as if she wanted to go back. She was in very good shape when I put her back into her crib.

On 30 April, Nadia expressed great joy when I arrived to collect her, jumping up and down in her crib, babbling, and trying to climb out of her crib to save time. The door of the consulting room was open; she laughed and leaned toward it.

She climbed down from my lap and sucked a piece of candy, then, standing in front of the table, she demanded that I should give her some cereal. While she was eating about half of it, she pushed the box down onto the floor, picked up the things that had been inside it, and put them back into the box, laughing. For a moment or two, she fingered the beads in the mug, then tipped it over, shrieking with laughter at the way the beads were scattered around.

She put the book on my lap *and turned the pages, laughing at the pictures and stroking them.*

After she had demanded a little more of the cereal, she went back to *the beads.* She played at picking one or two of them up and throwing them down, saying "caca . . . cou"; she was very dynamic and was really enjoying herself. *In the middle of this game, she urinated;* I did not change her, because I had noticed that she did not demand that I should do so if if she had just urinated, whereas she did when she had defecated. It was the differentiation between the aggressive urine and the gift of the excrement. However, for her it was not yet a question of an anal gift. I said so to her, adding what fun it was to scatter the beads in front of me while saying "caca"; I told her she did not want to give anything to me because I was not always there and because she held it against me, as she had held it against her mother, for not being there to feed her and to let her fill herself up with her. She started playing her game with the beads again and *farted,* which made her laugh. Then she sat down on the floor with the train, played the game of pushing it back and forth without letting go of it, then let go of it, and it ended up next to me. I pushed it back to her and Nadia shrieked with laughter. She played this game several times over.

She came up to me again and demanded a few spoonfuls of cereal; at the same time she knocked over the mug of milk. Although she was delighted to see the milk dripping onto the floor, *she did not like it when her hand got wet in it, and she held it out for me to wipe.*

Babbling imperiously, she went to put the train into the potty. She put it in, took it out, and then pushed it toward me so that I would roll it back to her, as I had just done. Great joy.

She came back to eat, and between spoonfuls, she made the most adorable exhibition of tenderness: she would tilt her head to one side, smiling and coming up to me so that I would caress her. She would go off across the room, frequently returning to snuggle in between my knees, but she stayed upright, free to go off again.

She was in excellent shape when I took her back. She clung onto my white coat and did not want to let me go. She was not anxious, but she wanted me to take her up with me.

On 1 May, while I was looking for her shoes and socks, the nurse absolutely insisted on changing Nadia's diaper because it was wet. Nadia could hardly bear it not being me who was doing it, since I was there, and she started crying. As soon as it was done, she threw herself into my arms and I dressed her. Not only did she help me, she even went so far as to hold out one of her shoes to me at the same time as her foot.

However, the session was tinged by the fact that she had been changed in front of me but not by me. There was no trace of anxiety. She ate as usual, but her interest was focused almost exclusively on the beads, which she threw around furiously. She got me to caress her more than usual, but more than that, she lay down on the floor so that I would pick her up. When I did, she laughed tenderly.

I took her back when dinner started; her face puckered up, but she did not cry.

On 3 May, Nadia was standing up; I put her coat on for her and noticed on her chart that she now weighed twenty-two pounds and measured thirty-two inches.

In the session, she started by eating a few spoonfuls of cereal, stretched out in my arms. She got down to take a cookie and wanted her diaper changed; she had defecated.

The emotional tonality of the session changed at that point, and I had the impression that this change was brought about by the correspondence between the color of the excrement in the diaper that I had just taken off her and the cereal—made of crackers crumbled into condensed milk—which even had a similar consistency. Everything that followed led me to believe that she thought I was making her reingest her excrement because she had done it during a session. Thus, she would take only one more spoonful of the cereal, only to spit it out again; she stuck her finger into what she had spat out, but did not suck the finger.

Then she went to play with the potty; eventually she put the piece of candy into it, took it out again and sucked it, and hurled the potty violently away from her.

When I took her back, she was quite relaxed, but it had had to be a short session.

During this session, *she had twice built a tower of three bricks.* Up to that point, she had only ever thrown the bricks around or shown no interest in them.

On 6 May, I arrived during supper. Nadia finished hers without any problem, while I got her things ready. I did not put her shoes on for her, because the nurse told me she had a blister on her foot. The fact that she was in her socks was to shorten the session; walking around without shoes, on the beads she had spread around, would be painful for her.

During the session, she wanted to eat some fruit puree, not from a spoon, but from my fingers, which she pushed deep inside her mouth and sucked, even after all the puree had gone from them. *She was creating the illusion of absorbing me,* which she needed to do in order to be able to give in return. I spoke to her about all that while I was feeding her.

She went off to scatter the beads around and then came back for me to change her diaper; but she was to urinate twice more into her clean diaper. I believe this aggressivity was caused by the fact that *she did not want me to put the clean diaper on for her.* For her, this would doubtless have signified a refusal on my part to let her give me her excrement, and this made her aggressive. I thought so because she was very agitated while I was doing up the clean diaper, doing everything within her power to make the job difficult; and also, because between the changes of diaper she was hurling the beads around furiously. Then she began to find it painful to walk on the beads. I was to see what would happen the following day.

I took her back.

On 7 May I came to see her in the morning, the first time I had done so for quite a while. *I found her sitting on her potty, as were four other children. They were all crying, except Nadia, who was watching the others with great interest, on the lookout for any toys she could snatch.*

As she had her back turned toward the door, she did not see me and I asked the nurse to dress her. There was no question of its being me who took her off the potty during this phase.

When I came back, she was ready. The nurse told me she was very pert and lively. I could feel that in her whole behavior she was trying to adapt to the daily life in the institution by being as unobjectionable as possible.

In the session, after she had eaten a few spoonfuls, she wanted me to take off her diaper. But on this day, she very clearly showed me that she did not want me to put a clean one on for her, because if I did, it would mean I was refusing her gift. *Without a diaper, her excrement would take on the value of a gift that a distinct individual could freely give or refuse to give,* since she would not have to ask me to take off her diaper. When I did put one on for her, she urinated in it twice, out of resentment, and showed me that was what she meant by scattering the beads and walking on them.

The whole of this session was taken up with this. But Nadia did something new: at one point, she bumped into the table and *a toy rabbit,* which had been upright on the table, *fell over; with very precise gestures, Nadia put it back into the upright position, picking it up by one ear, as she had often seen me do.* She was aware of what she had done, *because she turned to me with an enchanted look and came and snuggled tenderly between my knees.*

On 8 May, I arrived during supper. I sat down and waited for Nadia to finish eating, which she did without any problem. When I took her out, she was in great shape.

She started the session by getting me to feed her a little, as she sat in my arms, then, after she had scattered the beads, she got me to take off her diaper. I did not put anything back on her, but showed her that I had a clean diaper on my lap; it was at her disposal, according to her desire, and not to obey the rules of daily life, which I would have represented if, in virtue of my position, I had put on a clean one—which is how she would have interpreted it according to the meaning that had emerged in the preceding session. She spun around in the room, delighted at having a bare bottom in front of me.

Then she demanded that I feed her about half of the cereal. She came up close to me to look at the diaper on my knees and discontentedly went off to scatter the beads; she then urinated on the floor, showing me what she had done with some satisfaction. I interpreted for her.

She went off to play with the beads, saying "caca, caca" and then "potty-caca." I repeated what she had said. She came and stood in front of me, looked at the potty, then at me, and waited, repeating, "caca, caca, potty-caca." *She wanted me to sit her on the potty,* and as soon as she was sitting on it, she gave me a radiant and loving smile. She moved around, still sitting on the potty, so she could play with *the beads. She picked one up and gave it to me at the very moment when she defecated.* She came over so I could help her off the potty; she was radiant.

Then, sitting at my feet, she started to play the game with the train, only stopping to make a variety of gestures of tenderness or for me to give her a spoonful of food.

When she got up to bring me the book, *I put a clean diaper on her, so that she could clearly realize that I had understood* that she had given me a present and that the diaper was thus no longer a sign of refusal on my part.

She was very happy, and I took her back.

After the preceding period, during which she had structured her body and the orifices of that body, the problem of 25 April to 8 May once more concerned the object as a currency of exchange between her and me. It was now the status of the anal object that was in question.

Initially, the establishment of this status occurred via an oral object. As we saw, it was the pieces of candy, which she would suck after she had made me suck them and which participated in the change through the unwrapping of the paper that covered them. Hence, she was able to move on to the anal object, which she was to represent alternately with the beads and the little train, which she put into the potty. As to the beads, she was able to give one to me on 25 April, all the while babbling "caca-caca" very excitedly; but if she dropped them, it was to pick them up and put them back into the mug, in other words, not into the potty, but into an oral receptacle. And although she put the toy train into the potty, it was only so that she could tip it out by turning the potty upside down, and she did this several times in succession.

All this play, symbolic though it may have been, was nonetheless only too connected with her body, since she defecated in her diaper at the same time as she became violent, scattering the beads around and turning her back on me, not demanding that I should change her until the end of the session. At that point there was a momentary failure in the exchange system, which she confirmed when she went and put the train into the cradle and took out the baby doll, picking it up by its diaper, but fearfully. Instead of an exchange with me via an object disconnected from the dimension of the corporeal object, like the beads, she became hooked into a succession of metaphorical equivalents: excrement, train, doll. What was making a sign to her, and what made her frightened, was probably a return of the repressed, the *Unheimlich*. The beads having made the excrement into a metonymic object, the excrement in her diaper was returned to the dimension of the smearing of the body, as it had been before the mirror phase, at the moment when the body was only a surface.

We cannot avoid recalling the place of the anal infant in structure: a spreading out on the skin; or even the place of the autistic child

199 / *The Exchange*

for the mother: on the skin of the latter, insofar as it is a surface without holes.

In the course of the following sessions, Nadia found the way to exchange with me, first with the candy or the food, which created the pathway for the exchange with the train later on: she pushed it toward me and burst out laughing when I pushed it back to her.

As far as the beads were concerned, right up to the conclusion of the anal exchange on 8 May, although Nadia played a great deal with them, scattering them around, decanting them, all the while babbling "caca-cou, caca-cou," she refused to give them to me, to make an object of exchange out of them. And although her games with them were always varied and accompanied by constant babbling, they were also an opportunity for expressions of anger, when she scattered them around and urinated in her diaper while standing up. Even though she let me take off the diaper, she did not cooperate when I wanted to put a clean one on for her; quite the contrary. I wrote that she seemed to take the clean diaper I put on for her as a refusal on my part that she should give me her excrement and it made her aggressive. Eventually I understood; on 7 May, I took off her diaper and did not put on another one. On 8 May, with her behind bare, she first urinated on the floor, with obvious satisfaction, and then scattered the beads around saying "caca" and "potty-caca." It was at that point that she concluded with an astonishing synthesis: she gave me a bead at the very moment when she defecated into the potty, with a look of enchantment. She had given me the metonymic object of the real object of the body.

What was the meaning of her urinating in the sessions—which was never to happen again—if not of an imaginary phallic protest at what she considered to be my refusal to demand her excrement of her, when I put a clean diaper on her? Perhaps it took me rather a long time to understand what she finally made me realize. But was it not better, in the final analysis, that my demand reached her in this condition *a minima*, in order to disengage it from any compromise with the Real without an Other, which Nadia had always known? The long-drawn-out working toward the renunciation of the bodily object, from the oral point of view, had made me careful. It was thanks to the success of that work from the oral perspective that Nadia had all at once succeeded in achieving the metonymy of the anal gift, linking the Real and the signifier.

13/Life

On 14 May, supper had not finished when I arrived, and Robert the Wolf Child came into Nadia's room with me, holding my hand—he had met me in the corridor. He said "Hello" to Nadia and shook her hand quite hard. She looked at him with interest and smiled at him in spite of this rather brutal gesture. The nurse arrived with Nadia's dish and sent Robert out. The atmosphere was quite tense. I had to leave the room to take Robert back, but Nadia was not bothered by this! She was in the middle of eating, and what was more, I had left the little white overcoat on her crib. So she knew I was coming back. I took her off for a session a little later, and she was delighted.

In the session, she stretched out in my arms for a moment, demanded a spoonful of stewed fruit, then *demanded a second one so that she could turn her head away from it.* It was amusing to see how Nadia was behaving, managing now to put me in the position of a mother on whom one made demands in order to be able to refuse, whether it was a question of food or of the potty.

As to the potty, the first time she had sat on it, she had asked for my help and had defecated. In this session, she sat down on it by herself and stayed there throughout the entire session, going off around the whole room, propelling herself along on her potty; but she did not produce anything. Not only that, she did not want me to change her diaper anymore, either.

On 16 May I found Nadia in the garden, outdoors for the first time in her life, and she seemed very happy.

In the session, she noticed a new toy: the duck. She picked it up and was thrilled with its "quack-quack" when she pressed it. Sitting on the floor, she had great fun manhandling it in every possible way to hear this "quack-quack."

After that she demanded that I should feed her almost all the dish of stewed fruit. Then, rattling the mug of beads, she scattered them over the floor; then she sat down in order to pick them up and put them back into the mug. She came back up to the table so I would give her the whole of the other mug to drink, the mug of milk. I put the empty mug down, but Nadia seemed to be waiting for something; I emptied some of the milk from the bottle into the mug, and she drank it, then I did the same with the rest, and she drank that, too. After that, she used the mug to pick up the remains of the stewed fruit, and I had to give it to her to drink. I took her back into the garden, and she was very well.

On 17 May, when I took Maryse back into the garden after her session, I did not realize that Nadia was there until five minutes had elapsed. She had come right up to me. Although the consulting room was not ready for her, I took her with me, since she had walked up to me.

She came with me to fetch her things and then to put them in the consulting room. I left her briefly, because I had forgotten something, and found her eating the cereal, standing up at the table. She sat on my lap and demanded a few spoonfuls from me, then went off to play with the beads, shaking the mug until they were all scattered around. She amused herself by picking them up and putting them back into the mug, but also put some into the little truck.

Standing at the table, she ate a few more spoonfuls, then sat on my lap and gave me the spoon so that I would feed her, but then very quickly she got down again. Standing next to me, she alternately ate and fed me, with a very sweet look on her face. When the dish was empty, she held out her arms to me. As it was time for supper, I took her down to the dining room, and she was full of joy at eating with the bigger children for the first time.

On 18 May, I looked out through a window and saw Nadia in the garden, playing with her shadow, clapping with joy at the way it changed shape when she herself changed position.

I had other evidence of her spirit of initiative, her curiosity, her capacity for showing interest, her dynamism. She showed not the slightest anxiety or fear: she loved to go and discover things. She managed to get into the sandpit and to climb out of it without any help. Sitting in the sand, she enjoyed picking up fistfuls of it and letting it trickle down between her fingers.

She seemed to be really happy in the garden, seeking out the company of the oldest children, abandoning the little ones and the children she shared the room with.

On the evening of 20 May, I came to fetch her for a session at the end of supper, in the dining room. She was surrounded by about fifteen little children; one was asleep on the table, three others were crying, but she was smiling and munching an apple.

The session was short and she spent it almost entirely in my arms. She got me to kiss her and became absorbed in doing motor exercises. On the floor, she played at walking on all fours or at kneeling up, laughing all the while.

On 25 and 26 May, the children from her room did not go down into the garden. Nadia, who loved to go there, held me responsible for this throughout the session. She hit the book, then hit me quite hard on the knee with it. Nevertheless, she laughed when I interpreted to her what she was doing.

On 27 May I found Nadia in the garden because I had asked them to take her down there. She was halfway up the slide; I took her away, but in the session she expressed her anger at my depriving her of her exploratory activities.

I did not write up a number of sessions, which were characterized by their emptiness; for they were Nadia's reaction to the inevitable effort demanded of her in order that she could fit into nursery life. She lived there in the same rhythm as the others, taking her meals in the dining room, and returning to her room only for the afternoon nap and at night. She was the only child in her room to lead this particular life.

Thus she had to adapt to:

1. A different rhythm of life, comprising numerous changes of rooms and adults during the same day;

2. Other children who were nearly all older than her and whose behavior was often aggressive and violent. She was attracted by them, as she always was by other children, and being intelligent and wanting to do the things they did, she found herself in an inferior position because of her still somewhat unstable gait.

She was investing a great deal of energy and vitality in the work of adaptation, and for about two weeks the sessions were empty. One reason was that she was the last child I took for the sessions, very late, when she was tired out, and anxiety was not far below the surface; another was that she was interpreting the efforts required of her as a rejection on my part, all the more so as it was the first time she had seen me taking other children to and from sessions. That was why she refused to express herself and was incapable of demanding compensation from me in the form of food. It was only when she could reach that point that she emerged from this void, and she made a great leap forward.

Indeed, on 20 June, Nadia found her capacity for joy again. Just as she had done before this difficult period, she lay in my arms and babbled and wriggled her legs joyfully.

In the consulting room, as soon as she was on the floor, she went to fetch the pieces of candy and brought them over to me so that I would unwrap them, laughing happily, and put her head on my lap. Next, she climbed up to suck the candy and then got me to feed her all the cereal.

She went to get *the book and put it on my lap with the sole aim of demanding that I should turn the pages; she refused to look at the pictures, with joyful aggressivity.*

Back on my lap, she noticed a dollhouse that had been moved into the room. She went and squatted in front of it, and eventually, after pulling at everything in sight, chanced upon the door, which opened. She took out the beds, played around with them a little, put them back inside, closed the door, and turned her attention to the sand.

She put a *mug* next to the sandbox *and put about ten little pebbles* into it, which she had picked out of the sand. She came over to give me this mug and, as soon as I had it in my hand, *she pushed it over and burst out laughing.* Then she returned to the dish and herself finished off what little was left in it. When the dish was empty, *she said "More" to me* and waited. I went to fetch a little more cereal, which she came and ate, sitting on my lap. At first she was feeding herself, but then she wanted me to give her the rest.

When I took her back she was in great shape.

On 21 June, Nadia was overjoyed when I took her to the consulting room. She got me to unwrap the pieces of candy, sucked them while sitting on my lap, and wanted me to feed her a little cereal. She took the box of beads and shook it until they had all fallen out. But that did not satisfy her. She sat down on the floor and used her hand to scatter them to the four corners of the room, watching me and laughing, all of which seemed to be saying to me: "You've given me some food that I enjoyed and that keeps me alive, but I don't want to give anything myself; it's still up to you to give!"

She went and squatted in front of the dollhouse and amused herself by opening and closing it several times over; then she played with the nest of boxes, putting them inside one another and taking them apart again.

Then she got off my lap and climbed into the crib; she wanted me to open the window. Right until the end of the session, *she remained fascinated by the sight of what was going on in the street.* Whenever something in particular caught her attention she would turn to me and say, "Look!" It was the trees, a plane flying over, people walking along *the street, and above all the neighbor's canary,* whose cage had been put outdoors, on the gable, just a couple of yards away from us. The song of this bird overjoyed her, and from time to time she would come and hide her head on my shoulder for a moment, as if the happiness was too much for her.

She was looking radiant when I took her back, but her face puckered as she saw I was leaving her.

On 25 June we started with the usual scene with the candy, then Nadia climbed up into the crib to look out into the street. The bird was out there in its cage. Her attention was caught by the cars, the passersby, the trees, and the bird, and she showed the same joy as in the preceding session. But after five minutes she moved on to something else.

She sat down again in the crib, stretched out so that I would caress her a little, then wanted me to help her up and take her out of the crib. She sat on my lap and got me to give her two spoonfuls of her cereal, then she ate a good half of it herself, drinking milk from the mug in between mouthfuls. She was thrilled that she had spread a quantity of the cereal over her pinafore.

She brought a small cooking pot onto my lap. She took the lid off and found a piece of candy inside, which she gave me to unwrap before she put it into her mouth, delightedly. Then she started playing a game with the lid, which I had to join in: I put it on, she took it off; I put it back on, she turned it over, then showed me she knew perfectly well how to put it on the right way up, having taken it off once more.

Then she got me to play the same game with the dollhouse: I opened the door and she closed it again.

She brought the nest of boxes onto my lap and played at taking them apart and putting them back together; then she took them apart definitively and, laughing, made them roll along the floor.

She got back onto my lap to finish the cereal and the milk, but then she accidentally knocked over the mug of milk. She was annoyed and looked desirously at the other mug of milk, which was on the shelf. So I put it on the table; *Nadia took it in both hands and drank all the milk.*

I took her back down for supper, in very good shape.

On 27 June, I took her off for a session before her afternoon snack. She was silent, and I did not hear the sound of her voice at all. Even though she ate all the cereal by herself, through her silence she was expressing her interpretation of the facts to me: by taking her away just before her afternoon snack, I was depriving her of food, I was taking the bread out of her mouth, just as she had done so many times to me in the sessions, three months before.

The only way I could "find my way back to her" was in her behavior with the candy, which she brought to me with the same joy as always, for me to unwrap.

Then she threw everything surrounding the dish and the mug violently down onto the floor: the nest of boxes, the rabbit, and the spoon. She went to pick up the latter so that she could finish the cereal.

From this point on, I kept a record only of the important sessions. On 3 July, I did not tell Nadia I was going on vacation for three weeks, as I had done with the older children. One week before would be sufficient, and up to then the same rhythm of sessions would be maintained for her, contrary to what I had done with the others.

She came to the session dressed only in a pair of rubber pants; she seemed delighted with them. As we went to the consulting room, she was laughing, kicking with joy, but seemed to notice something abnormal in my face; then I realized I was wearing my sunglasses, so I took her with me to change them.

She started the session with the candy and ate the stewed fruit, either with the spoon or with the candy, which she dunked and then sucked.

She got down from my lap, *went to look at the baby doll in the crib, and, looking straight at me, tipped it over.*

Somewhat pacified, she came back onto my lap to eat the fruit, but that was still not what she wanted. She looked at the bottle for a long time and pointed it out to me imperatively, looking at me. I put the bottle on the little table and waited, talking to her. She came into my arms and stretched out, opening her mouth; I gave her the bottle to drink. At the beginning her expression was happy, then I saw her tense up and push away the bottle. I then realized that it was because it had a new nipple and someone had forgotten to make a hole in it. I remedied this and gave the bottle back to Nadia, but she furiously threw it down on the floor. I interpreted for her. So she went to pick up the bottle, drank two mouthfuls; but although she wanted milk, she did not want it from the bottle any longer. She also drank some from the mug, having got me to pour the milk from the bottle into it. Then she was able to enjoy drinking. I interpreted her rancor against the bottle; she thought I had wanted to deprive her of it.

She went and opened the door of the dollhouse, took out the beds and threw them into a corner, then opened and shut the little door several times. Then she played *with the nest of boxes, putting them inside one another over and over again.* The first time, she misjudged the sizes and could not get them to fit; furiously, she shook the whole thing but then tried again. In her subsequent attempts she seemed to have understood: she did not lose her temper anymore and looked for the box that fitted.

Then she noticed *the baby doll on the floor; she went and picked it up, looked at it dubitatively, then, holding it by its diaper, sent it flying,* and with peals of laughter, wanted to get into the crib. There, she lay down so that I would pick her up. Then she wanted to look out of the window, sitting in my arms.

When I took her back down, she was very cheerful, particularly after this final scene through which she had expressed to me that she did not want me to occupy myself with any children except her. As we went through the garden, she saw a cat and wanted to run after it; each time she tried to stroke it, it moved away, but she did not stop trying.

The session of 8 July was more or less the same as the previous one. But, after eating a little of the cereal with a cracker, Nadia took *a mixture of cracker and cereal out of her mouth and put it into mine,* very happy.

She tipped the beads out onto the floor and came over to give me one. Then she sat on the floor, picked up the beads, and put them back into the box. When they were all back inside, she rattled the box and sent it flying. She looked at me and started to collect the scattered beads around her, demanding my help; only a few of the beads got put back into the box. Then she came onto my lap to do some gymnastics; she was upset.

I talked to her about the food she had given me, and about the scene with the beads, and then I took her back, in very good shape.

On 9 July, the session started just as the previous ones had: candy and cereal.

Then Nadia emptied the beads into the potty and threw away the empty box. She picked up another box and poured the beads into it. She climbed into the crib, looked outside, and came back onto my lap to drink some milk from the mug, holding it in both hands. Then *she said "caca" to me and went to fetch the potty*. She got me to take off her pants—for the last week she had not had a diaper anymore, but just rubber pants—and *sat down on the potty*, leaning her back against my legs. She got me to play with her feet, holding them out to me one at a time, laughing, then she stood up. She had not done anything, and she sat down and *urinated*.

Then she climbed onto my lap and gave herself over to little tender games with me, stroking my face with her hand, leaning her head on one side so she could see me from all directions, hiding her head on my shoulder and laughing affectionately.

On 11 July there were two scenes that occupied the whole session. Sitting on the potty, Nadia looked inside the dollhouse, playing at opening and shutting the door. In the second scene, she was in my arms gazing for a long while at the neighbor's bird, enchanted by its song.

On 15 July, the nurse was changing Nadia's diaper—why? I stayed right beside her and everything was going well until Robert came up to me and I responded to him. Nadia immediately began to sob. She stopped only when she was in my arms and we had gone through the door of the nursery.

Even in the session she stayed on my lap for a long time after the unwrapping of the candy, eating or relaxing in my arms. Once she was completely sure that I was there for her and was not going to abandon her, she got down from my lap to abreact against what she had believed to be my abandoning her; she did so without anxiety, but angrily. She threw down everything from the table, except the mug of milk, which she drank. She got me to take off her diaper, took the potty, and showed me clearly that she was not going to sit on it by way of reprisal. Then, after playing briefly and violently with the dollhouse door, she picked up the baby doll and spent ten minutes trying to dismember it.

When I took her back she was much calmer, and smiling.

The last week's sessions were quite similar; however, once I had told her about my impending departure, she spent far more time in my arms and on my lap.

We realized she had made tremendous progress in her adaptation to a collective way of life.

During the month of August, they told me that she was easygoing and affectionate in the nursery. She showed an outstanding capacity to be active, running, dancing around, climbing on chairs, playing tricks on other children that would make her shriek with laughter. She was talking more and more and always trying to repeat new words. She never lost her temper.

She took the initiative with the smaller children, taking them by the hand, helping them to walk, making desperate efforts to help them up when they fell. She had a very high opinion of herself relative to one little boy and would often take great delight in putting a ribbon in his hair. She knew how to say "hello, bye-bye, gone" and the names of the people who looked after her.

She had neither diarrhea nor otitis. She was eating well, without bulimia.

When I came back from my vacation, I had a few more sessions with her. She had grown a great deal, and I noted how much she had changed in terms of height, her more stable gait, and her careful and precise gestures; her complexion, too, was illuminated by what she had become: a little girl of two (she had had her second birthday in August).

On 5 September, although everyone had told me how Nadia had been transformed, it was difficult for me to judge, for I was not to hear a sound or see a single movement, apart from her sucking the candy she was carrying as she left the nursery.

I kept her with me for ten minutes, during which she stayed in my arms, sucking the candy; at first she would not look at me. I spoke gently to her; after that, her eyes did not leave my face. *It was a profound look but in it there was, quite deliberately, not a single spark, as if she did not recognize me at all. She was relaxed and showed no anxiety.*

I took her back to the nursery. She had shown no interest in the objects in the consulting room; but I knew that by relaxing in my arms, she had been expressing her confidence in me rather than a refusal. On the other hand, through her look, she was expressing something like this: "You abandoned me; well, I won't show any joy at seeing you. You acted as if I didn't exist; now I'm going to refuse to share my progress with you, I shall stay passive!"

On 6 September, Nadia held out her arms to me so that I would take her out, but she adopted the same attitude as the day before. However, the pieces of candy she sucked were the ones from the consulting room and not from the nursery, as on the previous day. When I interpreted her behavior to her, she turned her head away for a second and smiled, then, after giving me an oblique look, squeezed the duck in her hand and looked at me, delighted with the sound it made; then she took the rabbit and said to me, "Robert," and started energetically sucking both its ears. She looked at the door and I took her down again. I had heard only the one sound from her in the entire session: "Robert."

On 8 September Nadia smiled and stamped joyfully when I came to fetch her.

Lying in my arms, she said "candy" and sucked the pieces with a serious expression. A moment later, *she kicked at the empty air.* I guessed these kicks were aimed at me, and I talked to her at length about her resentment of my absence. My explanation was punctuated with even more violent kicks when I told her that she thought that I had abandoned her because in the past . . .

When I took her back downstairs, she was relaxed, for the first time since I had come back.

On 10 September Nadia laughed as I carried her up the stairs. This session was nothing like the two preceding ones; she was to be very active, babbling, relaxed and, at the end, would manage to express her aggressivity directly. *This big change was in fact brought about by a terrible attack of diarrhea,* which she had had since that morning, which was the escape route for the anxiety triggered by my return, that is to say, by the violent emotions against me that she could not express. Indeed, she had not had diarrhea once during my absence. Paradoxically, this diarrhea did not stop her putting on weight after my return; while I was away, even without diarrhea, she had not put on any weight, although she had grown taller.

As before the holiday, the session started with the unwrapping of the candy, during which she was wedged between my knees. Then she came up to suck the pieces, lying in my arms.

After that she went to look inside each one of the nesting boxes until she found the one that had the beads in it. As usual she found the box on the shelf. *She took out a bead and wanted to eat it.* A few minutes before the session, she had seen Maryse coming back from her own session with a box of beads, which Robert had then eaten. I told her so, and she put the bead back in the box. *She spent a long time playing at giving me beads so that I could put them back in the box.* She put some into my white coat, too, with the same purpose. Then she put some on the floor and then picked them up. Eventually she looked me full in the face, *scattered them all over the place, and left them.*

She went to the shelf, *urinated in her diaper, and threw* all the toys around, *except the milk pan and the bottle.* She came back to me and said "drink"; I held out the mug to her and she drank the milk.

Then she wanted to get into the crib to look outside. She showed me the pillar where she had seen some cats before the holidays, and she said, "Look," because they were not there. She lay down, held out her arms to me, and I took her back downstairs, relaxed and babbling.

There was a trace of bulimia in the way she had drunk the milk and demanded more; I interpreted this to her as an attempt to fill the emptiness she felt in herself during my absence.

Her eyes showed a great subtlety of expression and divulged a high degree of emotional intensity, whether it was humor or seriousness, joy or refusal.

In another session, she suffered from diarrhea while she was with me, and I talked to her about the meaning of this diarrhea in relation to my absence. It was the last time she would have diarrhea.

The following day, *she gave me a bead, without having an attack of diarrhea*, and, after going to look outside, said to me, "Bye bye."

That was how Nadia put an end to the treatment, in agreement with me, and went on to invest every effort she made in her life in the nursery. She became especially attached to one of the nurses, at the same time no longer needing to express her questions within the framework of the transference.

She was to come across me often in the institution. Smiling, she would come into my arms and get me to kiss her and then would return to whatever she had been doing.

Following what I called the "conclusion" for Nadia with respect to her status as subject, on 8 May, whatever it was within the transference that had been the "enactment of the unconscious" no longer had its raison d'etre. The debate about her loss of object *a*, the residue, had been completed, since I guaranteed it with my own lack, as she knew.

She knew of my lack in two ways: through the signifier of her demand, which returned to her "in inverse form"; and through the symbol she was able to give me, the bead, as object of my desire, or more truly, cause of my desire. With this bead she gave me, she founded the certainty of the desire of the Other, and that is probably far more essential than the classic dimension of the "gift" used to assure oneself of the Other's love, this Other who is supposedly waiting for something in order to be completed. This is where we would need to examine obsessional structures.

In any case, Nadia was so little implicated in this perspective of the gift that, in the session of 14 May, she played on the question of demand and desire: although she demanded the stewed fruit, it was only to turn away her head; a demand in order to be able to refuse. She played the same game with the potty, later on. On this occasion, she went alone, traveling around the room on the potty, but produced nothing, a "nothing" that joined the nothing of the milk pan, from which she had pretended to drink.

On 20 May she gave the most poetic image of herself: through the window, I saw her in the garden, playing with her shadow, clapping with joy at the way it changed shape. Death was there, although she did not know it; it was life she was applauding.

From then on she withdrew more or less completely from the treatment, for now she was going to the nursery and becoming very involved in it. On 27 May, for example, lost in her game—or in her joy—on the garden slide, she was less happy to come for the session. In the session, moreover, she showed far more interest in external things and was enchanted by what was going on in the street. This interest in external things was parallel with the discovery she made, in her daily life, now she was twenty months old, of everything she had not known before.

From the beginning of May, we could say that she was completely available for this new life among other people, which she led in the nursery, and for constantly discovering new things. These things were not necessarily new objects, moreover; far more often—and this demonstrated how far she had progressed—they were old objects that she could now use without inhibition. Hence, the food-objects, rather neglected at the beginning of June, when her demand was withdrawn, were found again with joy, whether it was the candy Nadia sucked or the cereal she ate up completely, even saying to me, "more" and "wait." When she drank the milk, now, it was without any fear of spilling it on her pinafore. If she knocked the mug over, it was accidentally; she showed she was annoyed by this and demanded another one. The famous spoon was no longer anything but a simple utensil and had lost its old value.

The most striking thing was that she loved to laugh and she did not stint herself on this score. Her laugh was infectious, and I often laughed with her. The way she would burst out laughing was characterized on 20 June, when she put the pebbles she had picked out of the sand into the mug, put the mug into my hand, and then immediately knocked it over: here there was nothing but the outline of what she had done before in the potty, but now it was just for laughs, and what is more, not for real. The unconscious, the drive, was there, but present only in the wink she gave me, which made me laugh like her, without needing to add anything at all in the form of words. Our complicity in humor, the joke even, was enough to make us jubilant. And jubilation it certainly was, and it could arise only on the basis of what she had seen in the mirror, that is to say, from the separation, the alienation which are constitutive of the subject of the unconscious: the unconscious that now emerged only at certain privileged points in the relation to the Other: those that were marked by laughter.

Even on 3 July, when she found the earlier representative of the small other, the baby doll in the cradle, she was able, without hesitation and looking me full in the face, on the one hand, to tip over the cradle. Then, on the other hand, picking up the doll and looking dubitatively at it, as if to remind herself, she was able to pick it up by its diaper and fling it away, bursting out laughing; then she got into the crib as if to take its place for a moment. Her laugh and her ease showed clearly enough that she was no longer concerned by the image of the small other that had fascinated her; for now she had her own image, her ego. Schematically, we could say that the libido that had attached to the other before the mirror and that had caused her to despair had been siphoned off by the ego, after the mirror phase; this ego that cannot be other than specular and that, as Freud said, because it does not involve the drives, desexualizes external reality.

That is the point Nadia had reached, the point where the transference becomes exhausted. The transference, for her, was not only the enactment of the unconscious, it was also the place where the unconscious could emerge, the place where the subject "Nadia" could emerge, because I called her by her name, which brought about the primary repression.

What is shown here is that it is necessary for there to be an unconscious in order for the subject to cease being prey to the Real. The whole of the progress she made from then on was the pursuit of this relation to the Other that I was, initially too massive in her presence, though nonetheless necessary for the debate to take place. Eventually, I became for her the place of lack, the place of castration, the Symbolic dimension of which had delivered Nadia from pure privation. While identification had been functioning throughout Nadia's journey, the identification did not end with me, but with the lack she had affected me with.

Her ego, as a specular construction, was able not to include me anymore as her mirror, because she had found the real mirror. Hence, she was able to detach herself from me, or rather, to drop me, we could say, at the point where her specular narcissism could not include me, in other words, in the very place of the object of loss: *a* as nonspecularizable, *a* the separator. At the time I said, "We have nothing more to do together."

PART 2   *Marie-Françoise or Autism*

Marie-Françoise's history is one of a long series of changes that started the day her mother abandoned her at a welfare office *(Assistance publique)* at the age of two months.

She remained in the nursery until she was ten months old. Her health must have been the motive for serious concern, judging from the numerous hospitalizations she had to go through after a very brief placement in foster care between the ages of ten and twelve months. Hers were rather long hospitalizations: some of them took three to four months. The only thing we know about that period is that on one occasion she stayed at the Claude-Bernard Hospital with scarlet fever.

At two years of age Marie-Françoise arrived at Parent de Rosan, where Nadia was and where I eventually treated her. Her developmental quotient was 40, a very low score indeed.

She was thirty months old when I saw her for the first time, following the decision to entrust me with her treatment. This occurred after a discussion at whose conclusion the diagnostic categories of childhood schizophrenia and autism were raised.*

*Frances Tustin, in *Autism and Childhood Psychosis,* published in Great Britain in 1972 (London: Hogarth) and in France in 1977 (Éditions du Seuil; translated from English by Mireille Davidovici), presents in chart 3 (p. 140) the differential features of early infantile autism and childhood schizophrenia. We reproduce here the most significant traits.

In autism, withdrawal dates from early infancy. There may be fits of screaming and tantrums. Physical health is good from birth. The body is stiff and unresponsive; it remains stiff when being held. Avoidance of any form of contact with others. The child's gaze avoids the others. Mutism or echolalia. Deftness in the manipulation of objects. Lack of orientation, detachment: the subjects appear disinterested in the events around them; they are rather aloof and oblivious to their environment. Hypersensitive sense organs. They are fascinated by mechanical objects. They show perseveration in the use of autistic objects.

In schizophrenia, severe symptoms follow a period of normality. The pre-schizophrenic child is the "easiest to care for, the most quickly trained, the cleanest, and in short nearly a perfect infant" (B. Rimland, *Infantile Autism,* London: Methuen, 1964, 69). The child's physical health is often poor: respiratory and metabolic problems. When held, the child molds himself or herself like "plastic or dough," while clinging

Indeed, she presented the following clinical picture:

1. Her gaze was particularly striking: in the presence of adults it wandered in the void, eventually becoming lost. It was a dead gaze that gave the impression of a wall.

2. She did not establish any contact with the adults or children in her environment. In her relation with objects, she had difficulties with prehension: she could only touch them with the tip of her index finger and with her nose, which she employed as a substitute for her mouth.

3. She did not speak at all.

4. As to her motility, she did not walk on her own, but shuffled around on her bottom. She was capable of walking if somebody held her; but more often than not she refused.

5. She presented a very characteristic symptom: a swinging motion that generally involved her whole body, although sometimes it only included her head or arms.

6. Against a background of withdrawal into herself, she was capable of violent tantrums during which she would bang her head on the floor while screaming stridently.

7. She also had nocturnal crises, with grinding of her teeth, tensed face, screaming, drooling, her eyeballs rolled upwards. Her EEG, however, was normal.

8. She became bulimic after having been anorexic.

---

to people. Contact is pathologically invasive. Eyes are unfocused. Inarticulate language. Body movements are loose, uncoordinated. Clumsy manipulation of objects. The schizophrenic child appears to be disoriented, confused, and anxious. The child "often expresses deep concern about his relationship with his environment" (74). The child may use a transitional object and remain very attached to it.

When compared with these two clinical pictures, Marie-Françoise's state appeared to be entirely on the side of autism, in particular as regards her fits of screaming and tantrums, her stiffness, and the avoidance of any form of contact with others, even through the gaze.

Given that Marie-Françoise was abandoned at the age of two months and had a long series of hospitalizations, we must refer to hospitalism. Hospitalism, however, is only a clinical presentation, and one should bear in mind the differences in the clinical pictures exhibited by Nadia and by the Wolf Child, who had different pathologies. The diagnosis of autism for Marie-Françoise can therefore be posited as truly specifying her state, over and above the life conditions to which she was subjected.

14 / Madness—Neither "a" nor "A": Convulsions in Front of Food

The first session, on 30 September, was held beside the crib. I put some items on a small table that stood against the crib, with a small chair at its side. On the table there were two cookies, two pieces of candy, a rubber dog, a rubber baby doll, and a dish of cereal with a spoon. Those were the materials I chose for our first contact; soon they would become more varied, as a function of the content of the sessions.

Marie-Françoise looked at me and started to rock. Her rocking stopped dead when she noticed the table. She took the two pieces of candy and tried one, which she then put on the mattress. She crunched the corner of a cracker and then *ate the two crackers one after the other.* After this she ate the two pieces of candy.

She finished eating, looked at me for a moment, and for a minute became absorbed in the exploration of a small car lying in her crib. I felt that *this occupation was simply a diversion while waiting for something else.*

All of a sudden, she threw the car down and got up *without supporting herself* with the edges of the crib, so strong was the dynamic aggressiveness that pushed her toward me. Laughing, she smacked me on the head once, and then, after straightening up my face, *gave me a monumental slap,* her arm well extended, *without the slightest trace of inhibition.* Although her gaze did not change, she looked at me with a delighted, radiant face that contrasted with the preceding glum expression. Noticing my understanding smile, she proceeded to give me *five slaps,* all equally monumental and on target. She stood up in front of me, holding onto my shoulder with one hand only.

Satisfied, Marie-Françoise sat down again and looked at the dog; then, as she noticed the cereal, *took the spoon from the dish and threw it under the crib.* She had another look at the dog, started to rock, and then stopped all movement, with her head resting on the mattress. She remained in that position.

On the following day, 1 October, the nurse put Marie-Françoise in the crib in the room where we had our sessions before I had time to set up the equipment. I arranged the materials and sat down near the crib.

She started rocking, first without looking and then looking at me.

She stood up, took a piece of candy, licked it once, and showed it to me. She took the other piece of candy, licked it, offered it to me, then left it on the mattress. Following this, she took the spoon from the cereal and threw it down. She came to me, took my glasses, threw them down, and came back to look at me from a very short distance.

She could not make up her mind to ask me to put her on the floor. She noticed the *mug*, stood up, bent over to seize it, looked inside it to see what it contained, and then, disgusted and furious, *threw it out of her crib, as she did with the cookies and the candy* after licking one of them once more.

She seemed satisfied by having thrown everything around; she got up, remained in that position without any support, and looked at me; her face was lit up, but her gaze remained the same. She came close to me, pulled my hair, then *took my glasses and immediately threw them into the pool of milk.* In the course of the session she bent over several times to admire that pool where candy, crackers, and glasses were soaking, looking at me with an expression of defiance, making me bear witness to her exploit. The pool of milk was the center of her interest and prevented her from becoming absorbed in anything else. I felt she was restless, trying to find an exit for her internal chaos; but she did not succeed. Her state soon triggered violent rocking, accompanied by guttural screams, her eyes closed.

I did not persist and asked the nurse to take her. The session lasted ten minutes.

When I arrived for the third session, on 3 October, Marie-Françoise laughed as she looked at me. Also laughing, the nurse asked for the ball she had in her hands. Marie-Françoise defended it against the nurse, turning her back and throwing the toys around her. Then she looked at me and, excited, threw the ball into the room next door where we held our sessions.

As she approached the two steps, *she extended her arms to me* so that I would help her to climb down, *but only that.* She cast an incensed look at me. She once more stood up without help but fell down as she came close to the table and looked at me with an unhappy expression. She shuffled on her bottom to reach the table. Then she wanted me to put all the things lying on the table on the floor, next to her.

She threw the car against my leg violently, licked the two pieces of candy, and got up without support. She drooled as she stood up and then touched the juice of the candy on the floor with her index finger, in a straightforward movement, not the tapping she usually exhibited when touching objects.

Slowly, her interest shifted toward the dish of rice pudding on the floor. She threw the candy, looking first at the dish, then at me. Marie-Françoise shied away from her emotion-desire once again: she took the sailor, pressed it against her nose for a few seconds, and then threw it down.

She stood up and, holding onto the edge of the small table with both hands, bent her head as far as she could toward the dish, her arms wide apart, while making noises with her lips.

She was still looking for a substitute: noticing the cookies, she crouched down, picked them up, turned her back to me, nibbled a corner of a cookie, then violently threw the cookies far from her. She then went toward the table, stood up, and made me understand that I must put the dish on the table in front of her.

Then *there began an extremely painful scene* that would soon become unbearable. Marie-Françoise, who was bulimic and was dying to eat the rice pudding, was unable to do so, and her anxiety mounted very quickly. She could not understand her own reaction at all, so new was it to her. She stood upright in front of the dish, devouring it with her eyes. Her face came very close to it. *Her eyes bulging with desire, her hands clenched on the edge of the table, she produced loud sucking noises.* From time to time she turned her face toward me, her gaze lost, uttered a scream of appeal, and then returned to her posture of contemplation in front of the dish.

Her tension was such that she started to shake violently, her arms very tense. She moved back, picked up the candy, stood up, and still facing the dish but keeping herself at a distance from the table, *she clutched the pieces of candy tensely,* one in each hand. *Her arms went through an almost convulsive crisis.* The crisis spread over her whole face, which she turned toward the ceiling, her eyes closed, *her mouth open for a scream that did not come out.*

I let my voice be heard in order to break the unbearable tension. She let herself drop to the sitting position, turned her back to me, and, still holding onto the candy, *started to rock.*

I then went to ask the nurse to take Marie-Françoise back with the other children. This took some time, and I came back twice to tell her that I was looking for the nurse. It was hard for her, and the second time her face was strained with contained tears. The nurse arrived and I left.

The session lasted fifteen minutes.

Everybody found her more vivacious and considerably more alert.

I went to fetch Marie-Françoise on 4 October when she was being changed. I left the room and went to pick up the materials for the session. When I returned five minutes later, Marie-Françoise was trying to come out through the same door I had used.

She stopped trying to go to the corridor from the moment she saw me setting up the materials. She rocked as she looked at what I was doing. As I sat down, she started *to sputter violently*, her chin toward the ceiling, her gaze fixed on the materials.

I unwrapped the pieces of candy. She immediately seized them, put one in her mouth, sucked it only a little; she bent over, her face low, her arms stiff, a piece of candy protruding from each of her clenched fists. In that position, *she uttered a guttural, stifled song*.

She stood up, exchanged the pieces of candy for crackers, held a cracker against her nose; then she rocked. She stopped all movement, her body leaning to the right, her head inclined over her shoulder and her gaze focused on me. Hers was an empty gaze that did not reveal any life, not even in her internal world. She remained like that for over a minute.

Then she exchanged candy and cookies once again, so that she had a piece of candy in one hand and a cookie in the other. In the course of the exchange she cast *a look, her eyes bulging*, at the dish of rice pudding; but she abruptly turned her look away from the dish, thus voluntarily closing any opening to the emotional upheaval it had triggered the day before. She tried to forget by sucking the piece of candy a while; then she offered both the piece of candy and the cookie to me. Her gaze was at that moment alive. This was the only instance of recognition of my presence that she manifested that day.

The dish still obsessed her, and she found the way to approach it by rocking sideways. She finally stood motionless, her face six inches from the dish. She was unable to cast even a look at it. Suddenly, Marie-Françoise straightened herself up and held the piece of candy against her nose. Then, *her whole body started to shake and, as on the day before, her arms tensed with uncontrollable agitation*. She tried to scream in order to find some relief, but her cries remained in her throat. She turned her face toward the ceiling, her eyes closed, with an expression of unbearable suffering. She came to a halt abruptly, looked at me, and started to rock.

I asked the nurse to take her to her room, where her dinner was about to be served. The session lasted fifteen minutes.

This session created in me a very strong impression of schizophrenic behavior. She was not in contact with me except for a brief moment.

Given the change noticed by the nurses and the doctor, who found her much more alert and dynamic, it seemed to me that the evolution of her behavior in the session from the beginning could be summarized as follows: she established a rather shallow contact with me but simultaneously became assured of my passivity. The confluence of both factors allowed Marie-Françoise to experience her internal world, partly reassured by my nonintervention and partly protected by my presence.

Half an hour later Marie-Françoise saw me as I crossed her room and, smiling, waved good-bye with her hand.

Comparing Marie-Françoise and Nadia, I had good reasons for being amazed, as I put it, at Marie-Françoise's violence when she established bodily contact with me. Indeed, in Marie-Françoise's case it was not the exploration of the hole of my mouth—of my body with its holes—that was at stake; nor was it that she was threatened by the presence of a small other, as Nadia was. What characterized Marie-Françoise's object relation was that there was no Other—indeed, there was no small other either—and that for her I was an object among the other objects.

This does not mean that I was not in a way privileged.

In a first moment she was interested in food: she ate the two cookies and then the candy without any inhibition, insofar as those food-objects were completely cut off from any relation with me and my body. For Nadia, this relation was the source of inhibition.

On the other hand, in a second moment, she distinguished me from the other objects by treating me in a special way: my privilege was to receive a series of monumental slaps. As with the other objects, she did not show the slightest trace of inhibition in her aggression against my body. As far as I can tell, judging from the absence of expressivity in her look, which did not come to life at those moments, she even seemed to be completely satisfied by that aggression.

Such was the first contact that Marie-Françoise had with me on 30 September, which concerned the muscular more than the scopic and which, in that sense, aimed at destroying rather than seeing me. If there is inhibition, in the last analysis it is in the muscular that it must take place. Indeed, that day, and for a long time afterward, her activity turned against herself: she dropped into the sitting position, folding back into herself and, after some rocking, she ended up motionless, her head on the floor between her wide-open legs.

When comparing her and Nadia—this is something we shall often do in order to clarify the difference of structure, and we shall see that the very notion of structure must be questioned in the case of Marie-Françoise—we are immediately struck by the double absence of the Other and the other in Marie-Françoise. These two absences had separate destinies in the course of the treatment.

As regards the Other (which is immediately recognizable in its absence), I may not have emphasized sufficiently in my accounts of the sessions the profoundly pathological look of Marie-Françoise. The total absence of the gaze in her contrasted markedly with Nadia's lively and pathetic gaze. The absence of the gaze was permanent, except for those brief moments when Marie-Françoise showed the distraught look of a demented person. I spoke of chaos in this connection.

On one occasion, however, and after having pulled off my glasses, she fixed her eyes on mine at a distance of half an inch, at a moment that would become meaningful later.

Although it remained a sign of the severity of her state, certainly her gaze started to turn toward me often enough, so that I could say in the report of the third session, on 3 October, that she looked at me laughing when I arrived. But her gaze did not become alive. The muscular, in the form of gesticulations of her face, was the only expression of her reaction, and even of her demand: that I help her to climb down the steps, for instance. Her gaze immediately manifested her refusal and her face adopted an angry expression.

The difference from Nadia already stands out at first glance. Nadia continuously cast pathetic looks around her and at me in particular. Her gaze was an appeal to the Other—the opposite of Marie-Françoise's refusal. When Nadia was in a state of stress among the other children in the nursery, her gaze faded away and her body froze to the point of becoming almost catatonic. In a similar situation, Marie-Françoise would become absorbed in the endless tapping of any object. For Marie-Françoise, the world was either to be destroyed or it destroyed her. For Nadia, the world was either to be seen or it looked at her.

We have seen the importance of the scopic when it is predominant in the relation with the world, as in Nadia's case: without the subject's knowing it, a loss can be inscribed in the scopic and prefigure what Nadia encountered on 10 December in the form of primal repression. For Nadia, the muscular continued the structuring function of the scopic through the experience of the mirror, without, nevertheless, ever replacing it.

For Marie-Françoise, the predominance of the muscular did not create a similar opening to a loss at once possible and ignored; at the most, she only reached the exaltation of the destructive character of the drive, since whatever concerns the drive always has to do with the death drive. Marie-Françoise encountered the scopic drive and its impasse in relation to her from the third session, in a scene that soon became unbearable.

The scene in front of the dish of rice pudding involved three paths of the drive. In a first moment, her eyes and mouth simultaneously: her eyes were bulging with fascination as she made very loud sucking noises. When her eyes turned from the dish to me for a second, her gaze looked distraught and was accompanied by a cry of appeal. Then, in a third moment, the forefront of the scene was occupied by the muscular level, which was so predominant in Marie-Françoise. She started to shake violently and almost had a convulsive crisis. Her arms and face were affected by it: she turned her face toward the ceiling, her eyes closed, her mouth open for a scream that remained mute. The sound of my voice eased that unbearable tension. Marie-Françoise let herself drop to the sitting position, turned her back to me, and started to rock, her eyes full of tears that could not flow.

The same scene was reproduced the following day: in front of the dish once again, she kept her face motionless six inches from it. However, the scene was different this time, in that her body started to shake and her arms became agitated in an uncontrollable manner; but she could not look at the dish even once. Instead, she held a piece of candy against her nose. As on the previous day, she turned her face toward the ceiling, her eyes closed, an expression of intolerable suffering, a scream stuck in her throat. She finally started to rock.

Nadia never showed such intense suffering in front of the object. Although on 13 November, the first time she encountered the bottle in a session, she hesitated, Nadia soon overcame her inhibition: she turned toward me and, in contrast with what Marie-Françoise did, she was able to ask me for the bottle—since for her, I was present.

For Marie-Françoise, on the other hand, I was not there. There was no Other; her cry of appeal was only a hint that could not be sustained, since she addressed herself to the absence; and after uttering her cry once, she was not able to make it come out, to make herself be heard again. Finally, her gaze disappeared behind her closed eyes; her uncontrollable muscular tension, turned toward an impossible aim, led to convulsive movements, ending up in rocking.

The following sessions would show that Marie-Françoise's whole problem was in fact centered on the absence of the Other.

It must be noted, however, that there was a contrast between what she expressed in the session, namely, the absence of the Other, which was so painful, and the alertness that everybody noticed in her daily life. I was told that she was certainly more lively and in touch with reality. But what "reality" was this, when we knew she was prey to bulimia, whose only function was to reassure the adult who stuffed her with food? If we consider what emerged in the treatment, the enormous barrier that stood between her and food, we can easily see how her bulimia was only the other side of that barrier. For Marie-Françoise its intensity was proportional to her absolute inhibition, tied up with the absence of the Other.

As regards the difference between Nadia and Marie-Françoise at the muscular level, we could situate Nadia on the side of catatonia and Marie-Françoise on the side of convulsion. It is difficult, however, to know exactly the respective parts played by structure and age difference: Nadia was thirteen months old, whereas Marie-Françoise was thirty months of age. Would it then be a question of two different developmental stages? Marie-Françoise would have reached a muscular level of expression, with the sadistic drive as a predominant component. This is very likely; but it is totally insufficient to give an account of the essential difference between these two children.

Nadia came out of her muscular passivity, particularly between 10 December and 19 January. Although she showed an intense muscular violence against me, another level existed in her, that of tenderness: the destructive dimension of the drive, which implies the object *a*, was permanently counterbalanced by her love for me, for the Other that I was. Ambivalence evolved in her relation with me.

In Marie-Françoise, who was older and more advanced from a muscular point of view, ambivalence was absent. Her fascination was entirely centered on an object that, although oral in appearance, was in fact a scopic real object, and this despite the wall of her gaze before the external world—whether it was a question of objects or the Other.

By contrast, what fascinated Nadia was an image, the image that actualized at once the other and the Other, "a + A." Marie-Françoise was absolutely ignorant of that image, which cut her off, on the one hand, from all possible identification, and on the other, and more significantly, from all loss, the object of primal repression from which, and from which only, Nadia unfolded her ambivalence toward me, in a beyond of the image that led her to the mirror.

Marie-Françoise remained with the real object, and this had the effect of closing off the division of the subject, which Nadia discovered after the repression of 10 December.

15 / The Other—A Real Absence: The Call to the Window

7 and 8 October

On 7 October, once the materials for the session were set up, I sat down on the steps that linked her room with the consulting room and spoke to Marie-Françoise. She gave me a broad smile and extended her arms to take my glasses; but, seeing that I did not budge, she turned her back to me and remained furious for a minute. Then she moved very quickly toward me and stretched out her arms so that I could put her at the bottom of the steps.

I sat down. She looked at the children in the room she had just left, then at the materials for the session. She moved quickly toward the table, took the candy, and got up without support to look at the dish of rice pudding.

For ten minutes her gaze went from the dish to the mug, from this to the baby doll sitting on the table, and back to the dish. Each time her gaze returned to the dish and while it concentrated on it she made movements with her jaw as if she were chewing. These were not the sideways movements she had exhibited before, and were occasionally accompanied by sucking noises.

There was a significant emotional change in the behavior she displayed in front of the dish. She no longer exhibited the almost convulsive trepidation, the rocking, the guttural screaming, or the face turned toward the ceiling with her eyes closed and a painful expression. On the contrary, she was very much present, and I was also present in her gaze every time she turned to me with a radiant smile.

She looked at me, then at the dish, as if she desired to be fed by me; but I did not make any move in that direction. I reminded her of her behavior toward the dish in the previous sessions, of how atrocious it was to have the wish to eat and not to be able to do so without knowing why. As she herself did not know it, I would feed her only if she made the gesture of giving the spoon to me, since it was harmful to receive food from the other without truly wanting it.

From that moment onward, the scene—Marie-Françoise standing up in front of the table and maintaining a relation with the food—acquired a more profound meaning: *her gaze turned from the dish to the open window and she babbled in the direction of the latter in a tone of call and demand. She looked at the dish again and remained silent in front of it.* This actually seemed to be the call to an absent being, from whom she would precisely demand to be fed. I told her that she appeared to demand something from someone who was not there, but outside; someone invisible; and that she did not demand anything from myself, who was present in the room.

She sat on the floor, sucked her piece of candy once, looked at me, turned once again toward the window, got up, and for the first time *walked up to the crib without any support;* then she returned to the table, in front of the window. She repeated the scene in front of the window. There was an apple on the floor. She picked it up, took a bite from it while looking at me, threw it away, and, still sitting down, moved toward me. Halfway through, however, she turned her back to me and got up again to move *in front of the window, to which she again addressed her gibberish of appeal.*

She moved toward the exit: *she needed to run away from me.*

For a moment I remained at the entrance to the room next door. I saw her playing with another child and laughing. She kept laughing as she took refuge under the table, from where she came out for a moment to look at me, smiling, to then return to the same place.

On 8 October, the door between the two rooms was open while I was preparing the materials for the session. As another child came close to see what I was doing, Marie-Françoise expressed her annoyance very intensely by growling. She extended her arms so that I could put her at the bottom of the steps.

She took the two pieces of candy, sucked one of them just a little, and got up to walk the few steps that separated her from the table and dish. She looked at the dish, then at the baby doll, then at the dish again, and finally at me. After this the circuit became restricted to the dish and myself, and her gaze *was accompanied by jaw movements, as if she were eating.* I pointed this out to her. Her behavior changed then: her gaze continued to turn from me to the dish, but when it was focused on the dish *she kept her mouth open, as if she expected somebody to put the spoon into it.* From that position, her look at me had an air of appeal and soon returned to the dish.

In order to facilitate the comprehension of what I wanted to tell her, namely, that I was happy to feed her, but she should demand it because if she did not that would be harmful to her, I filled the spoon with rice pudding and left it beside the dish, close to her hand. She followed everything I did attentively and looked perplexed. She immediately turned her face away, toward the window, without uttering the screaming call of the previous day, and moved toward it.

At that moment she heard the voice of the doctor who was visiting the room next door. She then sat down in front of the door between the two rooms, turned around toward me, and said *"papa,"* her face full of excitement. Then she started to rock as she looked at the door. I opened the door and invited the doctor in. As soon as she saw him, Marie-Françoise got up and walked toward him, babbling and laughing. She sat on the floor and addressed her laughter alternatively to him and to me. She looked very happy and waved good-bye with her hand when he left.

Following that, she seemed to hesitate about what to do next. She looked as if she wanted to follow up the opening that she had created between the two of us. Indeed, it was as if she wanted *to go back with the other children, but she wanted me there as well.* So I put her at the top of the steps, inside the other room. The nurse asked her for one of the pieces of candy she had in her hand. Marie-Françoise addressed *a peremptory "non"* (no) to her and turned her back on her. The same scene took place with a little boy. She came back to me, *removed my glasses, not to keep them but so that I did not have them on my eyes,* to prevent me from seeing, as was attested by the fact that she dropped them near me and went back to a little boy whose face she stroked. She then moved back toward where I was and checked that my glasses were in the place where she had dropped them. Delighted, she looked at me, stretched out her arms to me, and shut the door of the consulting room. I said good-bye to her.

I learned that for the previous two days Marie-Françoise had been saying "non" very energetically, had not been rocking, and had been very much alive with the other children. The tapping she constantly used to perform on every object had disappeared. She kept doing it only on the edge of her crib in order to fall asleep. Evidently that was her only source of autoerotic pleasure, in the absence of thumb-sucking, of which she was psychologically incapable.

In the two sessions of 7 and 8 October, Marie-Françoise took a leap forward. She could take it because I refused to fall into the trap of occupying the place of the adult who gave her food without her truly demanding it, something that left her with a complete disinvestment of food, which is what bulimia really is.

She became bulimic after being anorexic, and we know how profoundly manifest the affirmation of the subject's own desire is in anorexia. Far from being a simple inertia, it is a totally active refusal, which links the child's desire with death; which in turn assigns a place to the child and the Other, the adult in front of him or her, both of them as being in the position of desiring.

By contrast, bulimia—which often appears after anorexia in those children who show the first signs of hospitalism—is the collapse of the subject's own desire, the collapse of the subject qua desiring subject, which implies the disappearance of the Other as a relational pole. From being active in anorexic refusal, the young subject becomes passive, letting itself be stuffed by the adult, which is pure passivity, rather than the manifestation of a drive with a passive aim.

It is at this point that the question of the status and register of the Other arises.

In anorexia the aim is the Other's anxiety; therefore, the Other's desire. In bulimia, it is no longer the Other's desire that is in question, since the Other as such is not there anymore. The adult performs the function of nourishment in reality in order to escape his or her own death anxiety. This means that, in what constitutes a primary narcissistic relation, the adult is reflected in the small subject and satiates the child in the real, in an admission of incapacity to question what the nourishment truly means for each, the adult as well as the child: it *(ça)* must be satiated so that it remains shut up.

The conditions of institutional life may well eliminate all true relation, as the adult, solicited by too many mouths to be fed can only, amongst all those cries, respond by getting rid of them. In this filling up of children, no clues are given to the child about what is really in question: a bodily relation in which the Other's body is the carrier of the object cause of desire, of which the child must deprive the Other.

In anorexia, the Other is still the carrier of the object. In bulimia, the Other no longer performs that function and the oral object falls into the Real, losing its meaning as object of the body.

Marie-Françoise wanted to reproduce with me and with the nurse a feeding situation in which she was completely passive. In the first sessions she gave only a few signs of such a reproduction. These were the signs that prompted my explicit refusal to feed her unless she demanded it. I was driven by the knowledge and certainty that I should not occupy the place of the feeding other so that she could come out of her passivity. It was necessary for me to be there and not to intervene with the gestures of my body in the Real.

The fact that I carried out these treatments in the course of my own analysis, at the moment of the emergence of my own relation with the lack, namely, the lack of object—and not with the lure of a good object to be found—certainly had an influence upon the centering of these children on the lack in their object relation. Evidently, I could not make the mistake of believing in the role of some oral frustration in these overfed children. Furthermore, my position as analysand was such that I was very sensitive to a gap that was opened up for them as it was for me. Going beyond any motherly confrontation, I was able to maintain and sustain my interpretation at the level of the lack, never at the level of the object.

The interpretation at the level of the object as such may well place the young analysand in a position of stopgap and even bring about the depression of the analyst; whereas the interpretation situated in the symbolic register of lack relieves the child, insofar as the analyst does not impose upon the child a real object of satisfaction, which would constitute a flagrant contradiction. A real object imposed in that manner inevitably becomes persecutory. If it is an oral object, for instance, it leads to the emergence of an anal object that is to be expelled against the analyst.

Thus, I had to be present and do nothing. In a certain manner, it was Marie-Françoise who gave me such a command, by turning her back on me and running away from me, as if on the one hand she abandoned me and reproduced actively what had been done to her when her mother abandoned her at the age of two months, and on the other hand as if she were able to say "no" to what she had known afterward, namely, the real of people and food.

Her refusal, which she introduced into the treatment from the outset, allowed her to rediscover a certain dimension of anorexia. But nourishment had been linked with passivity for too long, and her bulimia had relegated the oral to the impossible, as a result of its impossible articulation with the Other.

As a consequence, the scopic field, as the field where the relation with the other and one's own body is predominant, moved to the foreground. Although at the beginning her gaze was fixed and dead, it was through it that she initiated a move toward activity in the treatment. She effected a reduction of me, to the point of not seeing me when her eyes pointed in the direction where I was; and facing the dish of rice pudding she experienced the loss of her eyes, as organs popping out of their orbits.

As far as my person was concerned, a new aspect of the reduction of the other to nothingness appeared more clearly in relation to my presence: to have a body and not to exist points to a new dimension—that of the Other, says Lacan—where the real other of the psychotic fades away without the subject's being destroyed as a consequence. This is what occurs for other children; but Marie-Françoise was still far away from it.

There still remained my speech, with which I told her—inasmuch as it was possible, that is to say, by halves—the truth about my refusal to feed her unless she asked for it. Her response, which was almost immediate, was the half of the truth that I had not told her: she went to speak to the window, to the absence. At that moment she uttered her call; a call that was not for the Other, but for the real absence.

Neither the Other nor the other were present for Marie-Françoise. Nadia had shown that these two presences, or absences, are linked: she started off with the relation "$a + A$" to arrive soon, at the beginning of the treatment, at "$A + a$" through her transference to me qua Other.

It is not easy to know why Nadia, who had not known her mother, from whom she had been separated at birth, could nevertheless keep within herself the image of completeness "$a + A$," about which she expressed, on 16 January, that she could be the child-a fallen at my feet; whereas Marie-Françoise, who until the age of two months had known her mother—about whom she expressed the void of the real absence—did not show any trace of the image of the other in its relation with the Other.

We can say that this image of the other, combinatory of the Real and the image, of the placenta and the newborn, seems to be the path indispensable for the advent of the Other in the signifying order, as an anticipation of the loss that must affect the Other, which can be inscribed as the algorithm $\cancel{A}$ for the young subject.

On 7 October, Marie-Françoise introduced the other and made it enter her field for the first time when, at the beginning of the session, she turned around to look at the children in the room she had just left before engaging herself with the objects on the table. That was the same presence of the other that she met again at the end of the session when she went to play with another child and burst out laughing. Moreover, during the session her attention was attracted by the representation of the other in the form of the doll, which she included in the circuit of her gaze between the dish and myself, at the moment of her interrogation of the dish, still at a dead end.

However, Marie-Françoise had not yet reached the point of being able to connect the other with the A, since the dimension of the Other's body did not exist for her: it was only a derealized absence, invisible beyond the window. It could be said that it did not have a specular image, that is to say, it occupied entirely the place of object *a* qua nonspecularizable object—the place of the object whose carrier it should be. Yet it must have had some reality.

The nonexistence of a symbolizable reality appeared in the dimension of a hallucinatory Real, which was not far away when Marie-Françoise addressed her call to the window. In contrast to Nadia, it was not the object but the Other itself that Marie-Françoise was in a position to hallucinate, and this in my presence.

In other words, Marie-Françoise was confronted with an absent Other that returned in the Real as a consequence of its not having been symbolized, and with the Real of the Other constituted by me, a duplicate of the first Real. Had I failed to suspend its existence, the Real of the Other would have persisted in the place of the first Real. Indeed, the slightest haste toward her mouth open over the dish or a resort to mothering in a renewal of what Marie-Françoise already knew would have been sufficient; but the satiation of her need would have been at the price of eliminating her as a subject and she would have remained in her passivity. We have already seen, and we shall see it again, that she imposed this passivity on me in an effort to nullify me and deprive me of the dimension of the Real.

The session of 8 October ended up with the irruption of a signifier that was problematic in Marie-Françoise's mouth: "papa." It was the first one pronounced by her.

She did not take the spoon that I put in the dish of rice pudding within her reach, after a true gaze of appeal that she cast at me, her mouth open, in front of that dish that paralyzed her.

When, on 7 October, I spontaneously included the spoon in what I was telling her, I was positing the spoon as a third term. The following day, 8 October, I filled the spoon and put it at her disposal in order to make her understand what I was telling her, which aimed at eliciting her demand. That did not tell her anything; it only resulted in perplexity. We were far from Nadia's spoon. Nevertheless, as Marie-Françoise turned toward the window, she did not utter her cry of appeal as on the day before. It was as if she almost perceived that her call—her demand—could be addressed to the spoon and not to the window anymore.

In the silence that followed there emerged the voice of the doctor who was visiting the room next door. Marie-Françoise turned away from the window of absence and toward the door of what was "heard," the sign of a presence. She then turned toward me to say "papa," her face excited. At that point an unexpected question as to the origin of this "papa" emerged.

Two reactions followed her call. First, she rocked while looking at the door. Then, as I opened the door and invited the doctor in, Marie-Françoise got up and walked toward him, babbling and laughing. Sitting on the floor, she addressed her laughter to the doctor and me alternately, and then, looking very happy, waved "good-bye" with her hand as he left.

We were a long way from Nadia's first reaction under similar circumstances, on 28 October. On that occasion, Nadia had looked at the doctor and had certainly shared her attention between him and me; but very soon she had withdrawn into herself, sucking her thumb while hiding behind her other hand. We had to wait a long time, until the session of 5 February, for Nadia to show to the doctor that she possessed me. For Nadia, the presence of a third party had a reference to me, whether that presence cut her off from me or whether Nadia demonstrated what I was for her, that is to say, that I truly occupied the place of the Other.

For Marie-Françoise, the Other was the doctor. Was this because I was at the time in the place of the absence before which her cry of appeal was halted, as it was halted in her throat before the impossibility of the dish of rice pudding? But this does not explain why she recognized the absent Other in the doctor without hesitation.

Certainly, this presence manifested itself in a register other than the scopic, where the absence had previously appeared: in this case, it was what was heard that elicited the irruption of a presence and prompted Marie-Françoise to respond to it by saying "papa." The presence of the Other induced Marie-Françoise's presence. She made that presence manifest for me: she turned toward me as she uttered her signifier, as if I occupied the place of the signifier of absence and she were naming the Other beyond me.

This is the normative place of the father. We have already seen it in the case of Nadia. It could be said that this place included me in an absence that persisted. It was certainly a question of a beyond, since even in her joy, when the doctor came in, she did not repeat the word "papa," which one would have expected if it had been a question of a real person. It was indeed a question of a beyond the absence and of an opening to me qua pure absence.

Can we speak in relation to the emergence of "papa" of the primary identification with the mythical father of whom Freud talks? This is likely, but not very convincing, bearing in mind the way Marie-Françoise was and what emerged in the sessions that followed.

Be that as it may, soon afterward Marie-Françoise wanted to pursue the experience of that which was beyond me. She wanted to return to the other children, but she also wanted me to go with her. She was somehow driven to introduce the small other–object a in my presence and to attempt the "$a + A$" that Nadia had known as a condition of A, through the coupling of the small other and the A that I was. At that point a scene took place where it was touching, rather than hearing, that created an opening in relation to me. After putting in brackets the scopic linked to absence—by removing my glasses—she moved toward a little boy whose face she stroked.

The second scene poses a question as to the structural level at which Marie-Françoise's paradoxical "papa" must be inscribed.

If we were—as we have been—tempted to inscribe it immediately at the level of the promotion of the Other with a certain plenitude of effect, the stroking of the small other defines its scope in a different way; and it must lead us to establish a link with what we found in Nadia as regards the place of the Other in front of the mirror, an Other who was very much a part of the existence of the other and of its menacing *jouissance*.

16/The Real and the Hole of the Body: Mine and Hers

On 9 October, I set up the materials for the session and sat on the steps at the door between the two rooms. I heard a boy crying as his scalp was being treated for lice with salicylate. Marie-Françoise saw me, threw down the toy she was holding, and approached me to exchange a block for my glasses. Precisely at that moment the child who had just been treated was left on the floor, screaming. It was now Marie-Françoise's turn; she kept my glasses in her hand. I stayed where I was and waited. Marie-Françoise yelled nonstop during the whole painless operation, the site and manipulations of which reminded her of the electroencephalogram. *One could feel that she was very scared.* I did not say anything; she could not see me because I was on the steps, inside the other room. The treatment was finished and she was brought back to the place from which she had been taken, i.e., very close and in front of me. She kept her hand clenched on my glasses all the time and *yelled. She yelled for nearly ten minutes; yet she stopped dead when I spoke to her.* The contortions in her face and the tremor in her arms ceased, while her gaze remained focused on mine; then she started again. In that ostensive way she wanted to express *that she was accusing me.*

Twice I said to her a few words in relation to the electroencephalogram and my having nothing to do with it, neither to prevent it nor to protect her. When she stopped yelling *she tapped on my glasses* with her stereotyped aggressive gesture. I told her that she had acted as she did in order not to express that she had a grudge against me, but that did not bring her any relief. She suddenly approached me, violently threw my glasses into the consulting room, and, laughing, *gave me a monumental slap.* She waited for the effect, then *pulled my hair violently and, once she managed to tear out a bit of hair, showed it to me triumphantly.* Following this, she touched a mole on my cheek and pressed hard on it. This turned into scratching, *as if she wanted to tear out* the mole. The scratching-tearing then expanded to my nose, my cheekbone, and my eye.

She relaxed during this scene, abreacting her fear; I told her this.

When I felt that she had really calmed down, I announced that I would return the following day. I got up to tidy up the materials. While I was doing that, *Marie-Françoise shuffled down one step on her bottom* and grumbled so that I would help her to climb down the next step. Now she wanted a session.

I set up the materials for the session again and sat down. Marie-Françoise grabbed and dropped the pieces of candy without licking them; then she stood up to look at the dish. She directed a brief demanding look toward me, *her arms tensed up for a moment; then, turning toward the window, she addressed her demand to the absence:* she moved in the direction of the window, uttered her scream of appeal, looked at me, and turned toward the other room, where I left her. I then went away.

The violence she went through (was it an evocation of the electroencephalogram?) brought back the aggressive stereotyped tapping, the tension-tremor in front of the food, and the cries accompanied by shaking but without tears. However, the externalization of aggressivity against me did not trigger a reaction of anxiety and actually came to her even as a relief.

On 10 October, she heard me entering the consulting room to prepare the materials. I heard her grumbling after having shuffled down one step on her bottom. She extended her arms to me so that I could carry her into the room.

She grabbed the pieces of candy, started to lick them, and stood up in front of the table. Her gaze turned from the dish to the baby doll, from the doll to the dish, and from the dish to me. Her face then approached the dish closer and closer; when her nose almost touched the edge, her gaze abandoned the dish and turned at an angle toward the doll, which she contemplated. Then her arms started to tremble, her eyes to bulge; she moved back and dropped to the floor on her bottom, so as to flee from her distress. She ate half of a cookie and *became interested in the toys* around her. She took the rubber sailor and pressed it against her nose. She put it aside for a moment, again on her nose, and then gave it to me: she did not want to see it anymore. She took the two boxes that fit exactly into each other and tried to separate them; she became irritated *and gave the boxes to me so that I could do it.* Yet when I returned them to her, she hardly looked at them—just enough time to grab from the smaller box a block that she put to her mouth and then threw at me with violence.

After making the truck roll for a moment, she took the big cooking pot from the toy tea set. She looked inside, plunged her hand in it, and, disappointed at not finding anything there, hesitated about putting one of her pieces of candy inside it. She could not resign herself to do it and looked at me as she uttered a little scream of appeal. I put a piece of candy I had in my pocket inside the pot and she was delighted. *She took it and looked at it but did not lick it,* while eating one of hers at the same time.

She then got up and went back in front of the dish. There, and with her legs wide apart, she bent over, her forehead almost touching the floor, in a posture that seemed to correspond to *an act of adoration and at the same time a flight* from the dish.

She stood up to look only at the doll, then the window, and, without even glancing at the dish, *she crouched down* in front of the cooking pot. She became absorbed in herself in front of that pot. She turned it upside down, put her face close to it, and then pulled it back, tapping on the pot. Then she started all over again. She accompanied this game with a range of noises:

1. Soft sucking noises, which ended with her mouth wide open, as she had done in front of the dish;

2. Muffled growls, accompanied by movements of her bottom, *as if she were making efforts on the potty.*

After a long while, she got up and went back in front of the dish. She was then more explicit and could face it more easily. She looked at it, her mouth open, and then looked at me. That was not a look of appeal, but one aimed at increasing her sense of security through my presence. Putting *her mouth very close to the dish,* she looked at the doll, then the window, and again the dish, in front of which *she said: "maman-bébé"* (mama-baby). She came back to me and repeated the same words. She then got irritated: she would have liked to be able to eat the cereal, but she could not. *She kicked the cookies* and the boxes, uttering short raging screams. She went back to the dish, still with hope. But it remained impossible, and she definitively abandoned the direct attraction of the dish to become absorbed with the doll.

She then *took the doll and dropped to the sitting position* while holding it. She looked at it, pressed it against her face, put it at a distance, and looked at it again, her mouth open, as she had done just before in front of the cereal. Then, *she started to suck her index finger while keeping the tip of the little finger of the same hand on the doll's mouth, making sure that it was on the doll's mouth.* She looked at me briefly and then, still in the same posture with the doll, rocked for five minutes. Finally she got up and moved toward the door with the doll.

I put her back with the others.

This was the first time that she stayed in the session for so long, almost half an hour. With the exception of the last part, she did not present periods of emptiness. Her behavior with me remained very schizophrenic, despite her demand for my help with the boxes and the phrase that she pronounced. Nevertheless, within her own world she moved about with more freedom and looked more explicit.

If we considered only the behavior and object relation that became apparent more clearly during these two sessions, we could already assume a true emergence from psychosis, insofar as all the evidence suggested that now there was an Other for Marie-Françoise. Yet, as I have already pointed out, she gave me the impression of still being very cut off and schizophrenic in her presentation.

Having expressed this reservation, we must return to the dominant line of Marie-Françoise's path.

On 9 October, at the beginning of the session, as she yelled because of the treatment of her head, and although her arms were agitated with almost convulsive movements, she kept my glasses in her hand. Her accusation against me for what she had to endure was also a form of contact. But then she cut herself off from me and started to tap on my glasses; I told her this. At that point she threw my glasses down and took me as an object of aggressiveness.

Nadia had taken me as an object on 15 December when, after putting aside all the objects, she turned toward an object of my body—the buttons of my white coat. The difference between the two girls, however, was considerable. Indeed, Nadia evolved within the frame of ambivalence, which enabled her to employ a signifier of tenderness. While manipulating the buttons she said "ma-ma-ma." She also scrutinized my face immediately after rejecting me, as she babbled "non-non" and hit my leg with her hand. There was no ambivalence of this kind in Marie-Françoise, no tenderness to soothe the radical movement toward making a hole in my body; a movement that failed as it remained within a pure Real that could not be canceled out by a signifier. At no time did she promote the signifier.

She did not assign any special significance to the Real of my body in relation to the other objects. Thus, she turned immediately toward the Real of the dish of rice pudding, the impossibility of which almost caused a convulsion in her.

That was the same object, connoted by the Real of the absence, that she sought at the window. There, at least, her cry of appeal allowed for the expectation of a beyond of that Real.

On 10 October, the beyond appeared as her face moved closer and closer to the dish. When her nose almost touched the edge, her gaze became tangential in relation to the object and focused on the doll. Judging from her trembling arms, her bulging eyes, and the turmoil that invaded her, the attempt to escape the real object failed, sending her back to another object of the same order, which had nothing to do with an image.

Then, after calming down, she established another object—at least for that session, since it was not new for her, according to what we knew about her behavior when faced with objects. She took the rubber sailor and pressed it against her nose. We shall see later the fundamental place occupied by a surface object stuck to the nose.

The scene that followed concerned the relation with the object in another way. After taking the large cooking pot from the tea set, Marie-Françoise looked inside, plunged her hand into it, and explored the hole, which she hesitated to fill in with one of her pieces of candy. She turned toward me with a little cry of appeal, the sign that I existed for her. I then responded and filled in the hole with a piece of candy that I had in my pocket. But my existence was ephemeral and my response did not result in her licking the piece of candy that I had put in; she sucked one of hers. She remained alone, always alone. She showed it once more as she went back to the dish, in front of which she bowed down.

She certainly searched for an articulation other than flight. She looked at the doll, then at the window, and, without looking at the dish, she got absorbed in herself, facing the cooking pot, which she turned upside down so that it did not show a hole. She tapped on its bottom.

That was the representation of the Other without a hole to which she returned by deciding to turn the cooking pot upside down. At that time she made sucking noises, ending up with her mouth wide open; and she uttered muffled growls, moving her bottom as if she were on the potty. All of this indicated clearly that, if the hole was not in the Other, then it was her body that was radically holed. The only true hole of the body, the real gap that goes from the mouth to the anus, was revealed there. Her body was holed, whereas mine failed to be holed. Only the day before she had tried to make a hole in my cheek. At this stage we simply take note of the fact.

Nadia, too, had encountered the question of the hole on 24 December, when she doubted that my body was holed as she manipulated the buttons of my white coat and touched my skin. This left her dumbfounded, and when she manipulated the buttons again she avoided my skin. The buttons were the separable object that I carried. My skin was the sign that my body was not holed. She then went fiercely at my mouth, pushing my head back and poking her fingers into the skin of my neck, as if she wanted to make a hole there, as if it were necessary to make the other end of the hole of my body, so as to ensure that this was holed. At the end of that session, let it be remembered, she smeared herself with excrement for the first time. This had the sense of representing the integrity of her body as structured like a Möbius strip, a nonholed surface with one side only.

Marie-Françoise would go through the same experience of smearing herself with excrement; but it will be seen that in her case the meaning was different. As to the violence that impelled her to the attempt at making a hole in my cheek—a violence that can certainly be compared with that of Nadia—there was a striking difference. Even during the most intense moments Nadia kept her contact with me, maintaining her interrogation and her demand in a consistent discourse. Marie-Françoise, on the other hand, was always ready to turn toward an object other than me, as if all the objects, including myself, were undifferentiated; and the question of the hole of the body appeared as much on my body as on the cooking pot, without any indication that there was a question of metaphorical substitutes, but rather of a Real in all instances.

The scene with the cooking pot did not make her forget the dish, which she tried to link once more with the doll and the window. It was the window of absence that, in fact, gave the doll its meaning: she exclaimed "maman-bébé" in front of the dish; and turning toward me, she repeated "maman-bébé." How is it, then, that the dish remained impossible? Only because the window qua real absence did not permit the presentification of the Other in a symbolic alternation of presence and absence, and because the Other was sealed in the Real of its absence, a Real that contaminated the dish and rendered it deadly. We could think that the doll had started to acquire the status of an image, were it not for the fact that Marie-Françoise ended up the session with a scene in which the doll was far from being an image.

Exhausted by the impossibility of the dish, she dropped to the sitting position (as she always did in situations of impasse), holding the doll. As she had done with the sailor, she pressed it against her face; as with the cereal, she looked at it, her mouth wide open. At that moment she made an incursion into autoerotism with that double, mirroring herself in the doll narcissistically: she sucked her index finger and gave the little finger of the same hand to the doll, as if to make it suck.

But the charm was broken when she looked at me; she completely withdrew into herself and rocked for five minutes with the doll, always in the same posture. It was as if I were of no help to her; or rather, as if my gaze carried the prohibition: she got up and went toward the door with the doll.

17/Really Filling in the Hole of Her Body

On 13 October, Marie-Françoise extended her arms to me as I entered her room, so that I did not need to wait for the nurse. I put her on the floor, at the foot of her crib, helped her, at her request, to walk down the steps, and then sat down, leaving her free to do what she wanted—to keep in contact with her room, if the contact with me was only partially tolerable for her.

She grabbed my glasses as I took her from her crib. For five minutes she played with them, throwing and picking them up, looking at me and from time to time uttering little screams. It did not make a bad impression: *it amounted to making the glasses, a part of me, suffer what she would have wanted to make me suffer.* She made this intention clear *by extending her hand toward me* and opening and closing it, while uttering a little cry of appeal, as if she wanted to catch me. Immediately after that, she threw down the glasses more violently.

Following her call, I approached Marie-Françoise discreetly and sat down on a chair closer to her; but after a few minutes I had to return to my place, because in the second chair I blocked the way between her and the objects on the table. If she wanted to go toward them she had to pass in front of me, and she could not make up her mind to do so. Her gestures became more violent, and while she looked several times in the direction of the table, she showed that she was determined not to look at me. As soon as I sat down where I was before, she made up her mind.

She stood up and walked up to the table. Walking was difficult because she did not have her shoes on. When I picked her up, I put her shoes close to her; instead of giving them to me so that I could help her to put them on, however, she threw them into the room.

She took the piece of candy from the cooking pot, licked it, did not dare to look at the dish, and became absorbed in a conventional game with the cooking pot in order to escape the attraction of the dish. The game consisted in plunging her hand into the pot, as if she wanted to verify the void, and then turning it upside down to tap on it. She got up again and then sat in different places within the room to reproduce the same game.

During this scene her walk became more and more difficult as it was hindered by her diaper, which eventually fell. The nurse, who was walking past, put Marie-Françoise on her lap and fixed her diaper. Once again on the floor, Marie-Françoise was furious with me and played *a scene in two moments:* first, sitting in front of me, *she stamped her arms and feet while looking at me,* as if she were hitting me with her arms and pushing me away with her feet (and for the first time emotion was present in her aggressive movements against me). Following this, *she swiveled around herself* in the sitting position, like a weather vane in the middle of a tornado that cannot point in a single direction. She ended up staying motionless in front of me and then started the stamping again.

She wanted to go back to her room and thus finished the session herself, as if it were something unbearable. Yet she started to cry when she saw me moments later.

On 14 October she had a slight temperature, as did all the children in her room. The nurse told me that she had had a temper tantrum for no apparent reason and had refused all forms of consolation. It was a crisis of despair rather than a convulsive one, as she did not show any agitation or rigidity.

As I prepared the room, I heard Marie-Françoise's little cries of appeal; she had recognized my voice.

The nurse brought her and sat her on the small chair. Marie-Françoise did not say anything, took a piece of candy, and licked it; but she started to cry as soon as the nurse left. She calmed down immediately when I put her on the floor as usual. She licked her piece of candy and every now and then held it out to me, a big smile on her face, only to say "non" to me. This made her laugh.

Her interest turned to the basket, which contained some of the usual toys. She was slow in satisfying her curiosity. She moved forward, turned around herself to face the basket, tilted it slowly toward her, and, keeping it in that position, took from it a small milk pitcher and then a pot much smaller than the one with which she had played before and which had a *lid.* But she could not stay interested in an object of the external world for too long. After concerning herself with the lid for a moment, she stood up and moved toward the table.

She did that in order to look at the dish. She devoured it with her eyes for a second, almost sticking her face to the rice pudding. Then she looked at *the baby doll; near its mouth she put a cookie,* of which she had eaten a little, but stopped her movement just a few inches away from the doll's mouth. This innovation troubled her; she fled by dropping on the floor to the sitting position and becoming absorbed in the contemplation of the sailor.

This was not the contemplation of an object external to her: indeed, she almost pressed the sailor against her eyes, first on one, then on the other. *I had the impression that she incorporated that object, which thus became a projection of herself, her double, which did not have an atom of existence outside herself and which came from the external world.* It was her way of fleeing from an emotion. She threw it far away after five minutes, during which time she had been able to regain her internal balance. She stood up in front of the table once more.

Perhaps a bungled action, perhaps not: as she tried to grab the cup, *she knocked over the doll and its head went into the rice pudding.* She froze, took the doll by the diaper, looked at its face smeared with rice pudding, and fell on the floor to the sitting position, still holding the doll. She put it close to her face, as she had done with the sailor; but this was very brief, because the presence of the rice pudding prevented her from making of the doll her double. Keeping it at a normal distance, she cautiously put her finger on the smeared face, and then, intrigued, looked at her dirty finger. She started again and, *looking at me, she slowly moved the doll's head to her own mouth, which she opened and where she stuck the smeared head.* No sucking motion. One would say that she was biting in order to absorb. It was only after a minute, when she removed the doll from her mouth, that she perceived the taste that the rice pudding had left on her lips—which looked as if they had been painted with pudding—and moved her mouth like a wine taster.

She liked that and used the doll as an intermediary to satisfy the craving she had for the rice pudding. She stood up again, *sunk the doll's foot into the dish, and sucked it;* she repeated this three times in a row. She looked at me as I told her of the intermediary role that she was making the doll play, through which she avoided any demand addressed to me. The tension was too high; she dropped to the sitting position.

She picked up *the lid of the pot and wanted to put it on the doll's bottom.* But she did not do it; she hit the doll with the lid and threw the lid to then grab *the duck, which she made quack, with pleasure.* Then *she sunk the tip of the duck's tail into the rice pudding, sucked it,* and started again. She turned her back toward me and, *keeping the duck's tail in her mouth, she squeezed it to make it quack.*

The session had been long enough. She threw down the duck, picked up the cooking pot, into which she put the milk pitcher, and threw the whole thing in the air. She dragged the duck caught on her diaper as she went to pick up the potty. She stopped, sitting in front of the connecting door; then she moved toward it.

I heard her saying *"pipi"* (pee-pee) to the nurse who put her back in her bed. I knew later that, exhausted, she fell asleep before dinner.

Given the little contact that Marie-Françoise had established with me in the course of the preceding sessions, the little interest she had shown in my presence, on 13 October I decided to adopt a position of retreat, that is to say, to interrogate her demand for a session. She showed that beyond the absence of contact on her part, she was nevertheless searching for something, since she came without hesitation. Her drama was not, therefore, a refusal on her part, but rather the impossibility of formulating her demand due to the lack of means. Her refusal would have been the sign of ambivalence, to which, as we have seen, she did not have access. All she could do was to address a call to me that undoubtedly was not unequivocal and that was located rather within the frame of her impossible relation with the object, which excluded the true presence of an Other.

Moreover, if she played with my glasses it was not because, as in the case of Nadia, the glasses were a part of my body that she could use to question the separable object, thus foreshadowing the metaphor. For her, the object had a rather massive character: the glasses were my entire body. She showed this by extending her hand to me, opening and closing it as she uttered her little cry of appeal, as if she wanted to catch the totality of me.

In the scene that followed I was only an object that constituted an obstacle between her and the other objects. As these were what she wanted, she was tense; but she did not address any demand to me, not even a look: which confirmed that for her I was there or I wasn't, that is to say, I was a real object. I did not acquire the dimension of a representation for her.

She could not look at me as she could not look at the dish a little later. Then she renewed the game that she had already played with the potty, in which she isolated on one side the void and, by inversion, the fullness, tapping on the bottom. The fact that she played that game in different places of the room can be compared with the way in which, after the mirror, Nadia discovered the three-dimensional and containing character of the room, as well as the hole of that container, i.e., the window. To be sure, for Marie-Françoise the window was also of capital importance; but, did it have the same character of the hole that Nadia enjoyed as a function of the structure of the body that she had acquired? Certainly not. Marie-Françoise did not find in it an opening to a beyond, but the place of a call to a real absence, which simultaneously made of the window a real hole and of the object of her call qua real absence a massive object without qualities and unable to hold separable objects.

At the end of the session a scene took place that triggered Marie-Françoise's violence against me. For the first time her emotion was clearly manifest. We could associate her movements with the convulsive crisis in front of the food on 3 October. During that crisis the muscular discharge indicated the absence of another in the place where I was and where she could not see me. In the context of the session I was absent, in the same way as there was no other during the nocturnal crises that she had been having for quite some time. But in the session we are discussing there was an almost successful attempt at addressing to me the jerky motions of her arms and legs: Marie-Françoise did not have a convulsive crisis, but acted as if she were hitting and pushing me away, which made sense.

We still have to know why this occurred in connection with the diaper that a nurse put back on her, in front of me. Was it not for the same reason why, at the end of the session of 26 December, Nadia had not tolerated that the nurse left her bottom naked in front of me, had quickly crawled to her bed, without looking or listening to me, and the following day had smeared herself with excrement? The inferior pole of the body has to do with a hole. Nadia had posited that question in front of the mirror. Marie-Françoise did the same with the potty. That hole under my gaze had to do with the real gap of her holed body, as she showed on 10 October. That was also Nadia's fear: that my gaze made a hole in her.

In the case of Marie-Françoise, despite everything, my gaze placed me at the limit of the emergence of the Other. This became evident when she started to cry as she saw me moments after the end of the session. Did she cry like a child in front of an adult, in order to address a call to the adult, or did she cry because she had failed to make her call be heard, the call that never came out of her, like the scream that remained in her throat? This is also the question posed by the sense of the crisis of despair that she had the following day, before her session; a crisis that the nurse described as unmotivated and beyond any form of consolation.

Yet on 14 October, as I was preparing the materials for the session, I heard Marie-Françoise's short cries of appeal when she recognized my voice. That did not prevent her from crying at the beginning of the session, when the nurse sat her on a small chair instead of putting her on the floor. She calmed down as soon as I sat her down in the usual place—as if in the very problematic relationship with me only the spatial points of reference remained for her.

She then took a step that might appear to be decisive in her relation with me, as Nadia did when she uttered the signifier "mama" on 5 December, opening the path for the passage from the Real to the signifier in the bodily relation. With a broad smile on her face, Marie-Françoise offered me the piece of candy she had been sucking, only to say "non" and laugh. But her bodily relation remained short of the level at which Nadia was able to engage. In addition, she returned immediately to her manipulation of the objects in the basket, thus cutting off from me. It was not insignificant, however, that among those objects she chose a small pot with a lid. This lid attracted her attention; we shall see how she used it.

Her cutting off from me was even more evident when she returned to the dish, where she reestablished her only relation with the object, putting her face very close to the rice pudding. She attempted to establish a relation at a distance with the doll and tried to give it a cookie from which she had eaten a little bit. But she stopped her motion a few inches from the doll's mouth and dropped to the sitting position, as she usually did when confronted with the impossible. Finally she took the sailor and almost pressed it against her eye for about five minutes, in order to make her double, as I mentioned previously. We shall refer later to the central function of the double in Marie-Françoise's pathological deviance. The bungled gesture toward the cup, which made the doll fall into the rice pudding, left her frozen initially; however, she immediately abandoned the image of the smeared doll—the smearing preventing it from becoming her double—and turned it into an object that plugged the orifice of her mouth. The difference with Nadia was again evident in this instance, in relation to the smearing of the skin, whether this involved excrement or cereal.

Marie-Françoise then used the doll as an intermediary to eat a little rice pudding, sinking the doll's foot into the dish and sucking it three times in a row. In that way she avoided making any demand to me. That also represented an impasse and she dropped to the sitting position. In that respect her orientation was the opposite of Nadia's: Nadia had inscribed the oral in the register of the scopic, while Marie-

Françoise made the scopic object, the smeared doll, pass into the register of orality, where her demand to the Other was arrested.

Arrested, too, was the possibility of her inscribing, at the level of the Other's body, the separable object that she might find there to plug the hole of her own body, thus producing in the Other's body a hole left by what she might have taken from it. Nadia was able to make it, in the course of a debate that took her from the real body, where her impasse was evident, to the signifying inscription of the object of the body, which opened the way to her demand. She was able to make it because from the beginning there was no exclusion of the Other that I was; or, to put it in other words, because for her the signifier preexisted, anticipating the experience that she might have of it.

The signifier that preexists all other signifiers is what Lacan called "Name-of-the-Father," which in *The Ego and the Id* Freud postulated as the "Primal Father," the basis of primary identification, and which makes possible any mutation of the Real when it is not foreclosed. For Marie-Françoise it was foreclosed: she was searching for the same thing as Nadia, that is to say, the filling of the hole in her body, but only in appearance, since she remained in the initial real impasse, in the impossibility of the mutation of the Real into the signifier, the only path toward the demand to the Other. She had no option then but to always return to the demonstration of the impossible. She insisted in vain, since the insertion of the initial master signifier was foreclosed. The head of the smeared doll, although outlining her lips, could really fill in her mouth only because it failed to become the substitutive image of the object that she could have shown me and that would have been on the path of a demand addressed to me. No metaphorical substitution emerged. The Real closed up in itself and, as always, despair made Marie-Françoise fall to the sitting position.

The last scene, still in the absence of the Other, represented a last attempt to show that what was at stake was the plugging of the hole—the hole of the body—that goes from the mouth to the anus: after having tried to fill in her mouth, Marie-Françoise wanted to put the lid of the pot on the doll's bottom. But she did not do it; what she did instead might induce vertigo. She took the duck, made it quack by pressing on it, sank the tip of its tail into the rice pudding, sucked it, started again, and, turning her back on me, the duck's tail in her mouth, pressed on it to make it quack.

Vertigo, certainly, from seeing that object—which usually is a representative of the embryonic stages by virtue of its relation with water—plug in the hole of her mouth and become a sort of appendix that fed her. Nadia had used it in February to express a relationship between the exterior and the interior: the duck within the ball and herself within the room, with the hole formed by the window. That object sent out the cry that Marie-Françoise herself could not utter. She would have been able to utter that cry only through and toward the Other that I was; but she turned her back on me, since once more her demand, also represented by the cry, could not be addressed to anyone. She was reduced to show only in the Real the vain prolongation of her body, like a penis, which she might make cry but which was nothing other than the reverse side of the irreparable silence between her and me.

Nevertheless, in the last analysis the duck took her to the borders of the signifier, such is the way in which the Real is ordered and infiltrated by what cannot be said. After the session I heard her saying "pipi" to the nurse that put her back in bed. That "pipi" came to occupy the place of the impossible cry, like the demand that she was unable to address to me in the session. During the period of violence of the last days of December, Nadia's urine in the session had to do on a number of occasions with that which could not be said. But, in contrast with Marie-Françoise's, it had a representational function and it simply occupied the place of a temporary stumbling block in her discourse, since it was in the session that she addressed it to me. The urine as such had to do with a lack. Marie-Françoise's was in the order of the Real and had to do with a penis; but she was not able to show it except in my absence.

The sequence of the session of 14 October was fundamental. Marie-Françoise showed in it that her whole problem with the body was the filling in of the hole, a real hole that was to be really filled:

1. Just before the session her rectal temperature was taken; that is to say, a hole was "made" in her body. This happened immediately after an unmotivated and inconsolable tantrum.

2. A little later, she turned the sailor into her double, sticking it against her eye, displacing the filling in of the hole of her mouth, like a veneer, on the surface of her eye.

3. She filled in the hole of her mouth with the head of the doll, which had fallen into the rice pudding.

4. After filling in her mouth with the doll, she plugged the doll's bottom with the lid of the cooking pot.

5. Finally, she also closed up her mouth with the duck, making it send out the cry that she herself could not utter.

It was only in relation to her own body that the hole of the body was in question: her mouth or her eye. It was not at all a question of the hole of my body.

18 / The Real and the Signifier Separated: Psychosis and Structure

When I arrived on 15 October, Marie-Françoise was sitting on a table and a nurse was putting her shoes on. She held out her hand to me, opening and closing it, a gesture of appeal accompanied by a brief cry. As she was put on the floor, *she immediately moved on all fours to the consulting room.*

She stood up in front of the table and sat down again to suck the pieces of candy as she looked at me. Her gaze was very lively and very much in contact with me. Twice she held out a piece of candy to show it to me. She stood up again in front of the dish, and for five minutes *her gaze moved from the dish to me and to the window. Only at the end her gaze included the doll in the circuit, and at that moment she excluded the window.*

Moving quickly, she put her head near the edge of the dish. She stood up and, smiling, uttered a brief cry toward me. I could not perceive a tone of appeal in her softly uttered cry. She was smiling and her jaw was not protruding as usual. *Her brief cry was aimed at making me share an interest with her, rather than making me participate in an action.* She knew very well that I would not take any initiative; this made her emotion in front of the food less conflictual. The second time, instead of the short cry, which was not even a phoneme, she said *"maman,"* distinctly pronounced. From that moment her gaze aimed at the window and not at me anymore, and she also *remained silent.* I told her this.

Then she addressed herself to the doll, not to the void anymore. Her gaze went from the doll to me and back, without focusing on the dish. She took the doll and looked at it from a distance, without saying anything; in particular, without saying "bébé." *With the doll in her hands, she put the dish and the window in brackets* and, smiling, could look at me. Her entire face was *very relaxed.*

I reminded her of the scene of the day before. Holding the doll, she sat down again; unable to make up her mind, she looked at it from a normal distance, as if she hesitated to turn it into her double as she had done before. She did not know where to put it, then left it to eat a cracker and *become absorbed in the manipulation of the toy tea set.* She rummaged around inside the basket and took out a cooking pot, a teapot, and a lid. She held the lid with her teeth as she looked for a way of putting the cooking pot and teapots *one inside another.* Furious at not being able to get a result immediately, she threw the pots away, then played with the lid, throwing it in the air, hitting it against the floor, and making it roll. She had enough of that; she stopped and observed the lid. She stood up again to get the cooking pot, rubbed it against the floor, laughing, straightened it up, and *put the lid on it.* She was so delighted with her achievement that she turned around to make me admire it.

Still standing up, she went to get the teapot and once again tried to fit it into the cooking pot. After many attempts, she could place the cooking pot on top of the teapot, building a tower. She admired it; but when she added the lid to the cooking pot the whole thing collapsed. She started the tower again, fidgeting impatiently, furious because the objects were not obeying her, and got up to *displace her fury onto the lid,* which she hit on the floor as *she babbled with violence.*

Finally, she spread the three objects in different corners of the room and moved toward the door. On her way there, she kicked the teapot, and then also the lid, which she pushed in front of her. Once in front of the door, she opened it and looked at me hesitantly. I told her that she had had a good session and that it was indeed enough for the day. Her face showing relief, she playfully threw the lid at a boy in the room, in order to make her departure easier. I helped her to climb the steps and left her in very good shape.

On 17 October I was told that the previous day, as I did not take her for a session and she abandoned any hope of seeing me (probably she had heard me in the building), *she had smeared herself with excrement taken from her diaper,* covering her eyebrows, eyes, and the area around her lips completely.

She received me with her stereotyped gestures of arms and legs and an expression of bad mood on her face. When we were alone, she *rocked with violence.* She stopped when I said that she did not want me because I had been absent the day before and moved to take the pieces of candy on the table. She sucked one, then *held it against the tip of her nose* and held it out without giving it to me.

She left it and *grabbed the sailor, which she held a half inch away from her right eye, then against her nose, and against her right eye again.* I told her that because I had not come to see her the day before she was trying to ignore me, incorporating the sailor inside her, making of it her double in order to exclude me.

What did she understand? Whatever it was, she stopped her game, looked me straight in the eyes, first with an air of hostility, then with a smile, *and uttered in my direction a short cry of appeal-recognition,* on which she insisted, as if she wanted me to imitate her. I echoed her; delighted, she repeated it twice.

From that moment on there was more contact with me: my presence played a part in what she was doing. She rummaged inside the basket and took the milk pitcher and the cooking pot and its lid. In front of me, she put the cooking pot upside down on the floor and the milk pitcher on top of it. She wanted me to witness her achievement. *She put the lid in her mouth for a second* before placing it on the milk pitcher; then the whole thing collapsed. Furious against the lid, she picked it up, hit it against the floor, and placed it on the bottom of the cooking pot, after having thrown away the milk pitcher in the direction of the window.

She moved up to the table and sat down with the crackers, without looking at the dish or the doll. She threw a cracker after biting it a little, pretended to drink from the cooking pot, then fished out a piece of wood in the shape of a bridge and sucked it as she looked at me. I pointed out to her that she pretended to drink from something she knew was empty, that she never wanted to drink from a mug, that she threw the crackers that were there to eat, and that she sucked the piece of wood while looking at me. She then *moved toward the window, saying "maman,"* and threw the cooking pot in front of her.

She looked outside, *wanting to ignore me,* until the moment when I told her that she called "maman" in the direction of the window to tell me that since her mama was not there the food was empty, and that she did not want to have anything to do with me because I had abandoned her the day before. She turned around and started to move toward me, pushing the cooking pot in front of her. But when she heard an airplane, she dropped to the sitting position, uttered a cry, her jaw protruding in my direction, and raised her head toward the sky. I spoke to her about her fear of all the noises from outside; more calm, she stood up again, *but in doing so she banged her head against the glass.* She dropped to the sitting position and looked at me with hostility, accusing me of the damage she had suffered.

She got up once more and chased the cooking pot with fury; the pot ended up against my foot, from where she picked it up without hesitation. For a moment she stayed sitting at my feet, not knowing very well what to do. Her fury against the cooking pot was directed at me, and for the first time led her against my feet. That was something new, and it became evident that the novelty of her initiative triggered an upheaval even stronger than her fury. As usual, she escaped her emotion by cutting off from me as best as she could, that is to say, eating the cracker as she turned her back on me.

Once she calmed down, she got up and took the doll without looking at the dish. She put it on the floor *and came to take my glasses.* She sat down and explored my glasses with one finger, without tapping on them. Then she commenced with them the same game as with the lid, shaking them, throwing them to the floor, and picking them up. She threw out the glasses and picked up the doll; she looked at its diaper, then its face—as an evocation of what she had done to herself the day before—all this at a normal distance. She then held it against her eye *and finally put her mouth on the doll's mouth.* After this, she placed the doll further away and *touched its nose, mouth, then its eyes . . .* and this made her search for *my glasses* with her gaze. She brought the glasses close to her, touched the doll's diaper, *and then she sucked the glasses as she looked at the doll,* which she held all the time.

The emotion was too strong. I felt she was trying to flee from herself. After telling her a summary of the preceding scene, I said to her: "See you tomorrow." She waved good-bye to me when I left her room.

She took the doll with her; my glasses remained on the floor.

A little later I was told that Marie-Françoise responded with gusto to the nurse's calling phonemes, even when they were not addressed to her.

In this session I observed: (1) that she made me responsible for knocking herself as she was getting up; (2) that she used intermediary objects to express her aggressiveness toward me; and (3) that her fury led her to approach me for the first time. She was able to unload her anger on a part of me, my glasses, after making me understand that, since her mother was not there, she would not eat or drink. She made up her mind to suck the glasses after shaking them; but this only after putting her mouth on her double, the doll, which on a previous occasion had its face covered in cereal.

When I arrived on 18 October, a nurse was giving Marie-Françoise her afternoon snack. She was standing up, holding on to the adult's knees. She smiled as she saw me and immediately opposed resistance to eating. I told her I would come later.

When I returned, she dropped to the sitting position and rocked. My arrival while she was having her afternoon snack had disturbed her considerably. She expressed her resentment *by alternating between voluntary refusal and cutting off from me.*

She expressed her *voluntary refusal* by sitting down, her face toward the window, her back turned to me. She started to rock, and as soon as I spoke to her, her arms and legs shook violently, as if she were hitting and kicking me out. She had been drawn to the window by a call of the Wolf Child, who was in the garden, and cried "maman." I spoke to her of her reaction, connecting it with Robert's call and its meaning for her.* She then made her will clear by staying at least five minutes *sitting down, completely still and straight, facing the window, without uttering a sound or making a gesture, her back loaded with all her hostility.*

After a long while, she turned around to face me and, smiling, looked at me with an expression that was surprisingly powerful. It was as if she were telling me: "I know very well that you are there. You can see that I ignore you. I am very happy that you are close to me, because, as mama rejected me, I can now reject you!" She then turned around toward the window.

Her refusal was also expressed through her attempt *to drink from the exterior, the bottom side of the cooking pot* and the milk pitcher, to then throw them away violently. She also tried *to eat the lid,* thus displaying aggressiveness toward me: eating what was not edible and refusing to eat what she could eat.

She looked at the basket and spluttered intensely toward it for two minutes. After expressing her refusal in that way, she took *a white dog from the basket and put two of its legs in her mouth. She held it with her teeth as she looked at it and explored it with her finger.* Noticing the knotted end of the string *that served as one of the dog's eyes and was a bit loose, she tried to eat it.* As I verbalized for her the scene with the eye, reminding her that she placed the objects

---

*Translators' note: Rosine Lefort presented the case of Robert the Wolf Child at Jacques Lacan's seminar on 10 March 1954 (see *The Seminar of Jacques Lacan, Book I: Freud's Papers on Technique, 1953-1954,* edited by Jacques-Alain Miller, translated and with notes by John Forrester [Cambridge: Cambridge University Press, 1988], 89-106). See also Rosine Lefort and Robert Lefort, *Les Structures de la psychose: L'Enfant au loup et le Président* (Paris: Éditions du Seuil, 1988), where the case of Robert is discussed in great detail and compared with the case of Schreber.

very close to her eye when she wanted "to return them to herself" in order to cut herself off from everything, *she threw the dog at her feet and hit it with the palm of her hand.*

These scenes were interspersed with true breakdowns of her contact with me, at the times when she incorporated the objects so that these entered her internal world and did not contain a single portion of me.

The session had lasted for half an hour when she started to rock, looking at the door. She looked at me before stretching her arms to the nurse, smiling broadly, full of emotion. She sucked the pieces of candy but ignored the cookies, the dish, and the mug.

On 15 October, she held out her hand to me, opening and closing it, and her gesture of appeal was accompanied by a short cry as on 13 October. She repeated the cry addressed to me a little later, in front of the dish of rice pudding, when, after putting her face close to its edge, she got up and turned toward me, smiling.

Her cry was admittedly soft, and I have mentioned that I did not perceive in it a tone of appeal but the sense of making me share an interest. It concerned the dish, and that is why I think that her cry was not a demand that I feed her; that is to say, it did not aim at making me participate in an action. The Real of the dish remained excluded, impossible. That did not prevent Marie-Françoise from taking the step of uttering the signifier "maman," which she pronounced distinctly. Then her gaze turned toward the window, away from me; she remained silent, and I told her this.

Thus, what she did was only to return to a preceding scene, when, following an exchange of candy during which her gaze was for the first time very much alive and in contact with me, she remained motionless in front of the dish for five minutes, her gaze turning from the dish to me and from me to the window. At that moment, her gaze included the doll in the circuit but excluded the window.

Before turning to the part played by the doll, we may examine and clarify that first sequence by comparing it with the scene of 5 December, when Nadia said "mama" for the first time. Nadia's "mama" emerged only at the culmination of the scene where the violence of her desire had pushed her to take possession of the object of my body: it was by clutching her hands on my breast that all was resolved for her in her appeal to me. All was resolved in the passage from the real object of the body to the signifier. Whereas for Marie-Françoise nothing was resolved, since her cry of "maman" did not annul the object, which remained radically separated, excluded from the cry. The Real and the signifier remained each in its own camp, and the absence of any mutation of one into the other left Marie-Françoise confronted with the void. That is what she said when she turned her gaze to the window and did not turn to look at me again.

The void she found there was the absence, not of the Real, but of the signifier—which constitutes a void that could not be more real. That is to say, in the window there was no signifier that could return to her, in an inverted form, the demand that she had sent out.

Which signifier was lacking there? No other than the first of all, that of the primal repression, that which Nadia found on 10 December and which then founded all the signifiers for her in the locus of the Other, necessary guarantee for the "making herself heard" of the subject.

In the following scene, Marie-Françoise did not address herself anymore to the void, but to the doll. Previously the doll had excluded the window from the circuit of the gaze; it now excluded the dish. This is like a new attempt to exclude the Real—which resists, as we have seen, its being mutated into the signifier, as a result of the absence of the Other.

The attempt nevertheless had some effect, since with the doll, that small other, Marie-Françoise was able to put the dish and the window between brackets and could look at me, smiling, a clear expression of relaxation on her face. I wrote that although she could not name the doll, as if the previous failure of the "maman" prevented it, she was, however, able to look at it from a normal distance, without pressing it against her eye to make it into her double, as she had done with the sailor. But then she did not know what to do with it and left it. A new failure: she was not able to shift the doll to the dimension of an image in which she could recognize herself. This makes us think that the imaginary dimension cannot exist without the possibility of promoting the Real to the level of the signifier, that is to say, to the locus of the Other.

From the beginning Nadia told us that the image of the other was tied up with the Other, to the point that on 10 December she summed them up in the object of her fascination: "a + A" Marie-Françoise showed that without the A there can be no a.

The following scene involved a game of fitting in the cooking pot and teapot one inside the other, which could be seen as a game of container and contained. In reality, from beginning to end the main object was the lid. Like every other time she used the lid, it was a question of plugging the hole. Then, after giving up fitting the tea-pot inside the cooking pot, she built a tower and she wanted to add the lid on top of the tower, which made the whole thing collapse. At first she displaced her fury against the lid, then pushed it in front of her as she moved toward the door. As she was leaving, she threw it playfully to a boy.

Finally, she linked in a manifest fashion the lid qua stopgap to the other: a small other that she was not able, as Nadia was, to transform into a separable object of my body so that she could fill in the hole. But it did not work because I was not in the scene. Once again, in the absence of the articulation of the Real to the signifier, the artic-ulation between the other and the Other could not be made.

Nevertheless, on 16 October, I appeared, if I can put it this way, in the negative, when I could not see Marie-Françoise for her ses-sion. She probably heard me in the building. That evening, after los-ing all hope of seeing me, she smeared herself with excrement from her diaper. She covered her eyebrows, eyes, and the area around her lips completely. The nurse spontaneously remarked on the phenom-enon of the rim present in that smearing.

That rim poses some questions. What we described in the case of Nadia was considerably different: Nadia had smeared her body, in-cluding her face, with excrement, and had even eaten some. In oth-er words, for Nadia it was a question of a closed, nonholed, entire surface. We could say that her skin had to be a surface without fault or hole, all in one piece, without exterior or interior. That was the version, inscribed on her skin, of the image of 10 December: her skin represented the totality "$a + A$." My absence had brought about such a reaction, which placed in counterpoint the existence of a and A.

For Marie-Françoise there was neither A nor a: neither A, which was replaced by the real absence beyond the window; nor the small other, whose image could not be formed in the absence of the A in which to inscribe it. Consequently, her smearing was not the same as Nadia's. It only delimited the surface at the points where a hole, a real hole, was formed. Nadia affirmed that the surface of her skin should be without holes and that only my surface of A must be holed. Marie-Françoise could not say the same thing in relation to the sur-face of my body because I did not exist for her at the place of A. It is necessary to assume that there is a symbolic dimension in the require-ment that the body of the Other be holed: as Marie-Françoise could not find the hole symbolically in my body, that hole reappeared in the real of her own body.

We are tempted to discern in this an essential aspect of the *infans**
subject's psychosis: there is no hole as a result of the absence of the
Other. Could we not even say that it is not the Other, but the Other's hole, a hole of reception, the only place where the subject may
become, a place that is not in the Real—where the subject, and not
the Other, is holed?

On 17 October, after the smearing, which had as its sole effect the
outlining of the holes of her body—as the head of the doll fallen in
the rice pudding had served to outline its lips, that is to say, the rim
of its mouth's hole—she received me in a bad mood and rocked with
violence. As was pointed out, the rocking was so much tied up with
the Other that it was sufficient that I gave her an interpretation on
the basis of my absence the previous day to make her stop.

She then tasted a piece of candy, pressed it against the tip of her
nose, and held it out to me, but did not give it to me: an attempt to
make the hole of her body shift onto mine, with the piece of candy.
But she soon abandoned it to take the sailor, which she approached
and held at a distance of a half inch from her eye. I interpreted the
sense of that double and, once again, she stopped her game, to then
utter toward me a short cry of appeal-recognition, which I imitated.
Delighted, she repeated it twice.

The entire sequence between the piece of candy and the cry made
me perceive Marie-Françoise's limits: she heard very well what I told
her, but her response always remained within an enclosure that she
could not break. Indeed, if following her attempt to question a hole
in me—by refusing to give me the piece of candy that she had put
on her nose—she took the sailor and placed it against her eye, then
her nose, then her eye again, that was because she was searching,
beyond the hole in me, for the image of the other that would serve
her as an anchoring point, so that she could find her bearings in relation to me.

At this point we may recall the process that Nadia went through
in relation to the image *a* + A. For Nadia, however, the A was the
reference for the existence of the other, which could be inscribed in
the image. For Marie-Françoise, on the other hand, the other did not
have an imaginary existence because there was no Other. For her what
remained of the other was not an image but a real object, the sailor.

Nadia had attached the image to the surface of her eye in order not
to lose it. Although the sailor was not an image but a real object, Marie-

*Translators' note: *Infans* = unable to speak.

Françoise too attached it to her eye. On 10 December, my naming had unstuck the image from Nadia's eye, had made of it a repressed signifier, the primordial signifier of her primal repression. My interpretation to Marie-Françoise—that she made the sailor into her double in order to exclude me—was for her nothing other than a finishing-off stitch. Almost immediately, she made the shift to the signifier by means of her short cry of appeal; but she left a real gap between, on one side, the Real of the sailor, and on the other side, the signifier of her appeal to the other, with no mutation of the first into the second—the same thing had happened between the dish and "maman" on 15 October. While for Nadia the image of 10 December never returned, since as a signifier it had been repressed, the sailor could not be repressed but kept its role as a double attached to the eye.

For Marie-Françoise, my intervention, which she heard, remained isolated and did not entail the reorganization of the scopic as in the case of Nadia. Although what she heard led her to the limit of "making herself heard" through her short cry of appeal, this in no way aimed, as with Nadia, at the Other, but at the immediacy of her echo.

Marie-Françoise resumed the game of making a tower with the pieces of the toy tea set. She took me as a witness, but the beyond at which she aimed was always the lid that plugged the hole. As she failed in her attempt to place it on top of the tower, she was furious against me: she banged it against the floor and then put it on the bottom of the cooking pot.

A little later she pretended to drink from the cooking pot and, redoubling her game of pretense, she threw the crackers and sucked a block while looking at me. For Nadia, this kind of pretense had been a victory in her relation with the "nothing," that is to say, with the signifier. Marie-Françoise, on the contrary, when I told her what she was doing, answered—to put it this way—that the matter for her was not the "nothing" but the real of absence: she went to the window and said "maman." The real of absence suddenly acquired a strange, if not frightening, aspect, when from the same window came the sound of a flying airplane. Marie-Françoise fell to the sitting position as she uttered a cry, the echo of the sound she had just heard, for which she reproached me by turning her head toward where I was.

The scene that followed was the first true attempt at articulating an object of my body, my glasses, with the doll. But my glasses did not have at the time, and would not have later, the same polymorphous value as they did for Nadia.

At first Marie-Françoise associated them with the lid: she grabbed them, explored them with her finger, shook them, threw them down, and picked them up again. Can we say that then she evoked sufficiently the question of the hole in my body in order to be able to take the doll, after throwing the glasses? What she did with the doll remained undecided. She looked at the doll's diaper and then at its face—an evocation, I wrote down, of what she had done to herself the day before when she smeared herself. That is to say, she posed the question of the doll's holes, and consequently of those of her own body, the evidence being that she immediately pressed the doll against her eye and finally put her mouth on the doll's mouth.

Thus, there seemed to be a return to the usual point of encounter with the stopgap "double," as she went back to the preceding scene following the reverse direction: holding the doll at a distance, she touched its nose and mouth, then its eyes, and this made her search for my glasses with her gaze. She brought the glasses close to her, touched the doll's diaper, then sucked the glasses while looking at the doll, which she held all the time. At that moment her emotion became too intense, as if she had come too close to a decisive step that she could not take: that the doll became her own image in my eyes, the place where she made a hole by taking my glasses.

In the circuit established between her and the doll, on the one hand, and myself—where she made a hole by taking my glasses—on the other, the doll prevailed too much upon her as to come to plug the hole in my body. She had no alternative but to flee, and that is what she did: she fled from the risk of becoming my real stopgap. She took the doll with her and left the glasses.

On 10 December, Nadia had known this alternative: either to have her body closed up by the image or to occupy the place of a stopgap after I called her. But for Nadia this happened in another register, that of the signifier, where the danger was inscribed in metaphor and where metonymy allowed her, on the one hand, to refuse her body as a whole, so that she only held out a foot to me, and on the other, to reverse the situation, looking for an object on me, then uttering the signifier "mama" in response to mine ("Nadia"), signifiers that posed me as Other and she as subject. Evidently, Marie-Françoise, who was still entirely a prey to the Real, without metaphor or metonymy, was not at that point.

On 18 October, a nurse was feeding Marie-Françoise as I arrived, and she could not bear being fed under my gaze. Nadia could not bear having the afternoon snack that a nurse had given her at the session either; or at least she received it with her gaze turned down and absent. It was apparent that for Nadia food was only to be refused if it did not concern the Other: for her the object at which she aimed was not food but the hand that fed her. The refusal of food referred Nadia to the Other, which for her already had its status. For Marie-Françoise, in relation to food the question was the very void of the Other; that is to say, as the Other was not there she was sent to the void. Besides, when I returned, after her snack, she dropped to the sitting position and rocked.

The experience at the beginning of the session colored the rest of it with a refusal of the void where my gaze sent her while the nurse was feeding her. She rocked because there was no Other for her. From that moment, she could not accept that I spoke, and as soon as I did she agitated her arms and legs as if she were hitting me. She turned toward the window, all the more so since she heard Robert in the garden calling "maman." I mentioned the attraction that it had for her, but this did not put an end to her will to remain facing the window for a long time, without making any sound or gesture, turning her back on me.

That hostility was important insofar as she posited me as the Other, to whom she had to make so many reproaches. It was at least the sketch of a movement that Nadia had utilized—and I can say it was my desire, since I knew it represented a possibility for her. However, after smiling at me for a moment, Marie-Françoise returned to the window, putting an end to her address to the Other.

We could well say that, in its dimension as Real, the window was a wall—a wall from which she attempted to drink, as she had done with the exterior of the cooking pot and the teapot. In other words, it did not have any holes: what blocked the route to the Other was the fact that for Marie-Françoise the Other was without holes. Did she at least attempt to make a hole, perhaps, when she aggressively tried to eat up the lid, to destroy it, in front of me? She then returned to the basket, from which she took a white dog and tried to eat up the dog's eye. I connected for her the attempt to eat the dog's eye with what she expressed when she attached objects to her own eye. But it could be added that, since in the scopic structure the gaze can erase the dimension of the loss of the object, that was the only path open to her in order to avoid, not so much a loss, but a mutilation. It was still necessary that my gaze did not take away from her the object that she attached to her eye-organ.

This session was marked by her truly cutting off from me several times and by a kind of precipitation of her eye upon the objects. She finished it with her rocking, while looking at the door. Yet when leaving she held out her arms to the nurse, smiling.

19/ The Real, the Demand, and the Signifier: Surface Relations and Distance Relations

On 21 October, in view of the diversity of objects that Marie-Françoise had sucked during the previous sessions while not being able to touch the dish of rice pudding, I introduced a bottle of milk among the materials.

She must have heard me setting up the materials for the session before I arrived to pick her up. I found her tapping on a piece of rag with her index finger: she pretended to ignore me. This must have been a reaction to my presence, since it was not at all her usual behavior outside the sessions. According to everybody, indeed, she had changed considerably, even from the physical point of view. This made me think that hearing me, even without seeing me, was enough to make her adopt a behavior of schizophrenic defense, aimed at a reduction of my person to a livable-with other, which she tried in vain through her cutting-off symptom.

She retained the same attitude after I entered the room; then she gave up the cutting off and looked at me. She laughed and shuffled on her bottom toward the steps at full speed.

Once in the room, she went directly to the table, where at first she did not see *the bottle, as if she were cut off from it*: she showed no reaction. She paid some attention to it only, tangentially, when she went to grab the cookies, which were beside the bottle. She took the cookies and ate them, casting furtive glances at the bottle. I perceived a certain excitation mounting in her. She abandoned the cookies/substitutes and tried to become absorbed in the fitting in of different pieces of the toy tea set. But that could not really divert her from her *center of attraction;* she returned to it and stood up to look at it intensely. She stamped her feet while looking at me from time to time, furious against me, as I did not help her to make up her mind, but not in an unpleasant manner. That pushed her to find an outlet for her desire, in that part of it which represented absorbing something. But she could not reach that point yet.

She dropped to the sitting position again, went back to the bas-

266 / *Marie-Françoise or Autism*

ket, and, rummaging in it, ended up finding *a spoon*. She grabbed it, came back near me, and for a moment played at throwing it in the air, shaking it, and grabbing it again—a bit like the game she played with my glasses. *She finally put it in my hand,* stood up again, and, with her mouth open, looked at the dish and then at me as she made mastication motions. *In that way she ate it all up.* She indicated clearly that for her the dish was a substitute, as her gaze remained constantly attracted by the bottle, quickly turning away from it. She also looked at me from a very short distance as she smiled: *she ate me up with her eyes a little.*

She stayed in front of me for a long time, almost leaning on me, *and started to let out phonemes at my face, as she sputtered a lot, her jaw protruding, as if she were spitting out* the food on my face. Emotionally she was not in pain but rather playful.

I took her back with the other children.

On 22 October, as I arrived, I saw Marie-Françoise by the window. She looked at me with much interest, but because of the distance I could not tell whether she had actually realized that it was me—especially because I was not wearing my white coat.

As I set up the materials, I could hear her babbling intensely in the room next door; but I still had to make her wait.

As I opened the door, she moved toward me, made me put her at the foot of the steps, and hurried toward the table to grab the pieces of candy. She dropped to the sitting position and put all the candy in her mouth. As she was sucking the candy, she picked up a rabbit, which she looked at with great interest *without putting it too close to her face.*

She abandoned it and stood up in front of the dish. She devoured it with her eyes, trembling for a moment, moved her face very close to it, *and then her gaze went from me to the dish, letting out a cry of appeal toward me,* her jaw protruding markedly. She did this for a few minutes, kicking in the void, furious because I did not obey her desire.

In fact, her desire was ambivalent: her gaze turned from the dish to me, but it was aggressive and devouring when it focused on me. Although the day before she had been able to give me the spoon, now she made no gesture toward it. Her anger became more intense, but its emotional charge was not unpleasant. Her desire was to demand in an ambivalent way, so that I would not give in to her despite her demand and at the same time she would still be able to hold a grudge against me. She made her intention clear by dropping to the sitting position with an air of relief and joy addressed to me. Relieved because I did not give in. In that way I defended her against the harm that she demanded I do to her.

I explained all this to her. *Laughing, she came to me and grabbed my glasses.* She shook them, hit them, threw them down, and picked them up. She then felt ready for her usual game of fitting in pieces of the toy tea set. But this game did not last very long, and she moved toward the door, thus ending the session herself, as if she were running away from me.

I gave her a summary of the session, reminded her of the session of the day before, and interpreted her desire to run away from me. I took her back with the other children.

After the session I was told that on the same day, in the morning, she did not tolerate the presence of an adult who was in her room to observe another girl. She started to rock and a nurse had to take her to another room because she also began to scream.

On 23 October, I found Marie-Françoise lying on her bed looking tired. She sat down when she saw me and started to babble with impatience. She stood up in front of the table for almost the entire session, with a bodily ease that I had not seen in her before.

She sucked a piece of candy, her head between her arms, and *she drooled on the floor instead of swallowing the candy.* I remarked on this. She then crunched the piece of candy.

Slowly, her gaze turned from the dish to the bottle, from the bottle to the rabbit, then to the mug, and finally to the baby doll. She looked at me with the same attention she had given to each of those objects, as if I were one of them. Then she sat down with the doll, saying "bébé" to me *and wanting to look under the diaper,* a desire that she feared intensely. She approached the diaper with great reticence, looked at it for a long time, put her finger close to it, then tapped on the slit three or four times before trying to insert her finger in it. . . . She cast a questioning look at me and turned back to the *doll,* which she looked at with perplexity. *She put her mouth on the doll's for a long time.* Looking at me again, she uttered a series of words, her jaw protruding: *"Bébé, bibi, pipi, tété"* (baby, me, pee-pee, breast). As she said "tété," she looked at the bottle, stood up again and said *"parti, parti"* (gone, gone) in a violent tone.

With her gaze on the bottle once again, she opened and closed her mouth as if she were eating, *with no sucking motions.* I told her this, which made her attention turn to the dish. She then took my arm to put my hand close to the spoon. When this was full, she moved her wide-open mouth close to the spoon, and in that way *she ate up the contents of the dish.*

She ate me with her eyes as I fed her, not without a certain latent violence when her gaze focused on the bottle, which made me think that what I gave her was the substitute of the bottle that she could not demand.

She coughed several times while she was eating. As I said this to her, *she laughed and cleared her throat.* I told her that she behaved as if she wanted to throw up the food that she had asked me for.

During this scene, she sat down with *the sailor, which she pressed hard against her eye,* while keeping the doll in her other hand; but she did not incorporate the doll.

She was not happy when the dish was empty. She stamped her feet and bent over more and more toward the mug. As she had done with the spoon, she took my arm to make the mug move closer. I put the mug within her reach and waited. She timidly put her finger on it and tilted it to see what it contained. Having verified that it was milk, she sat up and *followed with her gaze the circuit formed by the mug, the bottle, and myself, while sputtering.* After an *energetic clearing of her throat,* she made up her mind and made me grab the mug, after opening her mouth on its rim. She wanted *to drink it all.*

The term *drink* is not exact: for the first time I noticed the difficulties she had with swallowing when she had to drink from a mug. In fact, she sucked; and while drinking from the mug *she looked at the bottle incessantly.* I think that her refusal to drink from the mug (while she could drink from the little spoon and be bulimic) had its origin in her unfulfilled desire to suck, as she had babbled previously.

She confirmed that was the origin in the following scene, where she absorbed all the milk from the mug spilled on the table *through three successive intermediaries:*

1. *Her fingers,* then the entire palm of her hand, which she sucked with delight as she looked at me. I pointed out to her that she sucked the milk on her hands, while she said to me "parti" in relation to the doll or mama.

2. *A cake* that she ate piece by piece, saturating it with milk each time.

3. *The glasses,* which she sucked after sinking them in the pool. At that moment she was not looking at me anymore, as if it were too much to suck the milk through a piece of my body. She licked

the rest of the pool and dropped to the sitting position, holding my glasses all the time.

She took the sailor again and looked at it through the glasses; that is to say, *she put a lens against the sailor's face and then put the whole thing against her eye, the lens in contact with her eye.* That seemed to me to be an interesting mechanism of symbolic incorporation of a part of me, a part she considered as having been taken from her at the time of the separation from her mother, during the period of breast-feeding.

But in that way she also cut off her contact with me. I thought the session had lasted long enough. However, she was not happy when I put her back in her crib: she took her shoes off and threw them across the room.

I have pointed out that I introduced the bottle on 21 October because Marie-Françoise had shown from the beginning a sucking activity that made me think that it was necessary that she return to the primary oral stage, blocked as she was in front of the dish of rice pudding.

The fact was that, from the first session, she did not have any inhibition in sucking the candy; and she also ate the cookies, that is, all the food, before giving me her slaps. In the following sessions she went on sucking the candy, which was in marked contrast to her inability to touch the dish of rice pudding.

At first she ignored the bottle—was it voluntarily, given the lack of expression on her face?—and then cast only a few furtive glances at it. But her excitation increased. Afterward in the session, and following some diversionary games, the bottle's presence was not alien to her firm design of rummaging in the basket to take the spoon from it.

After a game that consisted in throwing the spoon in the air, grabbing it back, and shaking it—the same game she had played with my glasses—she carried out what I had told her: that I would not feed her unless she asked me for it. She put the spoon in my hand as she looked at the dish with her mouth wide open; then she looked at me as she made chewing motions. It should be emphasized that what I expected of her was an active and unambiguous demand to be fed. I did not content myself with her mouth open and her eyes fascinated in front of the dish: if I had, it would have been like the repetition of the bulimia, where there was no Other or desire of the subject. Desire can only pass through a demand, even if the conclusion, as she put it after eating the whole dish of rice pudding, were that "it isn't it."

Although her demand was expressed only through gestures, she used her mouth to tell me that "it wasn't it" by sputtering on my face a whole sequence of phonemes, her jaw protruding aggressively. "It" was certainly the scopic object while she was eating the rice pudding. Her gaze was continuously attracted by the bottle, to then be quickly deflected from it. Sometimes it was attracted by me, coming so close that, as I said, she appeared to be eating me up with her eyes. In other words, her oral activity had much to do with the scopic, that is to say, an activity that involved a surface. This had been the case from the start, not only as regards the dish of rice pudding, which Marie-Françoise ate with her eyes more than once, sticking her face against it, but also in relation to her pressing an object—the sailor or the doll—against her eye to make it into her double. She also used the doll to plug the hole of her mouth.

The whole question oscillated, therefore, between the hole in the body and the surface. There is a hole in the body only through the Other: it is the Other who must be affected by it. In a first moment, the Other must be the only one with a holed body. This is what Nadia showed from the beginning by insistently exploring my mouth. Initially the small subject does not experience its body as holed because the hole in its body is plugged by the objects of the Other's body. The hole in the body appears only secondarily, at the oral level, with the loss that the subject experiences, making the demand to the Other emerge—under the condition, which is a primordial one, that the debate be at that moment inscribed in the signifier.

Insofar as it is nullified in its Real dimension by the signifying mutation, the object does not really fill in the hole, but must pass through the demand to the Other. After the nullification of the Real, this demand remains necessarily unsatisfied—how could it be satisfied, if no demand can emerge in the Real, and no Real can fill in the hole in the signifier, the compulsory path of demand?

Although after eating the dish of rice pudding Marie-Françoise said that it was not it by means of the phonemes that she sputtered at me, she was nevertheless following the reverse direction of the demand. That is to say, she made me understand that she wanted the rice pudding through gestures without, strictly speaking, articulating her demand; and in articulating her phonemes she only expressed her refusal.

The essential component of the scene was not that she ate the rice pudding but her gaze, incessantly attracted toward the bottle or me.

In other words, what the situation represented for her was not situated at the oral level but at the level of the scopic: to really have the object, attached to her eye in order to compensate for the loss that the oral activity of eating showed her at the level of her mouth's hole.

At the beginning, Nadia, too, had only her gaze to establish contact with her environment. In this respect we have commented extensively on the essential trait of the scopic function, which is the maximum reduction of any loss. Although it can be argued that this feature was present in Marie-Françoise, it is, however, necessary to give an account of a significant difference in relation to Nadia. Nadia was striking not only because of her gaze, but also because of the pathetic quality of that gaze, which we regarded as lively. Marie-Françoise's gaze was death. On the first occasions I saw her, it was devoid of all expression or emotion. Even when the sessions were apparently rich as a result of her contributions, as on 4 October, I concluded that her behavior and her gaze were cut off from any contact with me, as if she only wanted to make sure that I remained passive.

With Nadia, the scopic promptly joined the exploration of my mouth, which went on uninterruptedly almost until 10 December. The exploration of my mouth was Nadia's way of directly saying that I was a holed Other. We would even suggest that in the scene of transitivism on 7 November, when she vomited as I was biting a cracker, what she feared most was that the hole was filled in. She immediately made sure that it was not filled in by putting her finger into my mouth before I left. On the basis of the hole of my mouth she founded the existence of separable objects in my body, linked to other holes of my body that made her satisfaction possible. Which path did she take? Surely not that of a real object that she could have taken from me, but through the veiled object that she demanded of me on 5 December when, her hands tightly clenched on my breast, a resolution emerged in the form of the signifier "mama," which she addressed to me. For her, the Real of the objects had been promoted to the level of the signifier, and I was a carrier of objects insofar as these were signifying objects. Although on 10 December she underwent a massive return to the scopic through her fascination with the "A + *a*" and the Real became manifest in her sucking motions, the signifying dimension was possible when she heard—after resisting it—her name being called. This entailed the primal repression, which is based on the fact that there is a signifier. We must also note that what fascinated her had to do with an image, not with the Real. After that repression the marked predominance of the scopic ceased, even if later, during the mirror phase itself, she wanted to explore the surface of my eyes.

If Marie-Françoise's gaze was dead, it was because I did not have holes, no holes to explore, no objects separable from my body, at least symbolically—as the small other had been for Nadia when I took away my hand from the crib of the child next to her, at a time when this child was absent. That I had no hole meant for Marie-Françoise that there was no place in my body where the mutation of real objects into signifiers could be done. She was therefore entirely abandoned to the Real of the objects, and the loss that she knew could only be made good by real objects. These objects also corresponded to the filling in of the real absence with which she was confronted by the window.

Thus, the absence of holes in my body was correlative of the foreclosure of the register of objects at the level of the signifier—all objects, not only food-objects. As her entire debate with the bottle showed, Nadia had to associate different levels of the drive—scopic, oral, auditory—in her attempt to overcome the conflict, which orality took to a point of maximum intensity, between the object of the need and the object of desire, between the Real and the signifier, between all and nothing. Marie-Françoise too tried to link orality and its pitfalls to the scopic. But for her the object could not leave the register of the Real. When she came up against the oral object, her scopic fascination was of no help. Similarly, nothing was resolved when she ended up with a convulsive crisis. Marie-Françoise failed to include the object in her gaze; what is more, she was deprived of her gaze, as she could not include in it an object that remained real. She nevertheless showed that as her aim, even if what she encountered there was the impossible. From the beginning, indeed, she continuously stuck the real object on her nose. After the initial phase of the treatment, she stuck it successively on her nose and her eye. On her nose: this is how the initial picture of her relations with objects can be described. Instead of taking them to her mouth like any other child of her age, she held them against her nose. In other words, she converted the nose into the substitute of the hole of her mouth, as if she were denying the very existence of that hole in her body.

As from the second session she came to me to take my glasses, threw them down, and attached her face to mine, her eyes a half inch from mine. Did she make a hole in me by taking my glasses? I do not think so; she was rather searching for the contact of the surface of the eye-organs, surfaces without a hole for her or me, which only joined together in an organic adhesion, which neither posited me as Other nor was in the nature of positing the space of the gaze. I was one of the real objects, privileged only at the muscular level by means of her slaps.

This is, at any rate, what was manifest in the sessions. However, there must have been a beyond, which would explain, on the one hand, why she was so fond of coming to the session, which at times she expressed through her haste and a certain joy accompanied by lively mimicry, and on the other hand, as regards her life in the institution, the effects of the sessions, which were reported to me as involving a significant change vis-à-vis the others, both adults and children.

On 22 October, she encountered the dish of food again, but there was no repetition of the experience of the day before, when she had eaten it all up after actively demanding it from me. Eating it "was not it." "It" was sticking the object on her eye; and that is what she did by putting her face close to the dish, her gaze sliding toward me, as she also uttered a cry of appeal. Furious because I did not respond to her appeal, she was nevertheless relieved by my not giving her the rice pudding—which would have been imposing it upon her.

She became very relaxed as I explained all this to her. Laughing, she grabbed the glasses and shook, hit, and threw them down as she had already done with the spoon in the previous session. It is surprising to find once again, as with Nadia, the coupling of the spoon and my glasses. With Nadia, the connection was made during the mirror period, on 6 February, and had a particularly representational character: my glasses were an object of my body and her spoon an object of hers, as she experimented—by putting them in and then taking them out of the ark—with the acquisition of the notions of contained and container. That was a decisive step that she had taken with the mirror. Evidently, it was not the same for Marie-Françoise: as with the spoon, my glasses were not promoted to anything other than what they were: an object of my body, certainly, but one that did not and would not refer in any way to the exploration of my body. This lack of articulation led Marie-Françoise to confine herself to her usual fitting-in game. But this game did not last long and she moved toward the door as if she did not have the means to say anything else.

The news that after the session she did not tolerate the presence of an adult close to another girl in her room reminded us of Nadia's image, "A + *a*"; or rather, of that which Nadia could not bear seeing at the beginning of her treatment: the presence of another child close to an adult, myself in particular. Like Nadia at the time, Marie-Françoise started to rock and even to cry. They were both confronted with the same scene in an intolerable manner and they reacted to it in the same way. In the case of Nadia, we noted the impossible and Real character of the presence of the small other near me. But in fifteen days Nadia was able to come out of that real impossibility by interrogating my body and the hole that the lack of the other left in it, not only really but also symbolically.

On 23 October, Marie-Françoise was exhausted. Yet in the session she showed a much greater ease with her body. She started off by sucking a piece of candy, and for the first time, instead of swallowing her saliva she let it flow down to the floor, her head down between her arms leaning on the edge of the table. That went even further in the opposite direction of any oral satisfaction, or rather of any ingestion, as if intended to affect the hole of her mouth with a negation.

In the scene that followed, she quickly linked the hole of her mouth with the other end of the body's hole, which she could explore only in the doll, given the scopic component of her exploration. Since the doll had a diaper, Marie-Françoise's gaze stopped immediately; she was, on the other hand, afraid of seeing the hole. Her fear seemed to diminish following the prolonged gaze that she directed at the doll's diaper. We found there once again the function of the veil, whose importance Nadia had shown so precociously; that is to say, the need for a veil in front of the object to make possible the articulation of the Real with the signifier. Marie-Françoise showed shortly afterward that her exploration aimed, to begin with, at the existence or nonexistence of the hole. In the absence of a direct approach to the hole, after the prolonged gaze she put her finger closer to the doll and tried unsuccessfully to insert it in the slit of the diaper. She only managed to tap on the slit of the diaper three or four times, following her usual mode of defense when facing objects; a defense that, as we have mentioned, replaced even the sucking of her thumb when she went to sleep. In other words, she really avoided the hole of her mouth. For the time being she looked at me with an air of interrogation; then, perplexed, she looked at the doll and, returning to the hole formed by the doll's mouth, she put her own mouth on it for a long while.

This scene ended up with an explosion of signifiers, as if an excessive pressure had mounted and made it impossible to contain the signifiers that burst forth from Marie-Françoise's mouth in a flash that made sense: looking at me, her jaw protruding, she uttered "bébé, bibi, pipi, tété." As she said "tété," she looked at the bottle, stood up, and then said "parti, parti" in a violent tone. During that flash, the real of the absence was mutated into the signifier. The logic of the signifier carried Marie-Françoise along and she addressed her demand to me.

Unfortunately, her mouth became closed for the signifier, and it was only by leading my movements that she made me grab the spoon and fill it up in the dish. Thus she ate the contents of the dish, like the first time, but she showed that it was not it, judging from the tension that seized her when her gaze came upon the bottle, or even from the cough that shook her while she was eating. It was as if she wanted to refuse that food. It was the same refusal that she had expressed two days before by sputtering on me and throwing phonemes at my face.

But she stopped short of the step that had announced itself so clearly in the signifiers before she made herself be fed, as she sat down with the sailor, during the same scene, pressing it very hard on her eye while holding the doll with the other hand: surely, that food was not "it," it was not from my body, the Other was not involved in it, and Marie-Françoise was reduced to plugging the hole of her body with the sailor, the double, not putting it on her mouth but—sliding toward the scopic—sticking it to her eye.

The scene that followed was another attempt, again in relation to the bottle that she looked at but could not touch and toward which she sputtered, as she cleared her throat, before making me take the mug and leading my hand to put her mouth on the rim.

"Leading my hand" is peculiar to the autistic child's relation with the Other's body: the child manipulates the Other's entire body as an object. This is the signature of a relation to the Real of the Other's body that fails to extract objects from it: objects classically called partial, signifying objects, to put it more precisely, insofar as only the dialectic of the signifier makes the detachment from the Other's body possible. Nadia showed this at length through her inability to touch me or any object—I refer to her automatic gesture of letting go, and her hands with the palms in the air when I carried her—before her trajectory took her, through the path of the signifier, to the articulation of the demand for the object that I bore.

To return to Marie-Françoise: she wanted to drink the whole mug. In fact, she did not drink but sucked, her gaze fixed on the bottle. This means that with the mug she attained the substitutive object for the bottle, but not without coming up against an impossibility, since under the circumstances most of the milk got spilled on the table. She went to all possible extremes to absorb the spilled milk, using three means in succession. We can see in this her ultimate attempt to introduce a mediation in her oral relation with milk, within a frame about which she had so much to say: sucking, a primitive relation with the Other's body, was still a failure, insofar as, after involving her own body and then the cake, the use of my glasses to collect the milk was too much for her. She did not look at me again, returned to the Real of her body, licking the rest of the pool, and remained unable to establish her demand and address it to me.

Nevertheless, she still held my glasses in her hand when she dropped to the sitting position at the end of the session. Then, as usual, the failure of orality made her fall back on the scopic and the sticking on her eye. For the first time, however, something of me participated in the sticking: she pressed a lens against the sailor's face, as if my eye were also involved, and then put the whole thing close to her eye, with my glasses in contact with it.

In this passage we find once again what Nadia knew in relation to her eye and mine: on 10 December, after the unsticking of the image from her eye, she transposed that image onto the surface of my own eye, after my calling her by her name and the repression. She returned to my eye incessantly searching for the image, until the mirror finally unstuck the image from the eye, hers and mine, through the establishment of a distance, a three-dimensional space where the surface ceased being the only dimension of her object relation. This is precisely what Marie-Françoise was unable to attain.

What was it exactly that she was unable to attain, when substitutions of objects emerged manifestly over the entire succession of scenes? The food-objects in particular came to occupy the place of the bottle, as was revealed by the furtive glances she cast at it while she ate. Is this substitutive process not the principle of metaphor? Moreover, at every step Marie-Françoise's progress at this level makes us think of an exact replica of Nadia's progress. Everything was there, including signifiers, the sequence of which was in some instances much richer than the phonemes that Nadia employed—this being evidently connected with the difference in age between the two girls.

What was, then, the fundamental difference between Nadia and Marie-Françoise? It concerned entirely the relation to the Other. In Nadia, the relation to the object passed through the Other, whom she incessantly questioned. Thus, the object lost for her its Real dimension and was mutated into a signifier placed in the locus of the Other that I was. Her relation with the Other became so prevalent that every object relation went through that Other; at the same time, signification was produced there. It was the essential character of the object relation—its being a relation with the lack of object—which founded desire for Nadia. Nothing of that took place in Marie-Françoise, in whom we found the Real—plenty of it—and the signifier; but they remained separated because the signifier could not get inscribed in the Other, which for her was nonexistent as such. It was manipulated by her like any other real object; she made it pass from a real absence by the window to a not less real presence when she addressed herself to me. Thus, despite appearances, she failed at the level of the true dimension of all articulated speech which is metaphor, and *a fortiori* at the level of the other signifying structure, metonymy. Psychotic discourse, Marie-Françoise has taught us, can produce an exchange, but in it substitution is only supported by the Real of objects without the production of signification in the Other, which is absolutely indispensable for the existence of metaphor. This process determines the exclusion of castration, of which the psychotic, within these conditions, does not want to, or cannot, know anything.

20/The Double and the Real: The Loss Revealed in the Scopic and the Absence of the Gaze

25, 27, and 29 October

On 25 October the children in her room heard me tidying up the consulting room and gathered at the top of the steps. As she was not in the first row, Marie-Françoise, furious, babbled. As I approached her, she extended her arms to me above the heads of the other children.

Once inside the consulting room and on the floor, she cast a provocative look at the others and quickly shuffled on her bottom toward the table. She stood up there, took the pieces of candy, and started to suck them.

This session was a reaction to the previous one, which had been so important. As she had taken a step forward, in this session she moved a step backward. The session that followed the one in which for the first time she had asked for and received food brought back tremors, rocking, autistic behavior, tics, and the refusal of me. The same thing happened in this session, although in an attenuated manner: she utilized some acquired behaviors and some intermediary objects, even if they came from me. Her contact was less autistic. Yet after ten minutes she wanted to return to the other children.

She played the entire session around the *desire that I fed her without her demanding it actively.* Obeying that ambivalent desire on my part would have amounted to my being the one who cut off the contact between her and me—this, considering the autistic character of bulimia.

Nevertheless, she was able to demand food actively by putting the spoon in my hand and opening her mouth or by grabbing the mug. Her gestural participation was an attempt to make the food lose its autistic character. The scene could be summarized like this: she brought her face very close to the dish, her eyes bulging, her gaze moving from the dish to me; she uttered a cry of appeal, her jaw protruding, and she started to shake as she looked at the dish again. She reproduced the same scene with the mug. She stamped her feet, casting a brief look at the bottle. *I reminded her that she truly knew how to ask when she was not split in her desire.*

She took the doll and sat down at my feet with it. She did not know what to do with it. She looked at it with an absent look, put it close to her, and then got up again and took *my glasses*. She twice *dipped my glasses in the rice pudding and sucked them*; then she dropped to the sitting position again as she angrily looked at me. She showed me my glasses, hit them, threw them down as she laughed, and *left them, taking the sailor instead, which she placed against her eye* to incorporate it. *She started to roar* but was not cut off from me. Her aggressive roaring was addressed to me. Then she stopped and looked at me.

She ended the session herself. I heard her laughing with the others as I tidied up the room.

On 27 October she attempted to make herself be fed like the previous time. She looked at the dish while uttering cries of appeal. I spoke to her about the spoon, which she knew how to give to me when she wanted. *She looked at it*, hesitated, and *her gaze slid toward my glasses*. I reminded her that she had used them as a spoon. She then came very close to me, *put her hand on my knee*, and looked at me for a long time, opening and closing her mouth, as if she were eating me. I told her this.

Still leaning on my knee, she looked at the bottle and at the doll, and then she said: *"bébé, tété,"* looking at my glasses again. She slowly moved her hand forward to take them. She *made them slide down my nose gently until she could close her mouth on the nosepiece, while making sure that the end of an arm was against my lips.* As the arm moved a bit away from my mouth, she straightened it up so that it was exactly against my mouth. She did this for about ten seconds, looking at me intensely.

Then she dropped at my feet, shook my glasses a little, and got up in front of the dish, where she reproduced the same ambivalent scene of demand. It was evident that she desired my passivity.

She stamped her feet, took a cookie and ate a little of it, and then, looking at me, *threw it violently toward me*.

Once again, she looked at the dish, the bottle, the mug, and the doll. She repeated *"bébé, tété,"* bending her head toward me, her gaze on the bottle, her attitude very tense. She dropped to the sitting position, the doll—whose diaper she looked *at* with great interest—in one hand, my glasses in the other. She remained motionless, in a hieratic attitude.

I reminded her of the previous scenes with my glasses and when she put her mouth on the doll's mouth, her fear of my mouth at the beginning of the treatment and her correlative wish to eat me up.

She then came out of her state of contemplation, looked at me, threw the doll into a corner, my glasses into another, and the small milk pitcher she had just grabbed in yet another direction. She became hyperactive, took the different pieces of the toy tea set, very quickly fitting one inside the other, then separating them, and finally throwing them away. This was *flight activity*, since immediately after it she moved to the door.

I waited for a while and then approached her. She looked at me straight in the face, said *"Non,"* went back to the table at full speed, and *grabbed the spoon*. As she went past, she noticed *the potty* for the first time.

She had a very curious way of filling the spoon, which could be compared with the way she swallowed when drinking from the mug. She dragged the spoon on the surface of the cereal, the back of the spoon toward her, its bottom on the cereal. The spoon was filled after she did this three times. Then she ate and started all over again several times, until the spoon dragged a bit of milk skin: she looked at it hanging, put it back in the dish, tried to take it out; but her anxiety intensified and she dropped to the sitting position, looking at me with a very painful expression. I put the milk skin back in the dish. Marie-Françoise grabbed the spoon again and, without the slightest hesitation, took the skin out of the dish and dropped it on one side. She looked at me with delight, ate two or three spoonfuls, and then *started to throw cereal around with the spoon, on the table and on the floor,* in an increasingly violent manner.

Since I was struck by her painful expression while she was feeding herself, I told her how painful it is to reach the point of having to feed oneself at an age when food is still the mother, her presence, her warmth. In feeding herself in front of me during the session, she realized for the first time, since her mother was not there, how much she had to divest food of its true meaning—a gift to be received—to then reach the point of bulimia. Thus, furious against that food devoid of meaning—since she had given it to herself—she had put it everywhere: this, because I was not "an other" as yet.

She sat down to contemplate the small lumps of cereal spread out, and this brought about an extremely painful scene. She took the sailor, turned her back to me, and started to tremble, holding the sailor in one hand and the spoon in the other. *She put the sailor between her open legs, very close to her diaper, and hit it with the spoon. She moved her mouth close to the sailor,* which made her adopt the position of a frog on its belly, *trembling two or three times,* on top of the sailor, which was still against her diaper. Then she stood up again and, *roaring,* she scattered the lumps of cereal with violence.

Finally, she moved toward the exit door. As I opened it, she dashed toward *the water basin,* which she had ignored until that moment, and bent toward it as she had bent toward the dish. Then she left.

On 29 October, Marie-Françoise struggled against her feelings toward the dish of rice pudding, which had changed a little since the last experience. In the previous session, when she fed herself, she realized the affective void of the food with which she was filled up. Hence her fleeting painful expressions, testimonies of her becoming aware of that reality. In this session *she attempted to instill an affective sense into the food before filling herself up with it.* At least this is the feeling that the whole scene produced in me.

Facing the table, she started off by contemplating the rice pudding. Then her gaze focused on every object on the table in succession, before looking at me. She uttered a brief cry of appeal so that I made her eat, but this was not followed by any move toward the spoon. That semi-demand was more a ritual than a reality. *She came to me, leaned on my knee, and looked at me for a long while, her gaze very close to mine, as if she were incorporating me, using the same mechanism she had used with the objects that she wanted to transform into her double.* Her eyes bulged for a moment; then they became very gentle, without their devouring tone.

She did not touch my glasses except at the end of the scene, and this only to remove them, so that they would no longer play the role of screen between her gaze and mine. She stood in front of the dish once more, contemplated it, picked up my glasses, *dipped one of their arms into the rice pudding, and sucked it.* This was not what she was seeking either, and she dropped the glasses. *She even stood on top of the glasses,* and for the rest of the session *she kept a foot on one of the arms.*

She spoke to the rice pudding for a long time. She uttered a series of different phonemes, some of which were comprehensible, such as: *"parti, tété, bébé, pas maman, veux pas"* (gone, breast, baby, no mama, don't want) and others that sounded like the fusion of two verbs: *"demander"* and *"manger"* (to ask for and to eat). She pronounced these phonemes sometimes violently, her jaw protruding, and other times very gently, in a low voice. Some of them were addressed to me, which made me think that she was searching to give an affective meaning to the food. This became so evident to me that I told her so. She heard what I said, stopped what she was doing, looked at the bottle for a long time, and *said: "maman, parti,"* as she dropped to the sitting position, as if she were overwhelmed, overcome by what was happening to her.

Then, and for five minutes, she broke with the emotion of the scene and got interested in the pieces of the toy tea set, fitting one inside the other and then disassembling them, always following a logic, becoming immediately aware of the impossibilities. She expressed joy when she succeeded and showed it to me.

She looked at the basin of water several times. Once she bent over it; then, tense, she threw away the pieces of the toy tea set and went back to her position standing up in front of the dish.

She looked at the rice pudding as she approached me and eventually leaned on my knee. Suddenly, she made a decision: she moved close to the dish, *grabbed the spoon, and, maneuvering in the same way as the previous session, she started to eat, although she ate only three spoonfuls.* She looked at me as if she were looking for the role that she desired I play. It must have been that, since she dipped the spoon into the rice pudding again and *smeared my cheek and forehead with rice pudding three consecutive times.*

The smearing, which the first time was fairly violent and then quite gentle, done almost with love, made me think that she smeared me to prepare for what followed, that is to say, the licking of my cheek—therefore, the incorporation of food that found again its most primitive meaning.* I said this to her, reminding her of the similar scene with the baby's head.

Exhausted, she dropped to the sitting position, threw away a toy aggressively, stood up again, took the sailor, and started the same scene as the previous session; but then she stopped and returned to nourishment, the mug on this occasion. She tried to drink from it unavailingly, since she bit the edge of the mug and the milk ran down. Furious, she threw it far from her and dropped to the sitting position once more.

I spoke to her at the end of the session and went to open the door. She was not happy, *moved quickly toward the basin of water,*

---

*This is what I thought at the time, unconsciously referring to Nadia. As we shall see, it was not as I thought at all.

> *and tried to dip a small milk pitcher into it. But she could not make up her mind, threw it down, and moved toward the door.*

Our comments on the session of 25 October can be restricted to confirm what we have expressed previously:

1. The initial scene, with the easy victory by Marie-Françoise over the other children who gathered at the top of the steps, has nothing to do with the question of the small others in relation to me. They were mere objects that she eliminated, without posing such a question in any way (as Nadia had done at the beginning of her treatment: the place that she assumed the small other had for me inhibited her or sent her into despair because there was an Other for her). For Marie-Françoise, the other children were only real obstacles between herself and the objects on the table; I was practically absent, except, perhaps, as an instrument.

2. The session proceeded along these lines, the relation with the feeding objects not implying me qua Other. It was at that point that, despite her appeal, I refused the food that she did not actually demand, but in front of which she was ready to assume her initial attitude once more: cut off from me, she started to shake as she looked at the dish.

3. My refusal led her to attempt to reintroduce the other, in the form of the doll, between herself and me. But this was not an image; it was only a real object upon which she turned an absent gaze.

4. This failure drove her, finally, to address herself to my glasses, which in the last analysis could play the role of an object that she would want to take from me, which would make of that object a signifier. That was probably the sense of the whole effort that she made to follow me in what I told her and which she understood very well, as it were, as in the classical observation that the very young psychotics "understand" everything they are told. What kind of understanding is this, apparent as it may be? Marie-Françoise answered this when she showed me my glasses, bit them, threw them down, and left them to then take the sailor, attaching it to her eye, as she roared at me. It was as if she had perceived for a brief moment that she had made me lose something through the mediation of my glasses, a loss that was also hers and whose responsibility she assigned to me, while at the same time she refused that loss radically, filling it in by means of the sailor on her eye. The sailor was of the order of the Real; it was her double and defended her against the signifier of my body's object.

At the following session, on 27 October, she gave a hint of a bodily rapprochement with me when she put her hand on my knee, as she looked at me for a long while and made movements with her mouth. She then heard very well what I told her about her desire of eating me up, as she said, looking at the bottle and the doll: "bébé, tété." However, her movement toward the oral object stopped abruptly; connected as she was with the Real of the object, she could only return to the scopic register. Contrary to Nadia, who had sought refuge in this register—as this is, by its very nature, the one that least reveals the loss of the subject—Marie-Françoise took my glasses in order to plug her mouth and make a link with my lips, as if by means of it she revealed as little as possible, not her loss, but mine. When, following that, she returned to the food-object, without being able to request it, I observed that she desired my passivity and that she could not tolerate my giving her food, which would eliminate my passivity.

The same transitivism, in an inverted form, occurred when she ate a little of the cookie and threw it violently in my direction. That was a dead end: lacking the signifier, her demand could not be expressed, and Marie-Françoise could only move along the path of the real objects. She could not attain satisfaction, but simply the expression of that dead end: the doll in one hand, my glasses in the other, she remained frozen. In the last analysis, the doll was her, who remained separated from the object of my body.

Why this impossibility? She said it when she came out of her motionless attitude and vainly fitted in and disassembled the pieces of the toy tea set: "The small pegs in the small holes" activity, whose despairing futility she expressed by throwing away everything. The Real did not respond.

After an abortive attempt to get out, she returned to the dish of cereal. By sliding the spoon on the surface of the cereal and rejecting with anxiety the milk skin, perhaps she tried to show that a surface without a hole constitutes a wall, that through a hole in the surface one could attain the object: the milk skin is the skin of the Other, interposed between herself and the cereal. This is what Marie-Françoise expressed when, having dropped the milk skin outside the dish, she was able to eat two or three spoonfuls of cereal; however, she could not bear it for too long and spread out the cereal with violence. She made the Other's hollow skin into an obstacle because she could not tolerate her making a hole into it. The Other was the mother that she had lost. This is what I told her, and I added that it was painful having to feed herself at her age and having food deprived of its true meaning because I was not yet an Other.

In the following scene, painful as it was, Marie-Françoise showed once more that food was unable to plug the hole in her body, either her mouth or the inferior orifice of the hole. Food failed in its function of plugging, and she ended up splattering it completely while she roared. She bent over the sailor, her real double, which she attached, not to her eye or her nose again, but to her diaper, also adopting the posture of a frog so that it was close to her mouth, thus functioning as a plug for both orifices. For the first time, the relation between the sailor and the food became evident as, still holding the spoon in her hand, she bit the sailor as she had bitten the food. All evidence here is against any interpretation of the scene as having an autoerotic meaning: it was not a question of masturbation, as there was no thumb-sucking for Marie-Françoise. After her attempt to plug the hole in her body, she could only flee; flee from me, once she had confirmed what I told her—that for her there was no Other in the food. Since for her there was no Other in the food that she put in her mouth, she immediately indicated that there was no Other either in the other orifice of the hole in her body, and this was the reason why she attempted to close it up by means of her real double.

On 29 October, after arriving at the same impasse with the food to find her other, she once more took the path of the scopic: her eyes came so close to mine that she seemed to want to incorporate me, as she did with her double, the sailor. It was evident that she found there something like the outline of the Other since her eyes, which at the beginning were bulging as they had at the times when she stood in front of the dish of rice pudding, became very gentle, without their devouring tone.

She then attempted a rapprochement between the gaze and the food by dipping the arm of my glasses, which she had taken from me, into the rice pudding and then sucking it. But this attempt to link the oral object with me through the agency of my glasses failed. Nadia did it very often and at those moments her babble was addressed to me, namely to the Other that I was for her. Marie-Françoise also spoke at that moment; yet it was not to me but to the rice pudding that she addressed herself in principle. However, hers was no simple babble but almost a phrase that condensed her history: "parti, tété, bébé, pas maman, veux pas!" Without speculating too much, one can understand that she spoke of the loss of her mother when she was still a baby at the breast and that, without her mother, "she did not want." What was it that she did not want? We are tempted to answer by referring to the two condensed verbs that I thought I could hear in what she said: "demander" (to ask) and "manger" (to eat). "To ask" something from an Other who was not her mother, in whose place there was a real absence, that is to say, undialectizable: that was what she did not want; and she did not want "to eat" either because the Real of what she could eat did not contain her lost mother. This became so evident to me that I said it to her. Certainly, she heard it but it was looking once more at the object, the bottle, that she said: "maman partie" and dropped to the sitting position, overwhelmed by that Real.

We must stop for a moment here to interrogate those words of a child described as autistic and not without reason, not only because of the initial clinical picture that she presented, but also—as we have seen a number of times—because of that which cut her off from me radically, despite her waiting for the Other—which she sustained, as it was evident. Her words were full of signification and, one might say, of "awareness." But was awareness possible for her, when those words failed to posit me as an Other with whom, by regression, she could relive and recollect the trauma of her abandonment? She made me only into a witness, the witness of a real absence, but not of a loss. In a strict sense, it is the inscription of the loss in the Other that induces the demand, a signifying demand by the subject to the Other of the object of the body. However, Marie-Françoise promoted an object that was not signifying (the sailor) to the role of real double in order to respond to the real absence of the Other's body.

She actualized the case that we thought of in relation to Nadia, on the occasion of the first moment of the mirror; the case where, after losing her sailor, she would have turned around to see nobody. The risk of falling into psychosis would have been high. The confrontation with the Real of her loss would have taken the place of its metonymic image.

The whole question of the transference and the place of the analyst is at stake here: as an instrument for the restitution *ad integrum* of the body in the Real—which is the first part of the process of cure in psychosis—and as the witness of a loss—a signifying process, as it was for Nadia on 10 December, when I became the place of the loss that led to the metonymy of the body. It is necessary, therefore, that the loss be not only that of the subject, since in that case it remains in the Real. It is necessary that it pass through the Other, which as the locus of the signifier inscribes it and, as such, becomes in the same movement affected by it. For Marie-Françoise the real absence of the Other prevented the Other from being affected by a loss, which would be the effect of the inscription of the Real in the signifier in the place of the Other. The absent Other could not actually come to occupy that place. This occurred, no matter what the *primum movens* was (the old question of the chicken and the egg): the refusal of the signifier, which implies a loss in the Other, or the refusal of the Other, which for Marie-Françoise was not the really lost Other.

Following this scene, Marie-Françoise could only seek refuge in the fitting in of real objects, as in the previous session. However, she once more attempted an opening by approaching me. After grabbing the spoon and dipping it into the rice pudding, she turned toward me as if she were looking for the role that she wanted me to play: moving from the surface of the rice pudding to the surface of my skin, she smeared my cheek and forehead.

That smearing made me conjecture a few things in relation to the incorporation of a food of the body that could find its most primitive meaning, under the condition that she made it go through my body. I could not fail then to link this smearing with that of the head of the doll fallen in the dish of rice pudding. It was apparently the same smearing that Nadia used during the fruitful period of the mirror; a smearing that she began on her skin, to then become attached to mine, before our confrontation in the mirror. But Marie-Françoise did not smear herself to then smear me. It was only me that she smeared.

If the smearing had the same sense for her as for Nadia, that is to say, the presentification of the surface of an unholed body, it was not, as for Nadia, her own body that was in question, but mine. Yet, it is only a holed body that can found the Other in its presence vis-à-vis the small subject's body, which originally should not be holed. If she smeared me, it was not the Other that she attained. In her smearing with excrement, the Other was not present either, and she also missed the other, due to the incapacity of inscribing it as an image in the Other.

Then, exhausted, she dropped to the sitting position, and, grabbing the sailor, she reproduced sketchily the same scene as in the previous session. In that way she confirmed that the smearing of me had made of me an unholed body; the closing up of the hole in her body with the sailor was the only thing left to her. In the register of the Real, it was impossible for her to take from my body an object that would fill in the hole in her body, as Nadia was able to do within the register of signifying objects. However, the opening that she produced left a trace: she arrived at the scene with the sailor only in order to go back to food, in the form of the mug. That was the ultimate indication of what she was seeking: to plug the hole in her mouth by drinking milk. But her attempt was futile. She could not drink the milk that ran down the side of her mouth, and it was the real object, the mug that she bit before throwing it away, furious, dropping again to the sitting position. Nadia would have bitten my body. Marie-Françoise remained tied up with her own real loss, which she tried to fill up in the Real. She could not gain access to the loss of the Other that would inscribe the loss as such.

21 / The Temptation of the Other, Holder of the Object

31 October, 3 and 5 November

On 31 October, as I was preparing the materials, Marie-Françoise managed to climb down a step on her bottom; then she uttered a cry for help for the second step. I helped her to climb down. She went quickly to the table, on which I had not put anything as yet, and waited.

She looked at me with great interest as I unwrapped the candy. I could perceive that she had understood perfectly that she could not eat them unless I removed the paper. She grabbed the pieces of candy and put all of them in her mouth at once. I pointed out to her that if she put all the pieces of candy in her mouth she would not be able to taste or eat them and that she would only drool. She removed the pieces from her mouth and put them on the table; then she looked at the new cookies, which had a different shape, took one, and dropped it in the dish. Then *she looked at me and came close to me, leaning on my knee with one hand.*

During this session she came to me three times, seeking my contact and warmth. On each occasion she took a step forward toward establishing contact. I sensed a real emotion and a trust that relaxed her gaze to the point of making it very attentive and deep. That was a great novelty that appeared in this session.

She returned to the dish and uttered a brief cry of appeal so that I fed her. Then she came to take my glasses, dipped one of their arms into the rice pudding, sucked it, and dropped the glasses. She came back close to me and *took a pencil* that she noticed in my pocket. *She first used it as a spoon for herself, then for me.* But when she gave it to me, she licked it completely beforehand and *tried to make it enter my mouth, touch my teeth, and extract something from my mouth.* She did it so violently that she dropped to the floor in the sitting position, perplexed. She got up again to grab the spoon and eat; she put plenty of rice pudding on the table and smeared it on my cheek.

She let herself drop to the sitting position and engaged in *an aggressive game* with the three objects that she used to take the food: *my glasses, the pencil, and the spoon.* She threw them down, picked them up, shook them, and then, after looking at me, *finally threw them to the four corners of the room.*

She stood up again and for a long time looked at the bottle, the dish, with resentment, and then the mug, which she tilted toward her to see whether it was full. All these gazes charged with emotion culminated upon me. She came close to me, put one hand on each of my knees, and lifted her shoulders as if she wanted me to take her, but at the same time she bent her head more and more toward my breast. She remained a few moments in that position; then she straightened herself up, *opened my white coat with both hands, and buried her head in the opening.* She looked and would have wanted to abandon herself, but she could not.

Marie-Françoise got up, *looked at the dish,* and, bending over toward me again, she said to me in a very low voice: *"veux pas"*—like a painful confidence—and dropped to the sitting position overwhelmed, her troubled gaze focused on mine.

She found a diversion in an aggressive game with the spoon. Then she grabbed *a cookie and threw it violently into the water in the basin,* as she looked at me, stamping her foot and uttering a scream. She even emphasized her aggressive expression against me by turning her back on me, her hands on the floor, and *kicking in my direction.*

She sat down and moved toward the basin, but did not dare to touch it. She then returned to the fitting in of pieces of the toy tea set, which she skillfully managed to do in decreasing order. She took me as a witness to her success, to which she seemed to assign particular significance.

I wondered why, after looking at me with an aggressive air, she tried deliberately to make *impossible assemblies,* following *the same logic, reversing precisely the order of the three containers.* In *her will to refuse the fitting,* she ended up making an unstable tower. I thought that the meaning of that desire was given by the fact that she again stopped in front of *the basin while she jabbered aggressively.* She then returned to the toy tea set and hid its pieces under her crib.

I opened the door; she stamped her feet, furious, and then stretched her arms out to the nurse.

On 3 November, Marie-Françoise kept me waiting for nearly fifteen minutes before coming to the session: another therapist came to fetch a little girl and she was again disturbed by that picture of an adult and a child. For a while she ignored me and rocked. She then became very interested in the compact of one of the nurses and tried to open it. From time to time she looked at me, laughing, and then returned to the compact. She had to defend it against two other children and she managed very well to keep the intruders away. The nurse opened the compact and showed Marie-Françoise her image in the small mirror. Marie-Françoise got up, *looked at the mirror,* her jaw protruding, and uttered aggressive phonemes. I do not think she could identify what she saw as her image, her double, which would be particularly disturbing for her. Yet as she looked at herself *she touched the back of the mirror,* as if to verify whether it was a piece of glass or not.

The rest of the session was concerned with the problem of food.

Marie-Françoise began by eating the pieces of candy one by one for the first time. She then got interested in the dish, approached it very closely, and, straightening herself up, uttered "miam-miam" (yum-yum). She turned toward me and repeated her "miam-miam" as she had done in front of the dish. Then something very important occurred that concerned the role of speech in the treatment: I verbalized the meaning of the "miam-miam" toward the dish and then toward me in succession. She went back in front of the dish and *uttered a barrage of aggressive, incomprehensible phonemes.* I had the impression that they were *deliberately incomprehensible.* I noticed, as the scene progressed, that there was an *upsurge* of the phonemes every time *I spoke,* as if she wanted me to shut up. *Slowly, my silence led to hers.* I then adopted a policy of total silence, and this silence created the void indispensable to oblige her to project.

I linked the scene of the phonemes with the problem of her bulimia, on the basis that both had the same character of emotional void. In the phonemes, as in the food that she absorbed through bulimia, there was no signification, and this absence of signification had a relation with me.

She could not as yet absorb me through food. That was the problem which, transposed onto the verbal plain, prevented her from absorbing my words, which she perceived as devoid of sense. She reproduced this through her incoherent phonemes, at a time when she knew very well how to pronounce words in a manner intelligible and comprehensible to everybody.

My silence sent her into the void, confronted her with the absence of sense; *she then came to lean upon my knees, almost snuggling up against me, with a distraught face and she said to me, while looking at the dish: "veux pas, maman!"* with a very low and pathetic tone, as if she were confiding in me. She went back in front of the dish and looked at me. I responded only with a warm look. *Once again she almost snuggled up to me* and returned to the dish.

She grabbed the spoon and used it in her usual manner, even more clumsily, so that nothing reached her mouth, which did not seem to trouble her. After three times, she bent over and, very gently, *said to the cereal: "maman"* and got up.

She looked at the bottle and the doll and then started *to throw cereal on the table with the spoon.* She formed three heaps. Then she managed to eat a little cereal with the spoon.

At one time *a spoonful was emptied close to the bottom of the bottle.* From that moment onward the scene became visibly painful. Marie-Françoise dropped the spoon and had great trouble grabbing it again, thus presenting *the same difficulties in prehension as at the beginning, which made her moan and almost cry.* She could finally grab the spoon and used it to empty the rest of the cereal on the table. As she verified that there was nothing left in the dish, she started to moan again and dropped the spoon once more. She had the same difficulties with prehension, which made her face contract with pain. She finally left it all, dropped to the sitting position, and tried to calm herself down with the sailor, as she had done previously, and the pictures on the nesting boxes.

On 5 November, the beginning of the session was dominated by Marie-Françoise's hesitation between aggressiveness and the wish to come with me, the latter finally winning very clearly.

Sitting down on the steps as I waited for Marie-Françoise, I could hear her puffing like a seal as the time for the session approached. When she saw me sitting down and waiting for her decision, she took to her mouth the toy that she had in her hand (a frog) and then rocked. I did not show any reaction. She then stopped, uttering some aggressive phonemes, as she stretched her hand toward me, opening and closing it, as if to extract something. In the face of my passivity she stood up and came toward me, stretching her arms.

I took her to the consulting room. For the first time I did not have the impression, as I was holding her, that she was in a hurry to step on the floor again. Also for the first time, at the moment when I took her in my arms, *her face had a sweet expression.*

The atmosphere of the session was a novelty. I could not hear a single aggressive phoneme. She remained surprisingly silent and *I perceived a deep contact between her and me.* Everything she did was done slowly and with emotion.

Standing up in front of the table as usual, she slowly chewed the candy. Yet *her interest was directed toward the bottle,* and her gaze moved from it to the doll, then onto me. She contemplated the bottle for a long time, then *she started to shake in front of it;* and when she could not bear it any longer, she looked at me as if she were asking for my help.

In order to show her that I had understood, I lifted the bottle a few inches and immediately put it back in the same place and told her that I understood her emotion. She looked at it again, this time with a gaze that was more alive, as she produced a sucking noise. Then she started to shake and again asked for my help. I did the same thing as before.

She grabbed the spoon and touched the bottle and then the nipple. She did this with a certain restraint, without tapping it. She thus had the courage to touch the whole length of the bottle and the nipple. The drop of cereal that the spoon left on the nipple seemed to make her happy.

That was all she did with the bottle; she did not concern herself with it again during the session.

The novelty was that in order to extract herself from the interest that she preferred to ignore, she did not need to let herself drop to the sitting position and become absorbed in a more or less stereotyped game of diversion. She got the diversion by sucking a series of substitutes for the bottle and eating the cereal. The substitutes for the bottle were:

1. *The spoon,* which she held in her hand and with which she ate a little. She ate very slowly, poured cereal on the table, and then spread it with her hand, showing satisfaction.

2. *The rabbit's bottom,* which she soaked and sucked: another pole of the body, closing the circuit in an autistic fashion.

3. *My glasses,* which she started to smear with cereal using the spoon, as if she were feeding them, and therefore me through them. She then dipped the glasses completely in the cereal, smearing them with her hand. Following this, she either sucked the glasses or used them *to smear my face.* The first time she put them on my cheek, as if she were hitting me. But then she twice did it with intense emotion, as if she wanted *to make me absorb the food through all the pores of my skin*—and a food that would not be bad. This absorption of food through the surface of the body was the real act that she psychotically transposed into the absorption of objects, pressing them against her eye and cheek in order to make her double. *She was making me into her double.*

She evidently had to do the same in relation to herself, with:

4. *Her hand,* which she sank entirely into the cereal. She then sucked it and almost ate it, smearing her cheeks.

Now that I was identified with her through her rituals, she attempted to move forward in the process of incorporation that she wanted to make of me. Thus, she took from me:

5. *My watch,* which she pulled until I gave it to her. She looked at it and put it to her ear as she looked at me. She then sank it into the cereal and sucked and chewed the leather band, still looking at me. She repeated this sequence once and then put the watch on the bottom of the dish; she spread plenty of cereal on it with her hand.

Then, *she dropped to the sitting position,* but in a different way. Evidently, there was in her an emotional cutting off, but while up until now the cutting off was produced by an emotion that tortured her, in this session she gave me only the impression that she could not move beyond what she had just experienced.

The emotion, however, left her fairly disoriented, so that she was tempted to return to the sailor: she grabbed it and turned her back to me.

This very rich session lasted only twenty minutes. Marie-Françoise came back after it had finished and cried when she saw me taking the materials away.

On 31 October, I recorded that the great novelty of the session was the very alert, very deep, human gaze that Marie-Françoise directed to me. That gaze—which was new for her—made the possible loss present, insofar as the gaze is always the carrier of loss without the subject knowing it. This not knowing about the loss is the unconscious and concerns the whole question of primary repression.

This was the question that I put forward the first time that she pressed the sailor against her eye. I wondered if she had been able to see it—just to see it—from such a short distance. To see it was for her to fail to acknowledge the loss, or rather, to fill it in, effacing the gaze in favor of the surface of the eye.

We cannot help thinking of Nadia in relation to the next scene, when Marie-Françoise took a pencil from my pocket, used it as a spoon, for herself and me, and finally touched my teeth and proceeded as if she wanted to extract something from my mouth. Nadia had succeeded in this after pulling at my teeth on 1 November and after wanting to separate off one of my fingers on 28 October, thus making my body marked by a hole, necessary for my status as an Other.

It appears that Marie-Françoise took a step entirely in agreement with the advent of her gaze when, in a first moment, she entered an aggressive game with the three objects she used to hold food at the beginning of the session: my glasses and my pencil on the one hand, her spoon on the other. Once more she reminded us of Nadia's path, when Nadia associated my glasses and her spoon at the bottom of the ark. Marie-Françoise had not yet reached that point and contented herself with playing with those objects before scattering them around the room.

However, in a second moment especially, the food-objects (bottle, dish, mug) did not attract her gaze to the point of cutting her off from me. On the contrary, her gaze always ended up on me and her emotion was visible. At that moment she could approach me and put each hand on my knees, lifting her shoulders, as if she were requesting that I take her; she bent her head closer and closer to my breast. After remaining a few moments in that position, she straightened herself up, opened my white coat with both hands, and sank her head in the opening. She stayed in that position only very briefly, stood up, looked at the dish, and, bending over toward me again, said to me in a very low voice: "veux pas."

It was not clear whether that painful "veux pas" was addressed to the impossible character of the dish or, more probably, to the object of my body which, for the first time, she was able to approach in a determined manner. Her "veux pas" was not the Real and the impossible that cut her off from me any longer; it clearly was the negation of what she wanted: it was both the spoken and the prohibited (*l'inter-dit*).* The impossible of the Real led up to the most archaic and tyrannical superego, which overwhelmed her and made her drop to the sitting position, her troubled gaze focused on my eyes.

Certainly, her signifying expression could make her take into account, in an inverted form, her demand, which posited her as a subject. But the Real still showed through in that it imposed on her the negation of her fundamental demand to the Other.

Is there not present a way of entering into psychosis, insofar as the Real—for instance, that of the mother's absence—is metabolized in the small subject in the form of the ferocious prohibition of the archaic superego, leaving her overwhelmed and exhausted as she was confronted with the dead end of the impossible?

We can perceive there the *articulation* between the Real and the signifier, an articulation where the superego plants its roots in the subject's need to constitute itself through the signifier, thus annul-

---

*Translators' note: Literally, the "between-said," i.e., said between the lines.

ling the Real: a process of symbolization, where the Real is present against the background of possibly not being there.

The real loss of her mother at the age of two months left Marie-Françoise with the absolute Real of absence, blocking the way to any symbolization, the Real remaining real. If the signifier finds its path again, as Marie-Françoise found it in the scene that we are discussing, the absolute character of the prohibited at the level of the signifier corresponds to the absolute character of the impossible at the level of the Real. That which is not present in symbolization reappears in the Real, but with the possibility of a signification that is inscribed in the archaic superego.

Nadia had also opened my white coat to push her head into the opening on four occasions, between 30 December and 4 January. But Nadia's unsatisfied demand in no way had the effect of sending her into the state of despair derived from a real loss as Marie-Françoise experienced at the age of three months. Nadia had known that loss, but at birth, too early for the game of presence and absence in the symbolic register to cease and become frozen in the "all or nothing" of the Real and the archaic superego. Unsatisfied, Nadia did not hesitate in letting me know this by hitting my breast every time she made me kiss her tenderly. Nadia's ambivalence was the safeguard of the Other that I represented, which was not destroyed by her aggressivity and allowed her to pursue the search for the object *a* on my body: she reassured herself of this by addressing the hole of my mouth, which in turn referred her to her own unholed body.

Marie-Françoise overcame her despair in the scene that followed by becoming aggressive; first against the objects, not directly against me as yet: she took it out on the spoon and then threw a cookie violently into the water basin. She looked at me as she kicked and uttered a scream, but she could only attack me by turning her back to me and kicking out in my direction: an aggressivity that was simultaneously muscular and anal by virtue of her position, but which did not become defined.

Indeed, she fell back on the fitting in of the toy tea set. For the first time, she showed me the impossible in that game by reversing the order of three containers that she had made to fit in previously: refusal of the assembly that had to do with the refusal, or rather the impossibility, of the assembly of bodies, hers and mine, as a result of the indecision in which she still was as far as the holes of these bodies were concerned.

We could also refer to Nadia's refusal (after my naming of 10 December) to become the peg to fill in the hole of my own body by means of her whole body when, metonymically, she offered me only a fragment of her body—her foot.

Marie-Françoise could not gain access to the metonymy of her own body, which would have been properly signifying. She was only able to represent my body through the water basin, whose existence she had already noticed several times during the previous sessions, by briefly stopping before it with an interrogating look. In this session, she was even able to throw a cookie at it for the first time. After the fitting-in game, she stopped in front of the basin again, babbling aggressively. But it was not in the basin that she put the pieces of the fitting-in game. By hiding them under her bed, she was saying that they had to do with her own body, whose fragmentation (as in the case of Nadia, on 10 December) takes part in metonymy and would open the possibility of a search for unity in the specular image.

In contrast with Nadia, who had demanded it, Marie-Françoise met the mirror fortuitously on 3 November: a nurse showed her reflection to her in the mirror of a small compact with which she was playing. Marie-Françoise stood up and looked into the mirror, her jaw protruding, as she uttered aggressive phonemes. I have already said that she did not identify what she saw as her image. She looked for the object that she was watching at the back of the mirror, as if this were only a piece of glass.

What she saw was neither an image—as Nadia had perceived on the occasion of the first mirror to very quickly withdraw from it— nor her double, whose place was occupied by the sailor that, as we know, she stuck against her eye. She was not particularly disturbed by that encounter, which did not fall into any category that might question her in relation to her body. For Marie-Françoise the specular did not exist.

The session concerned her relation with the objects that had to do with food and occupied the place of the mirror and with the part played by speech in relation to them.

She first stuck her face against the dish of rice pudding, as she had often done. The experience with the mirror, which she still had to know, makes us think that the dish of rice pudding was closer to representing a kind of mirror than the mirror itself, insofar as what she found in it was at the place of the image of that which she lacked.

Until that moment the dish was only an impossible Real, but she now took the step Nadia had taken on 5 December, when the approach to the object (veiled, it is true) constituted by my breast was resolved by the emergence of the signifier "mama," followed by her tenderness toward me. Marie-Françoise, like Nadia, was able to refer to the signifier when confronted with the object constituted by the dish of rice pudding by uttering her "miam-miam." She was even able to turn toward me and repeat her "miam-miam," as she had done in front of the dish. But at that point the parallel ceases, since when I linked her "miam-miam" with the expression of a demand addressed to me and said it to her, it was not tenderness that she manifested but the annulment of her demand, in the form of a barrage of aggressive and incomprehensible phonemes.

What she rejected first was meaning. In a second moment, she even rejected the signifier: she made me shut up; she did not want me to talk. Thus she reproduced the absence of meaning in the food absorbed by bulimia.

Distraught by this repetition, she reiterated, although snuggling up to me, the painful negation of the previous session: "veux pas, maman," where the "veux pas" was in this case accompanied by the signifier "maman," even though she pronounced those words while looking at the dish. A few moments later, she addressed her appeal very gently to the cereal, after attempting to eat so awkwardly that she did not manage to get anything in her mouth. Although Marie-Françoise, like Nadia, was able to pronounce "maman," that is to say, to refer to the Other, a reference where, before the mirror, the mirage of the primary narcissistic identification can already play a part—as it did for Nadia—she could only see herself in the object, the cereal, to which she addressed the signifier.

But the cereal was not a mirror. It did not reflect any image for her and did not mask the loss, as a mirror does, either. The reverse occurred; and when she emptied the full spoon next to the bottom of the bottle, although strictly speaking it was not the object of the loss that was revealed there, it was at least the painfully impossible object. The spoon also became painful, and she dropped it and could not pick it up without moaning, finally to empty the cereal. In front of the void of the dish, where the "cereal-mama" was, she dropped the spoon; her attempts to pick it up made her face contract with pathetic pain.

This scene was the opposite of the conquest of the spoon, which Nadia won over me in order to make a metonymic object of it, even if at the beginning she had the same difficulties in prehension as Marie-Françoise—the automatic dropping of objects. While Nadia arrived through the spoon at the conquest of the external world, Marie-Françoise remained stuck with the Real of the lost object. This is what sent her back to her double, the sailor, but also to something new: for the first time she became interested in the pictures on the nesting boxes.

On 5 November, I noticed that the contact of her body with mine became considerably less conflictual, and I perceived that Marie-Françoise was far more trusting toward me.

Although she experienced the usual stumbling block of tension in front of the bottle, she was capable, shaking in the face of it, of calling me to her aid. Obviously, my presence for her was far more clear-cut than beforehand. She repeated the call for help a second time, and to show her that I had understood I lifted the bottle and put it back where it was as I spoke to her. She was then able to touch the bottle with the spoon, although with some inhibition; finally, she was happy because the spoon had left a drop of cereal, like a trace, on the nipple.

She withdrew from the bottle and went to eat the cereal using five objects in succession: the spoon, the bottom of the fluffy rabbit, my glasses, her hand, and my watch. During this scene the smearing and the spreading of the cereal prevailed. She spread it first on the table, after pouring it with her hand. Then she spread it on my glasses conscientiously, using them to smear me.

The scene repeated the relatively recent one of 27 October. In contrast to Nadia, she did not smear herself before smearing me, but smeared only me.

However, something emerged in what she did with my body: she was in the process of turning me into her double, as I have pointed out. By smearing me, Marie-Françoise made of me a beyond the double: perhaps without a hole, but still someone in whom she could look at herself narcissistically—in the same way as Nadia, after smearing herself, smeared me by pressing her smeared body against mine, going beyond the search for the hole in my body.

Immediately after this and in reverse order, Marie-Françoise smeared her cheeks for the first time as she ate the cereal with her hand. We did not arrive at the same point as with Nadia, when both Nadia and I were smeared in front of the mirror. However, a loss emerged in my body in the form of an object that Marie-Françoise could extract from it: my watch (was this an object already on the path of the signifier?), to which she listened as she looked at me, then dipped in the cereal and sucked, always looking at me. Was she not canceling out the loss that she made me suffer by then spreading a great deal of cereal on it? At least, what she then did was entirely symbolic.

She could not, however, go any further, such was the level of audacity that she showed.

A little later she cried when she saw me taking away the materials for the session—which were truly hers since the day before, when she hid them under her bed. This is very telling in relation to the division, which she still experienced, between her debate with me and the old path of the double.

22/The Mirror in the Real:
The Topological Inversion in Psychosis

I was not able to see Marie-Françoise for five days and on 10 November it was evident that she reacted to my absence, particularly after the significant session of 5 November.

I found her standing up at the top of the steps; she managed to climb down by herself.

She took the pieces of candy and ate them; however, after looking at the bottle, the doll, and the dish, she returned to the room from where she had come, taking a cooking pot with her.

On 12 November, unfortunately, our usual consulting room was occupied and I had to prepare another room on the same floor. A nurse brought Marie-Françoise from the nursery, where she had already started to cry.

As soon as she saw me in the new room, she stopped crying and wanted to be left on the floor. She walked to the table and started to eat the candy in the usual manner.

The session lasted rather a long time, as twice she vehemently refused to finish. This was a session of refusal, which for the first time she expressed in a more normal way, without stereotypes or attempts to cut herself off from me through the absorption of objects. She remained silent, passive, *with a gaze voluntarily distant and cold;* but she did not show once the gaze of a demented person.

She looked at me intensely while she ate the candy and I explained to her why we were in a new room. She inspected the room visually, focusing her attention for a long time on a picture of a peacock stuck on the wall, then on the portion of sky and the tops of the trees that she could see above the frosted part of the window.

Her gaze, focused on all the objects, was attentive, interested; I did not perceive any anxiety in it. When it focused on me, it was voluntarily distant but not absent. She did not cut herself off from my presence, but expressed her resentment to me.

Once the candy was finished and her inspection ended, her gaze moved to the bottle, the doll, and the dish. After contemplating the latter silently for quite a while, Marie-Françoise decided to take the spoon and eat. But she very quickly abandoned the spoon; she spread cereal all over the table; *she took my glasses, sank them entirely into the cereal, sucked them, and hit me with them.* She left the glasses in the dish, picked up *the spoon* again to hit my face very hard and *to try to poke it into my eye*, with a furious look: the eyes continued to be substitutes for the mouth. She finished what remained in the dish with her hand, licking it with delight. On a few occasions she came to pull my hair with her hand full of cereal and finally gave me a slap.

I thought of ending the session, but when I arrived at the door, she turned around, looked at me intensely, and said violently: "non, veux pas." I then sat down again. Once she verified that I had gone back to my position, for five minutes she ostensibly showed interest only in what she could see out the window. When I did the same as her, she looked at me, furious, and became absorbed again in her contemplation when my gaze moved back to her.

She ended the session by fitting in pieces of the toy tea set, after saying to me again *"non, veux pas,"* although in a more satisfied tone this time.

She stretched her arms to a nurse who took her back to the nursery. There she started to walk aggressively when another girl clung to my white coat and played at hiding behind it.

On 13 November, I prepared the same room as on the day before and decided to try to take Marie-Françoise from the nursery myself.

I found her sitting under the table with a toy. She babbled when I entered the room, started to aggressively wriggle her arms and legs and then, seeing that the girl of the scene of the previous day was moving toward me, she wanted to stand up and come to me, but hit herself very hard on the head and fell back to the sitting position. She looked at me furiously and started to cry. I went to her and she stopped crying and stretched her arms out to me. I then took her. She was calm and looked into the rooms during the short time that we moved along the corridor.

She removed my glasses. I put her on the floor after entering the room. *For the first time, she made me put her on the floor standing up* and walked quickly to the table. She took the pieces of candy and started to eat them as I closed the door and sat down. She looked at me and then ostensibly looked at the tops of the trees. As on the day before, if I did as she was doing she looked at me and stopped looking outside. This lasted for five minutes. I interpreted it to her and she laughed.

She explored the bottle and the nipple with her hand, using only two fingers. Although she showed reticence, a real interest in that exploration allowed her to arrive at a compromise with her fear. She then took the spoon, filled it, and licked it once; afterward, *she filled it again to then empty it on the nipple of the bottle* with joy, as if she were giving it something to eat—this is what I told her. She then abandoned the spoon to take my *glasses and use them to eat on two occasions.* She left them in the dish to give me a resounding smack.

She turned toward the baby doll, which she picked up, and sat down to look at it intensely. She got up, leaving it on the floor.

Marie-Françoise returned to the table and formed piles of cereal, which she spread with her hand. She took a cookie and started to eat it. She then looked at me and threw the two cookies down, one after the other, aggressively in the direction of the water basin, with a triumphant air.

She picked the doll up and put its face into the cereal as if she were making it eat. She left it there, took *a cookie, and started to eat it.*

I verbalized what she had done. She looked at me intensely and threw the two cookies aggressively in the direction of the basin. She turned toward me triumphantly again, picked up the doll once more, sucked its hands, threw it, and ate the remainder of the cereal with her hand, after pulling my hair very hard.

She preferred to remain in her autistic circuit, i.e., to eat herself up, rather than investing the food with an affective reality in relation to me. She compromised with her means of defense and I did not interpret them to her; yet she appeared to be surprisingly conscious of what she wanted to express.

She sat down on the floor, took two pieces from the toy tea set, and assembled and disassembled them.

She dropped the small milk pitcher into the basin. She deliberately put all the toys that were in the basket into the basin.

She stood up and became interested in the small blue chair, shaking it. I took her back to the nursery; she kept my glasses, which the nurse took back from her a few minutes later.

On 15 November, she stood up and walked toward the room next door—the old consulting room—as soon as she saw me. As she realized that the materials were not there, she turned toward me, stretching her arms.

As I left her standing up at the entrance to the new room, she walked quickly up to the table and took the candy, which she ate while looking at the tops of the trees through the upper part of the window. She held a piece out to me, almost touching my lips, put it back in her mouth, and *ate it, looking me in the eyes intensely for a long time.* Hers was a look that she voluntarily made cold and distant, although she needed minimal contact. Since she looked at me as she was eating, after bringing the piece of candy close to my mouth, there was in the association looking-eating a kind of attempt to put food in relation to me, to assign an affective value to it, *an attempt that she made defensively.*

Following that, she explored the bottle for a moment and ate just a spoonful of cereal. Using the spoon, she successively hit me on the nose and then stroked my cheek. She let herself drop, took my glasses, dipped them into the cereal once, without sucking them, and then abandoned them on the table. She took the doll.

She sat down with the doll and explored it, touching and shaking each hand and foot a little. *She sucked a hand briefly* and, looking at the bottle, she made loud sucking noises two or three times. She went back to the doll, which she continued to explore, this time around the face. *She pressed a little on each eye and tried to poke her finger into the mouth.*

She then turned, *looked at me, and threw the doll onto my lap* fairly violently. The doll slid and fell on the floor; she looked at it, but then did not pay any more attention to it. She stood up, took the spoon, and threw it violently toward my other side. Then it was the cookies' turn: she threw one at my feet *and the other toward the basin.*

I summarized the scene for her: exploration of the doll ending up in its mouth; aggressive rejection on my lap; aggressivity against the spoon used for eating and then against the cookies that she usually ate, as if she were furious against everything that had to do with food in its relation to me.

She went to grab *the objects in the basket and placed them in the basin.* First she put the small milk pitcher in it and then looked at me and continued putting other objects there: the pieces of the toy tea set, i.e., containers. I told her this. She also put the duck in the basin. *Finally, with great caution, she placed in the basin the cookie* that she had thrown in that direction previously. She had a look at all the objects inside the basin and then lost interest in them.

Her interest then turned for the first time *to the empty basket.* To begin with, she emptied it completely, throwing out a small plastic toy that she had brought the previous session, which she hit, loudly uttering "miam-miam" twice. Then *she explored the exterior of the wicker basket for a long time:* its handle, a piece of string left attached to it, and the design of the weave. Following that, *she made it rock* by pulling the handle toward herself and letting it go. The first time she burst out laughing; then her face became tense and I had the impression that the rocking was unpleasant to her, although there was a very specific aim that she wanted to attain by producing it. She wanted to see the external side of the bottom of the basket. She succeeded by tipping it over on one side. She then slid the palm of her hand along the bottom of the basket.

She stood up, walked up to her chair, and sat down on the floor again, *far from the basket.* Her gaze went from the doll to the basket; she hesitated. Finally, she got up again, took the basket by the handle, and pulled it over a yard before sitting down close to it.

She then moved to *explore the basket's inside. This was followed by a sort of taking possession of that inside,* pressing hard on the bottom with her two hands. In order to be able to press even harder, she stood up and with her legs straight and her upper body inside the basket, she put her palms on the bottom and pressed harder and harder. The movements of her behind reflected her effort and she stamped her feet a little. Her excitation increased and she uttered a few violent phonemes; finally, however, she dropped to the sitting position in front of the basket with an empty gaze.

Thinking that it was sufficient for the day, I went to open the door. She immediately stood up and went out.

On her way out she entered a room and looked with interest at the children lying in their cribs. She noticed a small bucket between two beds. She picked it up, *looked at its inside,* and then left it in a corner.

She moved back into the corridor, walking rather quickly, with a much better balance, toward the nursery. At the end, however, she fell down and quickly finished her journey on all fours. She did not go in to the nursery: she became attracted by the linen cupboard, which she opened and whose interior she explored with great interest. Her nurse came to pick her up.

On 17 November, I found her standing up in the nursery, her face full of animation. She moved toward the steps as soon as she saw me, but then dropped to the sitting position, as she did not see the materials in the room. She then turned and stretched her arms to me.

As I took her to the room, she grabbed my glasses and then made sucking noises. As soon as she saw the room, her body contracted. Once on the floor, she walked quickly up to the table and ate the candy.

When she finished the candy, she looked at me and saw that I had put on my glasses again. She then threw a piece of candy in the direction opposite to mine; it fell into the basket. She grabbed the spoon, ate a spoonful of cereal, hit my glasses once with the spoon, and threw it down. She looked for *the duck* in the basket and wanted to throw it into the basin. She missed; then she grabbed the duck once more *to throw it violently into the basin*. She contemplated it with joy. She returned to the table, *grabbed the cookies and the spoon, and threw them into the basin as well*. She then returned to the table to eat with her hands; she pulled my hair and *gave me a hard smack*. She went back to contemplate the basin.

As she was doing this, she noticed the bucket, which contained some sand. She moved on all fours up to the bucket, stayed in front of it, and *looked at the sand for a long time*. But she did not touch the sand or the bucket.

She returned to the basket, took all the small containers inside it, and put them in the basin; she also added a car and a wagon whose wheels she made go around with her finger. She approached the table again and took the doll, *dipped its behind, covered with a diaper, into the cereal, licked it, and threw it into the basin*. She returned to finish the cereal with her hands; then she took my glasses off and pulled my hair.

She sat down with my glasses and grabbed the sailor. She initially pressed the sailor directly against her cheek; then she interposed my glasses against her eye. She threw out my glasses and *pressed the sailor against her mouth very hard*. She stood up again, abandoned the sailor and the glasses to grab the rabbit, whose ears she dipped into the remainder of the cereal and then sucked. After looking at the hole of the squeaker in the rabbit's behind, she threw this out and came to pull my hair once more.

She returned to the basin to take *the doll, which she put into the empty basket after much hesitation*.

She quickly lost interest in this and moved on all fours back to contemplating the sand. As she was returning toward the table she stepped on the rabbit, which squeaked. She picked it up and amused herself by pressing its belly and making it squeak; this made her burst out laughing, a true laughter of joy for which she held me as a witness. She repeated this several times before giving me a good beating on the head with the rabbit.

She then shook the basket harder and harder, trying to make the doll fall out; but she did not dare to shake it hard enough to succeed. She gave up and removed the doll with her hand. *Now that the basket was empty, she expressed a certain aggressiveness against it,* which became increasingly manifest. For ten minutes, she shook the basket, hit it, and turned it upside down. At a certain point, the handle, moving back toward her, hit her on the nose. She was perplexed for a second and turned around *to look at me with fury, as if I were responsible, which was symbolically true.*

The empty basket, after having contained the doll, was undoubtedly the mother, who contained and then abandoned her.

As in the previous session, she went back to the nursery partly walking, partly on all fours.

On 19 November, when I went to fetch Marie-Françoise, she looked into the room next door and, seeing that the materials were not there, addressed an interrogating phoneme to me. I answered her as I opened the door to the corridor. She came toward me on all fours, stood up, and stretched her arms to me. She brought a rubber chicken in her hand.

As usual, she started with the pieces of candy; but she only ate one near the dish.

She threw the chicken and then all the containers, including the nesting boxes, into the basin. For the time being, therefore, she was playing almost exclusively with containers.

She moved toward the bucket of sand, looked inside, and, after much hesitation, plunged her hand into it and *took a small handful of sand, which she dropped at the side of the bucket.* This scared her, and she quickly returned close to the table.

She grabbed the spoon and ate a spoonful of cereal. She *hit me on the nose with the spoon,* grabbed my glasses, dipped one of their arms into the cereal, and sucked it; then she dropped the glasses. She grabbed the spoon again and used it to *hit me on the back of my hand, then on the palm. She ate a spoonful between each sequence of blows.* Each time a little cereal left on the spoon got spread on the palm of my hand. She noticed it and proceeded as if she wanted to fill in the spoon and eat it. This scene lasted for at least five minutes.

She grabbed the doll, inspected it, and dropped to the sitting position with it. She moved closer to the basket and left the doll in it. She repeated the same game as in the previous session, rocking and shaking the basket to make the doll fall out.

She seemed to hesitate; then, as if she had made a heroic decision, *she put a foot inside the basket, leaving the other on the floor,* and held onto a crib with her hands. She removed and put back inside the basket the same foot, three times in a row. She hesitated to put her other foot inside. She lifted it, brought it close to the edge of the basket, put it forward, and withdrew it with a hesitant movement, which then became a stamping of her feet. She looked furious at not being able to put herself into the basket. However, she finally was able to do it and *remained with both feet inside the basket for about five minutes, clinging onto the bars of a crib with both hands.*

She seemed perplexed at the start, as if she were in a state of great affective emptiness. Eventually, she came out shaking the crib. This was a stereotypical aggressive gesture which made the emotion emerge and rendered it tangibly conscious. Gradually she accompanied her gesture with a few phonemes uttered toward me. This was very different from what had happened on previous occasions. Her jaw was not protruding. Her phonemes were not screams. They were well articulated, separated one from the other, and reduced in number. Her utterances had nothing in common with the opening of a floodgate. But they were only partially addressed to me; she looked straight in front of her toward the upper part of the window as she produced them.

She came out of the basket and moved to the bottle, which she looked at and touched, her gaze directed at its inside. She noticed *the doll, grabbed it, and, with a furious gesture, threw it at my feet* as she said "bébé" violently. She then moved to the window, which she managed to open; *for five minutes she looked outside.* However, her interest was not in what she could see but in me, insofar as I was the culmination of the entire preceding scene, which she terminated by coming back into the room *to shake a crib aggressively.*

The whole thing evoked birth as the primary maternal rejection; a function of the proximity of the actual abandonment of Marie-Françoise at two months, the age of bottle feeding.

As she looked outside the window, *she tried to close the shutters behind her three times, thus attempting to isolate herself from me,* as if she wanted to deliberately cut herself off, as a consequence of the rejection that she had suffered in the past.

She returned to the room and shook the crib. Her diaper started to fall down to the point of hindering her walk almost completely.

She went to the bucket, put herself on all fours in front of it, and tilted it toward her. The bucket fell and *the sand spilled. She retreated hastily,* possessed by panic, stood up with difficulty, and moved back toward me *to pull my hair.*

Her movements became more and more hindered by her diaper, which had fallen to her feet; I removed it. She seemed to be uncomfortable, so I went to fetch a dry diaper. I put it within her reach so that I could see if she wanted me to put it on her. She took it, held it out to me, and waited. I put the diaper on her and *I was struck by the joy it brought to her.* She had a brief moment of joyful freedom that I did not expect.

She threw the cereal on the floor and then moved on all fours to look at the spilled sand. She became possessed by panic again and stood up to shake the small chair.

I opened the door and she went back to her room, making an incursion into every room in the course of her journey.

The session of 10 November was very brief as a reaction to my absence; yet it was marked by an event that was very much related to the end of the previous session: although Marie-Françoise left almost as soon as she had arrived for the session, she took a cooking pot with her. We have seen that the objects used in the session could now be hers; but, in addition, she could take them from me.

On 12 November, the tone of the session was centered on her presence, which she affirmed as she was confronted by my presence, and this in a new room. She said "non" to me in order to affirm herself. She did not once show the gaze of a demented person.

She repeated twice a scene during which her gaze remained focused for a long time, first on the wall, where a picture of a peacock was stuck, then on the sky and the treetops, which she could see through the upper part of the window. I noticed that the first time she did this she did not cut herself off from my presence, but expressed her resentment toward me through her remote, cold look deflected from me. In a very clear way, she rendered my presence absent by means of her gaze.

Rendering me absent was then accompanied by an intense aggressiveness against the food, which she spread around the whole table, then on my glasses. She dipped my glasses into the cereal completely. Finally, she directed her aggressiveness against me. She first hit me in the face with my glasses, which she had previously sucked, then with the spoon, which she even tried to poke into my eye. This meant that she was trying to make a hole. I have mentioned that the eyes always functioned as substitutes for the mouth. She was now able to obtain pleasure from licking her hand, with which she finished what remained in the dish; this was accompanied by aggression against me: she pulled my hair with her hand full of cereal and ended up giving me a smack.

The smack reminds us of the first session. However, whereas at the beginning it was a question of pure muscular aggressiveness and she was not truly addressing herself to me, now she attacked my body with the hand she used for eating. The big difference from Nadia lay in the absence of ambivalence in Marie-Françoise. However, especially since the beginning of the session on 12 November, there emerged a hint of an interrogation of my body and of what I held on my eye.

When I decided to finish the session, she told me violently: "non, veux pas." But this time she said "veux pas" as she looked at me intensely: it was to me that she was talking. She had addressed her first two "veux pas" to the rice pudding, on 27 October, and to the object of my body, after sinking her head in my breast, on 29 October.

The second scene in front of the window, which lasted almost five minutes, took place when she returned to the room and I was sitting down again. She looked through the upper portion of the window, toward the tops of the trees, only when I was looking at her; but she could not bear my looking through the upper part of the window as she was doing. It was necessary that I look at her looking. Is this not the typical scene of the mirror that we had discovered in Nadia, where the child looks at his or her image, which will found the exterior of the body under the gaze of the Other and which is indispensable to produce the passage to the specular proper: to apprehend in the child's own virtual image the implicit loss of the Other in order to be able to tolerate the child's own loss? For Marie-Françoise, however, although my gaze was required, the mirror was replaced by the window. Behind the window, the virtual space remained as a Real, even if that was no longer the place of her call to a real absence, but to the treetops. In other words, Marie-Françoise realized a mirror scene in the Real, without the elision or loss inherent to the encounter with the mirror. In demanding that my gaze focus on her she ensured her existence in my eye.

We find there the outline of what Nadia had realized in the pre-specular phase through the image of the other stuck on my eye, which not only indicated her own place in my eye but also posited me as her Other. A certain sensitivity to the other started to develop in Marie-Françoise when coming back from the session another child clung to my white coat: she started to walk aggressively around the room. It is to be noted that she did not hit me as in the session.

On 13 November, she ostensibly repeated the scene in front of the window, her gaze on the treetops, demanding my gaze upon her. However, on that occasion I was able to interpret and tell her that she wanted me to see that she refused to look at me. Her laughter confirmed that I had hit the right spot, to the point that this was the last time that she demanded my gaze as she looked at the treetops.

Three successive scenes defined then what I called her autistic circuit. They did not make sense by themselves but exclusively through the contrast they made with what Nadia had shown in her relation to the Other and the other.

The first one was a replica of the scene of 7 November, when I believed that an opening toward the establishment of the Other for Marie-Françoise had been made, as she was then able to take in cereal using different substitutes for the bottle, of which two—my glasses and my watch—were taken from me. But what she did on 13 November invalidated what had appeared to me as an opening. Instead of taking the step of moving the objects toward the body of the Other, she closed herself up completely in the relation with the objects, which had consequences for her relation with me. She ended the first scene by giving me a resounding smack.

The smearing in this case did not involve her body or mine but only the objects. We can even say that it was the bottle that she fed—she had already done it with my glasses and my watch on 7 November, but she seemed then ready to move on to the smearing of the body, although it was first with my body and then with hers, in reverse order when compared with Nadia. This was not at stake any more in the session of 13 November. The bodies were excluded, and she transported onto the objects the consistence of surface that Nadia attributed to the bodies by smearing them. It was the object—good or bad—that occupied the place of the body and of what could be inscribed there as relational. She concluded the scene with the destructive gesture addressed to the dead end represented by the pure Real of my body. This probably had been the sense of the series of smacks in the first session already: it was to my body that she addressed herself. Against the "all or nothing" debate in the background, she pointed at the intolerable character of my presence in the Real, of which she could not be saved by the real absence that deprived her of everything—her mother, who had abandoned her.

The second scene confirmed that her relation was established only with a real object. The fact that she picked up the doll and sank its face into the cereal, as if to make it eat, could be understood as the expression of her own desire to eat passing through the image of the doll. Thus, Nadia, both with the bottle on 4 January and the spoon on 27 January, had shown her oral desire by insinuating the gesture of feeding the doll. That had been only an attempt that ended up in great violence against the doll accompanied by violence against the bottle and the spoon. But Nadia clearly showed then that her expressions were addressed to the Other that I was; that is to say, they did not have the value of what is impossible, but of what is prohibited. Although Marie-Françoise looked at me and threw the cookies in the direction of the basin on two occasions, and even started to eat one of them—that is to say, to take in food that was in relation to me—she immediately stopped and only became triumphant in the radical refusal that she addressed to me: grabbing the doll again, she sucked its hands, threw it down, and ate what was left of the cereal with her hand, after pulling my hair very hard. The doll implied in her refusal of the Other was not an image linked to me; it was a real refuge against me, i.e., a "double" she reencountered at the oral level, as she had done at the scopic level.

The second scene clarified the first: the bottle occupied the same place of real double as the doll, and it was accompanied by the same mechanism of refusal of my body. In all this there was nothing of the order of a prohibition; nothing but the Real of an object that was not inscribed in the Other, successively posited and refused without any signifying effect.

The consequences of the lack of inscription of the object in the Other and the reduction of the Other to a real object are that:

1. Strictly speaking, there is no substitute for the object in the metaphorical sense.

2. Indeed, for Marie-Françoise the Other was not the holder of objects that cause desire. The Other itself was the object, which explains simultaneously the need that she had for me and the impasse in which she found herself in my presence, which she could refuse only through an "all or nothing."

3. Under these conditions, Nadia's ambivalence could not appear in Marie-Françoise, since such ambivalence is the oscillation between the love for the Other and the aggressive search for the object that the Other bears. Marie-Françoise was captive of an alternation between my real presence, which she expected and looked for, and her radical refusal in the session, which corresponded to the real absence

of her mother, to whom she addressed herself by turning toward the void of the window.

The third scene confirmed, first, her lack of the imaginary and specular dimension, both regarding herself and the doll and herself and me. The two pieces of the toy tea set that she assembled and disassembled showed the real relation that was in question. That she then put a little container in the basin full of water, followed by all the toys from the basket, could lead us to think of a real replica of an Other, represented by the basin that contained the objects. Was this a regressive movement toward a prenatal habitat? We shall return to this point.

The first part of the session of 15 November was concerned with myself and with the doll as a whole.

As regards myself, her starting point was the real absence: she ate all the candy while looking at the treetops through the upper part of the window. But she did not spend much time on it. On the contrary, in this session she turned toward me and, bringing a piece of candy almost to my lips, she focused a long and intense gaze on my eyes; I felt that her gaze was cold and distant. She attempted to re-establish the link between food and gaze, but only succeeded in making the bottle her double and in using the spoon for successively hitting and stroking me. We could think of ambivalence, but the impossibility she showed of sucking my glasses, which she took and dipped into the cereal, would disconfirm it.

She fell back on the doll, her double, which she paired with her other double, the bottle. Taking one of the doll's hands to her mouth, she looked at the doll while making loud sucking noises. In this session she went further with the doll when she explored its face, pressing a little on each eye and trying to poke her finger into its mouth. The exploration of the hole in the doll's mouth made it come out of its role as double—a role that it did not always have. She confirmed this by not withdrawing with the doll but turning toward me to throw it violently on my lap. She was not concerned that it fell on the floor. I did not pick it up, the same way I had not picked up Nadia's sailor after the first mirror; this, because neither the doll nor the sailor had a representational function. For Nadia, that was the opportunity for realizing a loss, whose fruitfulness we have seen throughout the experiences with the mirror that followed. For Marie-Françoise, the fact that I did not pick up the doll created a similar opportunity, since it was not her representative but a real object among all the other objects from which she separated. Unfortunately for her, the mirror was not at her disposal as a place where the loss could be signified. In place of the mirror she found the basket and the basin of water; in other words, containers, volumes, instead of the mirror's surface. I told her this. Nevertheless, the basin and the basket were not the same thing.

The water basin was the basin plus water, i.e., two terms. When she put all the objects that she took from the basket in it, those were not only the objects that she had known all along for what they were, i.e., real objects, but also objects added to the first two: the basin + water + the objects, a situation where there is a "three," the water being the intermediary and having the structural function of the derealization of objects.

The question of the prenatal habitat, referred to as soon as there is a container and water, only concerns an imaginary situation with two elements. Actually, it is a structure of three, insofar as the elements in it are signifying for the subject; this is indispensable to constitute a structure. We cannot yet arrive at a conclusion in relation to Marie-Françoise. Marie-Françoise did not arrive at any conclusion either: after cautiously placing a cookie and looking at the contents of the basin, she lost interest in it and moved onto the empty basket, which had contained the objects now in the basin. There, she quickly arrived at her aim: to see the outside of the bottom of the basket, along whose surface she slid her palm. That was the first time she explored the basket. Contrary to the basin, it was not on the occasion a container, but a surface. That was a great step; we did not know as yet whether it would be decisive, but we must note that it was the first time that she posited the surface as a dimension of an object to be explored. Certainly, she had approached the surface of my body at the beginning with some smearing. But the exclusion of her own body that had not been smeared had sent her back into her autistic circuit in the course of the sessions that followed. Was it, perhaps, that in this session she was able to interrogate the surface again because previously she had put the objects and one cookie in reserve and under the shelter of the basin? Was the basin a representation of the Other?

The exploration of the basket's surface, which was clearly manifest in a first moment, as the outside of the bottom of the basket was involved, was followed by the exploration of the inside. Such an exploration could be interpreted as the search for a container. Marie-Françoise bent over to lean with her hands on the bottom, within the inside, in such a way that one could think that she tried to make herself into the contents of the basket. In fact, in that session, after her efforts and an increasingly intense excitation, she dropped to the sitting position, as she had at the beginning when she was in despair; at the same time, her gaze became empty. Her exploration of the linen cupboard when she left the session was not conclusive evidence as to what she was searching for.

On 17 November, my glasses, the basin, and the basket were the pivotal objects of the session:

1. As I was carrying her to the consulting room, she took my glasses and made sucking noises. It was the first time that an object of my body was so clearly linked with her autoerotism, which was not frequently manifest in Marie-Françoise.

The place of my glasses as an object at the border of her desire was confirmed when, having put the candy into her mouth, she looked at me and saw that I had put my glasses back on. At that moment she threw one of the pieces of candy. She also ate a spoonful of cereal, hit me once on my glasses with her spoon, and threw it down. All this was done as if to express the necessary link between an object of my body and food, so that she could eat and so that it made sense.

2. As to the basin, she put inside it not only the duck, which she kept contemplating, but also the cookies and the spoon. Then she ate with her hands, pulled my hair, smacked me, and moved to contemplate the basin, in that order. The place of the basin was precise: when I put on my glasses again, she could not eat anymore; she was able to eat again only when she kept her objects in reserve within the basin. This placed the basin in the position of an Other in reserve and enabled her to attack me violently. In contrast to the relation of contemplation that she had with the basin, by attacking me she put me in the place of the one who abandoned her and deprived food of its sense: her mother. In this scene, Marie-Françoise's progress consisted in the opposition she established between the basin and me. This pair of opposites was the beginning of an articulation.

She pursued the issue in the scene that followed, as she took the doll, dipped it into the cereal, licked it, and threw it into the basin before attacking me again.

She then managed to establish a ternary situation between herself, my glasses, and the sailor, pressing the latter against her cheek and interposing my glasses. Her "double" became unstuck from her by means of an object of my body whose status was not, however, that of an object cause of desire. She returned immediately to the sailor after throwing down the glasses and for the first time pressed it very hard against her mouth: she made of it an object that plugged the hole of her mouth, as she had made of it the object that plugged the lower orifice of her body. She must have remembered it somehow, since when she took the rabbit she looked at its lower hole, just before pulling my hair. Her aggression ended up acquiring through its insistence the value of a reproach, which stated that she had a body with a gap, a holed body, in relation to which I had failed in the transference to plug the hole with an object such as my glasses.

3. It was then in the empty basket that she put the doll, which she took from the basin. She continued to shake the basket with increasing vigor to make the doll fall out; as she did not succeed, she removed it with her hand. Her aggressiveness against the basket became more prominent; its meaning could be inferred when, having knocked herself against the handle, she turned toward me to express her fury.

The sequence of the first part of the following session, on 19 November, was a repetition of that of 17 November, which led us to conclude that there was now a signifier in Marie-Françoise and not just a pure Real, which would not produce a repetition. This confirmed the signifying value of the pair of opposites, the basin and myself, which we pointed out previously. The basin was a ternary reserve for her objects; I became the holder of objects whom she attacked incessantly, since in the transference I refused her the objects. The initial stage, during which I had been the real presence of an equally real absence, without any object of my body that could acquire the quality of being a separable object, was surpassed. She demonstrated this when she grabbed my glasses, dipped one of their arms into the cereal, and sucked it; and also when, hitting me with the spoon that she used to eat the cereal, she wanted to take back the traces of cereal that she had left on my hand. However, we should not forget what she did with the bottle on 13 November, when she left some cereal on the nipple. This meant that, as in the case of the bottle, I could offer her only what she had given me: an inversion of roles that might cut off any demand.

In the session we are discussing, she returned to the game with the doll and the basket; on this occasion, having removed the doll, it was herself who, after many hesitations, wanted to occupy her place in the basket. Certainly it was not to find some comfort in it; on the contrary, she gave the impression that what she found there was a great void. Besides, when she uttered a few well-articulated phonemes, she addressed them to the absence, always at the same place, at the top of the window. And it was to the window that she went when she came out of the basket, after throwing the doll at my feet, saying "bébé" violently, as a reproach.

Once near the window, which she managed to open, she first looked outside for a long time, at the place of the absence, but also at me, who was behind her; her reproach was addressed to me. Finally, she wanted to close the window shutter, in order to actually be on the other side of the glass, that is to say, more and more on the side of the real absence of the Other. However, on this occasion, in front of me, she was on her way to identifying with that absence.

In the face of such repetition and progression, are we not justified in talking of discourse? Certainly, this was a discourse that did not exist at the beginning, when only a few defensive elements, like the "double," were present. Now it was not a question of the double anymore, but of her and me in a certain relation. What relation? I was an Other for which she had a need, which she searched for, but to which she could not address any demand because that Other was not the holder of a separable object. In that first form of identification, transitivism, Marie-Françoise only found the Other in the real absence behind the window. It was not surprising that she could not demand anything of that Other. That is why at the most she could occupy the place of the Other: thus, she became the "being of absence."

That position was at the basis of an inversion: when the structural void of the beginning was succeeded by a beginning of structuration, Marie-Françoise did not take the place of a small other in relation to a big Other, as in the case of Nadia, but the place of the Other. Her structuration was inverted to the point that, from a topological point of view, she had the holed body of the Other while I did not, like the small subject confronted with the big Other. Thus, the relation was defined more prematurely in reference to three-dimensional contents and containers, rather than in reference to a surface of the body where she would try to fill in the holes by means of objects taken from the Other's body, as Nadia did. Although she smeared the surface of her body, the holes in this surface remained. She had a body in the form of a torus without having passed through the body structure of a Möbius strip.

Is it possible to come out of psychosis other than through the reestablishment of a topological order of the bodies that includes a relation between the Other and the other? The case of the Wolf Child will provide the answer to this question.*

Marie-Françoise's structure was not frozen. Her evolution proved

*Translators' note: Cf. Lefort and Lefort 1988.

it, as well as the joy she manifested when at the end of the session I put a new diaper on her. I filled in and veiled the lower orifice of her body. A joyful freedom possessed her.

23/The Emergence of a Call to the Other

On 22 November, Marie-Françoise refused to have the session in the usual room and took me through all the rooms.

She returned to the room only in order to put everything in the basin, including the cookies and candy, and to try to make the mug and the bottle fall by vigorously shaking the mug. She finished by making the bottle fall. She was staggered for a moment; then she lost interest in it.

On 24 November, she stretched her arms out to me when she saw me in the nursery. A nurse changed her diaper; if I did not remain close to her and within her sight *she started to cry.*

The session was ambulatory, and through it she expressed that her interest for the external world was a refuge against me. She did not show any manifest anxiety, but she tried by all means to make the children in whom she became interested cry; they were all small boys.

She stayed in the consulting room for only five minutes, long enough to put the contents of the basket and my glasses into the basin. She pulled my hair and hit me with the spoon. She was scared of looking at the bucket. Then she stood up and banged the door until I opened it.

She took me into a room where she noticed a small boy in his crib playing with a purse. She contemplated him for a long while and then tried to take the purse from him.

As she was about to get it, she heard a child crying in another room and left at full speed. It was a small boy whose diaper was being changed. His behind was naked, and Marie-Françoise contemplated him with great interest, clinging to a corner of the table on which he was being changed. Back in his crib the boy continued to cry; Marie-Françoise looked at him, lost interest, and then went to inspect a toy that she found on the floor. A moment later, she noticed that he was not crying any longer. She stood up and shook his crib, inspecting his face closely and watching his tears, which had returned. She left the room as if she were satisfied.

Once on the landing, *she noticed that the linen cupboard* was open. She rushed toward it and took possession of every shelf, her hands on the piles of linen, and then turned around to look at me.

She made a few timid attempts to get completely inside the cupboard but had to give up. She tried to reach a higher shelf on tiptoes.

A nurse that she knew well went by; she looked at her, babbling. At the end of the session, when I left Marie-Françoise in the nurse's arms, *she started to sob and to push the nurse away, chanting "maman-maman."* The nurse could not console her while I remained there.

The last two sessions were not the end of Marie-Françoise's treatment—far from that. We cannot comment much on their meaning, as we do not know what happened after them. If we did, perhaps we would also know the reasons for her refusal of the consulting room. She stayed there for only a few moments, enough to put all the objects from the basket into the basin, once more confirmed as the container of all those objects. Was the basin a representative of the Other in the first degree—*Repräsentanz* and not *Vorstellungsrepräsentanz*? It had nothing to do, at any rate, with Nadia's ark, which contained metonymic representatives of her and me, i.e., *Vorstellungsrepräsentanz*, since among the representatives the signifier implied her as well as me. Marie-Françoise became interested in walking from one room to another. At the time I said—since that was how I felt—that her interest in the external world was a refuge against me—another difference in relation to Nadia.

For Marie-Françoise, certainly, the mirror concerned only a parallel register where she was not constituted, like Nadia, in the place of the Other that I was, on the same side of the mirror as myself. She remained radically on the other side of a mirror that was only a piece of glass and that could only make of me her double in the Real. She failed in relation to the Other.

As far as the small other is concerned, his tears did not produce distress in her as they did in Nadia, who was emotionally moved in echo. This was because for Nadia the small other existed from the beginning: not only as a fellow child in despair, the place of an impossible *jouissance,* but also in relation to the Other, from whom the child was to be separated.

In the scene of 24 November, none of these dimensions was present for Marie-Françoise. She did not interrogate the small other as a fellow child or as an object of the Other. He was only a pure Real, and as such subject to her destructive drive, which produced the sadistic tone of the scene, where she shook the child's crib and watched his tears, which she wanted to cause.

However, a question can be posed as to why she chose boys to attack. Her attentive curiosity and her scopic interest were focused manifestly on the small other's sex, and the sight of the penis in the other only stirred up her destructive drive, instead of referring her to the Other, where that difference could be inscribed in the register of lack. Without the Other, there is no *invidia* or jealousy but only isolated sadistic drive: at the limit, it was Marie-Françoise who could emerge at the place of *a* for the observer, as "the black fetish," to use Lacan's words.

But that would be at the limit. Her sobbing at the end, when I left her in the arms of a nurse that she knew well and she turned toward me calling "maman, maman" for the first time, made us think that the Other that I was could come to the place of a call, a call that would make of her, at that moment, the subject of a lack.

Unfortunately, after this first opening, I had to break off the treatment because I was moving overseas, after a brief preparation of Marie-Françoise for my departure. What were the consequences? I do not know.

Conclusions

In conclusion, I would like to reaffirm that I carried out these treatments before I had any theoretical training, which means that the analytical situation is exemplary, insofar as it was not a question of knowing what to do, but rather of an unconscious knowledge, which created itself in the place of the analyst through the fact of the analysand. It was a knowledge that brought into play the principal discovery of analysis: the transference. The analysand was in the place of the teacher—which, in Freud's case, was quite evident right from the start; and this was no less evident for me, for example, when Nadia led me through the winding pathways of the mirror stage, when in my own journey I was still well this side of it. One can only conclude, as I have already said, that these treatments were a part of my own analysis.

But what would have come of it if I had not written it all down? Every evening, after the sessions, I wrote at great length a detailed account of what had happened—as presented in this book—feeling as if I was being guided by some necessity. But what necessity? If not to respond to what these children brought to me in the way of challenges, taking it upon myself, and discharging myself of it by writing, which took the place of the Real of my body and allowed me to become available again to listen to what they had to say. The writing was a way for me to blot out the Real of bodies that had been of use to them in the sessions but whose transformation into signifiers remained my responsibility, so that these small analysands could carry on along their own paths. Writing appeared there as the place of transformation of the Real into signifiers, signifiers that recall the Real, as in metaphor, as we shall see.

It is the text that we have confronted here, which emerged from that writing and which required us to work slowly and laboriously to go beyond the content to reach the structure. This structure is the essential transformation of the Real into signifiers, following the entire course of the sessions, whether or not the transformation was actually realized.

That is why we were able to be guided only by the fundamental difference between the two treatments presented: one in which the transformation did take place, in the case of Nadia, and the other where it did not, that of Marie-Françoise, which was the counterproof—although the greatest possible regret one can have is that the treatment cease prematurely—very much so in this case: for was not the transformation about to take place?

There are two approaches that can account for this transformation: a topological approach and an approach that involves the structures of the signifier, metaphor and metonymy, which we shall examine successively, in order to clarify them, at the risk of a certain amount of repetition. We will finish with the elements that can more properly be called topological.

The Clinic and Topology

At the start of our work, it was neither our purpose nor our ambition to refer to topology. This reference imposed itself on us; let me explain how.

With Nadia, there were two events that puzzled us for a considerable time as to their meaning: on the one hand, that she smeared herself with excrement and even went so far as to eat it; and on the other, that she smeared herself with cereal in order to go in front of the mirror, having smeared me in the same way.

It has to be said that I had an intuitive feeling, as I wrote at the time, that this smearing had its importance, when I introduced a dish of cereal and a spoon into the session on 27 January. The closeness of the two episodes of smearing, with excrement and with cereal, offered us the key to what was at stake: she was spreading whatever concerned the inside of the body, excrement or cereal, over the outside surface, her skin. Thus Nadia was telling us that the surfaces of her body, internal or external, were joined, structuring her body as a surface, and in no way as a volume with a separate inside and outside.

So how could we avoid referring to topology, or defining the type of surface to which the child's body belonged? How could we not redefine the corporeal relations between the small subject and the Other in terms of surfaces and, correlatively, of holes?

We were very soon to notice how fruitful our research was with Nadia, as well as with Marie-Françoise, insofar as she was the counterproof, as we have mentioned. We were even to find it subsequently in our analyses of adults.

Topologically, the structure of Nadia's body, in other words, that of the small subject at the dawn of life, appeared to be a Möbius strip, a strip twisted in on itself, a surface with only one side, without an exterior or an interior, and, moreover, a surface that was topologically without holes. This raises the question of the real orifices of the child's body.

For Nadia, it was the body of the Other that had holes, and she had straightaway started to explore the hole of the mouth. Her own body did not have any holes, because the hole was plugged by the object of my body. It started with the stopping of her mouth with the same finger she used to explore my mouth.

The small subject's body was initially plugged, not by any real food-object, but by an object taken from the Other, from the field of the Other, in other words, a signifying object: the structure we are talking about is a signifying structure and can only exist as such. By means of this structure, a dialectic was established between the child and the Other that Nadia, for example, posited very rapidly as that of the object that could be separated from my body, from the Other that I was. It was a separable object that at the same time made a hole in me and a non-hole in her. As soon as there was an Other, with its signifying status of Other, there was a real loss, which the small subject ascribed to the account of the Other. In this way, initially, the small subject escaped this loss and did not have holes in her body.

But how could that be, since in the physiological Real, the baby functions essentially at the level of digestion, that is to say, through the only hole in the body that can be defined topologically, the one that runs from the mouth to the anus? All the other cavities in the body, sensory organs, urinary tract, female genitals, or penis, are *stricto sensu* only deformations of the surface, in other words, have to do with the external surface: the skin. The sensory organs, furthermore, are nothing but specialized formations of the skin. But, on the other hand, in order for the child to know nothing of the hole in its body, it has to be somewhere entirely other than in the Real as far as the child's knowledge of its body is concerned; it exists—it is born—only in the field of the Other; so the Other has to exist; that is to say, for the small subject, the signifier has to preexist.

It is quite clear, indeed, what was at stake for Marie-Françoise, for whom the Other did not exist, resulting in the failure of structure. At no time was she able to explore the hole of my mouth, as Nadia did; she was not able to stop up the holes in her own body with signifying objects taken from the body of the Other; not being able to stop up this hole, she negated its very existence.

For her, there was an absolutely exemplary stage of this problematic of the hole in the body when, taking no notice of her mouth, she kept on coming up against her eye, to which she would stick the object (the sailor) that she made into her double in an attempt to completely ignore the hole in her body. From then on, confronted with the dish of rice pudding, which both fascinated and tortured her, she showed that the food-object in the Real could not fill up this hole.

There, too, structure showed that it was signifying, and the psychotic child, in her failure, bore witness once again to the truth that *beyond the signifier, there is no structure. For her, it was a question of a-structure.*

The displacement of the hole of the mouth onto the surface of the eye, both in the case of Nadia, with the image of 10 December, and with Marie-Françoise, blocked when confronted with food, sticking her double to her eye, underlined the fact that the body's surface is the locus of structure from the very beginning of life. This never ceases to have consequences, from then on, for any subject. For example, the hysteric's being-in-the-world, connected entirely with the body's surface; or indeed, in the mother-child relation, with respect to the emergence of psychosis, where the child is called into the place of the object that plugs the hole in the surface of the mother's body.

This type of structure, where the surface has no hole, coupled with the body of the Other, which has holes, explains the considerable importance of the faltering of the oral drive, even its complete inhibition. In such a case, the subject is on the one hand linked to the necessity to satisfy its needs, and on the other, to maintain its own desire in the Other. We know that anorexia is the choice on the part of the subject to save its desire in contempt of its needs, even of its life; and that bulimia is the opposite: no more Other, no more desire.

The reason orality can so easily be inhibited is because it implicates the relation with the Other and the transformation of the Real of the food-object into a signifier. The oral object is what the subject appropriates from the holed Other and which entails the subject itself not having any holes. The dialectic, which is signifying, situates this oral object at the level of "nothing" and includes in it a loss, that which psychoanalysis has pointed out as being central in the denomination of the concept of castration; and this happens from the very start, from the oral phase.

Thus we are led to completely revise our notions of the "good object" and the "bad object," notions that could allow us to believe that a good object exists in itself, bearing real witness to the love of the Other; and that would be in perfect contradiction to the signifying dialectic that is in question. Indeed, if the Other does not have holes, the subject, like Marie-Françoise, can appropriate nothing from it, and the oral object remains in the Real.

There is only one type of object: the drive object; it is an object that takes its place in a montage, the circuit of the drives, which absolutely implicates the Other and deprives the object of its Real dimension by marking it with a loss. That, indeed, is why orality can never lead to intrinsic satisfaction, but to a structure that is constitutive of the subject in the signifier, as is the case with all the other drives.

There is one very special drive, however, and that is the scopic drive, which is privileged insofar as it reduces to a minimum the dimension of the loss of the object.

In Nadia's case, this was a position of waiting, at the beginning. But with Marie-Françoise, it was shown to be the only privileged drive, to the point of not articulating itself, in a certain coexistence, with the oral drive, but, rather, replacing it almost completely.

For Nadia, this waiting was for the Other; and if, in order to avoid loss, on 10 December she promoted the image of totality, "$a + A$," her sensitivity to my presence, as Other, maintained her in the realm of the signifier and led her to repression. What she showed us was how the scopic object functions in order to protect the subject from any loss: it functions by sticking the object onto the surface of the eye, i.e., to the external surface of the body. But what Nadia stuck to her eye was an image, a representative of the object. The unsticking of the image could then happen via the signifier that I introduced by calling her by her name, on 10 December.

Marie-Françoise, however, denied the existence of the hole of her mouth, which she could not plug with the object of the Other, which I was not for her. She showed us that it was very much a question of sticking the object onto the surface, when she stuck it right against her eye, the organ in the Real. Neither the signifier nor the Other was promoted in that action, but merely a double, which, since it was Real, could not be repressed.

There remains, however, what was identical in the approaches of Nadia and of Marie-Françoise, in the signifier and in the Real, or even in the relation to the Other and in the absence of the Other. Certainly, the evolution was very different in the two cases, with respect to the next phase, the mirror stage, as we saw: a mirror for Nadia and a windowpane for Marie-Françoise. But this early correspondence leads us to pose the question regarding the relation between the Real and the signifier.

Phenomenologically, both normal and psychotic children attempt in the same way to stick the object onto the surface of the body in order to plug the hole in it. This similarity would be deeply troubling in the approach we were trying to make, if one insisted on a radical separation of the Real from the signifier, reserving the side of the signifier for normal development, with its inscription of the debate in the field of the Other as place of signifiers as well as founding the structure of the body as signifying; and the side of the Real, with the complete absence of the Other, for psychosis.

Now, this separation was completely unthinkable in Nadia's case, even at the level of the Other that I was for her, whose body she was exploring at every moment in reality. Moreover, the objects she was separating from my body were real ones. This separation occurred very early on in Nadia's debate; they were objects that correlated with the real hole of my body (my mouth, which she explored), and they themselves, real inasmuch as they were separable, thus constituted objects *a* causing her desire. When she deprived me of them, they were real; when she sought them on my body, when she desired them, they were veiled; they had undergone transformation from the Real into signifiers. Thus the Other certainly participates in the two registers of the Real and of the signifier. But the objects it bears cannot, under any circumstances, reveal themselves as real in the signifier: whence the veil or the predominance of the scopic.

Such a passage between the object that was separable, although veiled, took place for Nadia in the scene of 5 December, as we saw; the passage from the real *a*, fragmenting my body, to the signifier that synthesized me in the place of "mama."

For Marie-Françoise, and in the case of psychosis, the side of the Real was no more isolated than was the side of the signifier in Nadia's case. For her, too, the signifier arose, as it had done for Nadia, when she was faced with the Real. She, too, said "maman"; except that it was when confronted with the dish of rice pudding, and not with the object of my body, which she did not seek to separate. Her "maman" had no effect for her as far as my place was concerned; it did not designate me, and what is more, Marie-Françoise turned immediately to the window, the place of real absence. In other words, what was lacking for Marie-Françoise was not the signifier, but the relation of this signifier to the Real of my body, that of the Other.

The Real and the signifier each remained in their own domain, and there was no transformation from one to the other, which left her faced with a void, a void that was situated as much in the real absence behind the windowpane as in the absence to which she consigned me when she was struggling with the unbearable Real of the dish, during the first sessions.

There was further evidence that this articulation was not taking place: Marie-Françoise was able to take objects from my body, my glasses, my pencil, but failed to do the questioning, which would have been signifying, of necessity, a questioning starting out from the Real of the objects, concerning the hole they left on my body and that indicated the place of the subject.

For Marie-Françoise, the Real always remained opaque and could not lack anything. In this case, my body could not be affected with a hole; and in particular, it could not lack *a*, the small other as well as object *a*.

But while Marie-Françoise perceived the Other as not having any holes, she herself did, and so did the world, the consulting room, with the hole of the window, the objects, the basket, the cooking pot, the rabbit. Everything really had holes; on the other hand, no signifier came to answer for her own position, because it is only the holed Other that can be the place of such a signifier. Everything was the wrong way around.

The subsequent phase was the arrival for the subject of a new structure, the specular structure.

For Nadia, the first step toward the mirror, which was to bring with it the change in her perception of the structure of bodies, was the image that unstuck itself from the surface of her eye.

1. The first perceptible point in the passage from one structure to another is distance.

First we should note that among the four objects *a*—breast, voice, gaze, feces—the former two belong to the Other, and the latter two to the subject. We have seen the extent to which the latter two become stuck onto the body. The body there appears in its structure only with one side. As to the breast and the voice, they intervene only with the appearance of the Other, as objects that are separable from the body of the Other and cause the subject's desire. And already, in any case, as far as the breast is concerned, being stuck on the body of the Other, a distance appears between the subject and the object of its quest. As to the voice, even though we cannot say, *stricto sensu*, that it is stuck to the body of the Other, it clearly introduces the notion of distance, while also having something to do with the hole of the mouth.

It is possible to gauge the importance of the difference between these two types of object, as far as establishing a distance is concerned, by comparing what happened in the two cases of Nadia and Marie-Françoise.

For Nadia, I was very quickly established in my position of Other.

Of course we can only speak of such an establishment within the transference, and not of the inauguration of an Other who would not have been there at all, who would not have preceded the scene. The signifier that preexists founds the Other in its being, and we have already mentioned the primary identification with Freud's Mythical Father, with the Name-of-the-Father.

For Nadia, distance inscribed itself in the separation she insisted on between *a* and the body of the Other, *a* that could be separated from my body. Meanwhile, the distance from the object became concrete in the form of the veil. When she pushed her head inside my white coat, there was nothing left for her but an object beyond the veil, unattainable as such, which made her furious, but whose truth she recognized, since she herself was to veil the bottle. As to my voice, we have seen how sensitive she was to it right from the start.

The veiled breast, the voice, whether Nadia was hearing or beginning to speak, created a distance in her relation to the Other. The gaze was the image stuck onto her eye; feces were the excrement stuck to her skin. The breast and the voice were to be unstuck from my body, not without violence, so that they could be united with the two other objects on her own body, in order to realize, almost in a hallucinatory fashion, the primitive image of the first structure of the body in the form of a Möbius strip, without holes. But this structure was signifying, and, to this extent, Nadia's search did not sever her from me; it made her oscillate between her search on my body and my image, which existed for her as an image, in which she saw herself reflected narcissistically and with pleasure.

Where Marie-Françoise's relations with other external objects were concerned, I was present only as a witness, without her asking me to participate in her debate. Certainly, she too wanted to stick objects onto her body, whether she was sticking them to her eye or whether she did not know what to do with the baby doll, for example, when she pushed it away from her. But that was not sufficient to found what we saw in Nadia's case: the structure of a Möbius strip. All she could do was to remain at the point of discovering the real hole in her body, without moving on, as Nadia did, through the signifier of the objects of the Other, in order to have a body without holes. So her body remained holed, in any case, although we cannot speak of a toric structure, any more than of a Möbius structure, for the same reason of register: the Real; and where signifiers lack, it is a question of an a-structure, as we have already mentioned.

However, even in this Real where she was developing, it seemed there was an attempt at a succession, which indicated an approach analogous to Nadia's, and which surely testified to her quest for the Other, or even for what she could have known in the past, either in the two first months with her mother or in the nursery: the presence of a true Other.

2. For Nadia, the experience of the mirror was to introduce something that would go radically beyond the sticking together of our bodies.

One could make an objection, however: while distance, in the Real of bodies, on the same side of the mirror, could be reduced to zero and correspond to the primordial desire for sticking together, there was still, on the other hand, the captivating mediation of the reflection, the latter being at a distance. The Other was at the same time real and other-than-the-real. Nadia's look bore witness to this, as well as the real kisses she gave me, which were just as much for the reflection.

So the surface of our bodies was both a surface of real contact and a surface beyond our grasp, in the reflection, since the surface of the mirror was interposed. This interposition, moreover, left Nadia with the shadow of a regret, when, excited, she hit it with a building block.

It remains to say that it was this surface which separated two spaces, by doubling real space in a virtual space, that led her to truly apprehend the former space as limited by the mirror, with a beyond that was virtual space.

That beyond was also the outside, for day after day, during this short but intense mirror phase, she experienced the consulting room as limited by a wall, with an interior, and a hole (the window) defining an exterior. There, too, I was on the same side as her, in the room. Later on she was to find great delight in being carried in my arms, as we had done in front of the mirror, to stand in front of the window and become absorbed in the spectacle of the outside world.

3. Following this doubling of space in the mirror, as well as the doubling of the distance of our bodies from the reflection, Nadia almost immediately discovered the notions of inside, outside, and hole.

On her body, something appeared of the order of the holed, i.e., the real hole of her body, from mouth to anus, was now able to be inscribed in the Other, and therefore in structure. Her mouth, in the mirror, served her to give me kisses; the little empty container, from which she drank, was also a hole. Finally, the other hole in her body, the anal orifice, which up to that time had been plugged by the potty, was no longer plugged, when she presented the separated potty in front of the mirror, and when she explored its rim and its inside.

She had inscribed, through the mirror, the upper and lower orifices of the hole in her body, in the place of the Other. Her body structure was now toric, with an inside, an outside, and a central hole.

That was to be the most fertile effect of the small subject's encounter with the mirror, as far as the structure of the body was concerned, but only in the presence of her Other. At that point she was to make the transition from the initial structure of a one-sided, two-dimensional strip to a toric structure, which was three-dimensional and had an inside and an outside.

How was this possible? As we have seen, Nadia had shown us on 16 January that the Real was completely unbearable in bodily relations; on the other hand, she had had to repress the image of 10 December. The mirror joined together the Real of 16 January and the imaginary of 10 December (or at least, its trace) and once more made everything possible. A new dimension was introduced into the foreground, the Symbolic, and she immediately brought it into play in the consulting room, on the one hand, and in her relations with the food-object, on the other hand, by pretending to drink from her little empty container, by drinking the "nothing."

As for Marie-Françoise, she showed us what happens when the questioning of bodies is not pursued with the help of a possible articulation between the Real and the signifier in the field of the Other, but remains in the Real alone.

It has to be said that this Real is not univocal and monolithic, but rather that it functions in terms of "all or nothing." Marie-Françoise showed this in her relation to me: she did not annul me, so that she could subsequently tell me what the loss of her mother had meant for her; rather, she opposed the "all" of my real presence to the "all" of an absence, no less real, that of her mother.

Under these circumstances, the only time she encountered a mirror, by chance, in the powder compact of one of the nurses, all it reflected back to her was Real, which she tried to find by clawing at the back of the mirror.

So, it was not surprising that she did not address herself to the mirror, but to the window; she could not see herself in it, it was she who was elided. However, she insisted that I look at her, while she looked, not at herself, but at the treetops: she demanded that I send her image back to her. My eyes were her mirror, my eyes as organs, but she could not see herself in them, she could only be my double. She took up the position, relative to my eyes, that the rubber sailor had relative to hers.

In the absence of a relation to the Other—the premature termination of the treatment meant that we were deprived of seeing what this relation might have been—her body was really holed, and all she could do was to deny the existence of this hole, seeking in the scopic field a double to stop it up. The fact that I was not holed for her, or that I was in reality, did not in any case permit her to articulate a structure in the field of the signifier.

For her, the world was really holed and the mirror was only a windowpane in which she and I, in a real space, were to remain irremediably separated, even though this windowpane, between her and me, made present some mirror on the horizon.

Metaphor and Metonymy

It was the topological approach that appeared to us first; but, in the early stages, we were not yet aware of all the consequences, because we did not radically posit that topology, beyond its formulation in terms of surfaces and holes, is also the body flowing into the signifier, and the latter structure turns into it.

From that point, were we not forced to question the structures of this signifier: metaphor and metonymy? That is what we did in a second phase, picking up the text of the commentary on the sessions step by step.

In doing this we returned to the very sources of analysis, that is to say, to the structures of the psychoanalytic discourse, as Freud had discovered them in *The Interpretation of Dreams,* even before the advent of linguistics, in the form of *Verdichtung* (condensation) and *Verschiebung* (displacement). He made this discovery by formulating in the same work the relationship between latent discourse and manifest discourse. It was not until thirty-five years later that Roman Jakobson made of metaphor and metonymy, which correspond in analytical discourse to condensation and displacement, the combinations that organize any form of the spoken word. To be sure, the newly born science of linguistics took account of the Freudian discovery, which had anticipated it, as Lacan pointed out. Nevertheless it remained a textual affair—even though Roman Jakobson based his formulation on two clinical types of aphasia, one of which concerned decoding—the selection of signifiers—and the other, encoding—the combination of signifiers. That is to say, metaphor and metonymy, respectively.

We are not concerned here with constituted texts but with the emergence of articulated words—even with the comprehension of language before such an articulation of words, given the age of the children—via the transformation of the Real of bodies into signifiers (whether this transformation is realized or not). This dimension of bodies, and of the relation to the Other, is what specifically concerns analytical discourse. It is not so much a question of linguistics as of *linguisterie*, as Lacan called it. The clinic imposes on us the impossibility of isolating the text, which in any case is rather scant, of the body; that is to say, to isolate the signifier of the Real of the body.

We know that metaphor is the substitution of one signifier for another—one word for another—and that metonymy is the connection of one signifier to another—one word to another.

In the case of Nadia, who had access to the signifier throughout her treatment, we were constantly confronted with the body and with the part of the Real it brings with it. If the Real was destined to be promoted to the level of the signifier, it was achieved only after a long detour, during which Nadia did not always know which side she was on, that of the signifier or that of the Real. This was a result of their constant alternation, and even of the intrusion of the Real of my body, which was always a possibility, and which took her by surprise and caused her to flee from it. It was a slow and laborious process she had to accomplish to tame this Real, in other words, to make sure that it no longer intruded in an unexpected and isolated fashion, but was incorporated into a knot on the same level as the Symbolic and the Imaginary.*

Before the mirror phase, transitivism meant that even though Nadia plugged a hole in her body with an object she had taken from

---

*This path of the three registers, Real, Imaginary, and Symbolic, did not seem to us to be the best way to specify the difference between Nadia and Marie-Françoise.

The reason is that in approaching the problem via categories that can be registered, there is a risk of getting lost in them, as the abundant literature on Schreber proves. We therefore kept to the question of the status of the Other, since it had the advantage of being at the source of the existence of the three registers and allowed us to approach it from a critical point of view, beyond all appearances.

Indeed, if the Other is no longer the respondent of a signifier, then this signifier will do no more than alternate with the Real, without as such promoting anything other than the Real, even if the unleashing of the signifier may give the impression of a symbolic or imaginary reflection of the external world.

This external world starts at the Other, there where the Real and the signifier find each other in the body of the Other, above all, where the signifier is born of a transformation of the Real not only because the Other speaks, but also because the small subject, on hearing the word from the Other, sends it back to this Other, as Nadia did on 10 December, after I called her by her name.

mine—a process that can only be signifying, as we saw—she could also offer herself, by reversal, to plug the hole of my body. Insofar as the mechanism here was metaphoric, the Real of bodies quickly returned and provoked, particularly in the oral mode of devoration, the greatest degree of inhibition or flight, even the psychosomatic reaction of the subject through the fusion of the primordial signifiers representing the subject and the Other.

This function of being the real mouth-stopper of the Other was the limit Marie-Françoise came up against: the Real alone presided there, there was no place for metaphor, or it was dissolved . . . at least, for the small subject. But for the mother of a psychotic child who herself is not psychotic, the small subject really comes to take the place of what is lacking in the maternal metaphor.

The fundamental difference between Nadia and Marie-Françoise, regarding the smearing with excrement, was decisive for the role of the Real in the metaphor. Nadia's smearing aimed to cover her skin to the point of plugging the hole of her body, in order to make of it a surface without holes, using the excrement that represented me, and to realize what she had just learned in the session, namely, that it was impossible to make a hole in my skin. Marie-Françoise, on the contrary, designated the rims of the hole of her body with this excrement, that is to say, the hole that I had failed to plug. In the former case, the meaning arose metaphorically only through the transformation of the real excrement into my representation insofar as I was absent. In the latter case, the way Marie-Françoise designated the hole of her body situated me as absent in reality.

What was the difference between these two types of representation? It was that, for Nadia, it was possible to substitute my absence with the excrement that reestablished the continuity of her surface as body; and for Marie-Françoise there was nothing but the realization of her holed body, since I radically failed to plug up the hole. If I plugged the hole in Nadia's body, it was because she had raised the excrement to the dignity of the signifier, and could thus, in that field, represent me symbolically as the plugger. In her case, excrement was truly a *Vorstellungsrepräsentanz,* with its two moments: (1) representative; (2) in the field of representation (signifier). For Marie-Françoise, while the excrement represented me, its efficacity as representative was nil for plugging the hole of her body, which remained real; all it did was define its limits.

Although it was not a question of a word, in Nadia's case, we could say that the excrement was the metaphorical substitute for my presence on her skin, structurally; while for Marie-Françoise this dimension of metaphorical substitution did not come into being; her only access to the signifier was via the Real of bodies. Thus she was reduced to the opposing pair of "all or nothing" of my presence or my absence.

If we move on from the rather material level of smearing with excrement to the signifying call, we find the same opposition between Nadia and Marie-Françoise, on condition that we question the structure.

When Marie-Françoise sent out her call "maman" on 15 October, her look was directed at the window and no longer at me. Put another way, the signifier only returned her to a real absence in front of which she remained silent. It was certainly not like the "mama" of Nadia, which came to take the place of the bodily object she wanted to take from me.

For Marie-Françoise, a signifier could not take the place of the object that I was; because for her I was not a signifier or the carrier of such signifying objects. She was returned to the Real of absence, that is to say, to the opposing pair of presence-absence that, in her case, left the signifier and the Real in their separate domains. There was no substitution of an object promoted to the rank of a signifier for another signifier (such as the demand or the call Nadia addressed to me) to create the effect of metaphor.

Thus, while phenomenologically Marie-Françoise's approach could have appeared to us to follow the pattern of Nadia's, the absence of the Other as signifier meant that she failed to make any metaphorical substitution. Certainly, signifiers were present and were in place with regard to objects; but she remained powerless to place them in the Other that I was not for her. In my place, there was a real absence. Perhaps, moreover, we cannot decide one way or another what had come first: abandonment by the Other and its real absence or the absence of the signifier in the Other that would make of it this real absence.

Thus the signifiers and the objects remained separate; throughout the session, they were merely the cause of successive circuits, in spite of my speech that aimed to bring about an articulation between these objects and any demand or desire. As she was unable to address herself to me, the objects remained isolated, split between the signifier of their naming and the ex-sistence of their Real.

How, then, in these circumstances, could there possibly be metaphor? And even less, metonymy.

But before we can tackle metonymy, we still have to question metaphor from a logical point of view, starting not with Nadia, who reached it, but with Marie-Françoise, who demonstrated its failure by never getting out of the Real of language.

Psychosis does in fact speak—Schreber is there to show us how much—but that speech loses itself in language that never ceases to send the psychotic back to its pairs of oppositional terms:* high-low, interior-exterior. Marie-Françoise was not caught up in these, but perhaps, to that extent, only arrived at the essential more quickly: presence-absence. The non-holed Other that I was, was a "total-presence" incapable of receiving her call, which she could only address to the "total-absence" of the window.

She defined this "total-absence" of Other when she appealed with a "maman" to the object, the dish of rice pudding, which was the key to a real world whose "total-presence" had as sole corollary the "total-absence" of the Other, an alternative of exclusion in which no subject whatever had a chance of coming into being. Marie-Françoise and her dish of rice pudding were like Schreber and his world: a world on the point of perishing, only inhabited by "cursorily improvised men" and where he, Schreber, remained the only living being; or, in pure opposition, the end of the world was deferred but Schreber himself read the notice of his own death in the newspaper.

"The reversal of the position of indignation which was first aroused in the person of the subject by the idea of emasculation is precisely that in the interval the subject was dead."†

In front of me Marie-Françoise was like Schreber before the world: I was complete presence and complete absence. Did her subject need to die? We do not know this with certainty, but what is sure is that she was not a subject. She stayed at the level of "being" before the subject, a being for whom the alternative of exclusion, "to be or not to be," was in play, as mortal mirror of my "total-presence or total-absence." For Marie-Françoise I was "total" and she outlined, without hope, the frame, in its absolute state, of what Nadia could question in metaphor: for Nadia did it between the Real and the signifier, between the Real that made me "all" and that she fled and the signifier that created us as "not-all." In this way the metaphor did not impose itself

*Cf. Charles Melman, "L'Aventure paranoiaque: Le Cas Schreber," *Analytica,* no. 18.

†Jacques Lacan, "D'une question préliminaire à tout traitement possible de la psychose," *Écrits* (Paris: Éditions du Seuil, 1966), 567.

on her at first because the Real of the body was still too close: it was at one and the same time a coffin and the condition for the Real and the signifier not being completely separated, as in psychosis.

There remains the task of exploring how Nadia was going to articulate the signifiers in relation to the Real of the body and within a metaphoric framework.

On 10 December the repression of the signifying image left her momentarily exposed to the Real of the body. Her response at that moment was of the order of the "not-all"; "not-all" for me when she stuck her body to mine, for she offered me only a fragment, a part of her body, and addressed herself only to a part of mine; so I too was "not-all." The elision of this real totality, both for her and for me, was the condition for her "mama" in echo of my "Nadia."

Of course, the ensuing path was long, during the pre-specular phase, when she attempted to cling to the lure of some totality: an object she could take from me that would fill her, make her "all." Her call of "mama" was not issued during this period and nothing prevents us from thinking that, had mine, "Nadia," not kept her in the signifier, she might have sunk into the opposition of "alls" that Marie-Françoise knew, but because of the name "Nadia" whose keeper I was, she could not succeed in letting the real object take over completely, even though she eliminated between the object and herself—so that it might make her "all"—the signifier "mama."

Her malaise even drove her to the point of taking the place of the object for me: unable to let the object make her "all," she made of herself the object fallen at my feet that would make me "all," in the horror of a metaphoric realization—masked by transference love when she asked me to pick her up.

The whole of this period of metaphor was centered on completeness, hers above all, mine by means of transitivism; completeness of the body, certainly, but where the signifier kept a foothold. Under those conditions, metaphor remained completely marked by the Real of the body, as did the signifier put forward from this basis. There could not yet be a question for Nadia of my not being supposed to know everything she asked of me; even if, both by the Real that remained unbroachable and by means of the signifier marked by a loss, I could not satisfy her.

What followed, that is, her demand for the mirror, would show that what she succeeded in, in making herself my object in a global fashion, was not her goal: to fill me up or become one with me in some fusional perspective; that was only a way of paying the price for her own aim of being filled up. In that instant, the Real of the body was still preponderant; but when she found herself in front of the mirror, this Real fell. The reflection she saw and from which she immediately turned away was a signifying image, like the one she had known before, on 10 December. This was the true step toward the establishment of lack, between the metaphor, marked by the Real, in which she made herself my object, and the metonymy with which this Real fell in the shape of the sailor. At the same time she also saw the unitary form of her own body, perhaps without mine, but with which she gained in being Nadia, that is "one" in the "One of the signifier" of her name, which she had heard from the beginning from my mouth. The fall of the Real—the sailor and my body—confronted her with what founds metonymy: the "word to word" of her name "Nadia" with her image of herself.

This "word to word" was only possible for Nadia because a whole metaphorical sequence had preceded it: between me and her there had been signifying permutations of objects, permutations that were only the expression of a lack which insisted. This lack was accomplished in front of the mirror and was compensated by the unity of the body. Marie-Françoise and psychotics only encounter a real counterpart in the mirror, and this double is as much "all" as they are, without loss, without unity either, which is counted only in the signifier.

Then, as we know, metonymy came very much to the fore, with the spoon. Before Nadia actually pronounced "cuillère" as her first recognizable word, this spoon was already a signifier with which she spelled the world, in a word to word in which objects were in some way transmuted by this spoon with which she baptized them.

This metonymic object helped her get over the impediments that the metaphoric object imposed on her when she addressed my body. Of course, she took the spoon off me, but contrary to the metaphoric object, which I was supposed to know she was looking for, the spoon remained at a signifying distance, relieved of the Real of the body, lost at the moment of Nadia's entry into specular metonymy; this distance was such that she could use the spoon freely to exercise her power over the external world, and without having to fear above all that this object would reveal what she was depriving me of.

If the loss inherent in the passage to metonymy had to do with the repressed, it would be at her expense that the spoon represented what she was depriving me of; but to judge by her jubilation and her freedom of movement, it was also at my expense that she wielded what this spoon represented for her and which she had taken from me. In this sense, metonymy, in its process of signification, gets the better of censorship and opens the way for desire, whose metonymic object has taken all its distance from the Real of the body.

In this way the spoon that Nadia brandished victoriously became the purified signifier of a lack coming in the place of the object, but only on the condition that neither she nor I knew which object had been lost. It was like a secret between us, one that would echo from mirror to mirror in a series in which I myself as much as she was to be marked by this lack involved in both of us having our image.

Yet this was still not enough.

If she lacked, if I lacked, what we both lacked was a third term. This third term was the signifier of lack and we know that this refers to the phallus.

Metonymic play was going to maintain itself at an extensive level for the duration of the period of the mirrors, and even beyond. For the pathway along which Nadia could let each new object pass over into this field of metonymy was cleared, after she and I found confirmation in it several times, Nadia with her spoon and I with my glasses, both reunited in the closed space of the ark.

Such was the second moment of Nadia's entry into the signifier. It only found its true mainspring in the relation between objects that had become, sometimes after many vicissitudes (as with my glasses), the signifiers that represented the subjects that we were, each to the other qua signifiers, as well as for other signifiers.

Does this entitle us to say that the introduction of the third term was a return to metaphor? We believe that such is the case, to judge only by the difficulties and inhibitions Nadia gave proof of in front of the reflection of this third term, in the shape of the trainee. She could only accept her after she had veiled her, just as the veil masked the objects she had been searching for on my body. Of course, the signifying play of metonymies was pursued in parallel and one should not forget that she could only truly accept the trainee as third term through the mediation of the trainee's reflection, there where the metaphor of the third term was sustained by metonymy.

We know that she had already announced this third term on 12 February when she uttered the most common word a baby of her age could utter, and would have been uttering for some time already, but which she only then said clearly for the first time: "pa-pa."

Was it an inauguration? Ultimately not, no more than the encounter between Nadia and me had inaugurated the Other in its fundamental place as locus of signifiers. We have already said so, this access to the signifier implies an anterior step that is originary, Nadia's relation to the "Mythical Father" of Freud, to Lacan's "Name-of-the-Father," that is, an original metaphor that was radically missing or dissolved in Marie-Françoise.

Yet what was Nadia actually doing with this metaphor present in her before her analysis, if not remaining in a state of waiting, scopically fixated? Under those conditions, her analysis was a trajectory whose argument culminated in the encounter with metonymy, which is necessary if a subject wants to be incarnated in the signifier. This was the encounter with her specular image.

Any analytic trajectory seems to us to go from metaphor to metonymy. A necessary condition, though, is that the paternal metaphor is present from the start and that the desire of the analyst—whether or not the analyst runs the course, like me, with the analysand—carries it too. In the face of the psychotic subject the analyst is in fact the only one who carries it.

Elements of Topology

We shall end with a more specific reference to topology and attempt to illustrate with diagrams what the clinic has imposed on us.* This can be formulated as follows:

1. The structure with which the subject affects its body is only the effect of a signifier articulating itself with the Real of the body. Without this conjugation of the signifier with the Real there can be no structure, as in the case of Marie-Françoise where they each remained isolated. Psychosis is an "a-structure."

2. We were able to distinguish two stages in this structure:
—a nonorientable surface structure, illustrated by a Möbius strip;
—the passage, via the mirror, to an orientable surface structure, illustrated by a torus (fig. 1).

The greatest difficulty is to give a topological account of this passage from a nonorientable surface to an orientable surface.

From one to the other there is, moreover, a passage from a two-dimensional structure that implies relations of sticking and unsticking†—such as the image of 10 December on the surface of Nadia's

---

*We would like to thank Jean Petitot and Michel Demazure for the help they have brought to this tentative elaboration.

†We are not glossing over the etymological difference of these two words: "sticking" (*accolement,* from *ad collum:* neck) and "unsticking" (*decollement,* from *colla:* glue), which eliminates the required symmetry; but we have not been able to find a

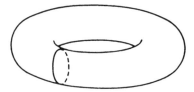

Figure 1. Möbius strip *(left)* and torus *(right)*.

eye or the clinging of her body to mine on 24 January—to a three-dimensional structure that divides the space of the body into an exterior and an interior.

First Stage: The Structure of Möbius and the Torus of the Other

We have seen how we were led to this notion of structure both by Nadia's smearing and by the fundamental difference between her and Marie-Françoise.

In this first stage the small subject structures itself as a Möbius strip, as long as the Other is duly structured as a torus.

If the relation to the Other does not allow of this signifying inscription of the subject onto the toric body of the Other, the subject remains holed: we have psychosis. The loss is revealed in the Real and nothing in the Other is brought forward as an object that could fill the subject. "To fill up" is an ambiguous term and has as such given rise to the observer's illusions in the Imaginary, when this articulation we are trying to effect, the one between the Real and the signifier, has not been made.

We end up with the following:

1. When the Real is not articulated, the small subject is holed whereas the Other is not, which prefigures the fact that the subject's castration persists irremediably in the Real.

2. When the Real and the signifier are conjugated, the body of the small subject finds itself filled by the signifiers of the body of the Other and this Other is holed in the Real.

In the case of Nadia, the dialectic between Möbius and torus was able to continue.

First, in the dialectic of sticking and unsticking of her body in re-

---

better representation of what is at issue, other than using the verb "to stick" as often as possible. Here again one can see the ambiguity of language since "beheading" *(decollation)* has to do with the neck.

lation to the surface of the torus that I was, on 16 January, she ended up separated, having fallen at my feet.

When she subsequently went in front of the mirror for the first time, she pitched the Möbius that she was, for a short moment, into space. There she encountered the impossible, topologically speaking; for a nonorientable surface, closed and without edges, cannot be pitched into a three-dimensional space; or else this compact surface without edges would become orientable (theorem).

We stumble here on the major difficulty constituted by Nadia's encounter with the mirror, yet we know that the next day, she was transformed by this encounter.

The clinic can at least tell us that during the complete process of this encounter with the mirror Nadia effected a loss on two levels:

1. A real level, with the sailor that she would give up in the mirror on the one hand, and of which, secondly, I deprived her.

2. A specular level, in which she could not see the image of my body, from which she had just unstuck herself.

It would be extremely difficult to account for her transformed state the next morning if one did not suppose her to have anticipated the unitary outline of her body, when she perceived it for a brief moment in the mirror, as a curve that located her and that already posed, like any curve that does not intersect itself, two areas on one plane: an external and an internal area, keeping in mind that she had eliminated their relation to the object and to my body.

So it was an anticipation that prefigured the separation of her body as gathered into a unitary image. In the structure that followed, Nadia would become toric, with an interior and an exterior, but this time in space.

In this first moment it was as if she had perceived her silhouette only on the plane of the mirror, that is, a new sticking of her body onto her plane image, we could say (fig. 2).

Walter von Dyck wrote, when he introduced the topology of three-dimensional spaces at the end of the last century: "one can construct closed surfaces that have either one or two sides, according to the space in which they are pitched" (fig. 3).

In this first encounter with the mirror everything happened as if Nadia were still in space, this side of the mirror, Real, without reversal, in which her Möbius structure could subsist.

She demonstrated this again after the second mirror when, after she had perceived her image stuck to my body, she confirmed the real and consistent character of my body by sticking herself to it again completely.

We saw how the next morning, when she wanted to stick herself

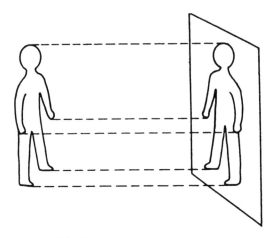

Figure 2. Plane image of the first mirror; no virtual space yet.

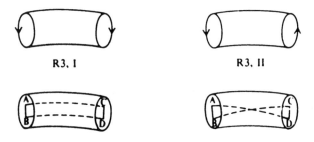

Figure 3. R3.I is an ordinary space limited by a ring.

R3.II is a double space (with immovable indicator) limited by a double surface.

The strip ABCD is placed in R3.I, then in R3.II, in such a way that AB ends up in CD. One obtains, in the case of R3.I, an ordinary cylindrical surface with two sides; in the case of R3.II, the surface has only one side.

If the construction is remade with a Möbius strip, in both cases one ends up with a surface having an immovable indicator, the one situated in R3.I, having one single side, and the one in R3.II, having two sides.

In analogous fashion, one could construct closed surfaces having two sides, according to the space in which they are pitched.

From Jean-Claude Pont, *La Topologie algébrique de ses origines à Poincaré* (Paris: PUF, 1974).

to me, a real loss appeared at the level of her body, in the form of a stool she passed in her diaper while she was leaning against me. She then proceeded to hit me, violently, as if a toric structure of her body had appeared when it was not part of the program. Something here indicates a similarity with what Marie-Françoise encountered, her holed body answering for the absence of a hole in my body. Nadia, however, answered to the real loss with the signifiers of her spoon and my glasses.

Yet things were not going to remain at this level, that is, where she would have a non-holed body whereas mine would be holed, following which our structure as a couple could maintain itself, as her Möbius stuck onto my torus.

Second Stage: Our Möbiuses

In this stage something decisive was going to happen during the third mirror: the transformation of the body of the Other into a Möbius. There were several reasons and conditions for this.

The most immediate reason was what I had just told her, on 31 January, when she had been sucking the tip of my nose and nibbling it as if she had wanted to absorb me: that there were two of us and that she could no more be inside me than I could be inside her. Her response had been to eat some cereal while smearing herself with it, to come into my arms while putting her arms around my neck, and to put her messy cheek against mine before demanding the mirror.

The condition that enabled her to understand so well what I had said was that the impossible I signified, when I posed the signifier, that there were two of us, articulated, like any law, the Real and the signifier. She could only understand the signifier of my interdiction against the backdrop of the real and toric consistency of my body, which she had experienced again during the second mirror. In other words, I was going to be grasped by Nadia in a surface structure only if she herself effected an active transformation on the basis of the experience she had of my body as toric.

This is shown by the impossible relation the small subject has with a nonarticulated Real—we are speaking of the Real as impossible here—when the Other it is confronted with, by dint of some psychotic or neurotic deviation, presents itself with a non-holed structure, like a Möbius strip. Then it is the subject who is holed, as Marie-Françoise showed; and, in the worst case, the subject cannot succeed at all in holing the body of the Other so that it might find there the signifying objects that would prevent the subject from being holed. Yet what occupies us above all at this point, the transformation of the Other into a Möbius so as to arrive at the mirror, a transformation actively led by the small subject, remains impossible. Only the body of an Other who has not been holed answers, behind the glass, to the subject's holed body.

The mirror is only possible in a combinatory of the Real and the signifier, the basis of structure, in which the sticking of Real bodies sends the subject back to the unsticking of the signifying image, to a distance.

There are two moments that need to be considered in this second stage in Nadia's case:

1. The sticking of Real bodies was inseparable from the signifying image of structure: because of this, Nadia and I had become two Möbius strips stuck together (fig 4).

2. We were both pitched in space. This space was divided by the mirror into a real and a virtual space.

To enable the small subject to pursue its articulation, it is important that it has at its disposal at the same time both the Real of the body of the Other, in whose arms the subject finds itself and to whom it is sticking, and the image of this body of the Other in the mirror together with its own.

The Other and the subject have to be on the same side: this is what happens with the mirror, where the relation of bodies in the Real can only occur in relation to the image. It is what cannot happen with the window, where the subject and the Other are each on one side, both remaining in the Real without reference to the image. This is what Marie-Françoise demonstrated when she searched for a plane that could cut space in two, as the mirror does. This failed because the window is only pitched in real space. It separated us, but, lacking a signifier, it had no effect on the structure: in place of the unitary outline of her body that Nadia encountered in the mirror, Marie-

Figure 4.

Françoise was referred only, in the window, to the real consistency of the body of the Other.

The function of the mirror is not only to cut space in two—the small subject and its Other, it has to be stressed, being on the same side—but to introduce a new parameter between the Real and its image; the left-right orientation. Looking at it closely one can see that this is a purely signifying orientation, as is proved by the fact that the mirror has no effect whatsoever on the Real of the high and low of the image it reflects. We know how precocious this mastering of laterality is, an apprenticeship that passes through the word of the Other. In this way the image in the left-right structure finds itself orientated, like the signifier of which it is the support.

However, we have to come back to the way Nadia stuck the two Möbius strips, our bodies, together. This sticking did not orientate these bodies. There was, we could say, at that moment, a topological identification between the small subject and her Other, shown by Nadia in her activity with an amazing certainty, as if it had been ineluctable, that is, logical: we could say that there, logic was the part of the Real that presided over the signifying operation.

This sticking, though not oriented in the Real, would become so in the signifier of the image.

For what follows, we will draw on an article on the reversal of the sphere.* It is demonstrated in this article that the union between two Möbius strips has to do with a unilateral surface: the Klein bottle.

It is not our intention here—we refer to the figures in the article that illustrate the reversal of the torus—to show how the Klein bottle with two leaves is a deformation of the torus in the course of its reversal: that is, how a bridge is established between a nonorientated unilateral surface and the oriented surface of the torus.

During the course of its reversal, the torus—one of the many cases of its reversal, for there is an infinite variety of ways of doing it in topology—"can be deformed into a lining with the two leaves of the Klein bottle (immersion of a surface obtained by the junction of two Möbius strips). One can then permutate the leaves of the lining and end up by running through the preceding transformation in the opposite direction, with a reversed torus."† If, on the other hand,

*Bernard Morin and Jean-Pierre Petit, "Le Retournement de la sphére," *Pour la science,* Jan. 1977.
†Ibid.

one were to stick the two sides opposite the two leaves, one would end up with a Klein bottle once more, that is, one would remain in the domain of the unilateral surface.

Two essential notions have to be posited in all the transformations of a torus—or any other surface—in the course of its reversal: the pitching of the surface and the immersion of the surface.

In pitching, an elastic membrane can be deformed infinitely without being either folded or torn, nor ever entering into contact with itself.

The deformations of immersion allow, on the other hand, the points of the surface to encounter each other and let these surfaces cross each other, as well as slide freely with respect to each other.

All these transformations have the character of a succession, which is also the mark of the signifier. This succession of transformations in space forms a sequence that introduces the notion of time. The sequence of transformations can be run through in one direction or another, which introduces into space the notion of reversal, and in time, the reversal of the sense of time, a notion that merits our full attention as regards its importance in the analytic process.

We are brought back to this in any case with the sticking Nadia effected, between me and her at first, and then with the game she played in front of the mirror involving the reciprocity of kisses, which illustrates the permutation of leaves. After this, going over in an opposite direction, the deformations undergone by the torus in one of its reversals, she ended up with a toric structure. We cannot say that she herself ran through the sequence of transformations of the torus toward the Klein bottle (with two leaves) since she inaugurated, on the contrary, a toric structure while starting from a unilateral surface that she composed with two leaves, hers and that of the Other.

One question here remains unanswered, concerning the structure of the Other. That it was holed for Nadia is certain, as we have seen; but that it was also toric from the start is an open question, unless we recognize there too, a certain anticipation, an anticipation that leaves space for a more leisurely return to a surface structure. Yet this could happen only, as Nadia had shown, if the relational impact was displaced from the signifying object sought on the body of the Other to an identificatory image, which it was all too clear, dominated the entry into the mirror: she made me a "surface" in her own image, before going to confront us in the mirror.

Third Stage: Toric Bodies

From that point on, two structural phases entered into play; on the one hand, as we have seen, an elision, that is, what was lost when from the Real of our bodies Nadia passed to the signification of the image, and, on the other hand, a new toric structure of bodies: the scission of space into two areas was conjoined with a certain scission of time, combining the past of the surface and sticking with the present of distance and separation, open to a future.

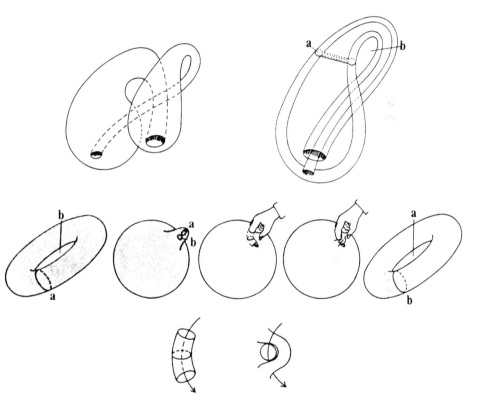

Figure 5. The two leaves in the form of a Klein bottle *(left)*. If they are not joined *(right)*, they form a torus (a: meridian circle of a torus; b: neck circle of a torus.) The reversal of the torus follows simply from the reversal of a sphere *(bottom)*. Starting from the torus, which is transformed into a sphere, supplied with a little handle, the sphere is then reversed (it becomes white) and the little handle is now on the inside: it is enough to extract this handle by passing a finger through it, in order to obtain a reversed torus. The meridian circle is once more around the finger and becomes the neck circle of the reversed torus, that is, what it is: the hole of the subject's body.

This future was sealed with the reversal of the torus, which was necessary to accomplish a toric structure giving the hole of the body from mouth to anus. The topology in fig. 5 taken from the aforementioned article gives us an account . . . not without the finger, useful in the demonstration, referring us back to that finger of Nadia's with which she explored the hole of my mouth, ready to want to deprive me of a finger, as if to actively reassure herself of the hole of my body that was a guarantee of her own non-holed body.*

Having been guided by this baby Nadia to the necessity of a topological approach, an approach that, as yet insufficient, we will carry further with other cases, we cannot help thinking that all we have done is follow the clinic. We have, moreover, the impression of always having been superseded, like archaeologists confronted with an unknown script, that, while they keep questioning it incessantly, does not cease to write itself for them as if it were a mirror sending them an image to decipher, because this image would not be a simple reflection, but the signifier graven on the Real of some slab of granite.

*Marie-Françoise, entirely occupied with the eyes, did not address herself to the hole of my mouth, but attempted to make a hole in the surface of my eye with a spoon.

Index

aggressive behavior: absence of Other and, 219–27; auditory drive and, 39; by Marie-Françoise toward food, 309–10; pre-specular ambivalence and, 53–55; as reaction to mirror image, 95–100, 117–31; realization of holed body and, 171–74, 183–84, 236–37, 240–43; transitive relation to the Other and, 31–36

alienation: Lacan's theories on, 50

ambivalence: about separation of Other, in Nadia, 51–75; absence of, in Marie-Françoise, 226–27, 247, 310; metaphorical place of the subject and, 83–91; as safeguard of the Other, 296

anal drive: connection with holed body, 168–71, 173–80, 182–90; object as currency of exchange, 189–99

analytic relationship: relation with lack in, 231, 323

anorexia: as active refusal, 231–33; in autistic children, 218. *See also* bulimia

anxiety: pre-specular ambivalence and, 53, 69

auditory drive ("getting heard" behavior), 39

autism: characteristics of, 217

autistic circuit: of Marie-Françoise, 302–3, 311–13

beads: as signifiers of anal drive, 181–82, 189–99

Beyond the Pleasure Principle, 47

biting behavior: development of separate images and, 99–102, 122–23

bi-univocal identification: realization of holed body and, 188–89

body contact: attempts at, by Marie-Françoise, 249–51; early attempts at, in Nadia, 6–8, 11–18; interruption of, in Marie-Françoise, 242–43; Nadia's ambivalence about, 89–91; Nadia's increased demand for, 27–36, 51–52, 67–69; oral drive in Marie-Françoise and, 284; scopic drive developed through, 19–25, 40; surface to spatial topology regarding, 132–33, 139–45; temptation of the Other and, 291–92, 298–99; violent component of, with Marie-Françoise, 219–27

bottle: as metonymic object for Marie-Françoise, 293, 298, 303–4; mirror image and, 134–35, 139–45; as object of demand for Nadia, 26–28, 34–35; as return to oral stage for Marie-Françoise, 265–66, 269–70; transition from metaphorical object to tool, 171–73, 183–84

bulimia: absence of, in Marie-Françoise, 221–22, 225–27; in autistic children, 218; as disinvestment of food, 228–31

castration (symbolic): construction of ego and, 208, 213; realization of holed body and, 173–74, 184; separation of the Other and, 47–48

coalescence: transitive relation to the Other and, 37

demand: absence of, in Marie-Françoise, 247–51, 265–77; bottle as object for, 26–28, 34–35; objects as mediators for, 22

Demazure, Michel, 341

Didier-Weill, Alain, 47

ROSINE LEFORT and ROBERT LEFORT are leading French psychoanalysts and students of Jacques Lacan. They have worked clinically and researched extensively in psychoanalysis with children, particularly in the treatment of childhood psychosis and autism. They are members of the Ecole de la Cause Freudienne and founders of the Network CEREDA (Centre de Recherche sur l'Enfant dans le Discours Analytique) in the frame of the Foundation of the Freudian Field.

Between 1969 and 1980 ROSINE LEFORT was an associate at the Experimental School of Bonneuil, directed by Maud Mannoni. In addition to *Birth of the Other*, she has written, in collaboration with Robert Lefort, *Les structures de la psychose: L'Enfant au loup et le Président*, a comparative study of the analysis of Robert the Wolf Child and the case of Schreber. She has also published numerous articles on psychoanalysis with children and other psychoanalytic topics.

In 1969 ROBERT LEFORT founded with Maud Mannoni the Experimental School of Bonneuil. He was the president of the Ecole de la Cause Freudienne in 1984–85. Apart from the works in collaboration with Rosine Lefort, he has published many articles on psychoanalytic topics and on education.

MARC DU RY is a psychoanalyst, member of the Centre for Freudian Analysis and Research in London. He is chief editor of JCFAR, the first Lacanian journal in the UK.

LINDSAY WATSON is a psychoanalyst practicing in London. She is a member of the Centre for Freudian Analysis and Research and of CFAR's Child Analysis Working Group.

LEONARDO RODRÍGUEZ is a psychoanalyst, a founding member of the Australian Centre for Psychoanalysis in the Freudian Field, and a member of the European School of Psychoanalysis. He is also a senior lecturer at the Department of Psychological Medicine, Monash University, Melbourne. He works in clinical psychoanalysis with adults and children and has published numerous articles on psychoanalytic theory and practice.

RUSSELL GRIGG teaches philosophy at Deakin University and is a cofounder of the Australian Centre for Psychoanalysis in the Freudian Field. He studied for his doctorate in the Department of Psychoanalysis (founded by Jacques Lacan) at the University of Paris, where he was also a member of the teaching staff. He has published widely on psychoanalysis. His translation of one of Lacan's seminars, *The Psychoses*, appeared in 1993.